Office for
National Statistics

120065

45.26
SJ4/08
ʌ

D0491416

Social Trends

COLEC
ABERG   YN.
ᴖANOᴵ   ᴸᴸYᴴᴵ⁻ ᴵ
         ᴱNᴿᴵ
         ᴺ

No. 38
2008 edition

Editor: Abigail Self

Assistant editor: Linda Zealey

Office for National Statistics

ISBN 978-0-230-54564-9
ISSN 0306–7742

A National Statistics publication

National Statistics are produced to high professional standards set out in the National Statistics Code of Practice. They are produced free from political influence.

Not all the statistics contained within this publication are national statistics because it is a compilation from various sources.

About us

The Office for National Statistics

The Office for National Statistics (ONS) is the executive office of the UK Statistics Authority, a non-ministerial department which reports directly to Parliament. ONS is the UK government's single largest statistical producer. It compiles information about the UK's society and economy which provides evidence for policy and decision-making and in the allocation of resources.

The Director of the ONS is also the National Statistician.

Palgrave Macmillan

This publication first published 2008 by Palgrave Macmillan, Houndmills, Basingstoke, Hampshire RG21 6XS and 175 Fifth Avenue, New York, NY 10010, USA
Companies and representatives throughout the world.

Palgrave Macmillan is the global academic imprint of the Palgrave Macmillan division of St. Martin's Press, LLC and of Palgrave Macmillan Ltd. Macmillan® is a registered trademark in the United States, United Kingdom and other countries. Palgrave is a registered trademark in the European Union and other countries.

A catalogue record for this book is available from the British Library.

10   9   8   7   6   5   4   3   2   1
17   16   15   14   13   12   11   10   09   08

Contacts

Editorial

For information about the content of this publication, contact the Editor
Tel: 01633 455931
Email: social.trends@ons.gsi.gov.uk

Other customer and media enquiries

ONS Customer Contact Centre
Tel: 0845 601 3034
International: +44 (0)845 601 3034
Minicom: 01633 812399
Email: info@statistics.gsi.gov.uk
Fax: 01633 652747
Post: Room 1015, Government Buildings, Cardiff Road, Newport, South Wales NP10 8XG

You can find more information about ONS, a downloadable version of this publication and our other statistics at
www.statistics.gov.uk

Publication orders

To obtain a print copy of this publication, contact Palgrave Macmillan
Tel: 01256 302611
www.palgrave.com/ons

Copyright and reproduction

Printing

This book is printed on paper suitable for recycling and made from fully managed and sustained forest sources. Logging, pulping and manufacturing processes are expected to conform to the environmental regulations of the country of origin.

Printed and bound in Great Britain by Hobbs the Printer Ltd, Totton, Southampton

Typeset by Academic + Technical Typesetting, Bristol

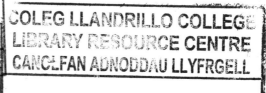

Contents

1: Population

2: Households and families

3: Education and training

4: Labour market

5: Income and wealth

Page

Page

12: Transport

13: Lifestyles and social participation

List of figures and tables

The 'last appeared' and 'previous number' columns refer to the Social Trends (ST) edition and location in which the same or similar chart or table last appeared. Page number refers to the page in which the table or chart can be found in Social Trends 38.

DATA Hover and click over tables and graphs on the online pdf of Social Trends and you can download them in Microsoft Excel. It's as simple as that.

www.statistics.gov.uk/socialtrends38

8: Social protection

9: Crime and justice

13: Lifestyles and social participation

Contributors and acknowledgements

The Editor would like to thank colleagues in contributing Departments and other organisations for their generous support and helpful comments, without which this edition of Social Trends would not have been possible. Thanks also go to the outgoing Social Trends team, namely Mario Alemanno, Simon Burtenshaw, Aleks Collingwood and Kwabena Owusu-Agyemang, for the smooth handover of work to the new team.

Authors:	Jenny Church
	Claire Collins
	Tania Corbin
	Anna Donabie
	Joanne Evans
	Steve Howell
	Francis Jones
	Ian Macrory
	Chris Randall
Production manager:	Ann Corp
Production team:	Victoria Chenery
	Angela Collin
	Julie Crowley
	Marc Evans
	Alessio Fiacco
	Tony James
	Saef Shah
	Dave Sweet
	Andrew White
Lead reviewer:	Paul Allin
Design:	ONS Design
Typesetting:	Academic + Technical
Publishing management:	Mark Bristow
Index:	ONS Library and Information
Maps:	Jeremy Brocklehurst
	Alistair Dent

Introduction

Welcome to the 38th edition of *Social Trends*, one of the flagship publications from the newly independent Office for National Statistics. *Social Trends* provides an up to date and comprehensive description of society in 2007, drawing on statistics from a wide range of government departments and other organisations to show how society is changing, as well as some of the factors which may be driving these trends.

Social Trends is aimed at a wide audience: policy makers in the public and private sectors; service providers; people in local government; journalists and other commentators; academics and students; schools; and the general public.

What's new?

Since the last edition, *Social Trends* has undergone several changes. In response to user feedback, we have introduced an overview page to highlight at a glance some of the key and emerging trends in today's society. This year's theme, 'measuring societal wellbeing' also receives its own spotlight. Both can be found as part of the new summary pages overleaf. We've also listened to your suggestions on signposting. You can now see how to access the data behind the charts and tables, at regular intervals throughout the book and we've revisited the list of tables and figures to highlight where data are new or have appeared in previous editions. Changes in design have also been introduced with the aim of making it easier to find your way around. Your views on these changes and suggestions on how *Social Trends* could be improved are welcomed. Please write to the Editor at the address shown below with your comments.

New material, definitions and terms

Each year, to preserve topicality around one-third of data used in *Social Trends* are new. The remainder, where possible have been carried forward from previous editions and updated.

Due to variations in coverage and definitions, some care may be needed when comparing data from more than one source. Anyone seeking to understand the figures and tables in detail will find it helpful to read the Appendix and Symbols and conventions pages towards the end of the book. A list of further reading and websites is also provided.

Availability on electronic media

Social Trends 38 is available electronically on the National Statistics website, www.statistics.gov.uk/socialtrends. The full report is available as an interactive PDF file where excel spreadsheets containing the data used in the publication can be accessed and downloaded by clicking on the relevant chart or table.

Contact

Abigail Self

Editor: Social Trends
Office for National Statistics
Room: 2.101
Government Buildings
Cardiff Road
Newport
Gwent
NP10 8XG

Email: social.trends@ons.gov.uk

In this year's edition...

- **The UK population is ageing.**
  The number of people aged 65 and over in the UK is expected to exceed the number aged under 16 in 2021.

- **Proportion living alone continues to rise.**
  The proportion of people living alone in Great Britain in 2007 (12 per cent) was double the proportion living alone in 1971.

- **Children happy at school.**
  In 2005, around eight in ten children aged 14 and 15 in England agreed that they were happy at school (82 per cent) and liked being at school (80 per cent).

- **Employment rates for men and women converging.**
  The UK employment rate of working-age men fell from 92 per cent in Q2 1971 to 79 per cent in Q2 2007, while the rate for working-age women rose from 56 per cent to 70 per cent.

- **Household net wealth doubled.**
  Household net wealth in the UK more than doubled in real terms between 1987 and 2006.

- **Nearly half have some form of unsecured debt.**
  In 2006, 42 per cent of individuals in Great Britain had some form of unsecured debt, 19 per cent owed money on a credit card, 16 per cent on a personal loan and a further 9 per cent on a car loan.

- **Increase in alcohol-related deaths.**
  Between 1991 and 2006, the number of alcohol-related deaths in the UK more than doubled from 4,144 to 8,758.

- **Nearly two-thirds believe there is more crime in the country than two years ago.**
  According to the 2006/07 British Crime Survey, 65 per cent of adults in England and Wales believed there was more crime in the country as a whole than two years ago.

- **Nearly half of all new dwellings are flats.**
  In 2006/07, 47 per cent of new dwellings completed in England were flats compared with 16 per cent in 1996/97.

- **Nearly one-third agree with non-environmentally friendly statements.**
  In England in 2007, nearly three in ten adults agreed or strongly agreed with the statement 'I don't believe my behaviour and everyday lifestyle contribute to climate change'.

- **Motoring relatively less expensive than a decade ago.**
  The 'All motoring' component of the retail prices index rose by 85 per cent in the UK between January 1987 and January 2007, compared with a rise in the 'All items' component of 102 per cent. The 'All fares and other travel' component rose by 130 per cent.

- **Nearly half believe it's more important to have close ties with family than with friends.**
  In 2006, 48 per cent of people in Great Britain felt it was more important to have close ties with family than to have close friends.

Overview

Social Trends provides a unique overview of the state of the nation. In this year's edition, staples such as trends relating to population change, family structures, our health and how we spend our money and free time have been updated. Also examined are attitudes towards various aspects of life in society today such as attitudes towards the criminal justice system, education and the environment, which together may begin to shed light on our 'societal well-being', the theme of this year's *Social Trends*.

Chapter 1: Population shows that the UK population continues to grow, age and diversify. In 2006, the UK population reached 60.6 million and projections reveal that by 2021, the number of people aged 65 and over is expected to exceed the number aged under 16. Population change is driven by natural change, migration and the diversity which this brings. In England and Wales in 2006, one in five (22 per cent) births were to non-UK born mothers, compared with one in eight (13 per cent) a decade before. Over the same period, the net outflow of Britons leaving the UK more than doubled to 126,000.

Family structures also continue to evolve, highlighting changes in attitudes of both individuals and society as well as perhaps, financial necessity. Chapter 2: Households and families highlights that more people than ever are living alone and that the proportion of births outside marriage are increasing, reaching 44 per cent in 2006 in the UK. The majority of such births are jointly registered and much of the increase was the result of increasing numbers of births to cohabiting parents. In 2006, around one-quarter of unmarried men and women were cohabiting in Great Britain, nearly double the proportion 20 years earlier, although marriage remains the most common form of partnership.

Chapter 3: Education shows that participation in education in the UK has increased between two and threefold over the last 35 years or so and that in England in 2005, around eight in ten children agreed or strongly agreed that they were happy at school. Schools are also embracing technology in varying degrees. In England in 2006, lap tops used for teaching and learning could be found in between 90 and 95 per cent of primary and secondary schools respectively. Take up of virtual learning environments (VLE) and networks for off-site working were less well used, with 24 per cent of teachers using VLE compared to 46 per cent of secondary schools reporting VLE capability.

The increased participation in education over the last 35 years was particularly notable among women, where enrolments in further education increased by three and a half times between 1970/71 and 2005/06. Over the same period, Chapter 4: Labour market highlights that there has been a marked increase in participation rates of women in the labour market in the UK, from 56 per cent in Q2 (April to June) 1971 to 70 per cent in Q2 2007, whilst overall working-age employment rates have remained stable. Recent years have also seen changes in working practices which may have contributed to the change. These include an increase in the proportion working part-time and the introduction of more widespread flexible working arrangements, enjoyed by more than one-fifth of full-time employees in Q2 2007 in the UK. We also learn that on the whole, employees in Great Britain in 2006 were satisfied with their work and pay.

As well as a convergence in the employment rates for men and women in 2007, Chapter 5: Income and wealth, shows that the pay gap between men and women has narrowed from 17 per cent in 1997 to 12 per cent in the UK in 2006. In addition, over the last 20 years to 2006, household net wealth has more than doubled in real terms and in spring 2007, nearly 9 in 10 adults in England were very or fairly satisfied with their standard of living. Fewer (around six in 10) were satisfied with their future financial security however.

The increase in household wealth is reflected in Chapter 6: Expenditure where the volume of expenditure by UK households has increased by two and a half times over the last 35 years, with particularly strong growth in expenditure on communication which grew more than nine times in real terms. Expenditure is not without debt however, and between 1993 and Q4 (October to December) 2007, the amount owed by individuals in the UK rose from £574 billion to £1,320 billion. In 2006, just over 42 per cent of adults in Great Britain had some form of unsecured debt.

Chapter 7: Health indicates that although we are living longer, we are spending more years in poor health. Initiatives for promoting healthy lifestyles and diet have had some impact, with higher proportions of girls and boys in England and Wales in 2006 having consumed at least five or more portions of fruit and vegetables per day than in 2004. Nevertheless, levels of obesity continue to rise in both children and adults and the proportion of alcohol-related deaths in the UK has more than doubled between 1991 and 2006.

Chapter 8: Social protection deals with the help given to those who are in need or at risk of hardship for reasons such as illness, low income, family circumstances or age. Over the last 30 years social security benefit expenditure in the UK has more than doubled in real terms to £134 billion in 2006/07. In this year, 2.9 million people in Great Britain were in receipt of Disability Living Allowance and 1.5 million received Attendance Allowance, both having increased by around 10 per cent since 2003/04. Charities offer another source of social protection in the UK. In 2005/06, the top 500 fundraising charities spent nearly £3.3 billion, an increase of £231 million from 2004/05. Of these, children's charities spent the most at £669 million.

In Chapter 9: Crime and justice, we find that overall levels of crime have remained broadly stable in the last few years. However, according to the 2006/07 British Crime Survey (BCS), 65 per cent of adults believed there was more crime in the country than two years ago and confidence in the criminal justice system is mixed. Nearly eight in ten interviewed as part of the BCS in 2006/07 were very or fairly confident that the criminal justice system (CJS) respects the rights of people who have committed a crime and treats them fairly but there was less confidence in the effectiveness in the CJS in dealing with young people accused of crime, protecting the public and dealing with victims.

Changes in household structures together with wider economic pressures have undoubtedly impacted on the size and availability of housing. Chapter 10: Housing shows that in England in 2006/07, nearly half of new dwellings completed were flats, compared with less than one-fifth in 1996/97, reflecting in part the increase in the number of one person households. Despite smaller new builds, access to the housing market remains a challenge for first time buyers. In 2006, 37 per cent of dwellings bought in the UK in 2006 cost over £200,000 with only 15 per cent costing less than £100,000. In the same year, average prices paid by first time buyers rose to three and a half times their average income, compared with two and a half times in 1996.

Chapter 11: Environment shows that in 2006, we are recycling more and that municipal waste disposed to landfill has fallen significantly over the last decade. However, domestic energy consumption has risen, possibly connected with the increase in smaller households which may have thwarted the gains to be had from more energy efficient practices. In contrast, energy use for cooking in the home has fallen by 35 per cent over the last 35 years or so, possibly indicating changes in technology, the availability of convenience food or even a tendency to eat out more often.

In Chapter 12: Transport, we find that the car remains the most popular form of transport in Great Britain in 2006, despite the UK being the fourth most expensive country in the EU-27 in which to buy a litre of petrol. Despite increased awareness of more environmentally friendly behaviour, such as sharing lifts or making greater use of public transport, the most common use of the car by car drivers was for commuting (28 per cent of all trips by car) while leisure was the main reason for trips made by car passengers. Indeed, in a survey which asked whether trips of less than 2 miles made by car could just as easily be walked, travelled by bus or bicycle, between 43 and 54 per cent of men and women disagreed or disagreed strongly.

Finally, Chapter 13: Lifestyles and social participation examines how we spend our free time. Watching TV is the most popular activity undertaken in free time, however 21 per cent of adults in England regularly took part in sport and active recreation in 2005/06. Spending time with family and friends is the second most popular way to spend free time with nearly half feeling that it was more important to spend time with family than with friends.

Societal well-being

The underlying theme of *Social Trends 38* is societal well-being. In this section we introduce the concept of societal well-being, explain why the theme was chosen, and give pointers to how societal well-being might be assessed on the basis of the content of this edition of *Social Trends*.

There is no single definition of societal well-being. The terms well-being, quality of life, happiness, life satisfaction and welfare are often used interchangeably, although there are some distinctions between them. Each of these terms conveys an attempt to assess 'how society is doing', or perhaps what progress we are making as a society, beyond the purely economic assessment captured in measures such as Gross Domestic Product (GDP), derived from the national accounts. One phrase often used, drawing inspiration from a speech by Robert Kennedy in 1968, is that 'there is more to life than GDP'.

Measuring societal well-being is one of ONS's current analytical priorities[1], along with children and young people, ageing and public sector productivity. It was identified as a priority issue and as the underlying theme for *Social Trends 38*, because for an increasing number of public policy needs, and in political and public debate, there *is* more to life than GDP. Sustainable economic growth and economic well-being remain important. However, international bodies such as the Organisation for Economic Co-operation and Development are, through the 2007 Istanbul Declaration, promoting debate about what progress means and how a shared view of societal well-being can be produced, based on high-quality statistics.

Economic well-being is measured through the national accounts and related indicators. These are well-established and internationally agreed measures. GDP per head is particularly used as a headline indicator of economic progress and to allow comparisons between countries. Chapter 5 of *Social Trends* covers income and wealth and Figure 5.1 shows that GDP per head in the UK more than doubled in real terms over the last 35 years, between 1971 and 2006. In 2005, the UK had the third highest GDP per head within the Group of Seven most advanced 'Western' economies.

GDP and the national accounts were never designed to measure wider aspects of societal well-being, so has the undoubted growth in economic performance resulted in a similar increase in well-being overall? We simply can't say, on the basis of the data collected here in *Social Trends*. It would be equally difficult to do so using other data until we have an agreed structure that would allow us to measure societal well-being consistently over time and place.

There is no shortage of relevant existing data to help build pictures of societal well-being and to assess our quality of life. However, we can only make sense of this data when we have a better and shared understanding of what well-being means and what its key components are. Clearly our overall well-being is likely to reflect health, education, culture, safety and a sense of community, among other things. But any of the strands may be valued more or less by individuals and groups within society. Looking back over 2007, for example, people affected by flooding or by uncertainties in the financial markets, may well reach a different assessment of quality of life in the UK than those of us less directly affected by these aspects of recent months. Similarly, while gun crime frequently makes the news, is this a significant indicator of a breakdown in quality of life across the whole of the UK?

One distinction that seems worth drawing is between objective and subjective well-being. Objective well-being refers to the material and social circumstances believed to foster – or detract from – an individual's or community's sense of well-being. Subjective well-being refers to an individual's self-assessment of their own well-being. Many of the statistics included in *Social Trends* can be used to describe objective well-being and we return to these shortly.

It has not been a tradition in *Social Trends* to measure subjective well-being, although two early editions did include articles on subjective measures[2] and satisfaction with standard of living is reported in Table 5.5 in this edition. The latest figures, collected in a survey in 2006, show that 85 per cent of people aged 16 and over were very or fairly satisfied with their standard of living, compared with 6 per cent who were fairly or very dissatisfied.

Other surveys indicate that this pattern has remained the same for at least 30 years. In particular, data for every year between 1973 and 2006 by Eurobarometer fluctuates closely around an average of 86 per cent of people saying they are very or fairly satisfied on the whole with the life they lead. This is an example of the Easterlin Paradox, following work on the relationship between GDP and life satisfaction or happiness. The strength of the relationship between income and reported levels of happiness declines rapidly after a certain GDP is reached. In the UK, as in the

United States and many other countries, life satisfaction overall has levelled off, despite increasing real economic wealth.

Life satisfaction might be seen as the ultimate performance indicator, distilling all aspects of well-being into a single response. There are different patterns of life satisfaction reported by different groups within society. However, given that we want to move on from a single measure of economic well-being, it hardly seems to present a more rounded picture if we are to rely on just another statistic, summarising life satisfaction. Rather, ONS is exploring the measurement of societal well-being drawing on a range of indicators. As well as providing a broader base, this will allow users to form their own conclusion, depending on the weights that they attach to particular aspects of societal well-being. We accept that presenting the whole volume of *Social Trends* as the data on which to draw an assessment of societal well-being is rather too open-ended and leaves the reader asking 'so what does it all add up to?'.

The state of UK society, particularly how society is diverse and dynamic, will be explored in depth in an article by the National Statistician to accompany *Social Trends 38*. Here in *Social Trends 38* we will therefore review a number of the potential components of societal well-being that are likely to feature in any more comprehensive review of the quality of modern life.

Health is widely accepted as a key component of overall well-being. Chapter 7 contains a number of indicators that could be included in a summary assessment of societal well-being. For example, there have been large improvements in expectancy of life at birth in the UK over the last century. However, while life expectancy at birth for men in 2004 was 76.6 years, healthy life expectancy was only 67.9 years, indicating an average 9.3 years spent in poor health. Similarly, disability-free life expectancy was even lower, at 62.3 years, with an average 14.6 years of total life expectancy likely to be spent with disability. Life expectancy for women continues to be higher than that for men. Both have increased, for a number of reasons, including a marked reduction in death from circulatory diseases. On the other hand, the proportions of people who are obese or overweight has been rising (see Figure 7.10), suggesting to some commentators that excess in the way we live now does not always lead to societal well-being.

Notable socio-economic inequalities still exist in health, as shown in Chapter 7. The extent of inequalities between groups within society more generally may be seen as another dimension to societal well-being. In the UK, the income distribution and the extent of inequality have changed considerably over the last three decades (see Figure 5.3). Inequality grew during the late 1970s and throughout the 1980s. There were only slight changes between the mid-1990s and 2005/06, though there is evidence of a marginal increase in inequality over this time.

There have been substantial changes in the pattern of household expenditure over the last 35 years. Trends in household expenditure provide an insight into changes in consumer preference, the growth of choices available to consumers and their increased purchasing power, standards of living, and wider changes in society. These are all summarised in Chapter 6. Figure 6.9 records how the ownership of consumer durables, from dishwashers to mobile phones, has extended rapidly to a greater proportion of households from when each kind of durable was first available on the market. For example, around two in three households owned a home computer by 2006, compared with less than one in three in 1997/98.

Figure 6.11 summarises how our total retail purchases have risen steadily. The volume of retail sales has increased every year since 1991, with an average annual rate of growth of 3.3 per cent over the last 20 years. Sales also always increase sharply in the build up to Christmas. This annual sharp spike in buying is both integral to the way of life of many of us, and acts as a yearly check on the state of the economy.

Since the early 1950s the number of dwellings in Great Britain has almost doubled, from 13.8 million in 1951 to 25.7 million in 2006. The rise in housing stock reflects a greater demand for homes caused partly by the increase in population, and more particularly a trend towards smaller households that has emerged since the 1970s. At least two aspects of quality of life are signalled by these statistics: our material living conditions, especially our homes, and changes in the nature of our households, including as a result of family formation, break-up and new relationships. These aspects of societal well-being are explored in Chapters 2 and 10.

Chapter 13 presents a wide range of statistics on lifestyles and social participation. What we do in our 'spare time', and how we engage with society, including through volunteering, charities and religious life, are important aspects of quality of life. The most common leisure activity, enjoyed by over 4 in 5 adults in England, is watching television, according to the 2005/06 'Taking Part' survey. Figure 13.1 indicates both the range of activities undertaken in free time and their relative popularity. Shopping and eating out at restaurants feature among the free time activities of most people, as do reading, listening to music and spending time with family and friends.

The quality of many people's lives is affected by crime, either directly, through suffering or loss, or indirectly through changes in actual and perceived levels of crime affecting their daily routines. The 2006/07 British Crime Survey (BCS) estimated that 11.3 million crimes were committed against adults living in private households in England and Wales (Figure 9.1). The number of crimes according to the BCS rose steadily throughout the 1980s and early 1990s, peaking in 1995. Since then there was a steady decline until 2005/06, before levelling out. In 2006/07 around 54 per cent of offences identified in the BCS involved some kind of theft or attempted theft. Vandalism accounted for more than one-quarter of all crime captured by the BCS in 2006/07 and this had increased by 10 per cent since 2005/06 (Chapter 9).

Comparisons with GDP, in which economic activity during a given period is accounted for, often means that we think about societal well-being in similar ways, for example how we spend our time when not contributing to economic activity. Another way of regarding societal well-being is to consider the levels of the stock of various forms of economic and other capital. Examples of this can be glimpsed in the pages of *Social Trends*. For example, the highest qualification held by people aged 16 to state pension age in 2007 is summarised in Figure 3.15. This shows that 23 percent of people had a degree or equivalent, and 8 percent had no qualifications. This level of human capital will change over time, not least because some people in 2007 were still in the educational system. The stock will only increase, however, if younger generations are gaining more educational qualifications than did earlier generations.

Coming to a conclusion about societal well-being and about progress is not going to be easy. It is rather sobering that academics are still debating whether Britain in the 1950s was a period of consensus or conflict. Did we really have it 'so good', or was it a decade in which differences of class, generation, ethnicity, gender, religion and region were sown?

Across the UK, the majority of people are generally satisfied with life. The selection of statistics quoted in this summary includes healthier lives and longer life expectancy. There are marked differences in the life-chances and capital available to different groups in society and between different parts of the country. In order to make sense of all of this, we will be working both to refine the questions and to reach some agreement on the key components of societal well-being and progress.

Your comments and contributions to this are welcome.

Please email: social.trends@ons.gov.uk

1 See 'Measuring societal well-being', *Economic & Labour Market Review*, Vol 1, No 10, October 2007 (pp46–52) for an overview of ONSs' approach to measuring societal well-being.

2 'Subjective social indicators' by Mark Abrams in *Social Trends No 4*, 1973, and 'Subjective measures of quality of life in Britain: 1971 to 1975', by John Hall in *Social Trends No 7*, 1976. Both authors were from the then Social Science Research Council Survey Unit.

Chapter 1

Population

- The number of people living in the UK increased from 55.9 million in 1971 to 60.6 million in 2006. (Table 1.1)

- The number of people aged 65 and over in the UK is expected to exceed the number aged under 16 in 2021. (Table 1.2)

- In 1996, around one in eight births in England and Wales were to mothers born outside the UK. In 2006, the figure had risen to around one in five. (Page 7)

- From 2001 the net flow of internal migration from south to north grew year on year peaking in 2003 at around 35,000 before declining to around 2,700 in 2006. (Figure 1.10)

- Between 1996 and 2006, the net outflow of Britons leaving the UK more than doubled from 62,000 to 126,000. (Figure 1.12)

- In 2006, there was a 32 per cent reduction in applications for UK citizenship compared with 2005, when new legislation relating to English language was introduced. (Page 10)

Download data by clicking the online pdf

www.statistics.gov.uk/socialtrends38

The number of births and deaths, and the number of people entering and leaving the country all affect the size, sex and age structure, and geography of the population. Reliable information on the size and structure of the population is essential for understanding many aspects of society and the economy, particularly household composition and the labour market. Changes in demographic patterns also have implications for public policy decisions in key areas, including housing, and the provision of health, education and social services.

Population profile

In 2006 the number of people living in the UK was around 60.6 million, an increase of almost 5 million since 1971 (Table 1.1). The populations of England, Wales and Northern Ireland all grew steadily over this period, by 4.4 million, 300,000 and 200,000 respectively, whereas the population of Scotland started declining slowly in the mid-1970s and has been broadly stable since the late 1980s. Despite rising in the last four years the population of Scotland stood at 5.1 million in 2006, lower than its peak of 5.2 million in 1971.

Population projections suggest that the UK population will continue to increase, growing by around 10.5 million between 2006 and 2031. As much as 47 per cent of this projected increase is expected to be the result of net migration, while the remaining 53 per cent is attributable to projected net natural change. Projections show that as much as 23 per cent of the projected increase may be the result of births to migrants. In total more than two-thirds (69 per cent) of population growth between 2006 and 2031 is projected to be attributable, either directly or indirectly, to migration.

The populations of England, Wales, Scotland and Northern Ireland as proportions of the UK population varied little between 1971 and 2006. In 2006, 84 per cent of the UK population lived in England (50.8 million), 8 per cent in Scotland (5.1 million), 5 per cent in Wales (3 million) and 3 per cent in Northern Ireland (1.7 million). However, projected trends vary for the constituent countries. Over the next ten years, the populations of all of the UK countries are expected to continue growing. Growth is expected to be 8 per cent in England, 7 per cent in Northern Ireland, 5 per cent in Wales and 3 per cent in Scotland. While the population is projected to rise in Scotland, fertility and life expectancy levels are projected to remain lower than in the rest of the UK (see also Chapter 7: Health).

More boys than girls have been born each year in the UK since 1922 (the first year that UK figures are available for the sex of babies born each year). In 2006, 105 boys were born for every 100 girls. However, there are more females in the overall population; 30.9 million females compared with 29.7 million males in 2006 (Table 1.2). This reflects differences in life expectancy as well as levels of both in- and out-migration. The age at which women start to outnumber men is getting younger, the earliest age that this has occurred since 1991 is in the 25 to 34 age group. This is primarily because males suffer higher mortality rates than females throughout their young adult lives (16 to 24 years of age).

Women have for many decades lived on average longer than men. In 2006, there were three times as many women as men aged 90 and over living in the UK with around 317,000 women compared with 106,000 men. Between 1971 and 2006, however, male death rates have reduced faster than female death rates from age 65 and over, meaning that male life expectancy is improving at a faster rate. The population size at these older ages is therefore projected to increase more strongly for men than for women. The increase in the number

Table 1.1

Population[1] of the United Kingdom

Millions

	1971	1981	1991	2001	2006	2011	2021	2031
United Kingdom	55.9	56.4	57.4	59.1	60.6	62.8	67.2	71.1
England	46.4	46.8	47.9	49.5	50.8	52.7	56.8	60.4
Wales	2.7	2.8	2.9	2.9	3.0	3.0	3.2	3.3
Scotland	5.2	5.2	5.1	5.1	5.1	5.2	5.3	5.4
Northern Ireland	1.5	1.5	1.6	1.7	1.7	1.8	1.9	2.0

1 Mid-year estimates for 1971 to 2006; 2006-based projections for 2011 to 2031. See Appendix, Part 1: Population estimates and projections.

Source: Office for National Statistics; Government Actuary's Department; General Register Office for Scotland; Northern Ireland Statistics and Research Agency

Table 1.2

Population:[1] by sex and age

United Kingdom

Thousands

	Under 16	16–24	25–34	35–44	45–54	55–64	65–74	75 and over	All ages
Males									
1971	7,318	3,730	3,530	3,271	3,354	3,123	1,999	842	27,167
1981	6,439	4,114	4,036	3,409	3,121	2,967	2,264	1,063	27,412
1991	5,976	3,800	4,432	3,950	3,287	2,835	2,272	1,358	27,909
2001	6,077	3,284	4,215	4,382	3,856	3,090	2,308	1,621	28,832
2006	5,912	3,696	3,940	4,587	3,876	3,512	2,379	1,792	29,694
2011	5,961	3,846	4,235	4,314	4,292	3,592	2,636	2,018	30,893
2016	6,187	3,647	4,707	4,043	4,487	3,642	3,052	2,324	32,088
2021	6,485	3,490	4,784	4,318	4,217	4,045	3,153	2,761	33,253
2026	6,557	3,670	4,553	4,787	3,957	4,238	3,230	3,322	34,313
Females									
1971	6,938	3,626	3,441	3,241	3,482	3,465	2,765	1,802	28,761
1981	6,104	3,966	3,975	3,365	3,148	3,240	2,931	2,218	28,946
1991	5,709	3,691	4,466	3,968	3,296	2,971	2,795	2,634	29,530
2001	5,786	3,220	4,260	4,465	3,920	3,186	2,640	2,805	30,281
2006	5,625	3,525	3,956	4,675	3,958	3,638	2,650	2,867	30,893
2011	5,682	3,613	4,200	4,375	4,413	3,744	2,883	2,958	31,868
2016	5,909	3,420	4,572	4,092	4,620	3,796	3,323	3,156	32,887
2021	6,202	3,272	4,591	4,321	4,323	4,242	3,438	3,549	33,938
2026	6,271	3,453	4,368	4,691	4,048	4,448	3,512	4,155	34,946

1 Mid-year estimates for 1971 to 2006; 2006-based projections for 2011 to 2026. See Appendix, Part 1: Population estimates and projections.

Source: Office for National Statistics; Government Actuary's Department; General Register Office for Scotland; Northern Ireland Statistics and Research Agency

of people aged 90 and over from 2006 to 2026 is projected to be nearly fourfold (360 per cent) for men and nearly double (190 per cent) for women.

The UK has an ageing population, a consequence of historically declining fertility rates and significant improvements in mortality, which mostly affects older age groups. Over the last 35 years, the population aged under 16 has decreased from around 14.3 million to 11.5 million while the population aged 65 and over has increased by 2.3 million (Figure 1.3 overleaf). In 1971 there were 14.3 million children aged under 16, which was around one in four of the population. By 2006 the proportion of under 16s had decreased to around one in five of the overall population, at around 11.5 million. The 2006-based projections suggest that this proportion of the population will stay broadly similar over the next 20 years, with 19 per cent of the population being aged under 16 by 2026. In contrast, the proportion of the population aged 65 and over has increased steadily over the past 35 years. This age group grew from

13 per cent of the overall population in 1971 to 16 per cent in 2006, and is expected to reach around 20 per cent by 2026. The number of people aged 65 and over is expected to exceed the number aged under 16 by 2021.

The ageing of the UK population, including an increase in the proportion of people claiming a state pension and the ageing of the working-age population, poses serious challenges, both socially and economically. In 2006, there were 3.3 people of working age (16 to 64 for men, 16 to 59 for women) for every person of state pension age. This figure is set to fall to 2.9 people by 2031. Without the forthcoming changes to the state pension age (rising from 60 to 65 for women between 2010 and 2020 and from 65 to 66 for both sexes between 2024 and 2026), this ratio would fall to 2.2 by 2031.

Having an ageing population is an issue in many of the 27 member states of the EU. In 2006 Italy, Germany, Greece, Bulgaria, Portugal, Latvia, Estonia, Spain and Slovenia all had a

Figure 1.3

Population:[1] by sex and age, 1971, 2006 and 2031

United Kingdom

Millions

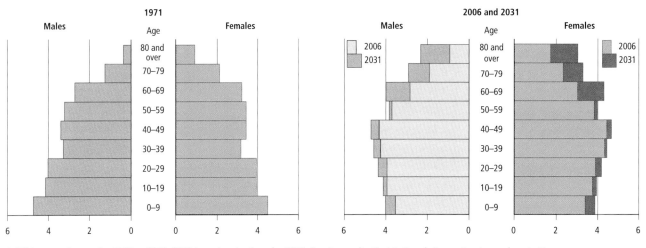

1 Mid-year estimates for 1971 to 2006; 2006-based projections for 2031. See Appendix, Part 1: Population estimates and projections.

Source: Office for National Statistics; Government Actuary's Department; Government Register Office for Scotland; Northern Ireland Statistics and Research Agency

greater proportion aged 65 and over than children aged under 16 (Table 1.4). Ireland had the youngest population, with almost 22 per cent of the population aged under 16 and around 11 per cent aged 65 and over, a proportion that has remained steady since 1960.

In 2006 the UK had a larger proportion of the population aged under 16 than the EU-27 average, 19 per cent compared with 17 per cent. The proportion of people in the UK aged 65 and over, at 16 per cent, was lower than the EU-27 average of 17 per cent.

Table 1.4

Population: by age, EU comparison, 2006

Percentages

	Under 16	16–64	65 and over		Under 16	16–64	65 and over
Italy	15.1	65.2	19.7	Slovenia	15.3	69.1	15.6
Germany	15.3	65.4	19.3	Lithuania	18.0	66.6	15.3
Greece	15.4	66.1	18.5	Denmark	20.0	64.9	15.2
Sweden	18.7	64.0	17.3	Romania	16.9	68.3	14.8
Bulgaria	14.8	68.0	17.2	Luxembourg	19.8	65.8	14.4
Belgium	18.3	64.5	17.2	Netherlands	19.5	66.2	14.3
Portugal	16.7	66.2	17.1	Czech Republic	15.9	69.9	14.2
Latvia	15.8	67.4	16.8	Malta	18.5	68.0	13.4
Estonia	16.5	66.7	16.7	Poland	17.7	69.0	13.3
Spain	15.5	67.8	16.7	Cyprus	19.9	68.1	12.0
Austria	17.1	66.5	16.5	Slovakia	18.1	70.2	11.7
France	19.9	63.9	16.2	Ireland	21.9	67.0	11.1
Finland	18.5	65.5	16.0				
United Kingdom	19.1	64.9	16.0	EU-27 average	17.2	66.1	16.8
Hungary	16.7	67.5	15.8				

Source: Eurostat; Office for National Statistics

Classification of ethnic groups

Membership of an ethnic group is something that is subjectively meaningful to the person concerned. Ethnic group questions are designed to ask people which group they see themselves belonging to. This means that the information collected is not based on objective, quantifiable information like age or sex.

There are two levels to the National Statistics classification of ethnic groups. Level 1 has five main ethnic groups: White, Mixed, Asian or Asian British, Black or Black British, Chinese or Other ethnic group. Level 2, the preferred approach, provides a broader breakdown than level 1 and is used in this chapter. For further information see Appendix, Part 1: Classification of ethnic groups.

Projections suggest that by 2050, the EU-27 will have almost twice as many people aged 65 and over than aged under 16. Spain and Italy are likely to have the oldest populations, with estimates that more than 35 per cent of their populations will be aged 65 and over and around 13 per cent will be aged under 16. Ireland, Sweden and Luxembourg are projected to have the youngest population profile, with around 18 per cent of their populations aged under 16.

Most ethnic minority groups in England have a younger age structure than the White British population. Estimates show that in 2005, around 19 per cent of the White British population was aged under 16 (Table 1.5), whereas children accounted for around 26 per cent of the non-White population.

The Mixed population had the youngest profile in England in 2005, with 46 per cent aged under 16. The Other Black, Bangladeshi and Pakistani groups also had young age profiles, with 35 per cent, 34 per cent and 32 per cent respectively aged under 16. In all of these groups, the estimates suggest there has been a decline in the proportion of under 16s since 2001. Census data showed that 50 per cent of the Mixed population, 38 per cent of both the Other Black and Bangladeshi groups, and 35 per cent of the Pakistani group were aged under 16. Care should be taken when comparing estimates from different sources. Comparisons drawn here are indicative based on the best available data and are deemed reliable in this context.

The fastest population growth between 2001 and 2005 in England was estimated to be in the Chinese ethnic group, with an average annual growth rate of around 11 per cent. However, the proportion of people in this group aged under 16 increased by 14 per cent, compared with an increase of almost 18 per cent for Black African children and 19 per cent for the Other White group. Most of the increase in the Chinese

Table 1.5

Population: by ethnic group and age, 2005[1]

England   Percentages

	Under 16	16–64	65 and over	All people (thousands)
White				
White British	19	64	17	42,753
White Irish	6	65	29	592
Other White	13	78	9	1,623
Mixed	46	51	3	791
Asian or Asian British				
Indian	19	74	7	1,215
Pakistani	32	64	5	826
Bangladeshi	34	62	4	324
Other Asian	21	74	5	310
Black or Black British				
Black Caribbean	18	69	13	590
Black African	26	72	3	659
Other Black	35	62	4	110
Chinese	13	82	4	347
Other ethnic group	15	82	3	325
All ethnic groups	19	65	16	50,466

1 These are experimental statistics. See Appendix, Part 1: Experimental statistics, and classification of ethnic groups.

Source: Office for National Statistics

National Statistics Socio-economic Classification (NS-SEC)

The NS-SEC was launched in 2001 to replace the Registrar General's Social Class measure based on occupation. The NS-SEC is an occupationally based classification but has rules to provide coverage of the whole adult population. The information required to create the NS-SEC is occupation coded to the unit groups (OUG) of the Standard Occupational Classification 2000 (SOC2000) (see Appendix Part 4: Standard Occupational Classification 2000 (SOC2000)) and details of employment status (whether an employer, self-employed or employee; whether a supervisor; number of employees at the workplace).

Further information on NS-SEC can be found in Appendix, Part 1: National Statistics Socio-economic Classification (NS-SEC).

Figure 1.6

Population: by socio-economic classification[1] and working age[2], 2007[3]

United Kingdom

Percentages

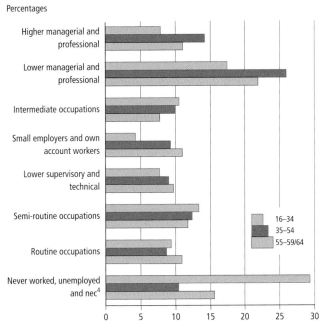

1 Population living in private households. Excludes those who did not state their current or last occupation, and those who had not worked in the last eight years. See Appendix, Part 1: National Statistics Socio-economic Classification (NS-SEC).
2 Men aged 16 to 64, women aged 16 to 59.
3 At spring.
4 People unemployed for less than one year are classified according to their previous occupation. Includes those not elsewhere classified (nec).

Source: Labour Force Survey, Office for National Statistics

population is among people aged between 16 and 64 and is largely because of net in-migration of people born in China.

Figure 1.6 shows that at spring 2007, working-age individuals in the UK were most likely to be in the lower managerial and professional socio-economic group (8.1 million) or in the 'never worked, unemployed and nec' group, which includes students and other occupations not classified or inadequately described (6.8 million), than in any other socio-economic group (see Appendix, Part 1: National Statistics Socio-economic Classification (NS-SEC)). In the youngest age group (people aged 16 to 34), more than 29 per cent were recorded in the never worked category and 4 per cent were classed as small employers and own account workers. People aged between 35 and 54 were most likely to be in the lower managerial group (26 per cent) and least likely to be either in routine occupations (9 per cent). Older workers aged between 55 and state pension age were also most likely to be in the lower managerial group than in any other category (22 per cent). They were least likely to be in the intermediate occupations (8 per cent).

Population change

The rate of population change over time depends on both natural change – the difference between the numbers of births and deaths – and the net effect of people migrating to and from the country. Table 1.7 shows that in the period 1951 to 2001 net natural change was the most important factor in

Table 1.7

Population change[1,2]

United Kingdom

Thousands

	Population at start of period	Annual averages				
		Live births	Deaths	Net natural change	Net migration and other	Overall change
1951–1961	50,287	839	593	246	6	252
1961–1971	52,807	962	638	324	–12	312
1971–1981	55,928	736	666	69	–27	42
1981–1991	56,357	757	655	103	5	108
1991–2001	57,439	731	631	100	68	167
2001–2006	59,113	701	595	106	189	295
2006–2011	60,587	780	565	215	220	435
2011–2021	62,761	802	551	252	191	443

1 Mid-year estimates for 1951–1961 to 2001–06; 2006-based projections for 2006–11 and 2011–21. The start population for 2006–11 is the mid-year estimate for 2006.
2 See Appendix, Part 1: Population estimates and projections.

Source: Office for National Statistics; Government Actuary's Department; General Register Office for Scotland; Northern Ireland Statistics and Research Agency

population growth in the UK. This began to change in the 1970s, with a lower number of live births than in earlier decades. The net inflow of migrants to the UK began to rise in the 1980s reversing the trend of the previous two decades when there was a net outflow of migration, before increasing rapidly in the 1990s. The combination of these two factors has considerably increased the influence of migration on population change. In the period 1951 to 1961, natural change accounted for 98 per cent of population growth in the UK. Between 2001 and 2006 this had fallen to 36 per cent. With the current trend in increased birth rates and a lower number of deaths, population growth between 2006 and 2011 is expected to be attributable to migration and natural change in roughly equal measures. Projections suggest that between 2011 and 2021 natural change is once again expected to become the more important factor influencing population change, accounting for around 57 per cent of the increase in population.

The two World Wars in the 20th century had a major impact on births in the UK. One million babies were born in 1915, falling to less than 800,000 in 1917 and 1918. The post-war baby boom was delayed by the 1918–19 flu epidemic, following which live births hit a peak of more than 1.1 million in 1920 (Figure 1.8). The number of live births then fell again to a low of 692,000 in 1933 before rising again to more than 1 million after the Second World War. Live births fell to 790,000 in 1955 but rose again and exceeded 1 million for a third time in 1964.

Figure 1.8

Live births[1,2]

United Kingdom

Millions

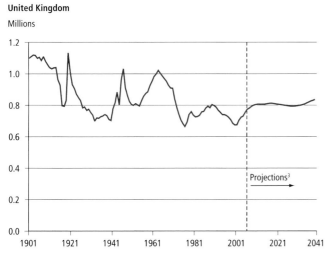

1 Babies showing signs of life at birth.
2 Data for 1901 to 1921 exclude Ireland, which was constitutionally a part of the UK during this period. From 1981 data for births in Northern Ireland exclude births to non-residents.
3 2006-based projections for 2007 to 2041.

Source: Office for National Statistics; Government Actuary's Department; General Register Office for Scotland; Northern Ireland Statistics and Research Agency

An important factor influencing the number of births is the number of women of reproductive age. By the second half of the 1980s the women born during the 1960s baby boom entered their peak reproductive years and this was reflected by an increase in the number of births from 719,000 in 1982 to 798,000 in 1990. The smaller cohorts of women born in the 1970s reached their reproductive peak in the 1990s and this, combined with lower fertility rates led to a decline in the numbers of births to below 700,000 by 2000.

The number of live births in the UK reached its lowest level since 1977 in 2001 at around 670,000, but has increased each year since then. In 2006 there were 749,000 live births in the UK, an increase of almost 12 per cent (80,000) compared with 2002. Projections suggest that the number of live births will exceed 800,000 by 2016 and will increase until around 2020, before beginning to slowly tail off. The last time the number of live births in the UK was this high was in 1972 when it reached 834,000. One factor in this recent change could be the increase in the proportion of births to mothers who were born outside the UK, as their patterns of childbearing could reflect those of their original country rather than the UK's fertility rates. In 1996 more than one in eight (13 per cent) births in England and Wales were to mothers who were not born in the UK. By 2006 this proportion had risen to more than one in five (22 per cent). Further information on births and fertility can be found in Chapter 2: Households and families.

With the exception of 1976, there have been fewer deaths than births in the UK every year since 1901. In 2006 there were 572,000 deaths in the UK (Table 1.9 overleaf), 472,000 in England, 31,000 in Wales, 55,000 in Scotland and 15,000 in Northern Ireland. Despite considerable population growth during the last century, the number of deaths remained fairly stable, fluctuating between 570,000 and 660,000 per year in the second half of the century. Current demographic patterns, including the increase in births and net migration, mean that natural change is projected to remain positive into the foreseeable future. Projections suggest that the number of deaths will stay below 600,000 per year until the late 2020s and then increase as the number of people born immediately after the Second World War and during the 1960s baby booms reach advanced ages. The number of deaths could exceed 700,000 deaths per year by the late 2030s.

As the population has increased and the number of deaths has remained broadly stable, so death rates have fallen considerably. In 1981 the crude death rate in the UK was 12.0 per 1,000 for males and 11.4 per 1,000 for females. By 2006 the rate had fallen to 9.2 and 9.6 per 1,000 respectively and is expected to be as low as 8.4 per 1,000 for males and

Table 1.9

Deaths:[1] by sex and age

United Kingdom

Death rates per 1,000 in each age group

	Under 1[2]	1–15	16–34	35–54	55–64	65–74	75 and over	All ages	All deaths (thousands)
Males									
1971	20.2	0.5	1.0	4.8	20.4	51.1	131.4	12.1	329
1981	12.7	0.4	1.0	4.0	18.1	46.4	122.2	12.0	329
1991	8.3	0.3	0.9	3.1	14.2	38.7	111.2	11.3	314
2001	6.0	0.2	0.9	2.8	10.4	28.7	96.6	10.0	288
2006	5.4	0.2	0.8	2.6	9.1	23.7	86.4	9.2	274
2011	5.3	0.1	0.6	2.6	8.5	19.5	75.4	8.6	264
2021	4.8	0.1	0.5	2.4	7.2	16.6	61.9	8.4	279
Females									
1971	15.5	0.4	0.5	3.1	10.3	26.6	96.6	11.0	317
1981	9.5	0.3	0.4	2.5	9.8	24.7	90.2	11.4	329
1991	6.3	0.2	0.4	1.9	8.4	22.3	85.0	11.2	332
2001	5.0	0.1	0.4	1.8	6.4	17.9	81.6	10.4	316
2006	4.5	0.1	0.3	1.6	5.7	15.2	76.1	9.6	298
2011	4.5	0.1	0.3	1.6	5.5	13.0	72.0	9.1	290
2021	4.1	0.1	0.3	1.4	4.6	11.2	58.0	8.3	280

1 2006-based projections for 2011 and 2021.
2 Rate per 1,000 live births.

Source: Office for National Statistics; Government Actuary's Department; General Register Office for Scotland; Northern Ireland Statistics and Research Agency

8.3 per 1,000 for females by 2021. Rising standards of living, changes in occupational structure such as the move away from hard physical labour to more office-based employment, and advances in medical technology and practice help to explain this decline in death rates.

Between 1981 and 2006, the populations of England, Wales and Northern Ireland all increased; by 8 per cent, 5 per cent and 13 per cent respectively. The population of Scotland fell by 1 per cent during this period (see Table 1.1).

At local authority level in England, the biggest net gains in population were recorded in Milton Keynes, where the population increased by more than 78 per cent between 1981 and 2006, followed by East Cambridgeshire and the London borough of Tower Hamlets, where the population increased by around 47 per cent in both areas. In Liverpool, the population fell by almost 16 per cent, closely followed by Knowsley, also in Merseyside, with a fall of 13 per cent.

In addition to births and deaths, regional populations are affected by international migration flows and by people relocating within the UK. Overall England had a net loss of nearly 15,000 people in 2006 through internal migration.

Northern Ireland gained almost 2,000 people, Scotland gained just under 5,500 and Wales gained around 7,500.

A recent study by the University of Sheffield looked at a series of different statistical, social, cultural and economic factors to come up with a definition of what constitutes north and south of the UK. Their conclusions placed the dividing line along a diagonal from just above Gloucester in the south west to just below Grimsby in the north east. During the 20th century there was a movement of population from the north of England, Scotland and Wales, where the coal, shipbuilding and steel industries were in decline, to the Midlands and the South East, where many light industries and service industries are based. This peaked in 1986, when there was a net gain to the south of around 71,000 people (Figure 1.10). So far the 21st century has seen a reversal of this trend, with a net gain to the north every year since 2001 and the south recording a loss of as many as 35,000 people in 2003.

Although the south, comprising the Government Office regions of London, the South East, the South West, East of England and the East Midlands, experienced an overall net loss of around 2,680 people in 2006, the South West saw the largest net inflow from internal migration in the UK

Figure 1.10

Net migration from north to south[1]

United Kingdom

Thousands

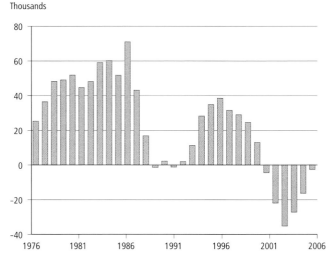

1 The south comprises the Government Office regions of London, South East, South West, East of England and East Midlands; the north is the remainder of the UK. See Appendix, Part 1: Internal migration estimates.

Source: National Health Service Central Register; General Register Office for Scotland; Northern Ireland Statistics and Research Agency

Many interregional moves are across relatively short distances; for example, one-third (33 per cent) of people who moved to London in 2006 moved from the South East and around two-fifths (43 per cent) of people who moved to the South East moved from London.

London has seen the greatest net loss through within-UK migration every year for at least the last three decades, losing an average of 60,000 people annually. Table 1.11 shows that in England and Wales the London boroughs dominated the list of the top ten areas losing population through within-UK migration. In 2006, Newham in east London recorded a net loss of around 9,500 people, accounting for almost 4 per cent of its population.

The authority with the highest net inflow of internal migrants in England and Wales in 2006 was Torridge, Devon, recording a net gain of more than 1,000 people, or less than 2 per cent of its population.

In Wales, Carmarthenshire recorded the highest net inflow with almost 1,250 more people (less than 1 per cent of the population) moving into the area rather than leaving, while Merthyr Tydfil saw the highest net outflow with more than 100 more people moving away (less than 1 per cent of the population). In Northern Ireland the local authority that recorded the largest percentage net gain was Carrickfergus, with around 350 people moving into the area in 2006, an increase of nearly 1 per cent. Belfast experienced the largest net outflow, with almost 2,250 people (nearly 1 per cent). Similar data are

(28,000 people). London experienced the largest net loss in the UK, with almost 79,000 more people moving from, rather than to, the capital. Of nearly 250,000 people who left London in 2006, more than three-quarters (194,000) stayed in the south.

Table 1.11

Internal migration:[1] net flows by local authority,[2] 2006

England & Wales

Percentages

Highest inflow			Highest outflow		
1	Torridge	1.57	1	Newham	−3.84
2	Oswestry	1.52	2	Brent	−2.44
3	West Lindsey	1.51	3	Ealing	−2.26
4	East Northampton	1.47	4	Haringey	−2.11
5	North Dorset	1.42	5	Lambeth	−2.10
6	North Somerset[3]	1.38	6	Hackney	−2.04
7	Suffolk Coastal	1.34	7	Luton[3]	−1.96
8	Tendring	1.34	8	Hammersmith and Fulham	−1.54
9	West Dorset	1.31	9	Waltham Forest	−1.49
10	Caradon	1.31	10	Southwark	−1.44

1 Net flow estimates are for year ending mid-2006 and are based on the patient register data system (PRDS) and patient re-registration recorded in the National Health Service Central Register (NHSCR). Rates are as a percentage of the mid-2006 population estimates for England and Wales population and represent flows of population to and from other areas of England and Wales.
2 Local authorities by top ten highest rates of internal migration inflows and outflows. See Appendix, Part 1: Internal migration estimates.
3 North Somerset and Luton are unitary authorities.

Source: Office for National Statistics

available for Scotland at NHS Board area level. The area with the largest internal net gain in 2006, with a 1.1 per cent increase was the Orkney Islands, whereas the Shetland Islands experienced the largest internal net loss with a 0.3 per cent decrease.

International migration

In 2006, the number of people arriving to live in the UK for at least one year was estimated to be 591,000, 85 per cent of whom were non-British citizens. Approximately 400,000 people left the country for at least one year and just over half of these people were British citizens. There was a net inflow of around 191,000 people to the UK in 2006, which is the equivalent of adding a little over 500 people to the population each day. London remained the most popular destination and its population decline due to internal migration was more than offset by the inflow of around 170,000 international migrants settling there. The South East was the next most popular destination, with more than 80,000 new arrivals.

Between 1998 and 2003, total net immigration to the UK remained fairly steady at around 150,000 a year. This increased sharply to 244,000 in 2004 but then eased off, with an estimate of 191,000 recorded in 2006. The higher levels of total net migration since 2004 can be largely attributed to increased net immigration from the EU. This was the year of EU expansion which granted free movement of people from Poland and other central and eastern European countries. There has also been a steady increase in net immigration from the New Commonwealth since 1996, and in 2006 it was 115,000 making it the highest of all the main citizenship groups. By contrast there has been a trend of higher net emigration of British citizens. This has increased from 62,000 in 1996 to 126,000 in 2006 (Figure 1.12).

London remained the most popular destination for immigrants to the UK and its population decline as a result of internal migration was more than offset by the inflow of around 170,000 international migrants settling there in 2006. The South East was the next most popular destination, with more than 80,000 new arrivals.

Provided they are working or are able to support themselves financially, nationals of the European Economic Area (EEA) (EU-27 plus Iceland, Liechtenstein and Norway) have the right to reside in the UK. Almost all other overseas nationals wishing to stay permanently in the UK need to apply for indefinite leave to remain. This entitlement granted for a fixed period of five years, can lapse and many people with this status go on to apply for full citizenship.

Applications for citizenship remained fairly steady during the 1990s, at around 60,000 applications a year. The introduction

Figure 1.12

Estimates of migration net flows: by citizenship[1]

United Kingdom

Thousands

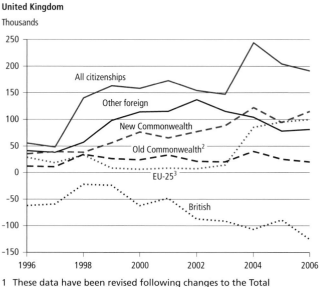

1 These data have been revised following changes to the Total International Migration (TIM) methodology. Therefore they may not agree with estimates that have been published previously. See Appendix, Part 1: International Migration Estimates.
2 Old Commonwealth comprises Australia, Canada, New Zealand and South Africa. New Commonwealth is the rest of the Commonwealth.
3 Up to and including 2003, estimates are for the EU-15. From 2004 onwards, estimates are for the EU-25.

Source: Total International Migration, Office for National Statistics

of new legislation in November 2005, which requires applicants to demonstrate knowledge of both the English language and life in the UK, coincided with a sudden surge in applications earlier that year. In 2006, 149,000 applications were submitted to the Home Office, 32 per cent less than in 2005 when around 219,000 applications were submitted.

Around 154,000 applications were approved in the UK in 2006, the first year since 1997 to see a fall in the number of persons granted British citizenship (Figure 1.13). Around one-half of the applications approved were granted on the basis of five or more years' residence in the UK. The number of citizenships granted on the basis of marriage continued to fall from a peak of around 40,000 in 2004. In 2006 around 28,000 people were awarded grants on the basis of being married to a British citizen for three or more years. The majority of the remaining grants were awarded to children and young people under the age of 18.

In 2006 there was a fall in the number of citizenships awarded to people from all geographic regions, with the exception of people from Asia, who accounted for more than two in five of all grants awarded. Citizenships awarded to applicants from the EEA fell by 6 per cent to just under 4,000. The largest proportion of these (16 per cent) were awarded to Polish applicants.

Between 2005 and 2006, the number of people seeking asylum in the UK, including dependants, fell by around 8 per cent to

Figure 1.13

Grants of British citizenship:[1] by basis of grant

United Kingdom

Thousands

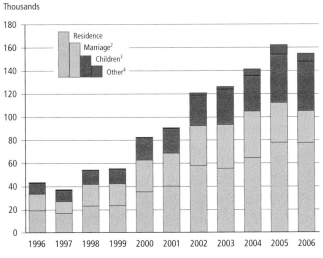

1 Data from November 2001 include grants of British citizenship in the Channel Islands and Isle of Man. See Appendix, Part 1: International Migration Estimates.
2 Marriage includes civil partnerships from 5 December 2005.
3 Children aged under 18.
4 Includes British Overseas Territories citizens from Gibraltar registered as British citizens under section 5 of the British Nationality Act 1981.

Source: Home Office

around 28,300. Applications have decreased each year since 2002, when they peaked at around 103,100. More than 80 per cent of applicants in 2006 were under the age of 35 and 3 per cent were aged 50 and over. The majority of applicants were men (70 per cent).

Almost 21,000 initial decisions on asylum were made in 2006, around 10 per cent of which resulted in asylum being granted, an increase from 7 per cent in the previous year. At the end of 2006, 6,400 applications were still awaiting an initial decision. Less than 21,000 individuals, including dependants, were declared to be failed asylum seekers in 2006, around one-half the number recorded for 2005 (45,200). In 2006 there were 17 per cent more removals of asylum seekers and their dependants than in 2005.

Including dependants, applications for asylum to the rest of the EU-27 (excluding the UK) fell by 21 per cent in 2006. Greece, Italy, the Netherlands, Spain, Sweden, Hungary and Malta experienced an increase in applications, while the number of applications in the other member states either fell or stayed the same.

France received the highest number of asylum applications of all the EU-27 countries in every year since 2003 and in 2006 received nearly 30,700 (Table 1.14). After France, the UK

Table 1.14

Asylum applications[1] including dependants: EU comparison, 2006

People

	Number of asylum seekers	Asylum seekers per 1,000 population		Number of asylum seekers	Asylum seekers per 1,000 population
Cyprus	4,500	4.5	Germany[2]	21,000	0.3
Malta	1,300	3.2	Hungary	2,100	0.2
Sweden[2]	24,300	2.7	Italy	10,300	0.2
Austria[2]	13,400	1.6	Spain[2]	5,300	0.1
Belgium[2]	13,200	1.3	Poland	4,400	0.1
Greece	12,300	1.1	Slovenia	500	0.1
Luxembourg	500	1.1	Bulgaria	600	0.1
Ireland[2]	4,300	1.0	Lithuania	100	-
Netherlands[2]	14,500	0.9	Romania	500	-
Slovakia	2,900	0.5	Portugal	100	-
France[2]	30,700	0.5	Estonia	*	-
United Kingdom	28,300	0.5	Latvia	*	-
Finland[2]	2,300	0.4			
Denmark[2]	1,900	0.4	All applications to EU-27	211,100	0.4
Czech Republic	3,000	0.3			

1 See Appendix, Part 1: Refugees. UK figures are based on Immigration Research and Statistics Service data. Unless otherwise stated, all other figures are based on United Nations High Commissioner for Refugees (UNHCR) data, including dependants.
2 Figures based on Intergovernmental Consultations on Asylum, Refugees and Migration Policies in Europe, North America and Australia (IGC) data but adjusted to include an estimated number of dependants.

Source: Home Office

received more applications for asylum than any other country in the EU-27. However, this amounted to less than one asylum seeker per 1,000 population, compared with almost five asylum seekers per 1,000 population in Cyprus.

International perspectives

In 2005 the world population was more than 6.5 billion people (Table 1.15). The most populous continent was Asia, with more than 3.9 billion people (60 per cent of the world's population) and this is projected to rise to more than 4 billion by 2010. More than 14 per cent of the world's population lived in Africa and 11 per cent lived in Europe. Asia was also the most densely populated continent, with 124 people per square kilometre. Oceania was the least densely populated, with four people per square kilometre. Oceania also had the smallest proportion of the world's population, at less than 1 per cent (33,410 million).

Throughout the world, population growth rates have been declining since the period 1970–75 and growth is expected to continue slowing over the next 20 years. In the period 1995–2000 the population of Europe stopped growing, the only continent in the world to do so. In the period 2000–2005, Europe experienced a positive growth rate of 0.07 per cent but a negative growth rate is expected in the future. In contrast, Africa recorded a growth rate of 2.32 per cent in this period and Latin America and the Caribbean recorded a growth rate of 1.29 per cent. The growth rate for all continents is expected to slow in the future.

Both in Europe and North America in 2000–05, the total fertility rate is below the replacement level of 2.1 babies for every woman of child-bearing age whereas African women

Total Fertility Rate

The total fertility rate (TFR) is the average number of children per woman a group of women would have if they experienced the age specific fertility rates of a particular year for their entire childbearing years. Changes in the number of births result in part from changes in the population age structure. The TFR is commonly used to look at fertility because it standardises for the changing age structure of the population.

Replacement level fertility

Replacement level fertility is the level at which a population would be exactly replacing itself in the long term, other things being equal. In developed countries this is valued at 2.1 children per woman to take account of infant mortality and those who choose not to have children.

bear an average of 4.98 children each. However, for every 1,000 live births in Africa, 93 infants will not survive beyond their first year. Those who survive childhood can expect to live to around 50 years, while in Europe and North America, where the infant mortality rate is less than 10 infant deaths per 1,000 live births, life expectancy at birth is around 75 years for men and 80 for women.

Across Europe, life expectancy at birth in the period 2000–05 averaged 69.6 years for men and 78.0 years for women. In the UK, this gap between the sexes widened in the 1980s but has narrowed in recent years, closing from 5.5 years in 1991 to around 4.3 years in 2006. Life expectancy at birth based on

Table 1.15

World demographic indicators, 2005

	Population (millions)	Population density (sq km)	Infant mortality rate[1,2]	Total Fertility Rate[1,2]	Life expectancy at birth (years)[2]	
					Males	Females
Asia	3,938	124	48.6	2.47	65.8	69.4
Africa	922	30	93.2	4.98	50.3	52.8
Europe	731	32	8.8	1.41	69.6	78.0
Latin America & Caribbean	558	27	25.4	2.52	68.8	75.3
North America	322	15	6.7	1.99	74.9	80.3
Oceania	33	4	28.6	2.37	71.6	77.3
World	6,515	48	53.9	2.65	63.9	68.3

1 Per 1,000 live births.
2 Data are for 2000–05, figures revised in 2006.

Source: United Nations

Table 1.16

Demographic indicators: EU comparison, 2007

	Population (millions)	Infant mortality rate[1]	Total Fertility Rate[2]	Life expectancy at birth (years)[2]			Population (millions)	Infant mortality rate[1]	Total Fertility Rate[2]	Life expectancy at birth (years)[2]	
				Males	Females					Males	Females
Austria	8.3	4.2	1.24	76.7	82.3	Lithuania	3.4	6.8	1.27	65.3	77.3
Belgium	10.6	3.8	1.67	76.6	82.4	Luxembourg	0.5	2.6	1.70	76.6	82.2
Bulgaria	7.7	10.4	1.31	69.0	76.2	Malta	0.4	6.0	1.71	77.3	81.4
Cyprus	0.8	4.0	1.40	76.8	81.1	Netherlands	16.4	4.9	1.40	77.3	81.7
Czech Republic	10.3	3.4	1.28	72.9	79.3	Poland	38.1	6.4	1.40	70.8	79.3
Denmark	5.4	4.4	1.80	76.0	80.5	Portugal	10.6	3.5	1.32	74.9	81.3
Estonia	1.3	5.4	1.50	67.3	78.2	Romania	21.6	15.0	1.26	68.7	75.7
Finland	5.3	3.0	1.77	75.6	82.5	Slovakia	5.4	7.2	1.80	70.2	78.1
France	61.5	3.6	1.92	76.8	83.8	Slovenia	2.0	4.1	1.25	73.9	80.9
Germany	82.3	3.9	1.34	76.7	82.0	Spain	44.5	3.8	1.35	77.0	83.7
Greece	11.2	3.8	1.33	76.8	81.6	Sweden	9.1	2.4	1.78	78.5	82.9
Hungary	10.1	6.2	1.31	68.7	77.2	United Kingdom	60.6	5.0	1.78	76.6	81.0
Ireland[3]	4.2	4.0	1.86	77.3	81.7						
Italy	59.1	4.0	1.31	77.8	83.4						
Latvia	2.3	7.8	1.31	65.4	76.5						

1 Per 1,000 live births, 2005 data, 2004 data for Italy.
2 Data are for 2005.
3 Population data for Ireland are for 2006.

Source: Office for National Statistics; Eurostat; national sources for Belgium, France and Italy

recent mortality shows women living 4.6 years longer than men, compared with 5.1 years in the period 1950–55. A similar pattern can be seen in other developed countries, such as Canada, France, Germany and the United States, where the gap reached a peak during the 1980s but began narrowing towards the end of the 20th century. Japan had the highest life expectancy in the world in 2000–05, with life expectancy at birth of 85 years for women and 78 years for men.

Historically, longer life expectancy and improved infant mortality rates have contributed to increased population sizes across Europe. In 2007, Germany had the largest population in the EU-27, at 82.3 million, almost 21 million more than the next largest country, France with 61.5 million (Table 1.16). The UK had the third largest population. Together, at around 205 million people, the total population of these three nations accounts for nearly half the population of the EU-27.

Chapter 2

Households and families

- Between 1971 and 2007, the number of households in Great Britain rose by 5.8 million to 24.4 million. (Table 2.1)

- In Great Britain in 2007 the proportion of people living alone (12 per cent) was double that of 1971. (Table 2.3)

- In 2005 there were just under 284,000 marriages in the UK, around 27,000 fewer than in 2004, and 197,000 fewer than in 1972, when the number of marriages peaked at 480,000. (Figure 2.8)

- Over the last 20 years, the proportion of unmarried men and women aged under 60 cohabiting in Great Britain rose from 11 per cent of men and 13 per cent of women to 24 per cent and 25 per cent respectively. (Page 19)

- One in ten men and one in four women forming a civil partnership in the UK in 2006 had been in a previous legal partnership, in nearly all cases a marriage. (Page 22)

- Married women giving birth for the first time were, on average, age 30 in England and Wales in 2006, compared with age 24 in 1971. (Table 2.14)

Home life, partnerships and other social relationships are important influences on personal development and well-being. Trends in household and family formation are of particular interest to policy makers, for example in determining housing needs. Traditionally the majority of people in the UK shared living arrangements with others in the same household. However, over the past few decades changes in the age profile of the population, in society's values and attitudes, and in social legislation have led to new structures and characteristics of households and families. More people are spending time living on their own, whether before, after, or instead of marriage or cohabitation.

Household composition

Households are defined, broadly, as people who live and eat together, or people who live alone. Families are defined by marriage, civil partnership or cohabitation and, where there are children in the household, child/parent relationships. Most households consist of a single family or someone living alone. However, not all people live in private households. Some live in institutions such as care homes, prisons, hospitals and other communal establishments and are not covered in this chapter.

Reference persons

Though the majority of households contain one family, some households contain multiple families, while others do not contain a family at all (for example, where the household consists of one person or of non-related adults). This chapter mainly refers to data based on the household reference person although some data are based on the family reference person. The UK Census 2001 defined Family reference person and Household reference person as follows:

Family reference person (FRP)

In a couple family the FRP is chosen from the two people in the couple on the basis of their economic activity in priority order of full-time job, part-time job, unemployed, retired, other. If both have the same economic activity, the FRP is defined as the elder of the two, or if they are the same age, the first member of the couple listed on the census form. In a lone-parent family the FRP is the lone parent.

Household reference person (HRP)

A person living alone is the HRP. If the household contains one family the HRP is the same as the FRP. If there is more than one family in the household, the HRP is chosen from among the FRPs using the same criteria for choosing the FRP. If there is no family, the HRP is chosen from the individuals living in the household using the same criteria.

Table 2.1

Households:[1] by size

Great Britain					Percentages
	1971	1981	1991	2001[2]	2007[2]
One person	18	22	27	29	29
Two people	32	32	34	35	35
Three people	19	17	16	16	16
Four people	17	18	16	14	13
Five people	8	7	5	5	5
Six or more people	6	4	2	2	2
All households (=100%) (millions)	18.6	20.2	22.4	23.8	24.4
Average household size (number of people)	2.9	2.7	2.5	2.4	2.4

1 See Appendix, Part 2: Multi-sourced tables, Households, and Families.
2 Data are at spring for 2001 and Q2 for 2007. See Appendix, Part 4: Labour Force Survey.

Source: Census, Labour Force Survey, Office for National Statistics

In 1971 there were more than 54 million people living in Great Britain and there were 18.6 million private households, with an average occupancy of 2.9 people per household (Table 2.1). By 2006 the British population had risen by more than 4.5 million (see Chapter 1: Population, Table 1.1). The number of households, however, rose by 5.8 million between 1971 and 2007 and the average household size fell to 2.4 people. Reasons for this increase in the number of households and the decrease in average household size include more lone-parent families, smaller family sizes and an increase in one-person households. In 1971, 18 per cent of all households in Great Britain were home to one person; this figure reached 29 per cent in 2001 and has remained stable each year since then. In contrast, 6 per cent of households in 1971 had six or more occupants; by 2007 this had fallen to 2 per cent.

The most common type of household in Great Britain is a couple family household, accounting for 56 per cent of households in 2007. One-half (28 per cent) of these are couples with children (Table 2.2). Between 1971 and 2007 the largest decline among households was in the 'traditional' household consisting of a private home with a couple and dependent children. In 2007 around one-fifth (21 per cent) of private households in Great Britain were home to two adults and dependent children, compared with more than one-third (35 per cent) in 1971. Over the same period, the proportion of households comprising one individual under state pension age (65 for men and 60 for women) more than doubled, from 6 per cent to 14 per cent. The proportion of households in

Table 2.2

Households:[1] by type of household and family

Great Britain   Percentages

	1971	1981	1991	2001[2]	2007[2]
One person					
Under state pension age[3]	6	8	11	14	14
Over state pension age	12	14	16	15	15
One family households					
Couple[4]					
No children	27	26	28	29	28
1–2 dependent children[5]	26	25	20	19	18
3 or more dependent children[5]	9	6	5	4	3
Non-dependent children only	8	8	8	6	7
Lone parent[4]					
Dependent children[5]	3	5	6	7	7
Non-dependent children only	4	4	4	3	3
Two or more unrelated adults	4	5	3	3	3
Multi-family households	1	1	1	1	1
All households (=100%) (millions)	18.6	20.2	22.4	23.8	24.4

1 See Appendix, Part 2: Multi-sourced tables, Households, and Families.
2 Data are at Q2 each year. See Appendix, Part 4: Labour Force Survey.
3 State pension age is currently 65 for men and 60 for women.
4 Other individuals who were not family members may also be included.
5 May also include non-dependent children.

Source: Census, Labour Force Survey, Office for National Statistics

Table 2.3

People in households:[1] by type of household and family

Great Britain   Percentages

	1971	1981	1991	2001[2]	2007[2]
One person	6	8	11	12	12
One family households					
Couple					
No children	19	20	23	25	25
Dependent children[3]	52	47	41	39	36
Non-dependent children only	10	10	11	9	9
Lone parent[4]	4	6	10	12	12
Other households[5]	9	9	4	4	6
All people in households (=100%) (millions)	53.4	53.9	54.1	56.4	57.3

1 See Appendix, Part 2: Multi-sourced tables, Households, and Families.
2 Data are at spring for 2001 and Q2 for 2007. See Appendix, Part 4: Labour Force Survey.
3 May also include non-dependent children.
4 Includes those with dependent children only, non-dependent children only and those with both dependent and non-dependent children.
5 Includes same sex couples from 2001.

Source: Census, Labour Force Survey, Office for National Statistics

Great Britain comprising more than one family remained constant, at 1 per cent, while the proportion of households with two or more unrelated adults sharing private accommodation fluctuated a little between 1971 and 1991 but has remained stable at 3 per cent since then.

While Table 2.2 shows that over half of households were headed by a couple in Q2 (April to June) 2007, Table 2.3 is based on people. It shows that there have been marked changes in the way people live in Great Britain since the early 1970s. In 2007 the proportion of lone parents as heads of households (12 per cent) was treble that of 1971 (4 per cent). The 2006 British Social Attitudes Survey found that more than two-thirds of people questioned did not think that they needed a partner to be happy and fulfilled in life. In 2007, the proportion of people living alone (12 per cent) was double the proportion in 1971 (6 per cent) (Table 2.3).

The proportion of people living in couples without children increased from 19 per cent in 1971 to 25 per cent of the

population in 1991 and has remained at this level since then. More than one-third of the population (36 per cent) lived in private households that consisted of couples with dependent children in 2007, compared with more than one-half (52 per cent) of the population in 1971. This trend has been driven by a number of factors including a tendency among young people to live alone or cohabit before having children and an increase in the number of older couples whose children have left home. Figures for Northern Ireland show that a larger proportion of the population live in households with children, compared with Great Britain. In 2007 more than 41 per cent of the population in Northern Ireland lived in the traditional single family unit with dependent children, around 20 per cent lived as part of a couple with no children, 12 per cent were lone parents and 11 per cent lived alone.

Family patterns differ between religious groups. In Great Britain Christian families are least likely of all families to have children living with them, closely followed by Jewish families. In 2001 40 per cent of Christian families and 41 per cent of Jewish families had a dependent child or dependent children at home (Figure 2.4 overleaf). In contrast, around 73 per cent of Muslim families had at least one dependent child living with them. This reflects the age structure of the population of these religious groups in Great Britain. In 2007, 34 per cent of the

Figure 2.4

Dependent children in family:[1] by number and religion, 2001

Great Britain
Percentages

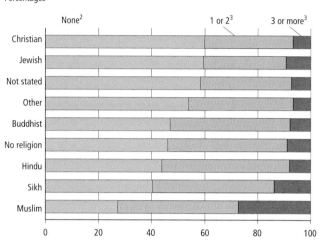

1 A family consists of a couple (married or cohabiting, including same sex couples) with or without children, or a lone parent and their children. See Appendix, Part 2: Multi-sourced tables, Households, and Families.
2 A small number of families consist of a couple without children where one member of the couple was under 16. These appear in the figure in the 'None' category. Includes those with non-dependent children.
3 Dependent children.

Source: Census, Office for National Statistics; Census, General Register Office for Scotland

Muslim population was aged under 16, double the proportion of Christians and Jews in that age group (17 per cent).

Muslim families tended to have the largest number of children, compared with families of other religions in Great Britain.

Apart from the younger age structure of the Muslim population, other cultural factors may also have an influence. Many Muslims have a Pakistani or Bangladeshi background and, in 2001, the average intended number of children among women of these ethnic groups was 3.4 and 3.6 respectively, compared with 2.1 children among White women (see Appendix, Part 1: Classification of ethnic groups).

Hindu families were the most likely to be headed by a married couple. In 2001, 87 per cent of Hindu families with dependent children were headed by a married couple, compared with 76 per cent of Muslim families and 65 per cent of Christian families. Of all Hindu families with dependent children 4 per cent were stepfamilies compared with 10 per cent of Christian families. Hindu families with dependent children were also least likely to be lone-parent families (11 per cent), compared with 15 per cent of Jewish and Sikh families, 21 per cent of Muslim families, 25 per cent of Christian families and 30 per cent of Buddhist families.

One of the most notable changes in household composition over the last few decades has been the increase in one-person households. There were more than 7 million people living alone in the UK in 2007. From the mid-1980s through the 1990s these households mainly comprised older women. This was a reflection of there being more women than men in the older age groups and, in particular, women outliving their husbands. In 2006 more than 60 per cent of women aged 75 and over lived alone in Great Britain, a similar proportion to 1986/87 (Figure 2.5). However, the proportion of men in this age group who live alone has increased over the years; nearly one-third

Figure 2.5

People living alone: by sex and age[1]

Great Britain
Percentages

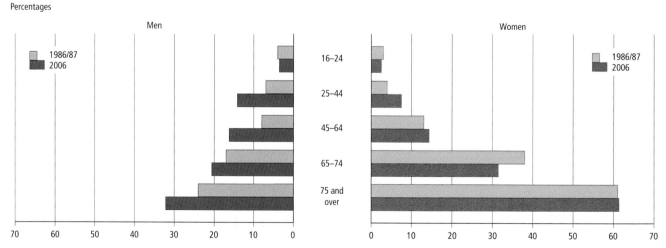

1 Data from 2006 onwards are weighted to compensate for nonresponse and to match known population distributions. See Appendix, Part 2: General Household Survey.

Source: General Household Survey (Longitudinal), Office for National Statistics

of men aged 75 and over lived on their own in 2006, compared with less than one-quarter in 1986/87. Part of the reason for this may be an increase in life expectancy for men (see Chapter 7: Health, Figure 7.1). In Northern Ireland the proportion of women aged 75 and over living alone rose from 43 per cent in 1986/87 to 56 per cent in 2006. However, the proportion of men living alone in this age group fell from 29 per cent to 27 per cent.

Typically, more men than women in Great Britain under the age of 65 live alone. Over the last two decades the proportion of people living alone doubled, from 7 to 14 per cent of men aged between 25 and 44 and from 4 to 8 per cent for women in this age group. There was a similar pattern in Northern Ireland, where the proportion of men living alone rose from 4 per cent in 1986/87 to 10 per cent in 2006 and for women the proportion rose from 3 to 7 per cent. This trend of people living alone looks set to continue; figures for England suggest that 70 per cent of projected household growth until 2026 will be because of single-person households. Many of these one-person households are home to people aged 65 and over, which is a reflection of the country's ageing population and an increase in average life expectancy. Other reasons for increased growth in one-person households may include an increase in the number of divorces, a tendency for young people to live alone before cohabiting

Table 2.6

Dependent children:[1] by family type

Great Britain					Percentages
	1972	1981	1997[2]	2001[2]	2007[2]
Couple families					
1 child	16	18	17	17	18
2 children	35	41	37	37	36
3 or more children	41	29	25	24	22
Lone mother families					
1 child	2	3	6	6	7
2 children	2	4	7	8	8
3 or more children	2	3	6	6	6
Lone father families					
1 child	..	1	1	1	1
2 or more children	1	1	1	1	1
All children[3]	100	100	100	100	100

1 See Appendix, Part 2: Multi-sourced tables, Households, and Families.
2 Data are at Q2 each year. See Appendix, Part 4: Labour Force Survey.
3 Excludes cases where the dependent child is a family unit, for example, a foster child.

Source: Census, General Household Survey, Labour Force Survey, Office for National Statistics

or getting married, rather than moving in with a partner directly from the family home, and an increase in international migration.

Despite considerable growth in the number of lone-parent families, the majority of dependent children still live in a family with two parents. The proportion of children in Great Britain living in a two-parent family unit has remained steady since the late 1990s and was 76 per cent in Q2 2007, compared with more than 90 per cent in 1972 (Table 2.6). Meanwhile the proportion of children living with one parent more than trebled over the past 35 years to 23 per cent in 2007. Over this period the proportion of children living with their fathers remained constant, at around 2 per cent, whereas the proportion living with their mothers rose from 6 per cent to 21 per cent.

The proportion of children in each family type has also changed since the 1970s. In 1972, 2 per cent of families with dependent children consisted of a lone mother and three or more children, compared with 6 per cent by Q2 2007. Over the same period, the proportion of children in two-parent families with three or more children almost halved, falling from 41 per cent to 22 per cent.

Partnerships

The pattern of partnership formation is also changing with a marked increase in the proportion of people cohabiting. In 1986 (the first year data are available on a consistent basis) 11 per cent of unmarried men aged under 60 and 13 per cent of unmarried women aged under 60 cohabited in Great Britain. By 2006 these proportions had roughly doubled, to 24 per cent for men and 25 per cent for women.

Higher proportions of divorced men cohabit in Great Britain compared with men in other marital status groups. In 2006, one-third (34 per cent) of divorced men were cohabiting, compared with 22 per cent of single men and 23 per cent of separated men. The proportions of men and women cohabiting differ according to their marital status. While one in three divorced men were cohabiting in 2006, less than one in four divorced women were doing so (Table 2.7 overleaf). In contrast 2 per cent of widowers were cohabiting, compared with 8 per cent of widows. Across all marital statuses there was a lower proportion of people cohabiting in Northern Ireland than in Great Britain. In 2006 more than one in four divorced men (27 per cent) and less than one in eight divorced women (12 per cent) were cohabiting in Northern Ireland. The same proportion of single men, single women and separated men were cohabiting (15 per cent for each group), together with 11 per cent of widows and 3 per cent of separated women.

2

Table 2.7

People cohabiting: by marital status, 2006[1]

Great Britain   Percentages

	Single	Widowed	Divorced	Separated
Men				
Cohabiting[2]	22	2	34	23
Not cohabiting	78	98	66	77
All men	100	100	100	100
Women				
Cohabiting[2]	27	8	24	9
Not cohabiting	73	92	76	91
All women	100	100	100	100

1 Aged 16 to 59. See Appendix, Part 2: General Household Survey.
  Includes those who describe themselves as separated but were, in a
  legal sense, still married.
2 Includes a small number of same sex cohabiting.

*Source: General Household Survey (Longitudinal), Office for National
Statistics*

Cohabiting couple families tend to be much younger than
married couple families. In 2001, one-half of cohabiting couple
families in the UK were headed by a person aged under 35,
compared with one in ten of married couples. This reflects the
greater acceptance of cohabitation by younger generations. It
may also help to explain the trend towards marrying later in life
as it is possible that many cohabiting couples see cohabitation
as a transitional stage and go on to (or expect to) get married.

In 2005 there were just under 284,000 marriages in the UK,
around 27,000 fewer than in 2004, and almost 197,000 fewer
than in 1972, when the number of marriages peaked at
480,000 (Figure 2.8). This peak was partly a result of babies
born in the post-war boom reaching marriageable ages
(see Chapter 1: Population, Figure 1.8) and also because at that
time people were marrying at a younger age than in preceding
years. In 1961, the mean age of men and women at first
marriage in England and Wales was 25.6 and 23.1 years
respectively. This fell to 24.6 years for men and 22.6 years for
women in 1971. By 2004, the average age had risen to
31.4 years for men and 29.1 years for women.

Despite the increase in the proportion of people cohabiting
and the decrease in the overall number of people getting
married, marriage is still the most common form of partnership
for men and women. In 2001 there were more than
11.6 million married couple families in the UK, compared with
around 2.2 million cohabiting couple families.

There is no requirement for UK citizens to register marriages
that take place abroad and there is some evidence that

Figure 2.8

Marriages and divorces[1]

United Kingdom

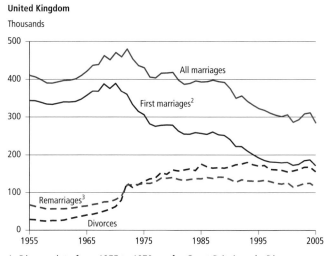

Thousands

1 Divorce data from 1955 to 1970 are for Great Britain only. Divorce
  became legal in Northern Ireland from 1969. Includes annulments.
2 For both partners.
3 For one or both partners.

*Source: Office for National Statistics; General Register Office for Scotland;
Northern Ireland Statistics and Research Agency*

marrying abroad is becoming popular, perhaps accounting for
up to 10 per cent of marriages in England and Wales. This may
partly explain the recent fall in marriages registered in the UK.

More than 60 per cent of marriages in 2005 were first
marriages for both partners, compared with 69 per cent in
1976. Although the number of remarriages remained fairly
stable over the last 30 years, there was a marked decrease in
the remarriage rate (the number of divorced men and women
marrying per 1,000 divorced people) over the same period. In
1976 there were around 124,000 remarriages and the
remarriage rate was 178.8 for men and 122.2 for women.
In comparison there were around 11,000 fewer remarriages
(almost 113,000) in 2005 but the remarriage rate had fallen to
40.2 for men and 29.5 for women. This reflected the increasing
size of the divorced population.

The number of divorces in Great Britain more than doubled
between 1958 and 1969, from around 24,000 to around
56,000. After 1969 divorce became legal in Northern Ireland
and between 1970 and 1972, the number of divorces in the UK
rose from 63,000 to 125,000. This increase was also partly a
result of the *Divorce Reform Act 1969* in England and Wales,
which came into effect in 1971. This Act introduced a single
ground for divorce – irretrievable breakdown – which could be
established by proving one or more certain facts: adultery,
desertion, separation (with or without consent) or unreasonable
behaviour. Following a fall in the number of divorces in 1973,
to around 114,000, the number of divorces in the UK generally

Table 2.9

Marriage and divorce[1] rates: EU comparison, 2005

Rates per 1,000 population

	Marriage	Divorce		Marriage	Divorce
Cyprus	7.8	2.0	Spain	4.8	1.7
Denmark	6.7	2.8	Germany	4.7	2.7
Romania	6.6	1.5	Estonia	4.6	3.0
Malta	5.9	-	Portugal	4.6	2.2
Lithuania	5.8	3.3	France	4.5	2.2
Finland	5.6	2.6	Netherlands	4.5	2.0
Greece	5.5	1.2	Hungary	4.4	2.5
Latvia	5.5	2.8	Luxembourg	4.4	2.3
Poland	5.4	1.8	Bulgaria	4.3	1.9
United Kingdom	5.2	2.6	Italy	4.3	0.8
Czech Republic	5.1	3.1	Belgium	4.1	2.9
Ireland	5.1	0.8	Slovenia	2.9	1.3
Slovakia	4.9	2.1			
Sweden	4.9	2.2	EU–27 average	4.9	2.1
Austria	4.8	2.4			

1 Divorce is possible in all EU-27 countries except Malta.

Source: Eurostat

rose over the next two decades, reaching a high of 180,000 in 1993. The number of divorces fell to around 155,000 in 2000 before rising for four successive years to 167,000 in 2004 and then falling once again to around 155,000 in 2005.

Similar trends in marriage and marital breakdown to the UK can be seen across Europe. The majority of countries in the EU-27 reported a decrease in the number of marriages over the last 30 years. In 2005 Cyprus had the highest marriage rate, at 7.8 marriages per 1,000 people, closely followed by Denmark with 6.7 per 1,000 (Table 2.9). Slovenia had the lowest rate, at 2.9 marriages per 1,000 people, followed by Belgium at 4.1 per 1,000.

In general, the increasingly common practice of cohabitation prior to marriage has been accompanied by rising divorce rates across Europe over the last few decades. The EU-27 average divorce rate rose from 1.4 per 1,000 population in 1975 to 2.1 per 1,000 population in 2005 and, also in this year, the divorce rate reached 50 per cent or more of the marriage rate in ten of the member states. Lithuania had the highest divorce rate in 2005, at 3.3 per 1,000, while Italy and Ireland had the lowest rates – numbering 0.8 per 1,000 population. Divorce is not legal in Malta although overseas divorces can be registered.

The *Civil Partnership Act 2004* (see Appendix, Part 2: Civil partnerships) enables same-sex couples aged 16 and over

to obtain legal recognition of their relationship. Almost 2,000 couples registered their partnerships before the end of 2005 in the UK (Figure 2.10), shortly after the Act came into effect.

Figure 2.10

Civil partnerships:[1] by sex, 2005–06

United Kingdom

Numbers

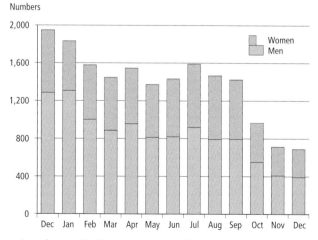

1 Data do not include civil partnerships of UK residents taking place abroad but will include non-UK residents who form a partnership in the UK. See Appendix, Part 2: Civil partnerships.

Source: Office for National Statistics; General Register Office for Scotland; Northern Ireland Statistics and Research Agency

Table 2.11

Stepfamilies[1] with dependent children[2]

Great Britain

Percentages

	1991/92	1996/97	2000/01	2001/02	2006[3]
Child(ren) from the woman's previous marriage/cohabitation	86	84	88	83	84
Child(ren) from the man's previous marriage/cohabitation	6	12	9	9	10
Child(ren) from both partners' previous marriage/cohabitation	6	4	3	8	6
Lone parent with child(ren) from a previous partner's marriage/cohabitation	1	-	-	-	-
All stepfamilies	100	100	100	100	100

1 Family head aged 16 to 59. See Appendix, Part 2: General Household Survey.
2 Dependent children are persons under 16, or aged 16 to 18 and in full-time education, in the family unit, and living in the household.
3 In 2005 GHS data collection changed from financial to calendar year.

Source: General Household Survey (Longitudinal), Office for National Statistics

In 2006 more than 16,000 civil partnerships were formed in the UK. Of these, 90 per cent took place in England, 6 per cent in Scotland, 3 per cent in Wales and 1 per cent in Northern Ireland. London remained the most popular region to form a partnership, accounting for 25 per cent of all UK registrations.

Male partnerships accounted for 60 per cent of civil partnerships formed in the UK between December 2005 and December 2006. Two regions registered more partnerships of women than men. These were Yorkshire and the Humber, and the East Midlands, where 52 per cent and 51 per cent respectively of all partnerships formed were between women. In Wales, partnerships between women accounted for 49 per cent of all civil partnerships. The lowest region in the UK for partnerships between women was London, where 24 per cent of registrations were made by female couples.

Women were more likely than men to have been married before forming a civil partnership. One in ten (10 per cent) men forming a civil partnership in the UK in 2006 had previously been in a legal partnership compared with around one in four (24 per cent) women. Almost all of these men and women had previously been married. A very small proportion of people forming a civil partnership in England had previously been in a civil partnership formed outside the UK.

Children live in an increasing variety of family structures. Parents separating can create lone-parent families or by remarriage or cohabitation, where stepfamilies may be created.

Following a separation, children tend to stay with their mother meaning that the majority (84 per cent) of stepfamilies in Great Britain in 2006 consisted of a stepfather and a natural mother compared with 10 per cent of families with a stepmother and a natural father (Table 2.11). The proportion of children living with their natural mother and a stepfather remained fairly stable (between 83 and 88 per cent) over the last ten years, whereas there were considerable fluctuations in the proportion of children living with their natural father and a stepmother. Between 1991/92 and 1996/97 the proportion of children staying with their natural father doubled, from 6 per cent to 12 per cent, although this proportion has since decreased. In 2006, 6 per cent of stepfamilies comprised children from both partners' previous relationships.

Family formation

For women born in the UK in 1920, the average number of children was 2.07 per woman (Figure 2.12). Almost one-third of women born in that year went on to have three or more children. The average number of children per woman increased to a peak of 2.46 children for women born in 1934, contributing to the 1960s baby boom (see Chapter 1: Population, Table 1.7). However family size has been declining in subsequent generations. The cohort of women born in 1961 reaching the end of their childbearing years in 2006 had on average, 1.96 children. The average number of children per woman is projected to decline to 1.84 for women born in the UK in the early 1990s onwards.

Figure 2.12

Completed family size: by year of birth of woman[1]

United Kingdom
Average number of children per woman

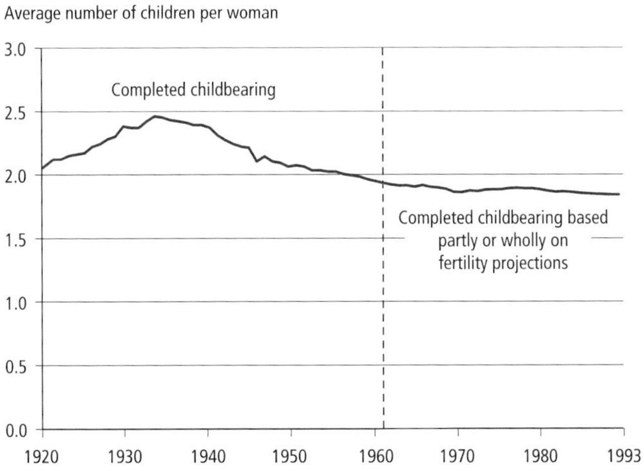

1 Women born in UK.

Source: Office for National Statistics; Government Actuary's Department

Table 2.13

Fertility rates: by age of mother at childbirth

United Kingdom   Live births per 1,000 women

	1971	1981	1991	2001	2004	2006
Under 20[1]	50.1	28.4	32.9	27.9	26.7	26.4
20–24	153.9	106.6	88.9	68.0	71.5	72.0
25–29	155.6	130.9	119.9	91.5	97.3	100.1
30–34	79.4	69.4	86.5	88.0	99.2	104.6
35–39	33.9	22.4	32.0	41.3	48.6	53.4
40 and over	9.1	4.7	5.3	8.6	10.2	11.1
Total Fertility Rate[2]	..	1.82	1.82	1.63	1.77	1.84
Total births[3] (thousands)	901.6	730.7	792.3	669.1	716.0	748.6

1 Live births per 1,000 women aged 15 to 19.
2 Number of children that would be born to a woman if current
   patterns of fertility persisted throughout her childbearing life.
3 Total live births per 1,000 women aged 15 to 44.

Source: Office for National Statistics

Not only are women born in the UK having fewer children than 30 years ago, they are also having them later in life. A number of factors, including the increased participation of women in the education and labour market (see Chapter 3: Education and training, Table 3.9 and Chapter 4: Labour market, Figure 4.17), the increased availability and use of contraception (particularly the pill), the trend since the 1970s for people to get married at an older age and a general shift in attitudes towards family sizes, have all contributed to the trend towards later child-bearing and smaller families. In 1971 fertility rates in the UK were highest for women in their late 20s, at 155.6 births per 1,000 women, compared with 79.4 for women in their early 30s (Table 2.13). However, as fertility rates for women in their 20s fell, rates for women in their 30s increased and, since 1992, the fertility rates for women aged between 20 and 24 were lower than rates for women aged between 30 and 34. In 2004 fertility rates for women aged 30 to 34 (99.2 births per 1,000 women) surpassed those for women aged 25 to 29 (97.3 births per 1,000 women), making it the age group with the highest fertility. The rates for these age groups stood at 100.1 births per 1,000 women aged 25 to 29 and 104.6 per 1,000 women aged 30 to 34 in 2006.

During the 1970s fertility rates for teenage mothers almost halved, falling from 50.1 births per 1,000 women to 28.4 per 1,000 by 1981. By 2006 there were 26.4 births per 1,000 women aged under 20 (see page 25 for more on teenage pregnancy). Fertility rates for women aged 40 and over have been rising steadily after an initial fall from 9.1 per 1,000 in 1971 to 4.7 per 1,000 in 1981, to a peak of 11.1 per 1,000 in 2006.

Over the past four years there has been rising fertility in the UK, with the Total Fertility Rate (TFR) (see Chapter 1: Population, Total Fertility Rate box) reaching 1.84 in 2006, up from a record low of 1.63 just five years earlier. However, this is still not as high as the TFR during the 1960s 'baby boom', which peaked at 2.95 children per woman in 1964. All four UK countries have experienced this rising fertility. In 2006 Northern Ireland had the highest TFR, at 1.94 children per woman. Both England and Wales had a TFR of 1.86, while Scotland's TFR remained lowest, at 1.67 children per woman. The increasing TFR of women in their late twenties and early thirties since 2001 has been contributed to by both UK and non-UK born women. However, the increase among women in their early twenties appears to have been driven by UK born women only.

Between 1971 and 2006, the average age of mothers at childbirth in England and Wales increased by more than three years for all live births, from 26.2 to 29.5, and by four years for first births, from 23.6 to 27.6 (Table 2.14 overleaf). Married women giving birth for the first time were, on average, age 30.2 in 2006, compared with age 23.9 in 1971, an increase of 6.3 years. The average age for births to unmarried women increased by 3.3 years over the same period. Unmarried women tend to give birth at younger ages than married women; the average age of unmarried mothers at childbirth was 27.0 years in 2006, compared with 31.4 years for married women.

Successive cohorts of women born in England and Wales since the Second World War have waited longer than the previous

Table 2.14

Average age of mother at childbirth[1]

England & Wales					Mean age (years)
	1971	1981	1991	2001	2006
All births					
All live births	26.2	26.8	27.7	29.2	29.5
All first births[2]	23.6	24.6	25.7	27.2	27.6
Births inside marriage					
All births inside marriage	26.4	27.2	28.9	30.9	31.4
First births inside marriage	23.9	25.3	27.5	29.6	30.2
Births outside marriage					
All births outside marriage	23.7	23.4	24.8	26.7	27.0

1 The mean ages shown in this table are not standardised and therefore take no account of the structure of the population by age, marital status or number of births.
2 See Appendix, Part 2: True birth order.

Source: Office for National Statistics

cohort before starting a family. More than two-fifths (44 per cent) of women born in 1931 had not had children by the age of 25 (Figure 2.15). This fell to one-third (33 per cent) for women born in 1941 but increased to almost two-thirds (64 per cent) for women born in 1981. Around 16 per cent of women born in 1931 were still childless at age 35, compared with 25 per cent of women born in 1971. This demonstrates a

Figure 2.15

Childless women[1] at selected ages:[2] by year of birth

England & Wales
Percentages

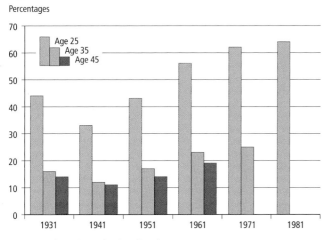

1 Women born in England and Wales.
2 Age 45 takes into account births to women at age 45 and over and therefore represents a final estimate of childlessness for women born in each year.

Source: Office for National Statistics

Figure 2.16

Births outside marriage[1]

United Kingdom
Percentages

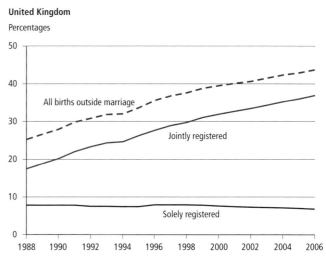

1 As a percentage of all births.

Source: Office for National Statistics; General Register Office for Scotland; Northern Ireland Statistics and Research Agency

trend of women delaying childbearing rather than not having children at all. The proportion of women who remained childless at age 45 rose from 14 per cent for women born in 1931 to 19 per cent for those born in 1961, the most recent cohort of women to reach the end of their childbearing years.

With the exception of the periods immediately following the two World Wars, few births occurred outside marriage during the first 60 years of the 20th century. Births outside marriage became more commonplace during the 1960s and 1970s and by 2006, 43.7 per cent of all births in the UK occurred outside marriage, compared with 25.2 per cent in 1988 (Figure 2.16). Much of this increase was the result of increasing numbers of births to cohabiting parents. The number of births registered by one parent remained quite stable throughout the 1990s, fluctuating between 7 per cent and 8 per cent. Since 1998 there has been a gradual decline in the number of solely registered births. In 2006, 6.8 per cent of births were registered by a single person. The proportion of jointly registered births has risen consistently, from 17.4 per cent in 1988 to 36.9 per cent in 2006.

Cultural differences and the way attitudes and values change over time mean that family patterns vary among EU member states. One factor common to almost all of the EU-27 is the increase in the percentage of births occurring outside marriage (Table 2.17). In 2005 slightly less than one in three of all births in the EU were outside marriage, compared with around one in six in 1991. Estonia had the highest proportion of births outside marriage, at 59 per cent (almost 8,400 births),

Table 2.17

Births outside marriage: EU comparison

Percentages

	1991	1996	2001	2005		1991	1996	2001	2005
Estonia	31	48	56	59	Germany	15	17	25	29
Sweden	48	54	55	55	Romania	..	21	27	29
Bulgaria	16	28	42	49	Lithuania	7	14	25	28
France	32	39	44	47	Luxembourg	12	15	22	27
Slovenia	26	32	39	47	Spain	10	12	20	27
Denmark	47	46	45	46	Slovakia	9	14	20	26
Latvia	18	33	42	45	Malta	2	3	13	20
United Kingdom	30	36	40	43	Poland	..	10	13	18
Finland	27	35	40	40	Italy	7	8	10	15
Austria	25	28	33	37	Greece	2	3	4	5
Hungary	14	23	30	35	Cyprus	1	1	2	4
Netherlands	12	17	27	35	Belgium	13	19	..	..
Ireland	17	25	31	32					
Czech Republic	10	17	23	32					
Portugal	16	19	24	31					

Source: Eurostat

followed by Sweden, at 55 per cent. Estonia and Sweden were the only two countries in the EU-27 to have a higher proportion of births outside marriage than within marriage.

In Sweden, babies born to married parents have been in a minority for the last decade. However, less than 3 per cent (around 1,400 babies) born outside marriage in Sweden were born to unmarried teenagers. This compared with 15 per cent (46,500 births) in the UK. In Malta more than one-third of all babies born outside marriage were born to unmarried women under the age of 20; this amounted to fewer than 300 births.

The only country not to see an increase in the proportion of births outside marriage was Denmark, where it has remained at between 45 and 47 per cent over the past 15 years (around 29,000 births in 2005). Cyprus remained the country with the smallest proportion of births outside marriage, at 4 per cent in 2005 (fewer than 400 births).

Despite the general trend towards later childbearing, there were more than 102,000 conceptions to females aged under 20 in 2005 in England and Wales (Table 2.18 overleaf). After the introduction of free contraception on the NHS in 1974, the rate of teenage conceptions for those aged 13 to 19

declined steadily for around a decade but rose by 23 per cent between 1983 and 1990. The rates began to fall in the early 1990s, increasing slightly between 1995 and 1998, before falling once again, to 60.1 per 1,000 females in 2005.

The number of conceptions among teenage females leading to a maternity varies by age; the likelihood that a pregnant teenager will have an abortion decreases in the older age groups. For girls aged under 16, 43 per cent continued with their pregnancy in 2005, compared with more than 50 per cent of 16 and 17-year-olds and more than 60 per cent of 18 and 19-year-olds.

The rate of teenage conceptions varies around the country and is considerably higher in deprived areas compared with affluent areas. Teenagers from affluent areas are more likely to terminate a pregnancy than those from deprived areas. The decision whether or not to terminate a pregnancy tends to be linked to economic and social issues, rather than the teenager's opinion of the morality of abortion. For example, women in deprived areas may consider early motherhood as an opportunity to change their lives, rather than as a barrier to further education or career development. Between 1999 and 2001 the highest proportions of teenage pregnancies ending in abortion were in Eden, Epsom and Ewell, and Rochford

Table 2.18

Teenage conceptions:[1] by age at conception and outcome, 2005

England & Wales[2]

	Conceptions (numbers)	Leading to abortions (percentages)	Rates per 1,000 females[3]		
			All conceptions	Leading to maternities	Leading to abortions
Under 14	327	*60*	1.0	0.4	0.6
14	1,830	*64*	5.4	1.9	3.4
15	5,773	*55*	17.1	7.7	9.4
All aged under 16	7,930	*57*	7.8	3.3	4.5
16	13,335	*46*	39.4	21.1	18.3
17	21,060	*42*	61.1	35.3	25.8
All aged under 18	42,325	*46*	41.4	22.2	19.2
18	28,044	*37*	82.5	51.6	30.9
19	31,943	*35*	93.5	61.0	32.5
All aged under 20	102,312	*40*	60.1	35.9	24.2

1 See Appendix, Part 2: Conceptions.
2 Residents only.
3 Rates for females aged under 14, under 16, under 18 and under 20 are based on the population of females aged 13, 13 to 15, 15 to 17 and 15 to 19 respectively.

Source: Office for National Statistics

(more than 70 per cent in each of these areas), while the lowest were in Merthyr Tydfil, Torridge and Derwentside (all less than 30 per cent).

In 2006 abortion rates across almost all age groups in England and Wales reached their highest levels on record. There were 193,700 abortions in England and Wales in 2006, a rise of nearly 4 per cent from 2005. Between 1969 and 2006, there was nearly a fivefold increase in abortion rates for the 20 to 24 age group from 7.0 per 1,000 to 32.5 per 1,000 (Figure 2.19). Similarly there was nearly a fivefold increase for women aged between 16 and 19, from 6.1 per 1,000 to 27.4 per 1,000. For women aged between 25 and 34, there was a threefold increase, with rates rising from 5.8 per 1,000 to 19.4 per 1,000 and for women aged over 35, abortion rates doubled, from 3.3 per 1,000 to 6.9 per 1,000. Trends in abortion rates have varied by the age of the mother to be since the *Abortion Act 1967* came into effect in 1968, but there was a marked increase in the number of abortions carried out for all age groups between 1995 and 1996, following a warning issued in 1995 by the Committee on Safety of Medicines that several brands of the contraceptive pill carried a higher than previously thought risk of thrombosis. Since the pill scare abortion rates continued to rise for all age groups except the under-16s; rates for this age group remained between 3.7 and 4.0 per 1,000 females.

Around 1 per cent of abortions in 2006 were carried out because there was a substantial risk that, if born, the child would be seriously disabled. Of these, nearly four in ten (38 per cent) were because chromosomal abnormalities such as Down's syndrome were detected, and almost one-half

Figure 2.19

Abortion rates: by age[1]

England & Wales
Rates per 1,000 females

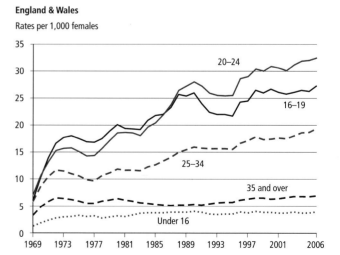

1 The rates for females aged under 16 are based on the population of females aged 13 to 15. The rates for women aged 35 and over are based on the population of women aged 35 to 44.

Source: Office for National Statistics; Department of Health

(47 per cent) were because of congenital malformations. The majority of abortions in 2006 (97 per cent) were carried out on the grounds that continuing the pregnancy would involve greater risk to the physical or mental health of the female than termination, although less than one-half of one per cent of these terminations were conducted because of a risk to the woman's physical condition.

As in 2005 nearly one-third (32 per cent) of females who had abortions in 2006 had undergone one or more abortions previously and nearly one-half (47 per cent) had at least one prior pregnancy that resulted in a live or stillbirth. Around one in seven (14 per cent) females had a previous conception that had resulted in either a miscarriage or an ectopic pregnancy (a pregnancy where the foetus is outside the womb).

There were around 13,000 abortions in Scotland in 2006, or 12.4 abortions per 1,000 females aged between 15 and 44. In Northern Ireland, abortions are only legal in extreme circumstances and data concerning these are not collected. Records for England and Wales show that almost 1,300 abortions were carried out on females usually resident in Northern Ireland and more than 5,000 abortions were carried out on females usually resident in Ireland. In total around 7,400 abortions for non-residents were carried out in hospitals and clinics in England and Wales in 2006.

It is estimated that as many as one in seven UK couples have difficulty conceiving, and infertility is the most common reason for women aged between 20 and 45 to see their general practitioner, after reasons relating to confirmed pregnancy. While the majority of women (around 95 per cent) who are trying for a baby will conceive naturally within two years, a minority will not. Many of these women will undergo fertility treatment, which is an important factor in the increase in the rate of multiple births in the UK. In 1975 the multiple birth rate was 9.9 per 1,000 maternities compared with 15.3 per 1,000 in 2006.

The biggest risk to both the mother and the baby from in vitro fertilisation (IVF) treatment is multiple births. For this reason, the Human Fertilisation and Embryology Authority revised its guidelines in 2004, restricting the number of eggs or embryos used at each IVF attempt from three to two for women aged 39 and under. However, the success rate of embryo transfers resulting in pregnancy is much lower for older women and for this reason, women aged 40 and over who are using their own eggs can have a maximum of three eggs or embryos transferred. In 2006, the rate of triplets as a proportion of all maternities in the UK was 0.6 per 1,000 maternities in women aged 40 and over (Table 2.20).

Table 2.20

Maternities with multiple births: by age of mother at childbirth, 2006

United Kingdom Rate per 1,000 maternities

	Maternities with twins only	Maternities with triplets or more
Under 20	6.7	0.0
20–24	9.5	0.1
25–29	13.1	0.1
30–34	17.8	0.3
35–39	21.4	0.3
40 and over	24.6	0.6
All mothers	15.1	0.2

Source: Office for National Statistics; General Register Office for Scotland; Northern Ireland Statistics and Research Agency

An alternative way to have children is through adoption. Children can be adopted from birth up to and including 17 years of age. In 2006 there were around 11.6 million people in this age group in England and Wales. In this year, fewer than 5,000 adoptions were registered compared with almost 6,000, ten years previously. These figures include a considerable number of adoptions by relatives and step-parents as well as adoptions from care. Over the last decade the number of adoptions of children in both the under one and the 15 to 17 years age groups have remained fairly stable, between 200 and 400 adoptions a year (Figure 2.21).

Figure 2.21

Adoptions: by age of child[1]

England & Wales
Thousands

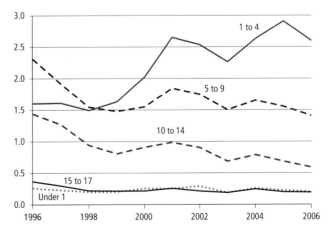

1 By age of child at entry of adoption order into the Adopted Children Register. Data for 2001 and 2006 include cases where the child was older than 17 years.

Source: Office for National Statistics

There was a decline in the number of adoptions of children aged between five and 14 years. In the 1990s children aged between five and nine were most likely to be adopted. Since the late 1990s the largest number of adoptions has been of children aged between one and four. This rose from around 1,600 in 1999 to almost 2,600 in 2006. During the second half of the last century, increased use of contraception, new abortion laws and changed attitudes to motherhood, had a negative impact on the number of children available for adoption. This number was further reduced by the introduction of the *Children Act 1975*, which required courts dealing with children of divorced parents to dismiss applications for adoptions if a legal custody order would be in the child's best interests. As at 31 March 2007, more than 64,000 children were in the care of local authorities in England and Wales. Around 4 per cent of these were placed for adoption.

Chapter 3

Education and training

- In 2006/07, there were nearly 33,900 schools in the UK, attended by 9.8 million pupils. (Table 3.3)

- The unauthorised absence rate for pupils known to be eligible for free school meals, in maintained secondary schools in England, was almost three times that of the rest of the school population in 2005/06. (Page 34)

- In 2005, around eight in ten children aged 14 and 15 in England agreed or strongly agreed that they were happy at school (82 per cent) and liked being at school (80 per cent). (Table 3.8)

- In 2005/06, there were 4.5 million further education students in the UK, more than two and a half times the number in 1970/71. (Table 3.9)

- In 2005/06, 59 per cent of pupils entered for the GCSE or equivalent exam in the UK achieved five or more GCSEs at grades A* to C or the equivalent, an increase of 14 percentage points since 1995/96. (Figure 3.13)

- In Q2 2007, employees in the UK who were graduates were more likely to receive job-related training than those with no qualifications, 20 per cent compared with 4 per cent respectively. (Table 3.18)

DATA

Download data by clicking the online pdf

www.statistics.gov.uk/ socialtrends38

For increasing numbers of people, experience of education is no longer confined to compulsory schooling. Early learning and participation in pre-school education is seen as being important for building a foundation for future learning, and most people continue in full-time education beyond school-leaving age. Qualifications attained at school are increasingly supplemented by further and higher education, as well as other training opportunities, to equip people with the skills required by a modern labour market and to keep these skills up to date.

Early years education

Early years education aims to ensure that all children begin their compulsory education with a basic grounding in literacy and numeracy and in key skills such as listening, concentrating and learning to work with others. The Government's ten-year strategy for early years and childcare published in 2004 outlined a number of key objectives for the foundation stage profile (see Appendix Part 3: Stages of education) including that all three and four-year-olds in England be entitled to a free part-time early education place for 12.5 hours per week (for 38 weeks of the year). From 2010 this will be extended to 15 hours a week. In Wales, Scotland and Northern Ireland, some form of free pre-school education is also available under different delivery strategies.

From September 2008 the foundation stage profile will be replaced by the Early Years Foundation Stage (EYFS). The six key areas of development for children in the EYFS will be: personal, social and emotional development; communication and literacy; problem-solving, reasoning and numeracy; knowledge and understanding of the world; physical development; and creative development. This provision will be delivered though a mix of maintained, private, voluntary and independent early years settings.

Since records began more than 25 years ago, data for the UK show a major expansion in early years education provided for young children in all settings. The proportion of three and four-year-olds enrolled in all schools in the UK rose from 21 per cent in 1970/71 to 64 per cent in 2006/07, although this is slightly down from a peak of 65 per cent in 2003/04 (Figure 3.1). The increase in participation partly reflects the growth in the number of places available – in 1970/71 there were 720 state nursery schools compared with 3,330 in 2006/07. The pattern of participation in pre-compulsory education varies regionally. The proportion of three and four-year-olds in maintained nursery and primary schools is generally higher in Wales and the north of England than in the south. In January 2007 twice the proportion of three and four-year-olds attended maintained nursery and primary

Figure 3.1

Children under five[1] in schools

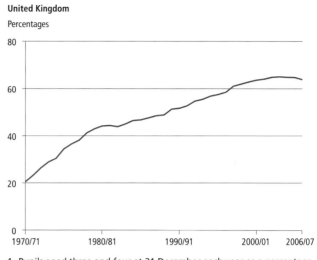

United Kingdom
Percentages

1 Pupils aged three and four at 31 December each year as a percentage of all three and four-year-olds, with the exception of Scotland where data are based on eligibility criteria. See Appendix, Part 3: Stages of education.

Source: Department for Children, Schools and Families; Welsh Assembly Government; Scottish Government; Northern Ireland Department of Education

schools in Wales (84 per cent) and the North East (83 per cent) compared with the South East and the South West of England (each 42 per cent). However, more children were enrolled with private and voluntary providers in the south than in other parts of the country (55 per cent in the South East and 61 per cent in the South West). It is worth noting that in England and Scotland any child attending more than one provider may have been counted twice.

In 2006 in England, 581,600 children aged between two and four were enrolled with full-day care settings compared with 378,900 children of the same age who were enrolled with sessional-day care. This was a reversal of the pattern in 2001 when 328,000 children in this age group were in full-day care and 532,400 were in sessional-day care (Figure 3.2). These two settings were by far the most common in both 2001 and 2006.

In 2006 there were 477,300 early years places in primary schools with nursery and reception classes in England, attended by 505,900 children aged under five. The number of children attending refers to the number of children actually attending a setting in a typical week rather than the number of registered places. The number of children attending can be greater than the number of places, as children who attend part time can share places. The number attending may also be lower than the number of places if providers are unable to fill all of their places. By comparison, there were 28,100 places

Figure 3.2

Children aged two to four enrolled with childcare settings:[1] by type of setting

England
Thousands

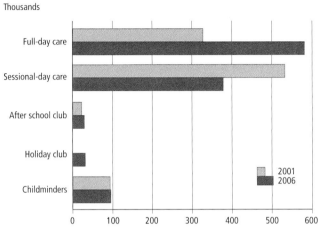

1 Children may attend more than one type of childcare setting.
   See Appendix, Part 3: Stages of education.

Source: Childcare and Early Years Providers Survey, Department for Children, Schools and Families

with 36,100 children attending in nursery schools. The total number of children aged under five from Black and ethnic minority groups in 2006 was around 127,600 in primary schools with nursery and reception classes, around 25 per cent of all children in these classes. This compares with 10,800 children of Black and ethnic minority origin in nursery schools, around 30 per cent of all children in nursery schools.

There are also children enrolled in early years education in England with either a special educational need (SEN) or a disability. In 2006 there were 46,700 children aged under five with either a SEN or a disability placed in primary schools with nursery and reception classes, averaging 9 per cent of children per setting. In nursery schools the equivalent number was 4,500 children, averaging 14 per cent of children per setting of this type. For data on total numbers of children with SEN in England see Figure 3.6.

Compulsory education

In 2006/07, there were nearly 33,900 schools in the UK, attended by 9.8 million pupils (Table 3.3). The peak year for pupil numbers was 1976/77 when 11.3 million pupils attended 38,500 schools. This peak occurred as the children of the cohort of women who were born in the baby boom after the Second World War, (see Chapter 1: Population) reached school ages. In 2006/07, 9.0 million pupils (92 per cent) attended public sector schools (not including special schools), while 0.7 million (7 per cent) attended one of the 2,500 non-maintained mainstream schools and 1 per cent of pupils attended one of

Table 3.3

School pupils:[1] by type of school[2]

United Kingdom   Thousands

	1970/71	1980/81	1990/91	2000/01	2006/07
Public sector schools[3]					
Nursery[4]	50	89	105	152	157
Primary	5,902	5,171	4,955	5,298	4,922
Secondary[5]					
Comprehensive	1,313	3,730	2,925	3,340	3,407
Grammar	673	149	156	205	219
Modern	1,164	233	94	112	103
Other	403	434	298	260	212
All public sector schools	9,507	9,806	8,533	9,367	9,021
Non-maintained schools	621	619	613	626	671
All special schools	103	148	114	113	106
Pupil referral units	.	.	.	10	16
All schools	10,230	10,572	9,260	10,116	9,813

1 Headcounts.
2 See Appendix, Part 3: Stages of education, and Main categories of educational establishments.
3 Excludes maintained special schools and pupil referral units.
4 Figures for Scotland before 1998/99 only include data for local authority (LA) pre-schools, data thereafter include partnership pre-schools. From 2005/06, figures refer to centres providing pre-school education at an LA centre, or in partnership with the LA only. Children are counted once for each centre they are registered with.
5 Excludes sixth-form colleges from 1980/81.

Source: Department for Children, Schools and Families; Welsh Assembly Government; Scottish Government; Northern Ireland Department of Education

the 1,400 special schools. These proportions have remained around this level since the 1970s. There were also around 490 pupil referral units (PRUs), catering for 16,000 pupils. PRUs aim to provide suitable alternative education on a temporary basis for some pupils. As well as pupils who have been excluded from mainstream schools and children with medical problems, PRUs may provide education for pregnant schoolgirls and school-aged mothers, school-phobics, and pupils awaiting placement in a maintained school.

Of the 2,500 non-maintained schools in the UK in 2006/07, 46 were academies in England. The academies programme in England was introduced in 2000 to promote publicly funded independent schools managed by sponsors from a range of backgrounds including universities, businesses, faith communities and voluntary groups. They are for pupils of all abilities, and are required to cover the key elements of the National Curriculum (mathematics, English and information and communications technology) and to specialise in other subject

3

areas. Most academies are located in areas of disadvantage and either replace existing schools or are established where there is a need for additional places. Although they still form a small proportion of the total number of non-maintained schools, by September 2007, the start of the next academic year, there were 83 open academies in England, with a further 50 projected to open in each of the next three years. This will contribute to the target of 200 academies open or planned by 2010.

Another characteristic school type is a publicly funded school with a religious character, popularly known as a faith school. Faith schools in some form have been present in England for more than 250 years – the first Jewish school for the poor was set up in 1732 and between 1811 and 1860 the Church of England founded 17,000 schools. Schools for Catholic children began in 1852. In 2007, among the 20,700 maintained schools in England, around one-third (6,842) were faith schools reflecting a number of world faiths, and were attended by 1.7 million pupils (Table 3.4). Although nearly all (99 per cent) of these schools were of a Christian denomination, there were also 37 Jewish schools educating 14,600 pupils, 7 Muslim schools educating over 2,300 pupils, 2 Sikh schools educating almost 800 pupils and 2 schools from other religious backgrounds. A higher proportion of maintained faith schools were at primary level in 2007 (91 per cent) compared with 80 per cent of maintained schools with no religious character. Faith schools are required to teach the National Curriculum and participate in National Curriculum tests and assessments as with all other maintained schools. The main difference is that faith schools have flexibility regarding the appointment of staff and pupil admissions (although they cannot refuse to admit

non-faith applicants if they have spare places). In Scotland there were 395 maintained schools of a religious character, all of which were Christian with the exception of one Jewish school. These schools are managed by local authorities in the same way as non-denominational schools. Alternative curriculum materials are produced for denominational schools where appropriate, for example religious education.

There were also around 900 independent schools in England in 2007 with a religious character, out of a total of more than 2,300 independent schools. More than 700 of these schools represented Christian denominations, followed by 115 independent Muslim schools and 38 independent Jewish schools. Independent schools account for 94 per cent of all Muslim faith schools and 51 per cent of all Jewish faith schools.

For several years reductions have been made in class sizes, particularly in the size of primary classes, in the drive to improve standards. The *School Standards and Framework Act 1998* aimed to reduce Key Stage 1 (five to seven-year-olds) class sizes in maintained schools in the UK to no more than 30 pupils by 2001/02. In 1995/96, 23 per cent of maintained primary schools in England had classes of 31 or more pupils at Key Stage 1. By 2002/03 this had fallen to 2 per cent and stayed at around this level through to 2006/07. Table 3.5 shows the breakdown of class sizes in 2006/07 for the Government Office Regions and devolved administrations (where data are available). In 2006/07 the average class size in Great Britain was 25 pupils for Key Stage 1 or equivalent and 27 pupils for Key Stage 2 (seven to eleven-year-olds). Key Stage 2 pupils were far more likely than Key Stage 1 pupils to be in classes of 31 or more pupils, 18 per cent compared with 2 per cent. More than one in four Key Stage 2 classes in the South West had 31 or more pupils in 2006/07 compared with less than one in ten classes in both Northern Ireland and London and an even smaller proportion in Wales. Northern Ireland had the smallest average number of pupils per class at both Key Stage 1 and Key Stage 2 in 2006/07. Average class size in secondary schools in England was around 21 pupils and in Wales, 20 pupils, despite secondary schools usually having more pupils than primary schools. This smaller average class size is in part because students choose different subjects in preparation for formal exams taken towards the end of their compulsory secondary schooling.

An alternative measure to class size is the pupil to teacher ratio, which is calculated by taking the full-time equivalent number of all pupils in a school (where a part-time pupil, for example in early years provision, counts as one-half) and dividing it by the number of full-time equivalent teachers employed (calculated using the total number of hours teachers worked). In 1995/96

Table 3.4

Maintained schools:[1] by religious character, 2007

England			Numbers
	Primary	Secondary	All
Christian	6,221	573	6,794
Jewish	28	9	37
Muslim	4	3	7
Sikh	1	1	2
Other religious	1	1	2
No religious character	11,106	2,756	13,862
Total	17,361	3,343	20,704

1 Includes middle schools. Depending on their individual age ranges middle schools are classified as either primary or secondary.

Source: Department for Children, Schools and Families

Table 3.5

Class sizes in schools:[1] by region, 2006/07

	Primary schools				Secondary schools	
	Key Stage 1[2]		Key Stage 2[2]			
	Average number in class	Percentage of classes with 31 or more pupils	Average number in class	Percentage of classes with 31 or more pupils	Average number in class	Percentage of classes with 31 or more pupils
Great Britain	25.3	2.0	26.9	18.0	..	..
England	25.6	2.1	27.2	19.6	21.3	7.4
North East	24.3	2.0	26.1	15.3	20.9	6.7
North West	25.2	1.8	27.3	23.7	21.1	8.2
Yorkshire and the Humber	25.4	3.1	27.3	21.1	21.2	7.5
East Midlands	24.8	2.4	27.2	24.0	21.3	7.4
West Midlands	25.6	2.0	27.2	17.5	21.1	7.3
East	25.6	2.4	27.2	18.4	21.3	7.0
London	27.1	1.7	27.3	8.5	21.3	5.8
South East	25.9	1.9	27.5	23.3	21.4	7.7
South West	25.3	1.6	27.3	25.5	21.4	8.6
Wales	24.3	3.2	25.2	4.8	20.4	9.5
Scotland	23.0	1.0	24.6	12.1	..	..
Northern Ireland	22.9	2.5	24.1	8.7	..	..

1 Maintained schools only. Figures relate to all classes, not just those taught by one teacher. In Northern Ireland a class is defined as a group of pupils normally under the control of one teacher.
2 Pupils in composite classes that overlap Key Stage 1 and Key Stage 2 are not included. In Scotland primary P1 to P3 is interpreted to be Key Stage 1 and P4 to P7, Key Stage 2. See Appendix, Part 3: Stages of education.

Source: Department for Children, Schools and Families; Welsh Assembly Government; Scottish Government; Northern Ireland Department of Education

there were 18.0 full-time equivalent pupils for every full-time equivalent teacher in the UK compared with 16.8 in 2006/07. The largest change in the pupils to teacher ratio was in maintained nursery schools – in 1995/96 there were 21.3 pupils per teacher. By 2006/07 this had fallen to 17.7 pupils per teacher.

In 2006/07, 270,600 pupils (2.8 per cent) in the UK had statements of special educational needs (SEN) or a co-ordinated support plan (CSP). Pupils with SEN have either significantly greater difficulty in learning than other children of the same age, or a disability that makes it difficult for them to use normal educational facilities. When a school identifies a child with SEN it must try to meet the child's needs, in line with provisions in the SEN Code of Practice. If the initial attempts do not meet the child's needs then an education authority or board may determine the educational needs for a child with SEN, and draw up a formal statement of those needs together with the action it intends to take to meet them. In Scotland, local authorities' responsibilities towards children with additional support needs are set out in the *Additional Support*

for Learning Act 2004, which also introduced the statutory document called the co-ordinated support plan (CSP). These plans are aimed at pupils whose support needs are complex and require support from a range of sources.

In January 2007 in England, the most prevalent need of pupils with statements in primary schools was help with speech, language and communication (23 per cent). In secondary schools the most prevalent need of pupils with statements was for moderate learning difficulties (25 per cent). These pupils have much greater difficulty than their peers in acquiring basic literacy and numeracy skills and in understanding concepts. They may also have low levels of concentration and under-developed social skills. For more information see Appendix, Part 3: Special educational needs data.

In England, the number of pupils with statements of SEN increased from 194,500 in January 1994 (representing 2.5 per cent of pupils) to peak at an estimated 258,300 (3.1 per cent) in 2001. Numbers have since declined with the total in January 2007 (229,100) representing 2.8 per cent of pupils. The number of pupils with statements of SEN in mainstream maintained schools increased from 100,600 in 1994 to an estimated 158,000 in 2001 but has since declined by around 27,000 to 131,000 in January 2007 (Figure 3.6). Over the same 13-year period the number of pupils in special schools and pupil referral units remained fairly constant, ranging between 88,000 and 95,000. In 2006/07, 15,300 pupils in Wales, 13,700 in Scotland and 12,500 in Northern Ireland had statements of special educational need (or the equivalent).

One reason why a child might not be in school is because of exclusion from school. In 2005/06, there were around 9,600 permanent exclusions from school, of children in England and Wales, compared with around 12,800 in 1997/98 when data were first available (it is worth noting that data are for the number of exclusions rather than number of pupils, as some pupils may be excluded more than once during the year). This represents a rate of 12 permanent exclusions for every 10,000 pupils in England and 10 permanent exclusions for every 10,000 pupils in Wales. In 2005/06, 87 per cent of permanent exclusions in England and Wales were from secondary schools; 11 per cent were from primary schools; and 2 per cent were from special schools. In Scotland there were nearly 43,000 exclusions of pupils from schools in 2005/06, although 99 per cent of these were temporary. In Northern Ireland in the same year there were 54 expulsions (permanent exclusions) and 5,600 suspensions (temporary exclusions) of pupils from school.

Figure 3.6

Pupils with statements of special educational needs (SEN):[1] by type of school

England

Thousands

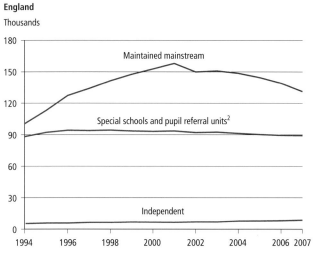

1 Data are at January each year. Estimates were made for 2001 because the SEN data were known to be incomplete. See Appendix, Part 3: Special educational needs data.
2 Pupil referral units did not exist before 1995.

Source: Department for Children, Schools and Families

Table 3.7

Children who missed school through truancy:[1] by sex and main reason, 2005

England   Percentages

	Boys	Girls	All
They were bored	24	20	22
They didn't like a particular subject or lesson	18	24	21
They didn't like school	16	13	14
They didn't like a particular teacher or teachers	15	12	13
Bullying	4	8	6
Other reason	15	15	15
They weren't sure why	7	8	8
All reasons	100	100	100

1 Children aged 14 to 15 who said that they played truant were asked 'When you played truant what was the main reason you did this?' Excludes those who did not want to answer.

Source: Longitudinal Study of Young People in England, Department for Children, Schools and Families

Another reason for a child to be out of school is unauthorised absence or truancy. In 2005/06, girls in maintained secondary schools in England missed a higher proportion of half days overall than boys, including both authorised and unauthorised absence (8.4 per cent of half days for girls compared with 8.1 per cent for boys). There was no difference between the sexes in unauthorised absence rates in 2005/06 – 1.4 per cent of half days missed by both girls and boys were missed because of unauthorised absence. The unauthorised absence rate for pupils who were known to be eligible for free school meals, commonly used as an indicator of family circumstances, was almost three times that of the rest of the school population (3.2 per cent of half days missed compared with 1.1 per cent).

In 2005, the Longitudinal Study of Young People in England asked children aged 14 and 15 who said they had played truant, why they had done so. The most common response cited by boys was that they were bored (24 per cent) while for girls the most common response was that they did not like a particular subject or lesson (24 per cent) (Table 3.7). A higher proportion of girls than boys said they played truant because of bullying, 8 per cent compared with 4 per cent, while 8 per cent of pupils overall said they were unsure why they truanted.

The same study also asked all children in the survey aged 14 and 15 a number of questions to gauge their attitudes to different aspects of school. Table 3.8 shows that in 2005 almost nine in ten (87 per cent) children in England agreed

Table 3.8

Children's[1] attitudes to school, 2005

England   Percentages

	Strongly agreed	Agreed	Disagreed	Strongly disagreed	Don't know
School work is worth doing	40	46	7	5	2
I am happy at school	22	60	11	4	3
I work as hard as I can	21	54	19	2	4
I like being at school	20	60	13	4	3
People think my school is good	19	49	19	7	6
I get good marks	15	67	11	2	5
I count the minutes in lessons	14	40	36	7	3
I am bored in lessons	10	36	43	6	6
Work in lessons is interesting	9	62	20	3	6
I don't want to go to school	7	24	44	21	3
School is a waste of time	3	6	37	51	3
The work in lessons is a waste of time	3	7	55	32	3

1 Children aged 14 and 15 were asked whether they agreed or disagreed with the above statements.

Source: Longitudinal Study of Young People in England, Department for Children, Schools and Families

that school work is worth doing (with 46 per cent agreeing and 40 per cent strongly agreeing), but fewer children (72 per cent) agreed overall that the work in lessons was interesting. Around eight in ten children agreed or strongly agreed that they were happy at school (82 per cent) or liked being at school (80 per cent). However there was also evidence of frustrations regarding school. Over one-half of children agreed or strongly agreed that they counted the minutes in lessons (54 per cent), and over two-fifths that they were bored in lessons (45 per cent). Almost one-third (31 per cent) of children said they didn't want to go to school and almost one in ten (9 per cent) went as far as to agree that school was a waste of time.

The Scottish Government carries out an annual Scottish Survey of Achievement, which asks both teachers and pupils (aged 5 to 14) about their attitudes to, and experiences of, teaching and learning. Each year the survey focuses on a particular subject area and in 2006 this was on the enquiry skills element of social studies (for example history, geography and modern studies). The survey found that overall, 77 per cent of pupils stated that they 'very often' wanted to do well in their work on this subject. However, this figure decreased from more than 80 per cent of pupils in the primary stages to less than 60 per cent for those aged around 13. Around 10 per cent of primary and 15 per cent of secondary pupils reported that their teacher 'hardly ever' helped them to make their work better. More than three-quarters of pupils agreed with the statement, 'everyone is expected to work hard in our class'.

Post-compulsory participation

In 2005/06 there were around 4.5 million further education students in the UK, more than two and a half times the number in 1970/71 (Table 3.9 overleaf), although it should be noted there have been changes to data coverage and methodologies over time (see Appendix, Part 3: Stages of education). This total comprised 2.6 million female further education students, more than three and a half times as many as in 1970/71, and 1.8 million male students, almost twice as many as in 1970/71. During this period, the proportion of further education students who were women increased from 42 per cent in 1970/71 to 59 per cent in 2005/06 and conversely the proportion of men has fallen from 58 per cent to 41 per cent.

Similar numbers of men and women study full time (more than half a million each) but the majority (76 per cent) of further education students studied part time in 2005/06. Women are more likely than men to study part time, 79 per cent and 72 per cent respectively of further education students. This contrasts to 1970/71 when a similar proportion of women (87 per cent) and men (88 per cent) studied part time.

There have also been substantial increases in the number of students in higher education in the UK (see Appendix, Part 3: Stages of education). In 2005/06 there were 2.5 million students in higher education compared with around 620,000 in 1970/71. The number of enrolments has increased for both

Table 3.9

Students in further and higher education:[1] by type of course and sex

United Kingdom   Thousands

	Men				Women			
	1970/71	1980/81	1990/91	2005/06	1970/71	1980/81	1990/91	2005/06
Further education								
Full-time	116	154	219	517	95	196	261	538
Part-time	891	697	768	1,325	630	624	986	2,071
All further education	1,007	851	986	1,842	725	820	1,247	2,609
Higher education								
Undergraduate								
Full-time	241	277	345	561	173	196	319	701
Part-time	127	176	148	267	19	71	106	458
Postgraduate								
Full-time	33	41	50	116	10	21	34	119
Part-time	15	32	46	140	3	13	33	177
All higher education[2]	416	526	588	1,085	205	301	491	1,456

1 Home and overseas students. See Appendix, Part 3: Stages of education.
2 Figures for 2005/06 include a small number of higher education students for whom details are not available by level.

Source: Department for Children, Schools and Families; Department for Innovation, Universities and Skills; Welsh Assembly Government; Scottish Government; Northern Ireland Department for Employment and Learning

sexes – for women, there were 1.5 million higher education enrolments in 2005/06, seven times as many as in 1970/71. For men, there were 1.1 million enrolments in 2005/06, an increase of two and a half times over the same period. The sharper increase in female numbers means the proportion of female higher education students increased from 33 per cent to 57 per cent over the 35 year period.

At the end of 2006, 1.5 million 16 to 18-year-olds (77 per cent) in England were in some form of education or training – the highest proportion since 1994, when it reached 78 per cent. There have been changes between the sexes in participation rates in recent years. In 1985 a larger proportion of young men than young women were in some form of education or training (63 per cent and 55 per cent respectively). In 1998 this trend reversed and by 2006, 75 per cent of men and 79 per cent of women in this age band were in education or training (Figure 3.10). For both young men and women the increases in participation were in the late 1980s and early 1990s. Since 1994 the proportions have remained relatively stable.

The overall participation rate in education or training for young people aged between 16 and 18 in Wales followed a similar pattern to England, with participation rates of over 75 per cent throughout the 10 year period to 2002. Since then there has

Figure 3.10

Proportion of 16 to 18-year-olds in education or training:[1] by sex

England
Percentages

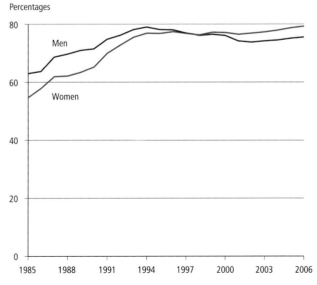

1 From 1994 there were changes in the source of further and higher education data. Participation estimates may be slightly underestimated for 16-year-olds between 1999 and 2000, 17-year-olds between 2000 and 2001, and 18-year-olds between 2001 and 2002. Data are at end of calendar year.

Source: Department for Children, Schools and Families

Table 3.11

People working towards a qualification:[1] by age, 2007[2]

United Kingdom   Percentages

	Degree or equivalent or higher	Higher education[3]	GCE A level or equivalent	GCSE or equivalent	Other qualifications	All studying
16–19	16	19	73	69	12	35
20–24	43	20	10	6	12	21
25–29	11	16	3	4	16	10
30–39	15	21	6	8	26	16
40–49	10	18	5	8	21	12
50–59/64[4]	4	6	2	5	13	6
All aged 16–59/64[4] (=100%) (millions)	1.8	0.5	1.4	0.9	1.6	6.2

1 For those working towards more than one qualification, the highest is recorded. See Appendix, Part 3: Qualifications. Excludes those who did not answer and those who did not state the qualification they were working towards.
2 Data are at Q2 and are not seasonally adjusted. See Appendix, Part 4: Labour Force Survey.
3 Below degree level but including NVQ level 4.
4 Men aged 16 to 64 and women aged 16 to 59.

Source: Labour Force Survey, Office for National Statistics

been a decline. In 2005 the participation rate was 73 per cent with a higher rate for young women than young men (76 per cent compared with 70 per cent). In Scotland the overall participation rate in 2006 was 79 per cent and there was very little difference in the proportions for men and women.

Following the end of compulsory education, not all young people go on to further education or training. In 2007 the Government set out its plans to provide funding to help young people in England who are not in education, employment or training (NEET). The Government also outlined its intention of increasing the school leaving age of pupils in England from 16 to 18 by 2015, to provide young people with more opportunity to gain qualifications. According to data from the Department for Children, Schools and Families, 10 per cent of 16 to 18-year-olds in England were NEET in 2006 and although this is lower than peaks of nearly 14 per cent in 1985 and more than 11 per cent in 1992, this proportion has been increasing from the most recent low of 8 per cent in 1999. A slightly higher proportion of young men (more than 11 per cent) than young women (9 per cent) were NEET in 2006.

Not everyone working towards a qualification beyond the age of 16 has worked their way continuously through the various levels of education. More than two-fifths (44 per cent) of working-age people (16 to 64 for men and 16 to 59 for women) who were studying towards a qualification in the UK in Q2 2007 were aged 25 and over. Around one-fifth (19 per cent) were aged 40 and over (Table 3.11). The age distribution varies according to the qualification being studied.

Working-age adults aged 25 and over comprised 25 per cent of those studying towards a GCSE or equivalent and 17 per cent of those studying towards a GCE A level or equivalent. The proportion for this age group rose to 61 per cent of working-age people taking higher education qualifications below degree level (such as a Higher National Diploma or Higher National Certificate), and 40 per cent of those studying at degree level or higher.

Educational attainment

Girls generally outperform boys at all levels of education in the UK from Key Stage 1 to higher education. Assessment at Key Stages in England and Wales is an essential component of the National Curriculum (see Appendix, Part 3: The National Curriculum). Scotland and Northern Ireland each have their own guidelines for the curriculum.

Pupils' performance is assessed by National Curriculum tests at Key Stages 2 and 3 in England. These tests measure pupils' attainment against the levels set by the National Curriculum and measure the extent to which pupils have the specific knowledge, skills and understanding that the National Curriculum requires pupils to have developed by the end of the Key Stage. There were improvements in attainment in these tests over the last ten years, although girls generally performed better than boys. In 1997, 57 per cent of boys and 70 per cent of girls reached the expected standard in English tests at Key Stage 2. By 2007 these proportions had increased to 76 per cent and 85 per cent respectively. The same trend

Table 3.12

Pupils reaching or exceeding expected standards through teacher assessment:[1] by Key Stage and sex

England   Percentages

	1997		2007	
	Boys	Girls	Boys	Girls
Key Stage 1[2]				
English				
Reading	75	85	80	88
Writing	72	83	75	86
Mathematics	82	86	88	91
Science	84	86	87	90
Key Stage 2[3]				
English	57	70	73	83
Mathematics	63	65	78	78
Science	68	70	84	85
Key Stage 3[4]				
English	52	70	68	81
Mathematics	62	65	78	80
Science	60	63	73	76

1 See Appendix, Part 3: Stages of education, and The National Curriculum.
2 Pupils achieving level 2 or above at Key Stage 1.
3 Pupils achieving level 4 or above at Key Stage 2.
4 Pupils achieving level 5 or above at Key Stage 3.

Source: Department for Children, Schools and Families

was true for science. However, in mathematics boys performed marginally better than girls – 63 per cent of boys and 61 per cent of girls achieved expected standards in 1997, compared with 78 per cent of boys and 76 per cent of girls in 2007.

In addition to tests, pupil's performance is also measured by teacher assessment. Between 1997 and 2007, although the proportion of girls reaching the required standard in each of the Key Stages by teacher assessment has generally been higher than that for boys in England, there have been improvements in the performance of both sexes (Table 3.12). At Key Stage 1 the proportion of boys who reached the required standard in reading, by teacher assessment, increased by 5 percentage points over the period to 80 per cent and for writing, there was an increase of 3 percentage points to 75 per cent. For girls the proportions also increased between 1997 and 2007 by 3 percentage points for both reading and writing (to 88 per cent and 86 per cent respectively).

In English at Key Stage 2 there were more marked improvements for both boys and girls. In 1997, 57 per cent of boys reached or exceeded the expected standard at this stage.

By 2007 this had increased to 73 per cent. For girls the proportion who reached or exceeded the standard increased from 70 per cent in 1997 to 83 per cent in 2007. There was a similar pattern of improvement for both boys and girls in mathematics and science although in all three subjects the performance against expected standards for both sexes was lower at Key Stage 2 than Key Stage 1. Similarly, although there were improvements between 1997 and 2007 for both sexes at Key Stage 3 in all three assessed subjects, the proportions who achieved the expected standard at this stage was generally lower than at Key Stage 2.

The differences in performance between boys and girls at Key Stages 1 to 3 continued through to GCSE. In 2005/06, 64 per cent of girls in their last year of compulsory education achieved five or more GCSEs at grades A* to C (or equivalent) in the UK, compared with 54 per cent of boys. This was an increase for both sexes since 1995/96, when the figures were 51 per cent and 41 per cent for girls and boys respectively.

Overall in 2005/06, 59 per cent of pupils entered for the GCSE or equivalent exam in the UK achieved five or more GCSEs grade A* to C or the equivalent, an increase of 14 percentage points since 1995/96 (Figure 3.13). As a result the proportion

Figure 3.13

GCSE or equivalent achievements:[1,2] by grade

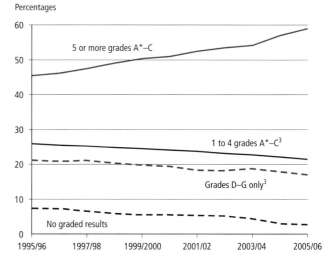

United Kingdom
Percentages

1 For pupils in their last year of compulsory education, i.e. pupils aged 15 at the start of the academic year; pupils in year S4 in Scotland. From 2004/05, pupils at the end of Key Stage 4 in England.
2 From 1990/91 National Qualifications were introduced in Scotland but these are not included until 2000/01. See also Appendix, Part 3: Qualifications.
3 Figures for 1997/98 refer to Great Britain only.

Source: Department for Children, Schools and Families; Welsh Assembly Government; Scottish Government; Northern Ireland Department of Education

of children who achieved lower grades fell as did the proportion who did not achieve a graded result, from 7 per cent in 1995/96 to 3 per cent in 2005/06.

The proportion of both young men and women in the UK gaining two or more GCE A levels (or equivalent) has also increased, but has been more marked among young women. Between 1990/91 and 2005/06, the proportion of young women gaining these qualifications more than doubled, from 20 per cent to 42 per cent (although in 2003/04 this figure reached 44 per cent). Over the same period, the proportion of young men gaining these qualifications almost doubled, increasing from 18 per cent to 33 per cent. In England in 2005/06, 25 per cent of young women achieved a grade A compared with 23 per cent of young men.

Table 3.14

Higher education qualifications attained:[1] by sex and class of qualification, 2005/06

United Kingdom			Percentages
	Men	Women	All
First degree			
First class	11	11	11
Upper second	39	47	43
Lower second	32	28	30
Third class/Pass	9	6	7
Unclassified	8	9	8
All (=100%) (thousands)	137.1	178.9	316.0
Higher degree			
Doctorate	15	12	13
Other higher degree	85	88	87
All (=100%) (thousands)	63.0	62.0	125.1
Other postgraduate			
PGCE[2]	32	44	40
Other postgraduate	68	56	60
All (=100%) (thousands)	26.7	46.5	73.2
Other undergraduate			
Foundation degree	8	7	7
HND/DipHE[3]	26	26	26
Other undergraduate	67	66	66
All (=100%) (thousands)	41.5	85.1	126.6

1 Full-time and part-time, home and overseas students. See Appendix, Part 3: Stages of education.
2 Post Graduate Certificate of Education.
3 Higher National Diploma or Diploma in Higher Education.

Source: Department for Children, Schools and Families; Department for Innovation, Universities and Skills

In 2005/06, 316,000 UK and overseas domiciled students obtained first degrees at higher education institutions in the UK (Table 3.14). Of these first degrees, 11 per cent were graded first class with similar proportions of men and women achieving this level. A higher proportion of women than men achieved upper second grades, 47 per cent compared with 39 per cent, while similar proportions of men and women achieved lower second class grades, 32 per cent of men compared with 28 per cent of women. Overall 7 per cent of first-degree students achieved a third class (or pass grade) and 8 per cent were unclassified. In the same year around 125,000 higher degrees were awarded (around one in eight of which were at doctorate level) and of the 73,000 other postgraduate qualifications attained, two in five were for a Post Graduate Certificate in Education. There were also 127,000 other undergraduate qualifications awarded in 2005/06.

In 2007 working-age people in the UK were more likely to be educated to at least degree level than to be without formal qualifications. Figures for working-age people in Q2 2007 show that 20 per cent of people held degrees or equivalent compared with 14 per cent with no qualifications. Differences emerged when attainment was analysed by sex and age. Among working-age women, those aged 50 and over (24 per cent) were more likely than women in other age groups to hold no qualifications. Among working-age men, around one-fifth (18 per cent) of men aged 50 and over, and almost one-quarter (23 per cent) of 16 to 19-year-olds held no qualifications; both higher proportions than men in other working-age groups. It should be noted that the high figure for 16 to 19-year-olds is largely accounted for by the fact that the majority of those who are 16 in Q2 will not have had their year 11 results and therefore will not yet have qualifications. When 16-year-olds are not included in the calculation the figure (for 17 to 19- year-old men) falls to around 10 per cent who held no qualifications.

In Q2 2007 working-age men in the UK were almost one and a half times as likely as women to be qualified to at least GCE A level or equivalent standard (27 per cent and 19 per cent respectively). This could be in part because of the far higher proportion of men than women who are qualified in trade apprenticeships, which, in this analysis, are all treated as being the equivalent of GCE A level. The difference between the sexes virtually disappeared among those with a degree or equivalent with 20 per cent of working-age men, and 19 per cent of working-age women qualified to this level.

Qualifications are also linked to occupations. In Q2 2007 those in professional occupations were by far the most likely of all

Table 3.15

Highest qualification held:[1] by occupation, 2007[2]

United Kingdom

Percentages

	Degree or equivalent or higher	Higher education qualifications[3]	GCE A level or equivalent	GCSE grades A* to C or equivalent	Other qualifications	No qualifications	All
Managers and senior officials	33	13	23	18	8	4	100
Professional	70	11	10	4	4	1	100
Associate professional and technical	34	20	21	16	7	2	100
Administrative and secretarial	15	9	25	37	10	4	100
Skilled trades	4	6	45	19	13	12	100
Personal service	8	12	29	31	13	7	100
Sales and customer service	7	5	28	36	12	12	100
Process, plant and machine operatives	2	3	21	25	29	20	100
Elementary	4	3	19	27	25	23	100
All occupations	23	10	24	22	12	8	100

1 Men aged 16 to 64, women aged 16 to 59. Excludes those who did not state their highest qualification. See Appendix, Part 3: Qualifications.
2 Data are at Q2 and are not seasonally adjusted. See Appendix, Part 4: Labour Force Survey, and Standard Occupational Classification 2000 (SOC2000).
3 Below degree level.

Source: Labour Force Survey, Office for National Statistics

occupations to have a degree or equivalent (or higher) qualification (70 per cent) (Table 3.15). Those who were in employment as managers and senior officials, or in associate, professional and technical occupations (such as nurses, financial advisers and IT technicians) were the next most likely occupations in which people were qualified to this level (33 and 34 per cent respectively). Workers in elementary occupations formed the group most likely to have no qualifications (23 per cent). However, around one in twenty-five who worked in this group was qualified to degree level or higher.

An alternative to the more traditional and academic qualifications are National Vocational Qualifications (NVQs) and Scottish Vocational Qualifications (SVQs), which were introduced in 1987 (see Appendix, Part 3: Qualifications). There has been an increase in the take up of these qualifications as shown by the numbers awarded. In 2005/06 around 622,000 NVQs and SVQs were awarded in the UK whereas in 1991/92 around 153,000 were awarded (Figure 3.16). The number of NVQ/SVQs levels 2 (equivalent to five GCSEs at grades A* to C) to 5 (equivalent to a higher degree) awarded in 2005/06 were the highest ever.

In 2005/06, 23 per cent of all NVQs and SVQs awarded in the UK were in health, public services and care and this sector subject area accounted for 31 per cent of all level 3 NVQ/SVQs. More than one-half (55 per cent) of all NVQ/SVQs, in any sector subject area, were awarded to those aged 25 and over,

with 25 per cent being attained by people aged over 40. The higher NVQ/SVQ levels were most likely to be awarded to older students – people aged 25 and over attained 36 per cent of level 1s, 54 per cent of level 2s, 58 per cent of level 3s and 88 per cent of levels 4 and 5. Women gained 70 per cent of NVQ/SVQs at levels 4 and 5, and 63 per cent of level 3s. For the lower qualifications of levels 1 and 2, there was

Figure 3.16

NVQ/SVQs awarded:[1] by level of qualification

United Kingdom

Thousands

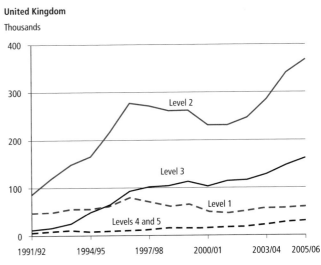

1 Data for 2000/01 are NVQ awards only. See Appendix, Part 3: Qualifications.

Source: Department for Children, Schools and Families

approximately a 50 per cent split between the sexes. The sector subject areas showed a difference between the sexes with the majority of awards for health, public services and care; retail and commercial enterprise; and business, administration and law going to women whereas the majority of awards for engineering and manufacturing technologies; and construction and planning and the built environment were attained by men.

Adult training and learning

Unlike Table 3.9, which reports numbers of further education students in further and higher education institutions in the UK, Table 3.17 reports Learning and Skills Council (LSC) funded further education in England (excluding higher education institutions that deliver further education provision). In 2006/07 there were 2.1 million LSC-funded adult learners (defined here as aged 19 and over) in further education institutions in England, and of this total 61 per cent were women (Table 3.17). The total number of adult learners in further education has decreased by 40 per cent since 2002/03, when there were 3.5 million studying in England. Total numbers of adults participating in further education have fallen away in recent years, reflecting a shift away from short courses towards longer ones, which is in line with current government policy.

In 2006/07 the number of LSC-funded learners decreased with age although there were still more than twice as many adult learners than younger learners (defined here as aged under 19) in this form of further education in England. Across all ages (including both adult and younger learners) the most common subjects studied overall were in the preparation for life and work group. However, there were some differences between the age groups in other sector subject areas. For example, there was a higher proportion of adult learners (14 per cent), compared with younger learners (6 per cent), studying information and communications technology (ICT) courses. This could be in part because younger learners will have gained more experience of ICT through use of computers in school, which has increased in recent years (see the Educational resources section later in chapter for more on computers in schools), or their use of ICT for other purposes such as accessing the Internet. Adult learners, particularly women, were also more likely than younger learners to be studying in the health, public services and care subject areas, (20 per cent of women aged 19 and over compared with 16 per cent aged under 19).

Table 3.17

Adult participation in further education compared with younger learners: by sex and sector subject area, 2006/07

England   Percentages

	Aged 19 and over			Aged under 19		
	Men	Women	All	Men	Women	All
Preparation for life and work	31	27	29	16	13	14
Health, public services and care	10	20	16	4	16	10
Information and communication technology	14	14	14	9	3	6
Business, administration and law	6	7	6	6	7	6
Arts, media and publishing	5	7	6	12	14	13
Languages, literature and culture	5	6	6	3	6	4
Retail and commercial enterprise	3	6	5	2	12	7
Engineering and manufacturing technologies	8	1	4	10	1	5
Construction, planning and the built environment	7	-	3	10	-	5
Leisure, travel and tourism	4	2	3	8	6	7
Science and mathematics	1	2	1	7	9	8
Other area[1]	6	8	7	12	14	13
Total (=100%) (millions)	0.8	1.3	2.1	0.4	0.4	0.8

1 Includes agriculture, horticulture and animal care, history, philosophy and theology, social sciences, and education and training. Also includes cases where sector subject area was not known. See Appendix, Part 3: Adult education.

Source: Learning and Skills Council, Department for Children, Schools and Families

Through the Lifelong Learning Wales Record, the Welsh Assembly Government also collects data on those aged 16 and over who are continuing with learning at further education institutions, through community learning providers or through work-based learning provision. In 2005/06 there were around 311,100 people aged 16 and over learning in Wales through these types of provision and of this total, 42 per cent of learners were men and 58 per cent were women. Men outnumbered women at all ages below 20. However, the proportion of women aged 20 and over was 62 per cent higher than that for men. The most popular subjects for all learning activities were care/basic skills (26 per cent), information technology (16 per cent), media (9 per cent), and health (8 per cent).

In Q2 2007, 14 per cent of employees of working age in the UK had received job-related training in the four weeks prior to being interviewed in the Labour Force Survey (Table 3.18). In general, greater proportions of women (17 per cent) than men (12 per cent) received job-related training, and the proportion was higher for younger than for older employees. Among people aged 16 to 24, 20 per cent of men and 21 per cent of women received job-related training, compared with 8 per cent of men aged 50 to 64 and 13 per cent of women aged 50 to 59.

Employees in the UK who already held high qualifications were more likely to receive job-related training in Q2 2007 than those with lower or no qualifications. In Q2 2007, 20 per cent of employees (particularly women) with at least a degree as their highest qualification received some form of job-related training. The same was true for those qualified with at least a higher education qualification. However, around one in seven

employees whose highest qualification was either GCE A level or GCSE grades A* to C (or equivalents in both cases) received this training and this proportion went down to one in twenty-five for those with no qualifications. It appears therefore that people with the highest qualifications were more likely to gain more work-related skills and experiences, aiding their career prospects, compared with those with low or no qualifications.

In 2006 the Workforce Training in England survey questioned employers about the volume, type and pattern of training they provided for their employees. Overall, three-fifths (61 per cent) of employers reported that they had provided some employee training (at the workplace) during the previous 12 months.

For employers who had provided training, health and safety (79 per cent) and job specific skills (76 per cent) were the most likely types of training to be provided in England (Figure 3.19). Two-thirds (67 per cent) provided induction training. Almost one-half (49 per cent) funded or arranged training to develop management and leadership skills and a similar proportion (47 per cent) sought to develop interpersonal skills through training. Basic skills training had been arranged by one in eight (12 per cent) of employers that provided training, equivalent to 7 per cent of all employers.

The 2006 Workforce Training survey asked the employers that had provided basic skills training whether the training had covered literacy, numeracy, English language skills and/or other

Table 3.18

Employees[1] receiving job-related training:[2] by sex and highest qualification already held,[3] 2007[4]

United Kingdom			Percentages
	Men	Women	All
Degree or equivalent or higher	17	23	20
Higher education	14	24	20
GCE A Level or equivalent	12	18	15
GCSE grades A* to C or equivalent	13	13	13
Other qualifications	8	11	10
No qualifications	4	4	4
All employees receiving training	12	17	14

1 Men aged 16 to 64, women aged 16 to 59.
2 In the four weeks prior to interview.
3 Excludes those who did not know their highest qualification. See Appendix, Part 3: Qualifications.
4 Data at Q2 and are not seasonally adjusted. See Appendix, Part 4: Labour Force Survey.

Source: Labour Force Survey, Office for National Statistics

Figure 3.19

Training funded or arranged by employers for staff: by type of training, 2006[1]

England
Percentages

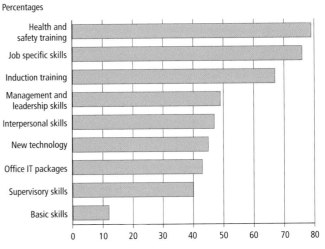

1 Training provided by employers for staff in the 12 months before employers' interview. Data are type of training provided as a proportion of all training provided. Employers could cite more than one type.

Source: Workforce Training in England Survey, Department for Education and Skills

areas. Literacy and numeracy were the most likely basic skills to be offered by these employers, at 71 per cent and 67 per cent respectively, while one-half (49 per cent) provided English language skills training. Other areas where basic skills training had been provided were ICT (7 per cent of those providing any basic skills training), job specific (5 per cent) and customer service (2 per cent). When considering the proportion of all employers that provided basic skills training the survey showed the most common training was for literacy (5 per cent), numeracy (5 per cent) and English language skills (3 per cent).

Educational resources

In 2006/07 public expenditure on education in the UK was 5.5 per cent of gross domestic product (GDP), the equivalent of £71.5 billion (Figure 3.20). This is the highest ever spend over the time series from 1978/79, the lowest period being 1998/99 when spending dipped from a peak of 5.2 per cent in the early 1980s to 4.4 per cent.

In 2004, for public expenditure on education, Denmark spent the most of the 18 EU member states for which data were available on education as a proportion of GDP, at 8.4 per cent. Greece spent the least (3.3 per cent). In the same year the comparable figure for the UK was 5.3 per cent of GDP.

The majority (70 per cent) of teachers in maintained mainstream schools in 2005/06 were women. In this year, the

Figure 3.20

UK education spending as a proportion of gross domestic product[1]

United Kingdom
Percentages

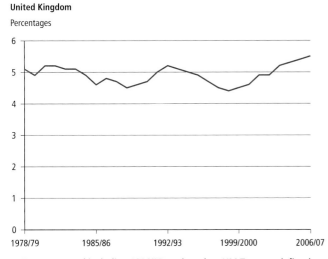

1 Data up to and including 1986/87 are based on HM Treasury defined functions; those from 1987/88 are based on the UN Classification of the Functions of Government (COFOG). Data are public expenditure only. See Appendix, Part 3: Classification of the Functions of Government (COFOG).

Source: HM Treasury; Department for Children, Schools and Families

Figure 3.21

Full-time teachers:[1] by sex and type of school

United Kingdom
Thousands

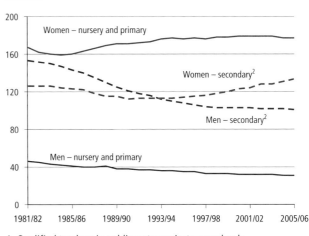

1 Qualified teachers in public sector mainstream schools.
2 From 1993/94, data exclude sixth-form colleges in England and Wales, which were reclassified as further education colleges on 1 April 1993.

Source: Department for Children, Schools and Families; Scottish Government; Northern Ireland Department of Education

number of female teachers in mainstream schools in the UK was at its highest level in the last 24 years at 310,000, while the number of male teachers fell to its lowest level over the same period, to 132,000 (Figure 3.21). This fall mainly affected secondary schools, where the number of male teachers fell from 153,000 in 1981/82 to 101,000. In nursery and primary schools, female teachers accounted for 85 per cent of teaching staff, while in secondary schools the difference between the sexes was less marked, with 57 per cent of teachers being women.

The number of support staff, such as teaching assistants and technicians, in maintained schools in England, increased by 7 per cent from 225,000 in 2006 to 240,000 in 2007. The majority of support staff were in primary schools, accounting for 55 per cent of all support staff in 2007 (Figure 3.22 overleaf). The number of teaching assistants has increased steadily over time, from around 57,000 in 1996 to 163,000 in 2007. Teaching assistants providing special needs support accounted for 30 per cent of all teaching assistants in 2007.

In 2005/06 there were around 165,000 academic staff in higher education institutions in the UK and of these 58 per cent were men. Around one-third (32 per cent) of all academic staff were lecturers and of these, 53 per cent were also men. In the senior positions (professors, senior lecturers and researchers) the gap between men and women increased, with men accounting for 83 per cent of professors and 66 per cent of senior lecturers and researchers.

Figure 3.22

Support staff:[1] by type of school

England

Thousands

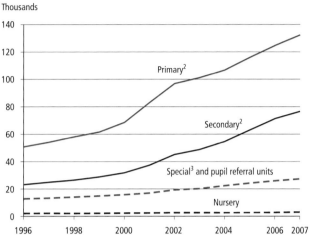

1 In maintained schools. Includes teaching assistants, technicians and other support staff but excludes administrative staff. Includes both full-time and the full-time equivalent of part-time support staff. Data are at January each year.
2 Includes middle schools. Depending on their individual age ranges middle schools are classified as either primary or secondary.
3 Includes non-maintained special schools.

Source: Department for Children, Schools and Families

Classroom resources have also changed. The Becta Harnessing Technology Review 2007 indicates that the average number of pupils per computer (used mainly for teaching and learning) in maintained schools in England has decreased steadily over the period 2000 to 2006. The ratio in primary schools dropped from 12.6 pupils per computer to 6.2, and in secondary schools from 7.9 to 3.6 pupils. By comparison, the EU-25 average was 8.8 pupils per computer overall in 2006. The lowest ratio was in Denmark with 3.7 pupils per computer, the highest was in both Latvia and Lithuania with 16.9 per computer. The UK ranked joint third with Luxembourg out of the 25 member states, with 5.1 pupils per computer.

There has also been an increase in the availability of laptops (used mainly for teaching and learning) in both primary and secondary schools in England, with availability in 90 per cent of primary schools and 95 per cent of secondary schools in 2006. In both primary and secondary schools laptop computers were located mainly within the classroom as opposed to a dedicated information and communication technology (ICT) room (77 per cent and 70 per cent respectively). However desktop computers for both school types were more likely to be located in dedicated ICT rooms (51 per cent for primary and 77 per cent for secondary level). There was also some level of wireless network in 49 per cent of primary schools and 82 per cent of secondary schools. The most common reason for implementing wireless in schools is to facilitate the use of ICT in classrooms other than dedicated ICT rooms.

Schools do not appear to fully exploit the possibilities for learning and teaching offered by technology, especially learning platforms such as virtual learning environments (VLE – a web-based software package used by teachers to manage courses for students) and networks to enable off-site working online. Whereas 46 per cent of secondary schools report having a VLE, 24 per cent of teachers report using it. This can be attributed to various reasons such as problems with technology support, lack of teacher knowledge, and access difficulties.

There has also been a rapid spread of interactive whiteboards in primary schools. All primary schools surveyed reported that they now had an interactive whiteboard, compared with 39 per cent in 2002. The average number per secondary school increased from 18 in 2005 to 22 in 2006.

Chapter 4

Labour market

- In Q2 2007, 15.7 million men and 13.3 million women were in employment in the UK. (Table 4.2)

- The UK employment rate of working-age men fell from 92 per cent in Q2 1971 to 79 per cent in Q2 2007, while the rate for working-age women rose from 56 per cent to 70 per cent. (Figure 4.4)

- Employment rates for disabled working-age people in the UK increased from 46 per cent in Q2 1999 to 50 per cent in Q2 2007. (Page 49)

- More than one-fifth of full-time employees in the UK had some form of flexible working arrangement in Q2 2007. (Table 4.12)

- In 2006 nine in ten employees in Great Britain said they were satisfied with their work, and seven in ten said they were satisfied with their pay. (Table 4.13)

- The number of economically inactive working-age men in the UK increased by 2.4 million to 3.2 million between Q2 1971 and Q2 2007. For working-age women, the number fell by 1.5 million to 4.8 million. (Page 57)

DATA

Download data by clicking the online pdf

www.statistics.gov.uk/ socialtrends38

Many people spend a large proportion of their lives in the labour force, so their experience of work has an important impact on them. Although still large this proportion has been falling. Young people are remaining longer in education and older people are spending more years in retirement, a contributory factor to this being the increase in life expectancy (see Chapter 7: Health). Employment in service industries continues to increase while employment in manufacturing continues to fall. There have also been differences between the sexes in the trends of those not in employment, including both unemployed people and those who are economically inactive.

Labour market profile

Since 1971, when Labour Force Survey (LFS) records began, the number of economically active people (aged 16 and over and either in work or actively looking for work) in the UK increased from 25.6 million in Q2 1971 to 30.7 million in Q2 2007. This equates to nearly two economically active people aged 16 and over for every economically inactive person. For those of working age (16 to 64 for men and 16 to 59 for women) the number of economically active people in the UK increased from 24.8 million to 29.5 million over the same period (the equivalent ratio of nearly four economically active people to every economically inactive person of working age).

Due to an increase in the total working-age population from 31.9 million in Q2 1971 to 37.4 million in Q2 2007, the increase in the number of economically active working-age people has had little impact on the economic activity rate. For example, using Q2 data, the working-age economic activity rate (see Glossary on opposite page) was relatively stable at 78 per cent in 1971 and 79 per cent in 2007, with the lowest rate in 1983 at 77 per cent and the highest in 1990 at 81 per cent (Figure 4.1).

The economically active population comprises those who are either in employment or unemployed. As those in employment make up the majority of these two groups, the working-age employment rate between Q2 1971 and Q2 2007 has followed

Labour Force Survey (LFS)

The LFS is the largest regular household survey in the UK and much of the labour market data published in this chapter are measured by the LFS. Calendar quarter 2 (Q2) data from the LFS refers to the months April to June in a given year. The earliest year for which LFS data are available is 1971 but only for limited time series. Where time series data are quoted in this chapter the earliest comparable year which is available has usually been used. For more information on the survey, including differences between calendar and seasonal quarters, see the Appendix, Part 4: Labour Force Survey.

Figure 4.1

Economic activity and inactivity rates[1]

United Kingdom

Percentages

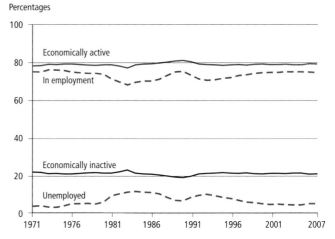

1 Data are at Q2 each year and are seasonally adjusted. Data are as a proportion of men aged 16 to 64 and women aged 16 to 59 with the exception of unemployment rates, which are as a proportion of people aged 16 and over. See Appendix, Part 4: Labour Force Survey.

Source: Labour Force Survey, Office for National Statistics

a similar trend to the economic activity rate, and shows the associated fluctuations in the economic cycle. The proportion of the working-age population in the UK who were in employment (the employment rate) decreased from 76 per cent in the mid-1970s to a low of 68 per cent in Q2 1983. Since then employment rates have generally risen. Although there was a slight fall following the recession of 1990 and 1991, the employment rate in Q2 2007 was 74 per cent, compared with 75 per cent in Q2 1971.

Similarly the unemployment rate (the percentage of the economically active who are unemployed) reflects fluctuations associated with the economic cycle over the period (see also Figure 4.14).

Because someone must be either economically active or economically inactive (see Glossary) the trend for the working-age economic inactivity rate has mirrored that of the economic activity rate over the period. With the lowest rate of economic inactivity in 1990 at 19 per cent and the highest in 1983 at 23 per cent, there was little change over the period as a whole, with proportions ranging from 22 per cent in Q2 1971 to 21 per cent in Q2 2007 (see also Figure 4.17).

Historical estimates back to 1971 for the Labour Force Survey are not yet available for subgroups of the population, other than by sex and for key age groups. LFS data by employment status are only available from 1992 (see Appendix, Part 4: Labour Force Survey). In Q2 2007, 29.1 million people were in employment in the UK. Comparing the labour market in

Glossary

Economically active (or the labour force) – those aged 16 and over who are **in employment** or are **unemployed**.

Economic activity rate – the percentage of the population, for example in a given age group, who are **economically active**.

In employment – a measure, obtained from household surveys and censuses, of those aged 16 and over who are **employees**, **self-employed**, people doing unpaid work for a family-run business, and participants in government employment and training programmes. The number of participants in government employment and training programmes is obtained from household surveys and includes those who said they were participants on Youth Training, Training for Work, Employment Action or Community Industry, or a programme organised by the Learning and Skills Council in England, the National Council for Education and Training for Wales, or Local Enterprise Companies in Scotland.

Employment rate – the proportion of any given population group who are **in employment**. The main presentation of employment rates is the proportion of the population of **working age** who are in employment.

Employees (Labour Force Survey measure) – a measure, obtained from household surveys, of people aged 16 and over who regard themselves as paid employees. People with two or more jobs are counted only once.

Self-employed – a measure, obtained from household surveys, of people aged 16 and over who regard themselves as self-employed, that is, who in their main employment work on their own account, whether or not they have employees.

Unemployment – a measure, based on International Labour Organisation guidelines and used in the Labour Force Survey, which counts as unemployed those aged 16 and over who are without a job, are available to start work in the next two weeks, who have been seeking a job in the last four weeks or are out of work and waiting to start a job already obtained in the next two weeks.

Unemployment rate – the percentage of the **economically active** who are **unemployed**.

Economically inactive – those aged 16 and over who are neither **in employment** nor **unemployment**. For example, those looking after a home, retirees, or those unable to work because of long-term sickness or disability.

Economic inactivity rate – the proportion of a given population group who are **economically inactive**. The main presentation of economic inactivity rates is the proportion of the population of **working age** who are economically inactive.

Working age – men aged 16 to 64 and women aged 16 to 59.

Working-age household – a household that includes at least one person of **working age**.

Working household – a household that includes at least one person of **working age** and where all the people of working age are **in employment**.

Workless household – a household that includes at least one person of **working age** where no one aged 16 and over is **in employment**.

Q2 2007 with 15 years earlier in Q2 1992, the number of people in employment has risen by 3.5 million (Table 4.2 overleaf). This is because more people, especially women, are working, and fewer people are unemployed. In the same period the population aged 16 and over also increased by 3.5 million. The number of people who were full-time employees rose from 16.5 million in Q2 1992 to 18.7 million in Q2 2007. Of this total, 11.6 million were men (an increase of 9 per cent since 1992) and 7.1 million were women (an increase of 21 per cent over the same period). The number of people who were part-time employees also increased over the period from 5.1 million in 1992 to over 6.3 million in 2007. Of this total 1.3 million were men, more than double the number in 1992, and 5.1 million were women, an increase of 14 per cent. Of the 3.8 million people who were self-employed in 2007, the majority (73 per cent) were men, a similar proportion to 1992 (74 per cent) when there were 3.5 million self-employed people in the UK.

Over the last 15 years the number of unemployed people in the UK has fallen from 2.8 million in Q2 1992 to 1.7 million in Q2 2007. The fall was more marked for men than women but this should be viewed in the context of the economic cycle. Unemployment levels in 1992 were nearing their most recent peak (in Q2 1993), a peak that was higher for men than for women. After this peak unemployment levels for both sexes fell almost year on year although there was a slight increase between Q2 2005 and Q2 2006.

Figure 4.1 showed an increase since the mid-1990s in the employment rate in the UK. One of the outcomes of increasing employment is a rise in the number of working-age households that are working (that is, households including at least one person of working age where all persons of working age are in employment). There were 10.9 million working households in Q2 2007, an increase of 262,000 compared with five years ago. Working households as a proportion of all working-age

Table 4.2

Economic activity: by employment status and sex, 1992 and 2007[1]

United Kingdom

Millions

	1992			2007		
	Men	Women	All	Men	Women	All
Economically active						
In employment						
Full-time employees	10.6	5.9	16.5	11.6	7.1	18.7
Part-time employees	0.6	4.5	5.1	1.3	5.1	6.3
Self-employed	2.6	0.9	3.5	2.8	1.0	3.8
Others in employment[2]	0.3	0.3	0.5	0.1	0.1	0.2
All in employment	14.1	11.5	25.6	15.7	13.3	29.1
Unemployed	1.8	0.9	2.8	0.9	0.7	1.7
All economically active	16.0	12.4	28.4	16.7	14.1	30.7
Economically inactive	5.7	11.0	16.6	6.9	10.9	17.8
of which, working age[3]	2.4	4.9	7.4	3.2	4.8	7.9

1 Data are at Q2 each year and are seasonally adjusted. People aged 16 and over. See Appendix, Part 4: Labour Force Survey.
2 Those on government-supported training and employment programmes, and unpaid family workers.
3 Men aged 16 to 64 and women aged 16 to 59.

Source: Labour Force Survey, Office for National Statistics

Table 4.3

People[1] in working-age households:[2] by ethnic group and household economic status, 2007[3]

United Kingdom

Percentages

	Working households	Households with both working and workless members	Workless households
White	57.7	31.5	10.9
Mixed	46.8	32.1	21.1
Indian	39.2	50.8	10.0
Pakistani or Bangladeshi	14.3	64.3	21.3
Other Asian	38.5	45.8	15.7
Black Caribbean	46.4	34.1	19.5
Black African	42.8	34.6	22.6
Other Black	53.4	24.9	21.7
Chinese	37.6	37.4	25.0
Other ethnic group	38.0	39.1	22.9

1 By ethnic origin of working-age person (aged 16 to 64 for men, aged 16 to 59 for women).
2 A working-age household is a household that includes at least one person of working age. Not adjusted for households with unknown economic status.
3 Data are at Q2 and are not seasonally adjusted. See Appendix, Part 4: Labour Force Survey.

Source: Labour Force Survey, Office for National Statistics

households were stable at 57 per cent between Q2 2002 and Q2 2006. However in the 12 months to Q2 2007 there was a small increase, to 58 per cent.

In Q2 2007 there were 3.0 million workless households (that is, households in the UK where at least one person is of working age but no one is in employment). The proportion of households that are workless has remained stable over the last five years, at around 16 per cent since Q2 2002.

The proportion of working-age people living in workless households in the UK was highest for the Chinese ethnic group, at 25 per cent, and lowest for the Indian ethnic group, at 10 per cent, while 11 per cent of people in the White ethnic group lived in a workless household (Table 4.3). Those from the White ethnic group were most likely of all ethnic groups to be living in working households (58 per cent) and those from the Pakistani or Bangladeshi groups were most likely to be living in households containing both working and workless members (64 per cent).

Employment

Although Figure 4.1 showed a fairly stable trend in employment rates between 1971 and 2007, this has been accompanied by a convergence of the employment rates for men and women in the UK (Figure 4.4). Over the period the

Figure 4.4

Employment rates:[1] by sex

United Kingdom

Percentages

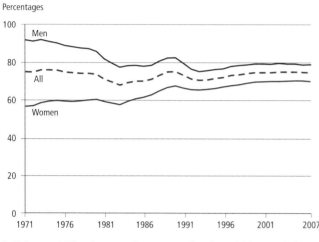

1 Data are at Q2 each year and are seasonally adjusted. Men aged 16 to 64, women aged 16 to 59. See Appendix, Part 4: Labour Force Survey.

Source: Labour Force Survey, Office for National Statistics

Table 4.5

Employment rates:[1] by sex and highest qualification, 2007[2]

United Kingdom   Percentages

	Men	Women	All
Degree or equivalent or higher	89	86	88
Higher education	87	84	85
GCE A level or equivalent	79	73	76
Trade apprenticeship	84	75	82
GCSE grades A* to C or equivalent	77	69	73
Qualifications at NVQ level 1 and below	74	61	67
Other qualifications	81	65	75
No qualifications	54	39	47
All[3]	78	70	74

1 The percentage of the working-age population in employment. Men aged 16 to 64, women aged 16 to 59.
2 Data are at Q2 and are not seasonally adjusted. See Appendix, Part 4: Labour Force Survey.
3 Excludes those who did not state their highest qualification.

Source: Labour Force Survey, Office for National Statistics

employment rate of working-age men fell from 92 per cent in Q2 1971 to 79 per cent in Q2 2007, while the rate for working-age women rose from 56 per cent to 70 per cent.

Before 1993 there were different trends in the employment rates between the sexes. The male employment rate fell from 92 per cent in Q2 1971 to 86 per cent in Q2 1980. Over the same period the female employment rate generally rose from 56 per cent to 60 per cent. During the early 1980s the rates for both sexes fell although the fall was more pronounced among men than women. The employment rate recovered in 1984 and increased for both sexes until the beginning of the 1990s, with the increase being more evident for women. Following the recession in the early 1990s employment rates for men fell to a low of 75 per cent in 1993 – the lowest male rate since LFS records began in 1971. The employment rates for working-age men and women since 1993 have shown a similar pattern.

The presence of dependent children can also influence labour market participation. In Q2 2007, the employment rate for married and cohabiting mothers in the UK was 72 per cent, up 1 percentage point from Q2 2002. For lone parents (including fathers) with dependent children there has been a more marked increase – in Q2 2007 the employment rate was 57 per cent, up 4 percentage points from five years earlier.

There are differences between the employment rates of men and women depending on educational attainment. In Q2 2007, 88 per cent of working-age people in the UK with a degree or equivalent were in employment compared with 47 per cent of

those with no qualifications (Table 4.5). This relationship was more marked for women than for men – 86 per cent of women who had a degree were in employment compared with 39 per cent of women who did not have any qualifications, whereas 89 per cent of men who had a degree were in employment compared with 54 per cent of men who did not have any qualifications.

Around 3.5 million working-aged disabled people in the UK were in employment in Q2 2007 (representing around one in eight of all working-age people in employment). This represented an employment rate for disabled people of 50 per cent compared with 46 per cent in Q2 1999. Employment rates for disabled men increased by 3.8 percentage points over the period and the rate for disabled women increased by 3.2 percentage points. For those who were not disabled, employment rates were around 80 per cent through the period Q2 1999 to Q2 2007.

Employment rates differ across the UK. Figure 4.6 overleaf shows working-age employment rates by region and country, and the highest and lowest local or unitary authority district employment rates within these regions and countries. In 2006 the highest regional working-age employment rate in England was in the South East (78 per cent) and the lowest was in London (69 per cent). At a country level rates were highest in Scotland (76 per cent) and England (74 per cent) whereas in Wales the rate was slightly lower (71 per cent). The overall employment rate for Northern Ireland was 69 per cent.

Figure 4.6

Employment rates:[1] by region,[2] 2006[3]

Great Britain
Percentages

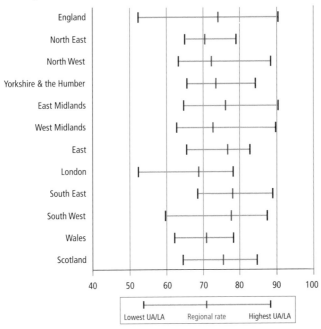

1 Men aged 16 to 64, women aged 16 to 59.
2 By region and lowest and highest unitary authorities or local authority
   districts. Excludes the Isles of Scilly.
3 January to December. See Appendix, Part 4: Annual Population Survey.

Source: Annual Population Survey, Office for National Statistics

Differences in employment rates between local or unitary authorities within Great Britain are often greater than differences between the English regions and between England, Scotland and Wales. In 2006 the greatest contrast between local authorities within a region was in the South West, with a difference of 28 percentage points between the highest and lowest working-age employment rates. London contained three of the four areas in Great Britain with working-age employment rates lower than 60 per cent: Tower Hamlets (53 per cent); Newham (58 per cent); and Hackney (59 per cent). The fourth was West Somerset (just under 60 per cent). The local authority with the highest employment rate in Great Britain was South Northamptonshire with a rate of 90 per cent. Around 90 local and unitary authorities in Great Britain (over one-fifth) had an employment rate of 80 per cent or higher.

NUTS (Nomenclature of Units for Territorial Statistics) is a hierarchical classification of areas that provide a breakdown of the EU's economic territory. Although employment rates are not available for all of Northern Ireland's local authority districts, NUTS data are available and figures for 2006 show that the highest working-age employment rate in Northern Ireland was Outer Belfast (74 per cent) while the lowest was North of Northern Ireland (62 per cent).

In March 2000 the Lisbon European Council agreed an aim to achieve an overall working-age employment rate in the EU of

Table 4.7

Employment rates:[1] by sex, EU comparison, 2006

Percentages

	Men	Women	All		Men	Women	All
Denmark	81.2	73.4	77.4	Luxembourg	72.6	54.6	63.6
Netherlands	80.9	67.7	74.3	Lithuania	66.3	61.0	63.6
Sweden	75.5	70.7	73.1	France	68.5	57.7	63.0
United Kingdom	77.3	65.8	71.5	Greece	74.6	47.4	61.0
Austria	76.9	63.5	70.2	Belgium	67.9	54.0	61.0
Cyprus	79.4	60.3	69.6	Slovakia	67.0	51.9	59.4
Finland	71.4	67.3	69.3	Romania	64.6	53.0	58.8
Ireland	77.7	59.3	68.6	Bulgaria	62.8	54.6	58.6
Estonia	71.0	65.3	68.1	Italy	70.5	46.3	58.4
Portugal	73.9	62.0	67.9	Hungary	63.8	51.1	57.3
Germany	72.8	62.2	67.5	Malta	74.5	34.9	54.8
Slovenia	71.1	61.8	66.6	Poland	60.9	48.2	54.5
Latvia	70.4	62.4	66.3				
Czech Republic	73.7	56.8	65.3	EU-27 average	71.6	57.2	64.4
Spain	76.1	53.2	64.8				

1 See Appendix, Part 4: Eurostat rates.

Source: Labour Force Survey, Eurostat

70 per cent, and a female employment rate of more than 60 per cent, by 2010. In March 2001 the Stockholm European Council added two intermediate targets; that the overall working-age employment rate should be 67 per cent by 2005 and, for women, 57 per cent.

In 2006 the overall EU-27 employment rate was 64 per cent, short of the target set for 2005 (Table 4.7). The UK had one of the highest employment rates (72 per cent) after Denmark (77 per cent), the Netherlands (74 per cent) and Sweden (73 per cent) and was one of 11 out of the EU-27 with an employment rate above the 2005 overall target. It was also one of five with a rate above the 2010 overall target.

The average employment rate for men in the EU-27 was 72 per cent in 2006 and the UK had the fifth highest rate (77 per cent) across the member states. Employment rates for men ranged from 61 per cent in Poland to 81 per cent in Denmark.

The employment rate for women across the EU-27 was 56 per cent in 2005, short of meeting the target of 57 per cent set at the Stockholm Council. However in 2006 the overall employment rate for working-age women reached the target of 57 per cent. The UK had the fifth highest female employment rate (66 per cent) in 2006. The lowest employment rates for women were in the southern European countries of Malta, Italy and Greece and together with Poland, these countries all had employment rates below 50 per cent. In contrast, the north European countries of Denmark (73 per cent), Sweden (71 per cent), the Netherlands (68 per cent) and Finland (67 per cent) had the highest employment rates for working-age women.

There is a range of factors underlying these differences. As well as economic cycle effects, which vary across countries in a given year, employment rates are also affected by population structures and differing cultures, retirement ages and participation in post-compulsory full-time education across the EU.

Patterns of employment

In Q2 2007, 15 per cent of people in employment in the UK were employed as managers or senior officials – the largest occupational group – followed by 14 per cent who were employed in associate professional and technical occupations. In Q2 2001 the largest groups were managers and senior officials and administration and secretarial, each comprising 14 per cent of people in employment (see Appendix, Part 4: Standard Occupational Classification 2000 (SOC2000)). In Q2 2007 between 7 and 8 per cent of those in employment were employed in each of process, plant and machine

occupations, sales and customer services, and personal service occupations.

The pattern of occupations followed by men and women is quite different. In Q2 2007 men in employment were most likely to be employed in skilled trades (19 per cent) whereas women in employment were most likely to be employed in administrative or secretarial occupations (20 per cent) (Figure 4.8). The proportion of women employed in these occupations has fallen in recent years from 23 per cent in Q2 2001, while there has been little change in the proportion of men in employment who worked in skilled trades.

A higher proportion of men than women were in employment as managers or senior officials in Q2 2007 (19 per cent compared with 11 per cent). However, since Q2 2001 the proportion of men who were employed in this group increased by 1 percentage point compared with an increase of 2 percentage points for women.

Around one in seven (14 per cent) women in employment worked in personal service (for example, hairdressers and child care assistants) and around one in nine (11 per cent) worked in sales and customer service – occupations that were far less common among men. The professional occupations, associate professional and technical occupations (such as nurses,

Figure 4.8

All in employment: by sex and occupation, 2007[1]

United Kingdom

Percentages

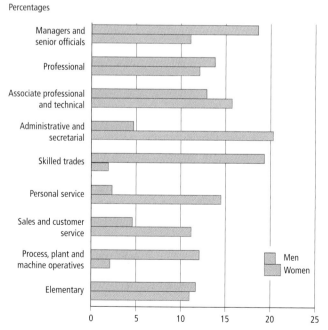

1 Data are at Q2 and are not seasonally adjusted. People aged 16 and over. See Appendix, Part 4: Labour Force Survey, and Standard Occupational Classification 2000 (SOC2000).

Source: Labour Force Survey, Office for National Statistics

Labour market participation by country of birth

People living in the UK who were born overseas are an important feature of the labour market. In Q2 2007, they accounted for 12 per cent of the working-age economically active population, 12 per cent of working-age employment, and 18 per cent of working-age unemployment. Most were born in countries outside the EU-27 area, and this subgroup accounts for much of the recent growth in the UK household population of working age. The number of people in the UK who were born in the eight central and eastern European countries that joined the EU in 2004 (A8 countries) has increased considerably since these countries joined the EU, although the number is much smaller in comparison with the number of those born outside the EU. The vast majority of those born in A8 countries and living in the UK are in employment (81 per cent). The employment rate for people born in the UK remained fairly constant over the four years to Q2 2007, at around 75 per cent.

When interpreting the Labour Force Survey results, users should bear in mind that the survey is not designed to cover everyone who is present in the UK. The Office for National Statistics (ONS) has a current programme of work to improve migration and population statistics. Further developments are also being considered to provide better information about migrant populations and their participation in the UK labour market. Details of this programme of work, and regular updates on progress, are available on the Improving Migration and Population Statistics Project (IMPS) website (http://www.statistics.gov.uk/imps).

financial advisers and IT technicians), and the elementary occupations (such as catering assistants, bar staff and shelf fillers) were likely to be followed by both men and women in similar proportions.

Since the late 1970s the UK economy has experienced structural change. In 1978, when the series began, 6.9 million employee jobs (29 per cent) in the UK were in manufacturing industries. By 2007 this had fallen to 3.0 million (11 per cent) (Figure 4.9). The largest increase in employee jobs has been in the finance and business services, where the number of employee jobs more than doubled between 1978 and 2007 from 2.5 million to 5.7 million. There were also large increases in employee jobs in public administration, education and health which increased by 2.2 million to 7.3 million (the industry with the largest number of employee jobs in 2007) and in the distribution, hotels and restaurants industry (up by 1.8 million to 6.5 million).

These overall changes are reflected in the industry breakdown of employee jobs by sex. In 1978, 34 per cent of male

Figure 4.9

Employee jobs:[1] by industry, 1978 and 2007

United Kingdom

Millions

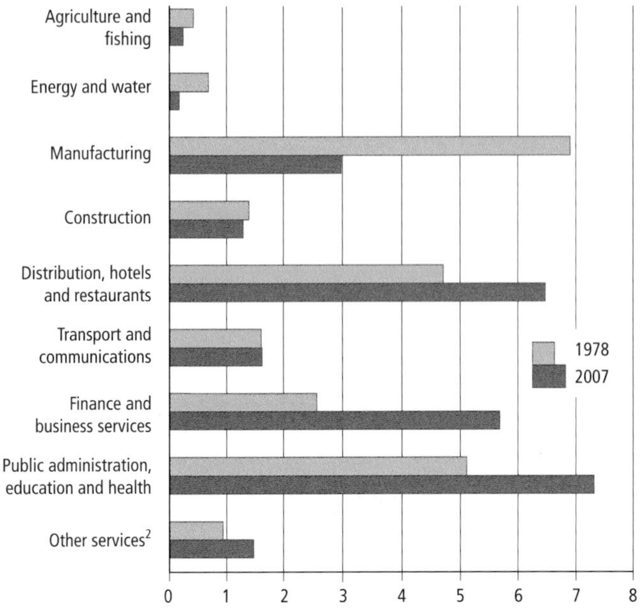

1 Data are at June each year and are not seasonally adjusted.
2 Community, social and personal services including sanitation, dry cleaning, personal care, and recreational, cultural and sporting activities. See Appendix, Part 4: Standard Industrial Classification 2003.

Source: Short Term Employment Survey, Office for National Statistics

employee jobs were in manufacturing. By 2007, the proportion had more than halved to 16 per cent. The proportion of female employee jobs in the manufacturing sector also fell over the period, from 21 per cent to 5 per cent. The largest increase in both male and female employee jobs was in the finance and business services industry, which accounted for around one in five of both male and female employee jobs in 2007 compared with around one in ten employee jobs in 1978.

In 1978 men accounted for a higher number of employee jobs than women (14.0 million compared with 10.3 million). However, by 2007 the gap between the sexes had narrowed to 0.2 million jobs with 13.7 million employee jobs performed by men and 13.5 million performed by women. Figure 4.9 is based on jobs rather than people – one person may have more than one job, and jobs vary in the number of hours' work involved.

The majority of people in employment (around 80 per cent) in the UK work in the private sector. The remainder work in the public sector, which comprises central government, local government and public corporations (for example, British Nuclear Fuels plc and Royal Mail). The number of people employed in the public sector fell during the 1990s from

Figure 4.10

Changes in public sector employment[1]

United Kingdom
Thousands

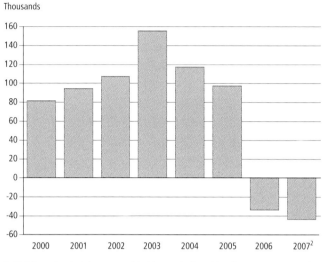

1 Public sector totals are provided by central and local government, and public sector organisations. Data are seasonally adjusted, annual changes in public sector employment measured at Q2 each year. Headcount of people aged 16 and over. See Appendix, Part 4: Public sector employment, and Labour Force Survey.
2 Annual decrease partly reflects removal of 10,000 duplicate records from the National Health Service in Q3 2006. Estimates for Q4 2006 to Q2 2007 are based partly on projections for some sources.

Source: Office for National Statistics; public sector organisations

around 6.0 million in Q2 1991 to around 5.2 million in 1998 (not seasonally adjusted). The earliest year for which seasonally adjusted data are available is 1999 and these data show that the number of people employed in the public sector increased from 5.2 million of Q2 that year to a peak of 5.9 million in Q2 2005. There then followed a fall of 1.3 per cent to 5.8 million in Q2 2007. This distinct downturn in recent years in the total number of people in public sector employment can be seen in the annual changes. Between Q2 1999 and Q2 2005 public sector employment increased each year with the largest increase in the 12 months to Q2 2003 (155,000) (Figure 4.10). The trend then reversed, with decreases of 34,000 in the 12 months to Q2 2006 and 44,000 in the 12 months to Q2 2007.

Central government employment increased from 2.1 million in 1999 to peak at 2.6 million in 2005 and then fell to 2.5 million in 2007. Local government employment, however, has increased year on year from 2.7 million in 1999 to 2.9 million in 2007.

Data for 2006 show nearly one-half of those working in the public sector in the UK were educated to at least either degree level (32 per cent) or other higher education qualifications beyond A level or equivalent (16 per cent). More than one-quarter of people employed in the private sector had qualifications to at least these levels (19 per cent to degree

level and 8 per cent to at least higher education qualifications beyond A level or equivalent).

Table 4.2 showed differences in full- and part-time employment levels among employees and self-employed people in the UK. The Labour Force Survey asks people to classify themselves as working either full time or part time, based on their own perceptions. Distinguishing only between full- and part-time working masks differences in usual working hours, which are also asked for in the survey. Table 4.11 shows the distribution of usual weekly hours of work, including regular paid and unpaid overtime, for both men and women in Q2 1992 and Q2 2007. The most common length of working week for both male and female employees was between 31 and 45 hours, 61 per cent and 49 per cent respectively in 2007, with similar proportions in 1992. The next most common length for male employees was more than 45 hours, whereas for female employees it was between 16 and 30 hours. Over the past 15 years, the proportion of male employees who were working more than 45 hours has fallen whereas for female employees there has been a slight increase. Female employees were more likely than male employees to work shorter hours – around four in ten female employees worked

Table 4.11

Distribution of usual weekly hours of work:[1] by sex and employment status, 1992 and 2007[2]

United Kingdom   Percentages

	Employees[3]		Self-employed	
	Men	Women	Men	Women
1992				
Less than 6 hours	1	3	1	8
6 up to 15 hours	2	15	2	17
16 up to 30 hours	3	25	8	25
31 up to 45 hours	60	49	36	25
More than 45 hours	33	8	53	26
2007				
Less than 6 hours	1	2	1	7
6 up to 15 hours	3	11	4	18
16 up to 30 hours	7	29	13	32
31 up to 45 hours	61	49	44	28
More than 45 hours	28	9	39	16

1 People aged 16 and over. Time rounded to the nearest hour respondents worked on their main job. Includes regular paid and unpaid overtime. Excludes employees who did not state their usual hours.
2 Data are at Q2 and are seasonally adjusted. See Appendix, Part 4: Labour Force Survey.
3 Full-time employees.

Source: Labour Force Survey, Office for National Statistics

up to 30 hours a week compared with one in ten male employees in 2007.

The self-employed follow different work patterns to those who are employees. A higher proportion of the self-employed worked longer hours than employees, with 39 per cent of self-employed men in Q2 2007 working more than 45 hours compared with 28 per cent of male employees. This proportion was smaller than in Q2 1992 when more than one-half (53 per cent) of self-employed men worked more than 45 hours a week. Self-employed women were most likely to work from 16 up to 30 hours in Q2 2007 whereas in Q2 1992 they were more likely to work longer hours, particularly more than 45 hours a week. A higher proportion of self-employed women than female employees worked less than 6 hours.

The opportunity to work flexible hours can help people to balance home and work responsibilities. Regulations introduced across the UK in April 2003 gives parents of children aged under 6, or parents of disabled children under 18, the right to request a flexible work pattern. This could be a change to the hours they work; a change to the times when they are required to work; or the opportunity to work from home. Employers have a statutory duty to consider such requests seriously, and may only refuse on business grounds. In 2006, two-thirds (65 per cent) of working parents with young children in Great Britain were aware of their right to request flexible working and more than two-fifths (42 per cent) of employees in Great Britain were aware that the Government intended to extend the right to request flexible working to carers of adults. This right was introduced in April 2007.

More than one-fifth of full-time employees and more than one-quarter of part-time employees had some form of flexible working arrangement in the UK in Q2 2007 (Table 4.12). These proportions were almost unchanged from those of Q2 1997 when the series began. The most common form for full-time employees of both sexes was flexible working hours. This was also the most common arrangement among men who worked part time and second most common for women, with term-time working the most popular option for them.

In the Third Work-Life Balance Employee Survey in 2006, employees in Great Britain who had worked in one or more flexible working arrangement were asked, 'What have been the positive consequences of you being able to work with a flexible arrangement?' Among the most frequently cited were having free time in general (34 per cent) and having more time to spend with family (33 per cent). More than one-half (52 per cent) of the employees who had worked with a flexible arrangement said they experienced no negative consequences.

Table 4.12

Employees with flexible working patterns:[1] by sex and type of employment,[2] 2007[3]

United Kingdom   Percentages

	Men	Women	All employees
Full-time employees			
Flexible working hours	10.1	14.9	12.0
Annualised working hours[4]	5.2	5.1	5.1
Four and a half day week	1.3	0.7	1.1
Term-time working	1.1	6.1	3.0
Nine day fortnight	0.4	0.3	0.3
Any flexible working pattern[5]	18.3	27.4	21.8
Part-time employees			
Flexible working hours	7.4	9.2	8.9
Annualised working hours[4]	3.1	4.2	4.0
Term-time working	4.5	11.4	10.0
Job sharing	1.0	2.4	2.1
Any flexible working pattern[5]	17.8	28.0	26.0

1 Percentages are based on totals that exclude people who did not state whether or not they had a flexible working arrangement. Respondents could give more than one answer. People aged 16 and over.
2 The Labour Force Survey asks people to classify themselves as either full time or part time, based on their own perceptions.
3 Data are at Q2 and are not seasonally adjusted. See Appendix, Part 4: Labour Force Survey.
4 The number of hours an employee has to work are calculated over a full year allowing for longer hours to be worked over certain periods of the year and shorter hours at others.
5 Includes other categories of flexible working not separately identified.

Source: Labour Force Survey, Office for National Statistics

The most frequently cited negative consequence was receiving less money (19 per cent).

The same survey also asked employees about how satisfied they were with different aspects of their work, including the hours they work. In 2006 nine in ten employees in Great Britain were satisfied with the work itself and more than eight in ten (82 per cent) were satisfied with their working hours (Table 4.13). Of the five aspects covered, employees were least likely to be satisfied with their pay (68 per cent). This was mirrored by the proportion who said they were dissatisfied with their pay (23 per cent) (see also Figure 4.22). Further analysis revealed that employees who expressed a higher satisfaction with their job security were also more likely to be satisfied with pay and that male employees were more likely than female employees to be satisfied with pay.

In 2004 the Workplace Employment Relations Survey asked employees in Great Britain to consider their effort and feelings of stress from work using three related questions. The analysis

Table 4.13

Employee satisfaction[1] with different aspects of work, 2006

Great Britain

Percentages

	Satisfied	Neither satisfied nor dissatisfied	Dissatisfied
Work itself	89	5	6
Current working arrangements[2]	87	6	6
Job security	86	6	8
Hours worked	82	6	12
Pay	68	9	23

1 All employees were asked how satisfied they were regarding each aspect. Data for satisfied include those who said they were satisfied or very satisfied, and data for dissatisfied include those who said they were dissatisfied or very dissatisfied.
2 The number of hours worked, as well as when and where those hours are worked.

Source: The Third Work-Life Balance Employee Survey, Department for Trade and Industry

found that around three-quarters (76 per cent) of employees in the survey agreed with the statement that their job required them to work hard, around 40 per cent agreed with the statement that they never seemed to have enough time to get work done, and around 27 per cent agreed that they worried a lot about work outside work hours.

Unemployment

During periods of economic growth the number of jobs generally grows and unemployment falls, although any mismatches between the skill needs of the new jobs and the skills of those available for work may slow this process. Conversely, as the economy slows and goes into recession so unemployment tends to rise. The unemployment rate in Q2 2007 was 5.4 per cent (equivalent to around 1.7 million people aged 16 and over) although there have been fluctuations in the rates since 1971 reflecting the economic cycle (Figure 4.14). During the early 1970s the unemployment rate in the UK was low, at around 4 per cent (equivalent to around 1 million people). From Q2 1974 unemployment increased and after levelling off to around 5 per cent in the late 1970s, it started to increase again to a peak of 11.9 per cent in Q2 1984 (equivalent to 3.3 million people). The late 1980s saw an economic recovery and unemployment fell back to 6.9 per cent in Q2 1990 before a recession in 1990–91 drove it up to 10.4 per cent in Q2 1993 (equivalent to 2.9 million people). Since then unemployment rates have generally fallen – in Q2 2004 and Q2 2005 unemployment rates reached their lowest level (4.8 per cent) since 1975 and after an increase

Figure 4.14

Unemployment rates:[1] by sex

United Kingdom

Percentages

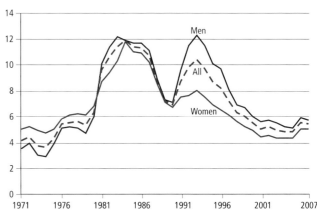

1 Data are at Q2 each year and are seasonally adjusted. People aged 16 and over. See Appendix, Part 4: Labour Force Survey.

Source: Labour Force Survey, Office for National Statistics

to 5.5 per cent in Q2 2006, the rate fell again in Q2 2007 to 5.4 per cent.

The first peak in male unemployment since Labour Force Survey (LFS) records began in 1971 was in Q2 1983, when the rate was 12.2 per cent, equivalent to 1.9 million unemployed men. The peak for female unemployment was in Q2 1984 when the rate was 11.8 per cent, equivalent to 1.3 million unemployed women. The recession in the early 1990s had a much greater effect on unemployment among men than among women, and the unemployment rate for men peaked to its highest level (12.3 per cent) since the series began. At the same time the unemployment rate for women showed a lower peak of 8.0 per cent.

In Q2 2007 more than one-half of unemployed men (53 per cent) and two-thirds of unemployed women (66 per cent) in the UK had been unemployed for less than six months (Table 4.15 overleaf). Younger employees were more likely than older employees to be unemployed for this length of time. Across all age groups unemployed men were more likely than unemployed women to have been out of work for 12 months or more (long-term unemployed). Older employees were also more likely than younger employees to be long-term unemployed – 41 per cent of unemployed men aged 50 and over and 29 per cent of unemployed women in the same age group were long-term unemployed. This compares with 11 per cent of unemployed 16 to 17-year-old men and 5 per cent of 16 to 17-year-old women.

Unemployment rates vary by the occupation held before a person became unemployed. In Q2 2007 unemployment rates

4

Table 4.15

Duration of unemployment: by sex and age, 2007[1]

United Kingdom   Percentages

	Less than 6 months	6 months but less than 12	12 months and over	All (thousands)
Men				
16–17	69	20	11	95
18–24	58	19	23	279
25–49	50	16	35	353
50 and over	44	14	41	163
All men	53	17	30	891
Women				
16–17	74	21	5	76
18–24	72	16	12	195
25–49	63	15	22	321
50 and over	52	20	29	84
All women	66	17	18	676

1 Data are at Q2 and are not seasonally adjusted. People aged 16 and over. Excludes those who did not state their duration of unemployment. See Appendix, Part 4: Labour Force Survey.

Source: Labour Force Survey, Office for National Statistics

were lowest for those who were previously in professional occupations (1.4 per cent) and the highest unemployment rate was for those who were previously in elementary occupations (9.1 per cent). People previously employed in elementary occupations were also more likely than those previously employed in other occupations to have been unemployed for 12 months or more (32 per cent).

Unemployment rates in 2006 were 5.4 per cent in England, 5.2 per cent in Scotland and Wales, and 4.9 per cent in Northern Ireland. As with employment rates, differences in unemployment rates within the English regions and countries of the UK are greater than differences between them (see also Appendix, Part 4: Model-based estimates of unemployment). The local authority areas with the lowest unemployment rates in Great Britain were Eden in the North West (2.1 per cent) followed by Cotswold and Purbeck, both in the South West (2.4 per cent) and Ribble Valley in the North West (2.4 per cent). Four areas had unemployment rates over 10 per cent – the east London boroughs of Tower Hamlets (14.2 per cent), Newham (11.8 per cent) and Hackney (11.6 per cent), and South Tyneside in the North East (10.2 per cent).

NUTS data (see also page 50) for 2006 show that the lowest unemployment rate in Northern Ireland was Outer Belfast

Table 4.16

Unemployment rates:[1] by sex, EU comparison, 2006

Percentages

	Men	Women	All		Men	Women	All
Denmark	3.3	4.5	3.9	Romania	8.2	6.1	7.3
Netherlands	3.5	4.4	3.9	Hungary	7.2	7.8	7.5
Ireland	4.6	4.1	4.4	Portugal	6.5	9.0	7.7
Cyprus	4.0	5.4	4.6	Finland	7.4	8.1	7.7
Luxembourg	3.5	6.2	4.7	Belgium	7.4	9.3	8.2
Austria	4.4	5.2	4.7	Spain	6.3	11.6	8.5
United Kingdom	5.7	4.9	5.3	Greece	5.6	13.6	8.9
Lithuania	5.8	5.4	5.6	Bulgaria	8.6	9.3	9.0
Estonia	6.2	5.6	5.9	France	8.7	10.4	9.5
Slovenia	4.9	7.2	6.0	Germany	10.2	9.4	9.8
Italy	5.4	8.8	6.8	Slovakia	12.3	14.7	13.4
Latvia	7.4	6.2	6.8	Poland	13.0	14.9	13.8
Czech Republic	5.8	8.8	7.1				
Sweden	6.9	7.2	7.1	EU-27 average	7.6	8.9	8.2
Malta	6.5	8.9	7.3				

1 See Appendix, Part 4: Eurostat rates.

Source: Labour Force Survey, Eurostat

(3.8 per cent) and the highest was North of Northern Ireland (7.6 per cent).

In 2006 the average unemployment rate in the EU-27 was 8.2 per cent, ranging from 3.9 per cent in both Denmark and the Netherlands to 13.8 per cent in Poland (Table 4.16). The UK (5.3 per cent) had the seventh lowest overall unemployment rate of the EU-27. However, unemployment rates for men and women in the UK, when compared with men and women in other member states in the EU-27, ranked differently. The rate for men in the UK (5.7 per cent) was the tenth lowest male unemployment rate in the EU but still below the EU male average (7.6 per cent). The rate for women in the UK (4.9 per cent) was the fourth lowest female unemployment rate in the EU, well below the EU female average (8.9 per cent). The differences in unemployment rates between the sexes were greatest in the southern European countries of Spain and Greece, where rates for women were between 5 and 8 percentage points higher than for men. For the majority of the other EU countries, including the UK, the differences in rates between men and women were no more than 2 percentage points.

Economic inactivity

People aged 16 and over who are neither in employment nor unemployed are classified as economically inactive (see Glossary on page 47). There were 7.0 million people of working age in the UK who were economically inactive in Q2 1971. By Q2 2007 this had risen to 7.9 million people of working age, and of this total 60 per cent were women. The overall economic inactivity rate (the proportion of the working-age population who were economically inactive) fluctuated around 21 and 22 per cent throughout the 1970s and was accompanied by a convergence of economic inactivity rates for men and women (Figure 4.17). Economic inactivity increased during the early 1980s and peaked at 23 per cent in Q2 1983. As the economy improved in the late 1980s the inactivity rate began a downward trend, dropping to 19 per cent in 1990 before rising again following the recession in the early 1990s. Since 1992, the rate has returned to similar levels to the 1970s and in Q2 2007 the inactivity rate among working-age people in the UK was 21 per cent.

Although the number of economically inactive working-age people in the UK has risen by 0.9 million over the period Q2 1971 to Q2 2007, all of this overall increase is caused by the rising trend among economically inactive working-age men, which increased by 2.4 million to 3.2 million. In contrast the number of economically inactive working-age women fell by 1.5 million over the period to 4.8 million. As a result, the inactivity rate among working-age men rose from 5 per cent in Q2 1971 to 16 per cent in Q2 2007. Over the same period, although the

Figure 4.17

Economic inactivity rates:[1] by sex

United Kingdom
Percentages

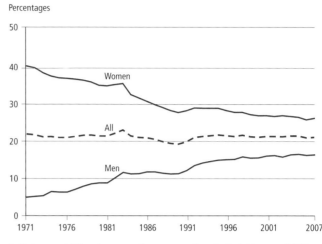

1 Data are at Q2 each year and are seasonally adjusted. Men aged 16 to 64, women aged 16 to 59. See Appendix, Part 4: Labour Force Survey.
Source: Labour Force Survey, Office for National Statistics

inactivity rate for working-age women remained far higher than that for men, it fell from 41 per cent to 26 per cent.

Economic inactivity rates vary by age. From Q2 1992 (the earliest year for which seasonally adjusted economic inactivity rates by age are available) to Q2 2007, the biggest change was for 16 to 17-year-old men. In this age group, the economic inactivity rate decreased in the mid-1990s from 46 per cent in Q2 1993 to 40 per cent in Q2 1998 and then rose by 17 percentage points to reach 57 per cent in Q2 2007 (Figure 4.18 overleaf). Although a smaller proportion of 18 to 24-year-old men than 16 to 17-year-olds were economically inactive between Q2 1992 and Q2 2007, the rate for this group also increased – from 16 per cent to 22 per cent. Inactivity rates for older men aged 25 to 34 and 35 to 49 showed slight increases over the period, whereas there has been a slight decline in inactivity rates among men aged 50 to 64 over the last 12 years from 29 per cent in Q2 1995 to 25 per cent in Q2 2007.

The inactivity rates for working-age women over the period showed a different pattern. Between Q2 1992 and Q2 2007, inactivity rates among women aged 25 and over fell, the largest fall being for those aged between 50 and 59 (from 38 per cent to 29 per cent). Inactivity rates for women aged 18 to 24 were relatively stable over the period, ranging between 28 and 31 per cent. The rate for young women aged 16 to 17 has shown a trend similar to young men in this age group – the rate fell from 46 per cent in Q2 1993 to 38 per cent in Q2 1997, but since then there has been a gradual rise. By Q2 2007, 53 per cent of these young women in the UK were economically inactive.

4

Figure 4.18

Economic inactivity rates:[1] by age and sex

United Kingdom

Percentages

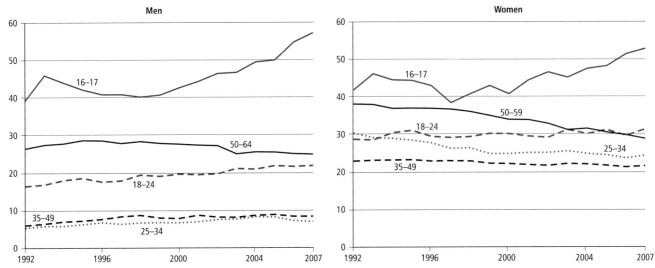

1 Data are at Q2 each year and are seasonally adjusted. Men aged 16 to 64, women aged 16 to 59. See Appendix, Part 4: Labour Force Survey.

Source: Labour Force Survey, Office for National Statistics

Although the proportion of young people who are economically inactive has increased in recent years the proportion of these who were inactive because they were studying remained at around 9 out of 10 for those aged 16 to 17, and 6 out of 10 for those aged 18 to 24, between Q2 1997 and Q2 2007. Over the same period the number of inactive students as a proportion of the working-age inactive population increased from one in five to one in four. This equates to the number of economically inactive students increasing by around 458,000, to around 2 million.

Figure 4.19

Reasons for economic inactivity: by sex[1]

United Kingdom

Percentages

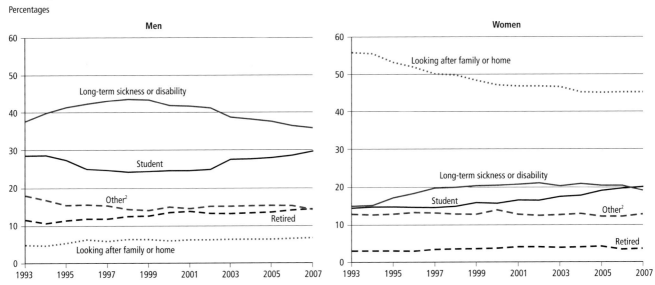

1 Data are at Q2 each year and are seasonally adjusted. Men aged 16 to 64, women aged 16 to 59. See Appendix, Part 4: Labour Force Survey.

2 Includes a small number of temporary sick and discouraged workers (people whose reason for not seeking work was that they believed no jobs were available).

Source: Labour Force Survey, Office for National Statistics

There are, of course, other reasons for economic inactivity than being a student. In Q2 2007 long-term sickness or disability was the main reason for economic inactivity among working-age men in the UK (36 per cent) although this proportion has fallen since Q2 1998 (44 per cent) (Figure 4.19). Among working-age women, looking after the family or home was the most common reason for inactivity; 45 per cent said this was their main reason for not seeking work although this proportion has also fallen from 56 per cent in Q2 1993 (when LFS data began).

Reasons for economic inactivity vary by age. In Q2 2007 long-term sickness or disability was the main reason for economic inactivity among men aged 35 to 49 (60 per cent). Looking after the family or home was the most common reason for inactivity for women aged 25 to 34 (73 per cent). For those approaching state pension ages, men were more likely than women to be economically inactive because of retirement – 33 per cent of economically inactive men aged 50 to 64 were retired compared with 14 per cent of women aged 50 to 59.

Industrial relations at work

Over the last decade the proportion of employees in the UK who were members of a trade union (trade union density) has fallen from 32.6 per cent in 1995 to 28.4 per cent in 2006. Among female employees, union density has been fairly stable over the period at between 28 and 30 per cent and in 2004 was higher than men for the first time (due to a general fall in the union density rate for men as opposed to an increase for women). This trend continued and in 2006 the rate for women was 29.7 (Figure 4.20). The fall in trade union density for male employees occurred almost year on year over the period (from 35.3 per cent in 1995 to 27.2 per cent in 2006). It must be noted that data from 1995 to 2005 are measured at autumn (September to November) each year and 2006 data are measured at Q4 (October to December). Comparisons should therefore be treated with caution (see also Appendix, Part 4: Labour Force Survey).

Data from LFS showed that union density in Q4 2006 was 10 per cent for employees aged 16 to 24, but was considerably higher among older employees (34 per cent for those aged 35 to 49 and 35 per cent for those aged 50 and over). In terms of working patterns, 31 per cent of full-time employees were union members compared with 21 per cent of part-time employees. In professional occupations women had a higher union density than men, 60 per cent compared with 36 per cent. Similarly female managers had a higher union density than male managers in 2006, 38 per cent compared with 25 per cent.

Across the UK, Northern Ireland had the highest union density (40 per cent of employees) in Q4 2006. In Wales it was

Figure 4.20

Trade union membership of employees:[1] by sex

United Kingdom
Percentages

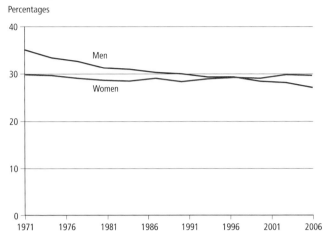

1 Union membership (including staff associations) as a proportion of all employees. Excludes members of the Armed Forces. Data are at autumn each year (with the exception of 2006 which are at Q4) and are not seasonally adjusted. People aged 16 and over. See Appendix, Part 4: Labour Force Survey.

Source: Department of Trade and Industry

36 per cent and in Scotland, 35 per cent. Union density was lowest in England (27 per cent). In the English Government Office regions, the South East had the lowest union density (21 per cent) and the North East the highest (39 per cent).

One of the aims of a trade union is to represent and assist people who feel they have been treated unfairly in the workplace. According to the First Fair Treatment at Work Survey, 1.6 million or 6.9 per cent of employees in Great Britain in 2005–06 said that they had personally been treated unfairly at work in the last two years. Those with a disability or long-term illness were twice as likely as other employees to say they had personally experienced unfair treatment at work (15.1 per cent) as were employees whose sexual orientation was gay, lesbian or bisexual (13.8 per cent).

Older employees were less likely than younger employees to report unfair treatment at work in 2005–06, 5.6 per cent of employees aged 45 or over, compared with 7.7 per cent of those aged under 45. When considering age as a basis for citing unfair treatment, employees aged 16 to 24 were more than twice as likely as those aged 45 or over to report age discrimination.

The First Fair Treatment at Work survey in 2005–06 looked at reasons given by respondents for unfair treatment at work. Reasons cited are presented as a proportion of all those who said they had been treated unfairly (respondents could cite more than one reason). The most common reason reported was age

Figure 4.21

Employees who personally experienced unfair treatment at work:[1] by cause, 2005–06

Great Britain
Percentages

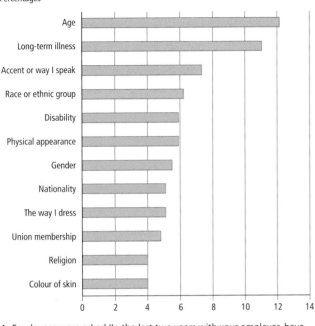

1 Employees were asked 'In the last two years with your employer, have you personally been treated unfairly because of the following?' and were shown the above options. Employees could choose more than one option. Data are as a proportion of all employees who said they had been treated unfairly at work. Forms of unfair treatment involving fewer than ten cases are not shown.

Source: The First Fair Treatment at Work Survey, Department of Trade and Industry

(12.1 per cent), followed by long-term illness (11 per cent). Two of the least common reasons cited by respondents were religion and colour of skin (both 4 per cent) (Figure 4.21).

In 2006, 754,500 working days in the UK were lost from 158 recorded stoppages associated with labour disputes (see Appendix, Part 4: Labour disputes). This was higher than in 2005, when 157,400 working days were lost. The 2006 total was also higher than the average number of working days lost per year during the 1990s (660,000), but lower than the average for both the 1980s (7.2 million) and the 1970s (12.9 million). Single disputes during the 1970s and 1980s accounted for large proportions of the total working days lost; a miners' strike in 1972 accounted for 45 per cent of the 24 million days lost during that year and a strike by engineering workers resulted in just over one-half of the 29 million days lost

Figure 4.22

Working days lost:[1] by principal cause of dispute, 2006

United Kingdom
Percentages

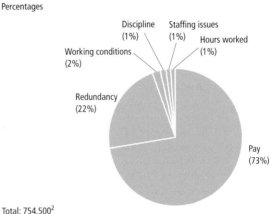

Total: 754,500[2]

1 See Appendix, Part 4: Labour disputes.
2 Includes 2,300 days lost from disputes arising from trade union matters.

Source: Office for National Statistics

in 1979. Another miners' strike in 1984 was responsible for over 80 per cent of the 27 million days lost that year.

The increase in the number of working days lost between 2005 and 2006 reflected the number of workers involved; 92,600 workers in the UK were involved in labour disputes in 2005 compared with 713,300 in 2006. Some 14 per cent (22,600) of the working days lost in 2005 were as a result of 13 stoppages in public administration, whereas this same sector accounted for 83 per cent (626,600) of working days lost in 2006 as a result of 18 stoppages.

In 2006, 552,200 (73 per cent) of working days lost were because of disputes over pay, followed by 166,700 (22 per cent) days lost to issues involving redundancies (Figure 4.22). Working conditions accounted for 15,700 days lost, discipline issues for 8,500, staffing issues for 5,000, and working hours for 4,100 working days lost.

Another way of putting strike statistics into a wider context is to consider working time lost through strikes as a proportion of time actually worked. In 2006 an estimated 42.2 billion hours were worked in the UK. Comparing this with the 5.9 million hours lost through strikes shows that around one in every 7,200 potential working days was lost through strikes in 2006. The equivalent figure for 2005 was one in every 33,800.

Chapter 5

Income and wealth

- In 2005 the UK had the third highest Gross Domestic Product per head within the G7, whereas in 1991 it was lowest in the group. (Table 5.2)

- Household net wealth in the UK more than doubled in real terms between 1987 and 2006. (Figure 5.4)

- In spring 2007, 85 per cent of adults in England were very or fairly satisfied with their standard of living and 63 per cent were satisfied with their future financial security. (Table 5.5)

- In April 2007 the median hourly earnings excluding overtime of women working full time in the UK were £10.46, 87 per cent of the median earnings of men. (Page 68)

- Payments of personal income tax and employees' social contributions amounted to 26 per cent of Gross Domestic Product in Denmark in 2005, compared with 16 per cent in the UK. (Figure 5.12)

- Around one in three families in the UK had no savings in 2005/06, but one in five couples where one or both were aged 60 or over had savings in excess of £20,000. (Table 5.21)

Overview

The UK, as a market democracy, shares a commitment with the other 29 members of the Organisation for Economic Co-operation and Development, to sustainable economic growth and employment, a rising standard of living, maintaining financial stability and contributing to the development of the world economy. The national accounts, and in particular gross domestic product (GDP) in total and per head, are often used as summary measures of economic well-being. Although for some years and for an increasing number of public policy needs there is an acknowledgement that 'there is more to life than GDP' (a phrase attributed to the late Robert Kennedy), GDP continues to be used as a proxy measure for societal as well as purely economic well-being.

GDP measures the overall level of economic activity in a country. The total income generated is shared between individuals (in the form of wages and salaries), companies and other organisations (for example, in the form of profits retained for investment), and government (in the form of taxes on production). If GDP is growing in real terms (after adjustment to remove inflation), this means that the economy is expanding. GDP per head in the UK more than doubled in real terms between 1971 and 2006 (Figure 5.1). Over this period there were times when the economy contracted, for example in the mid-1970s at the time of the international oil crisis, and again during periods of world recession in the early 1980s

Figure 5.1

Real household disposable income per head[1] and gross domestic product per head[2]

United Kingdom
Index numbers (1971=100)

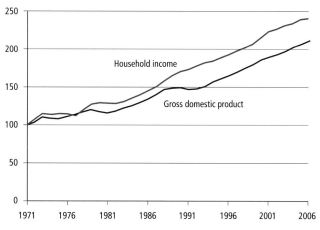

1 Adjusted to real terms using the expenditure deflator for the household sector. See Appendix, Part 5: Household income data sources.
2 Adjusted to real terms using the GDP deflator.

Source: Office for National Statistics

Table 5.2

Gross domestic product[1] per head: G7 comparison

US$ per head

	1991	1996	2001	2005
United States	23,460	28,780	35,290	41,670
Canada	19,640	23,330	29,340	34,060
United Kingdom	16,740	20,940	27,092	32,900
Germany	18,470	22,680	26,350	30,830
Japan	20,020	23,530	26,200	30,770
France	18,700	21,660	27,250	30,350
Italy	18,800	22,200	26,820	28,170

1 Gross domestic product at current market prices using current purchasing power standard and compiled on the basis of the System of National Accounts 1993.

Source: Organisation for Economic Co-operation and Development

and early 1990s. The UK economy has grown each year since 1992.

The Group of Seven (G7) are the world's seven largest industrial market economies, whose finance ministers meet several times a year to discuss economic policy. In 2005 the UK had the third highest GDP per head within the G7 (Table 5.2). This reflects a considerable increase since 1991 and 1996, when the UK GDP per head was lower than any other of the G7 member countries. The United States had the highest GDP per head throughout the period shown in the table, and Japan showed the biggest downward shift in position, moving from second place in 1991 and 1996 to fifth in 2005.

If a country's economy is growing then there is more 'cake' available for distribution across the population, which itself may be increasing in size. Household disposable income per head represents the average amount of this cake that each person has available to spend or save. This measure is commonly used to summarise people's economic well-being, rather than the economic well-being of the country as a whole. Household disposable income comprises income derived directly from economic activity in the form of wages and salaries and self-employment income, as well as transfers such as social security benefits. It is then subject to a number of deductions such as income tax, council tax (domestic rates in Northern Ireland), and contributions towards pensions and national insurance.

Household disposable income per head in the UK, adjusted for inflation, increased by nearly 150 per cent between 1971 and 2006 (Figure 5.1). During the 1970s and early 1980s growth fluctuated, and in some years there were small year on year falls, such as in 1974, 1976, 1977, 1981 and 1982. Since 1982 there has been growth each year. Over the period 1971 to 2006 as a whole, growth in household disposable income per head averaged 2.5 per cent per year compared with that in GDP per head of 2.2 per cent. However, there were years when this pattern was reversed, most recently between 2005 and 2006 when the growth in real household disposable income per head was considerably lower than that in GDP per head (0.6 per cent compared with 2.3 per cent), and much lower than the average annual growth rate of 2.5 per cent between 1971 and 2006.

Real household disposable income per head measures how people's incomes have been changing on average. However, income is not evenly distributed across the population, and people at different points in the income distribution may experience different levels of income growth. This is demonstrated in Figure 5.3, which shows how incomes have changed at the 90th and 10th percentiles of the distribution, and at the median (see the analysing income distribution box for an explanation of these terms). During the 1980s, there was little change in income in real terms at the bottom of the distribution, while income at the top of the distribution showed strong growth in real terms. The early 1990s were a period of economic downturn, when there was little real growth in incomes anywhere in the distribution. Between 1995/96 and

Figure 5.3

Distribution of real[1] disposable household income[2]

United Kingdom/Great Britain[3]
£ per week at 2005/06 prices

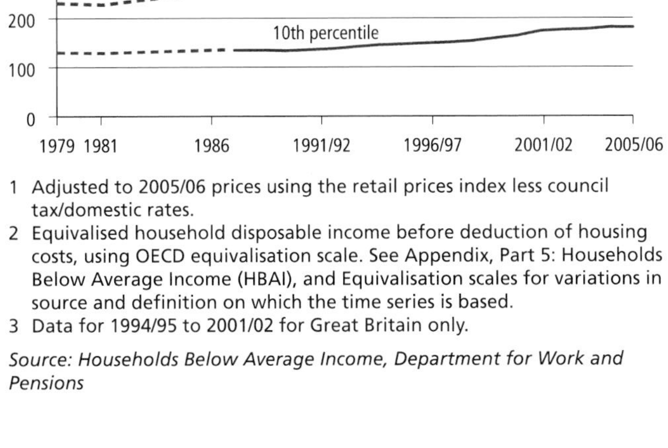

1 Adjusted to 2005/06 prices using the retail prices index less council tax/domestic rates.
2 Equivalised household disposable income before deduction of housing costs, using OECD equivalisation scale. See Appendix, Part 5: Households Below Average Income (HBAI), and Equivalisation scales for variations in source and definition on which the time series is based.
3 Data for 1994/95 to 2001/02 for Great Britain only.

Source: Households Below Average Income, Department for Work and Pensions

Analysing income distribution

Equivalisation – in analysing the distribution of income, household disposable income is usually adjusted to take account of the size and composition of the household. This recognises that, for example, to achieve the same standard of living a household of five requires a higher income than a single person. This process is known as equivalisation (see Appendix, Part 5: Equivalisation scales).

Quintile and decile groups – the main method of analysing income distribution used in this chapter is to rank units (households, individuals or adults) by a given income measure, and then to divide the ranked units into groups of equal size. Groups containing 20 per cent of units are referred to as 'quintile groups' or 'fifths'. Thus the 'bottom quintile group' of income is the 20 per cent of units with the lowest incomes. Similarly, groups containing 10 per cent of units are referred to as 'decile groups' or tenths.

Percentiles – an alternative method also used in the chapter is to present the income level above or below which a certain proportion of units fall. Thus the 90th percentile is the income level above which 10 per cent of units fall when ranked by a given income measure – this is also known as the top decile point. The median is then the midpoint of the distribution above and below which 50 per cent of units fall.

2005/06, income at all three points in the distribution grew by very similar amounts in real terms, with median income increasing by one-quarter.

The extent of household income inequality can also be regarded as an indicator of societal well-being, inasmuch as social equity is seen as a goal of social policy. In the UK, the income distribution and the extent of inequality have changed considerably over the last three decades. In Figure 5.3, the closer the percentiles are to the median line, the greater the equality within the distribution. Inequality grew during the late 1970s and throughout the 1980s. During the first half of the 1990s, the income distribution appeared to be broadly stable, though at a much higher level of income dispersion than in the 1970s. The Gini coefficient, a widely used measure of inequality (see Appendix, Part 5: Gini coefficient), has fluctuated only slightly between 1994/95 and 2005/06, though there is evidence of a marginal increase in inequality.

Researchers at the Institute for Fiscal Studies (IFS) investigated possible explanations for the changes in inequality observed between 1979 and 2005/06. They found that changes to the labour market played an important role. In particular, inequality rose during the 1980s when the incomes of the higher paid grew much more rapidly than those of the lower paid or of households where no one was working. Growth in self-employment income and in unemployment was also found to be associated with periods of increased inequality. It appears that demographic factors such as the growth in one-person households made a relatively unimportant contribution compared with labour market changes. However, the IFS found that changes in the tax and benefit system had made an impact. The income tax cuts of the 1970s and late 1980s worked to increase income inequality, while direct tax rises in the early 1980s and 1990s, together with the increases in means-tested benefits in the late 1990s, produced the opposite effect.

Between 1996/97 and 2003/04, income growth was much more evenly spread across the whole of the income distribution, with exceptions at the very top and bottom of the distribution. Changes at the bottom of the distribution are difficult to disentangle from measurement error. However, there is evidence, based on the Family Resources Survey (FRS), and also from data from tax returns, that there was much more rapid growth in the top 1 per cent of incomes than for the rest of the distribution. The reasons for this growth are not yet well understood, but possible explanations include changes in the nature of executive remuneration. More information about the distribution of income may be found in the section on Income Distribution later in this chapter.

Income represents a flow of resources over a specified period of time received either in cash or in kind – for example, earnings or the use of a company car. Wealth on the other hand describes the ownership of assets valued at a particular point in time. Thus although the terms 'wealthy' and 'high income' are often used interchangeably, they relate to quite distinct concepts. People's ownership of wealth, such as savings, a house or pension rights, is another important aspect of their economic well-being, in that wealth may provide financial security as well as in some cases providing a current income flow (for example, interest on savings).

The UK National Accounts indicate that the wealth owned by the household sector (net of liabilities) totalled £6,900 billion in 2006, or an average of £114,000 per head. Household net wealth more than doubled in real terms between 1987 and 2006 (Figure 5.4), but there has not been steady growth over the period. Two of the main components of household net wealth are residential housing (less the value of the loans outstanding on their purchase) and stocks and shares, and so the trends reflect both the state of the housing market (see Chapter 10: Housing) and that of the stock market. More information on household wealth may be found in the section on Wealth later in this chapter.

Figure 5.4

Real household net wealth per head[1]

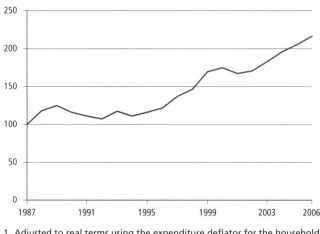

United Kingdom
Index numbers (1987=100)

1 Adjusted to real terms using the expenditure deflator for the household sector. See Appendix, Part 5: Household income data sources.
Source: Office for National Statistics

As with income, it is not only the overall level of wealth that is of interest but how equally it is distributed between individuals. Estimates of wealth distribution produced by HM Revenue and Customs indicate that wealth is very much less evenly distributed than income. In 2003, the latest year for which data are available, one-half of the population owned 7 per cent of total wealth and this proportion has scarcely changed since 1991. Conversely, the share of the wealthiest 1 per cent of the population was 21 per cent in 2003, having risen from 17 per cent in 1991.

Income and wealth provide access to goods and services and are thus important to people's overall well-being. People's satisfaction with their income and their financial prospects will depend on their material needs and expectations and the extent to which they feel that the income available to them will be able to meet these. Table 5.5 shows that in spring 2007, 85 per cent of adults in England were very satisfied or fairly satisfied with their standard of living, while 6 per cent were fairly or very dissatisfied. There was some variation according to age, with the proportion who were very satisfied being highest among the 16 to 21-year-olds and among those aged 60 and over (34 per cent for both groups), but lowest among those in their 20s and 30s (26 per cent).

Satisfaction with future financial security was lower than satisfaction with current standard of living, with 63 per cent of individuals overall being very or fairly satisfied. Satisfaction with future financial security rose with age, with satisfaction being lowest among those aged 16 to 21 (50 per cent very or fairly satisfied) rising to 78 per cent among those aged 60 and over.

Table 5.5

Satisfaction with standard of living and financial prospects: by age, 2007[1]

England   Percentages

	16–21	22–29	30–39	40–49	50–59	60 and over	All individuals
Satisfaction with standard of living							
Very satisfied	34	26	26	28	32	34	30
Fairly satisfied	49	58	54	56	52	55	55
Neither satisfied nor dissatisfied	13	10	12	9	9	6	9
Fairly dissatisfied	4	4	6	5	6	3	5
Very dissatisfied	0	2	2	1	2	1	1
Satisfaction with future financial security							
Very satisfied	16	13	14	14	20	24	18
Fairly satisfied	34	40	44	44	44	54	45
Neither satisfied nor dissatisfied	28	27	21	20	20	12	20
Fairly dissatisfied	15	16	14	16	8	7	12
Very dissatisfied	7	3	8	5	8	3	5

1 Data are as at spring 2007.

Source: Omnibus Survey, Department for Environment, Food and Rural Affairs

Composition of income

Alongside strong growth in household disposable income per head seen in Figure 5.1 there has been considerable stability in its composition since 1992. In 2006, 51 per cent of total household income in the UK was derived from wages and salaries, with social benefits the next largest source of income at 19 per cent of the total (Figure 5.6), compared with 49 per cent and 21 per cent respectively in 1992. Income from investments fell from 15 to 13 per cent over the period, while income from self-employment rose from 11 to 13 per cent of the total.

The data in Figures 5.1, 5.4 and 5.6 are derived from the UK National Accounts, whereas Figure 5.3 and the tables and charts in most of the remainder of this chapter are derived directly from surveys of households or surveys of businesses. There are a number of definitional differences between these two different types of data source. Appendix, Part 5: Household income data sources, describes the main differences between household income as defined in the National Accounts and as defined in most survey sources.

The composition of income varies between different types of households according to factors such as age, geographic location, family composition and ethnicity. Wages and salaries are the largest component of gross (before any deductions) household income in the UK whatever the household's ethnic group (Table 5.7 overleaf). However, the importance of wages and salaries varied from 73 per cent of the income of Indian households to 54 per cent of that of Pakistani/Bangladeshi households, averaged over the years 2003/04 to 2005/06. Conversely, social security benefits (other than the state retirement pension) formed 26 per cent of the income of Pakistani/Bangladeshi households compared with 7 per cent

Figure 5.6

Composition of total household income, 2006

United Kingdom
Percentages

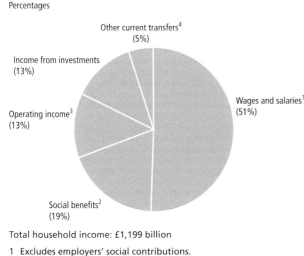

Other current transfers[4]
(5%)

Income from investments
(13%)

Operating income[3]
(13%)

Wages and salaries[1]
(51%)

Social benefits[2]
(19%)

Total household income: £1,199 billion

1 Excludes employers' social contributions.
2 Comprises pensions and benefits.
3 Includes self-employment income for sole-traders, and rental income.
4 Mostly other government grants, but includes transfers from abroad and non-profit making bodies.

Source: Office for National Statistics

Table 5.7

Sources of gross weekly income: by ethnic group,[1] 2003/04–2005/06

United Kingdom

Percentages

	Wages & salaries	Self- employment	Investment income	Retirement pensions[2]	Private pensions	Other benefits[3]	Other income	All income
White	65	9	2	6	7	8	2	100
Mixed	71	9	1	2	2	13	3	100
Asian or Asian British	67	10	1	2	2	13	5	100
Indian	73	9	1	3	2	7	4	100
Pakistani/Bangladeshi	54	11	1	3	1	26	5	100
Black or Black British	70	5	-	3	2	15	4	100
Black Caribbean	68	7	1	5	3	15	3	100
African/Other Black	72	4	-	1	1	15	6	100
Chinese or Other ethnic group	66	10	1	2	2	9	10	100
All households[4]	65	9	2	6	7	9	2	100

1 Of the household reference person. See Appendix, Part 1: Classification of ethnic groups.
2 Includes any payments of income support or pension credit.
3 Includes disability benefits and tax credits.
4 Includes households where the reference person is a full-time student, and those whose occupation was inadequately stated or not classifiable.

Source: Family Resources Survey, Department for Work and Pensions

of that of Indian households. Self-employment income was around twice as important to White, Mixed, Asian or Asian British and Chinese or Other ethnic groups, at between 9 and 11 per cent of gross income, than it was to Black or Black British households, at 5 per cent of gross income. The state retirement pension formed 6 per cent of gross income of White households and 5 per cent of that of Black Caribbean households, compared with 2 or 3 per cent for the other ethnic groups, reflecting the younger age structure of their populations. However, private pensions were important only for the White ethnic group, at 7 per cent of gross income, compared with 3 per cent or less for all other ethnic groups.

The composition of income also differs according to age. Pensioners, in particular, tend to have different sources of income from the working-age population. Benefits, including the state retirement pension and pension credit, are the largest source of income for pensioner families in the UK. However, the average levels and sources of income vary with age and marital status, with single pensioners aged 75 and over having the lowest gross income of the groups shown in the table, and couple pensioners under 75 having the highest incomes (Table 5.8). Two-thirds of the gross income of single pensioners aged 75 and over came from benefits in 2005/06, compared with less than one-third of gross income for pensioner couples where the head was aged under 75. Earnings and occupational pensions together formed more than one-half of the income of such couples and, although occupational pensions were equally important for

single pensioners under 75, earnings were much less important for them.

Personal pensions (pensions provided through a contract between the individual and a pension provider) play a relatively minor role overall in pensioner income – 4 per cent for couples irrespective of age in 2005/06 and 2 per cent for single pensioners. However, they have been the fastest growing source of pensioner income between 1996/97 and 2005/06. Average receipts of investment income fell over this period for each of the marital status and age groups shown in the table, reflecting the difference in stock market values between these two years. More information on investments may be found in the wealth section of this chapter, and information on pensions and the benefit receipts of older people may be found in Chapter 8: Social protection, Tables 8.15 and 8.16.

Pensioner incomes have grown faster than average earnings across the economy as a whole over the last ten years or so, (see Appendix, Part 5: Pensioners' income). The gross income of pensioner families averaged over all ages and family compositions rose by 37 per cent in real terms over the 11 years between 1994/95 and 2005/06, compared with an increase of about 17 per cent in real average earnings, with single pensioners recording slightly higher increases than couples. Note, however, that changes in average income do not simply reflect changes experienced by individual pensioners; they also reflect changes in the composition of the group, for example as new retirees with greater entitlement to occupation and personal pensions join the group.

Table 5.8

Pensioners'[1] gross income: by age and source

United Kingdom/Great Britain[2]   Percentages

	Couples[3]		Single	
	1996/97	2005/06	1996/97	2005/06
Under 75				
Benefit income[4]	34	31	58	55
Occupational pension	28	25	25	23
Personal pension income	1	4	1	2
Investment income	12	11	10	8
Earnings	24	28	6	11
Other income	0	1	1	1
All gross income (=100%)				
(£ per week at 2005/06 prices[5])	408	529	193	255
75 and over				
Benefit income[4]	55	54	70	67
Occupational pension income	27	30	19	21
Personal pension income	1	4	0	2
Investment income	13	9	10	7
Earnings	3	3	1	1
Other income	0	1	1	1
All gross income (=100%)				
(£ per week at 2005/06 prices[5])	302	381	164	220

1 Pensioner couples where one or more are over state pension age (65 for men and 60 for women), or single pensioners over state pension age.
2 Great Britain for 1996/97 and United Kingdom for 2005/06.
3 Classified by age of head of family unit.
4 Includes basic and second tier state pensions, widow's pension and widowed parent's allowance, income related benefits and tax credits, disability benefits, winter fuel payments and carer's allowance.
5 Adjusted to 2005/06 prices using the retail prices index less council tax/domestic rates.

Source: Pensioners' Incomes Series, Department for Work and Pensions

Earnings

Income from employment in the form of wages and salaries is the most important component of income overall (see Figure 5.6). If earnings across the economy as a whole rise rapidly, this may indicate that the labour market does not have enough employees with the right skills to meet the level of demand within the economy. In addition, a rapid rise may indicate that wage settlements are higher than the rate of economic growth can sustain and thus create inflationary pressures. Slower earnings growth may be a reflection of reduced demand within the economy and may be a warning that GDP is about to fall and unemployment is about to increase. The relationship between earnings and prices is also important. If earnings rise faster than prices, this means that

Annual Survey of Hours and Earnings

The source of data in this section is the Annual Survey of Hours and Earnings (ASHE), which replaced the New Earnings Survey (NES) in 2004 (see Appendix, Part 5: Earnings surveys for a summary of the differences between the two). In Figures 5.9 and 5.10, a series has been used that applies ASHE methodology to NES data for 1997 to 2004. ASHE includes supplementary information that was not available in the NES (for example, on employees in businesses outside the PAYE system), and data for 2004 are presented both with and without this supplementary information. Data for 2005 onwards include the supplementary information and so care should be taken in comparing these with estimates for 2003 and earlier. For 2006 and 2007 ASHE results, ONS has also introduced a small number of methodological changes. These include changes to the sample design as well as the introduction of an automatic occupation coding tool. Again, care should be taken when comparing these estimates with those for 2005 and earlier, as the changes introduce a small discontinuity.

employees' pay is increasing faster than the prices they have to pay for goods and services and that all things being equal, their purchasing power will rise and they will be 'better off'.

Over the period 1998 to 2006, the growth in median gross weekly earnings in the UK outpaced the retail prices index (RPI) in each year except 2005 (Figure 5.9). Median gross weekly

Figure 5.9

Annual growth in median weekly earnings[1]

United Kingdom

Percentages

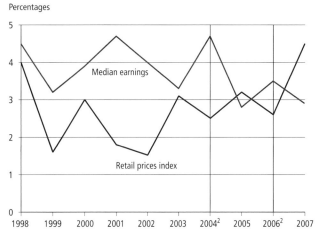

1 Weekly earnings of full-time employees on adult rates at April each year, whose pay for the survey period was unaffected by absence.
2 Vertical lines represent discontinuities in 2004 and 2006 ASHE data. See box on Annual Survey of Hours and Earnings.

Source: Annual Survey of Hours and Earnings, Office for National Statistics; Retail prices index, Office for National Statistics

earnings of full-time employees at both the top and bottom decile points (see the analysing income distribution box on page 63) of the earnings distribution also increased above the RPI throughout the period shown on the chart, except for the bottom decile point in 2005, and the patterns of growth at the top and bottom were generally similar. Between April 2006 and April 2007, median gross weekly earnings of full-time employees increased by 2.9 per cent to £457, compared with an increase of 4.5 per cent in prices as measured by the RPI, indicating a fall in purchasing power in real terms.

Legislation in the 1970s established the principle of equal pay for work that can be established to be of equal value to that done by a member of the opposite sex, employed by the same employer, under common terms and conditions of employment. The impact of this legislation, together with other factors such as the opening up of more highly paid work to women, has been to narrow the differential between the hourly earnings of men and women, though it has not yet been eliminated (Figure 5.10). The pay gap between men and women, defined as the difference between the two as a percentage of men's earnings, fell from 17 per cent in the UK in 1997 to 14 per cent in 2004, and then fell a further 1.9 percentage points between 2004 and 2006. In 2007, using the new ASHE methodology, the gender pay gap fell by 0.2 percentage points. In April 2007 the median hourly earnings excluding overtime of women working full time in the UK were £10.46, 87 per cent of the median earnings of men.

Figure 5.10

Pay gap between men's and women's median hourly earnings[1]

United Kingdom

Percentages

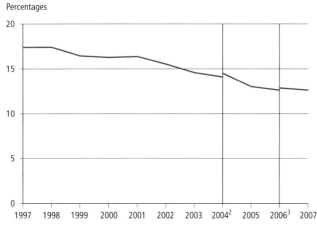

1 Full-time employees on adult rates at April each year, whose pay for the survey period was unaffected by absence. Excludes overtime.
2 Higher percentage includes supplementary information. See Appendix, Part 5: Earnings surveys.
3 Discontinuity in 2006 as a result of further methodological changes. See box on Annual Survey of Hours and Earnings.

Source: Annual Survey of Hours and Earnings, Office for National Statistics

On average part-time employees receive lower hourly earnings than full-time employees, and the hourly earnings differential between men and women working part time is smaller than that for full-time workers. In April 2007 part-time women's median hourly earnings excluding overtime in the UK, at £7.29, were slightly higher than those of men (£7.18). This is partly because a higher proportion of women than men work part time throughout their careers.

Wage rates vary considerably between industrial sectors. Agriculture has traditionally been a relatively low-paid sector in the UK, and this is still the case, with median earnings of full-time employees in this sector of £352 a week in April 2007. However, the hotel and restaurant sector was the lowest paid industry, with median earnings of £288 per week. At the other end of the scale, median earnings of full-time employees in the mining and quarrying sector were £589 per week. This was £15 per week more than the second highest – the electricity, gas and water supply sector. Over the period 1997 to 2007, the electricity, gas and water supply and financial intermediation sectors have also featured as the highest earning sectors. However, the weekly earnings for the mining and quarrying sector and also the electricity, gas and water supply sector are boosted by longer paid hours worked by employees than those worked in the financial intermediation sector.

Earnings also vary by occupation. In April 2007 the highest paid occupational group in the UK was directors and chief executives of major organisations, with median gross pay for full-time employees of £1,917 per week, followed by senior officials in national government at £1,236 per week. These high earners contrast with market and street traders and assistants who, with median gross earnings of £202 per week were the lowest paid of all full-time employees.

From October 2006 there were three rates for the national minimum wage: one for those aged between 16 and 17 (£3.30 per hour, increased to £3.40 from 1 October 2007), one for those aged between 18 and 21 (£4.45 per hour, increased to £4.60 from October 2007) and one for those aged 22 and over (£5.35 per hour, increased to £5.52 from October 2007). Young people are more likely to be in jobs paid below the national minimum wage. In April 2007, 4.1 per cent of jobs in the UK held by those aged 16 to 17 were paid below the relevant rate, compared with 2.5 per cent of those held by people aged 18 to 21, and 1.0 per cent of those held by people aged 22 and above. Part-time jobs were more likely than full-time jobs to pay less than the minimum wage. However, it is important to note that these estimates do not measure non-compliance with the National Minimum Wage legislation as the ASHE does not indicate whether jobs are exempt from the legislation, such as apprentices or new trainees. The increased likelihood of young people being in jobs paid below the minimum wage is likely to be at least in part because they are more likely to be in a job that is exempt from it.

Taxes

People's incomes are subject to a number of deductions over which they have little or no control. The main ones are income tax and social contributions. Social contributions, in the form of national insurance contributions, are paid according to an individual's earnings rather than their total income, and for employees, payments are made both by the individual and by their employer. In 2007/08, employees with earnings less than £100 per week in the UK paid no contributions, and neither did their employers. Employees paid Class 1 contributions equal to 11.0 per cent of their earnings between £100 and £670 per week, and an additional 1.0 per cent on earnings above £670 per week. Employers paid contributions equal to 12.8 per cent of earnings above £100 per week. According to the UK National Accounts, in 2006 around 10 per cent of total gross household income was paid out in employees' national insurance contributions, compared with 17 per cent paid out in income tax.

Under the UK income tax system, every individual is entitled to a personal allowance and those with an annual income below this do not pay any income tax. For 2007/08, the personal allowance was set at £5,225 for those aged under 65, with further allowances for people aged 65 and over. The income tax regime on earnings for 2007/08 includes three different rates of tax. Taxable income of up to £2,230 (that is, after the deduction of allowances and any other tax relief to which the individual may be entitled) is charged at 10 per cent. Taxable income above £2,230 but less than £34,600 is charged at 22 per cent, while income above this level is charged at 40 per cent. Special rates apply to income from savings and dividends.

HM Revenue and Customs estimated that in 2007/08 there will be around 31.6 million taxpayers in the UK (Table 5.11), 0.4 million more than in 2006/07. Given the progressive nature of the income tax system, the amount of tax payable increases as income increases, both as a proportion of income and in cash terms. The average rate of income tax for taxpayers with taxable incomes between the personal annual allowance of £5,225 and £7,499 was 1.7 per cent compared with average rates in excess of 30 per cent for taxpayers with incomes of £100,000 and over.

All countries in the EU-27 raise government revenue through both personal taxation and employee social contributions.

Table 5.11

Income tax payable: by annual income,[1] 2007/08[2]

United Kingdom

	Number of taxpayers (thousands)	Total tax liability after tax reductions[3] (£ million)	Average rate of tax (percentages)	Average amount of tax (£)
£5,225–£7,499	2,460	263	1.7	107
£7,500–£9,999	3,630	1,330	4.2	365
£10,000–£14,999	6,380	7,000	8.8	1,100
£15,000–£19,999	4,890	10,500	12.4	2,150
£20,000–£29,999	6,670	24,400	14.9	3,660
£30,000–£49,999	5,220	33,700	17.1	6,460
£50,000–£99,999	1,750	28,200	24.5	16,200
£100,000–£199,999	418	17,200	30.8	41,200
£200,000–£499,999	123	12,000	34.0	98,200
£500,000–£999,999	22	5,230	35.6	241,000
£1,000,000 and over	8	6,370	35.8	782,000
All incomes	31,600	146,000	18.1	4,630

1 Total income of the individual for income tax purposes including earned and investment income. Figures relate to taxpayers only.
2 Based on projections in line with the March 2007 Budget.
3 In this context tax reductions refer to allowances given at a fixed rate, for example, the Married Couple's Allowance.

Source: HM Revenue and Customs

However, the size of these deductions in relation to the size of each country's economy, as measured by their gross domestic product, varies widely, as does the balance between the two types of deduction (Figure 5.12 overleaf). Taking personal income tax and employee social contributions together, the payments made by people in Denmark amounted to 26 per cent of GDP in 2005, compared with 16 per cent in the UK and only 4 per cent in Poland and Romania. In Denmark, the majority of these payments were in the form of income tax, with employee social contributions amounting to only 1 per cent of GDP. People in Austria paid the highest proportion of GDP in social contributions, at 8 per cent, followed by France, Malta, Italy and the UK, at 6 per cent. Personal income tax as a proportion of GDP was 10 per cent in the UK compared with an average of 9 per cent across the EU-27, and ranged from 25 per cent in Denmark to 2 per cent in Romania.

These figures reflect a wide variety of policy choices by governments, as well as differences in incomes. They depend on the size of public provision of services, and thus the extent to which revenue has to be raised. They also reflect policy choices about the methods used to raise revenue – for example, the emphasis put on raising taxes and social

5

Figure 5.12

Personal income tax and social contributions as a percentage of GDP: EU comparison, 2005

Percentages

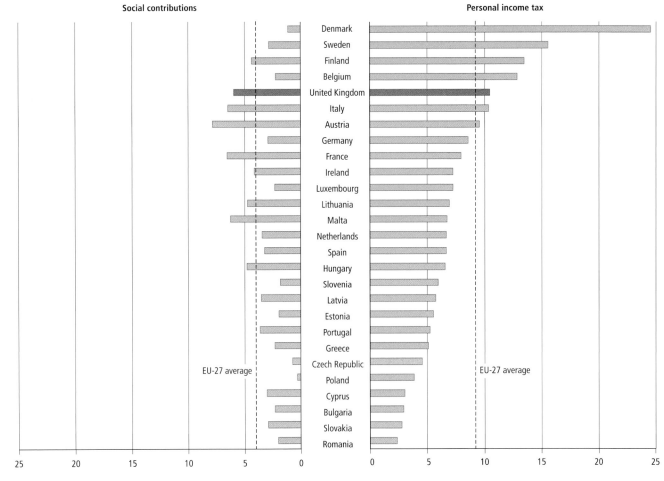

Source: Eurostat

contributions from individuals compared with businesses, and the balance between raising revenue for general purposes compared with raising revenue specifically for social protection through social contributions. Taking taxes and social contributions as a whole, whether raised from individuals or businesses, Sweden was the highest taxed country in the EU-27 in 2005, with total taxes/social contributions amounting to 51 per cent of GDP. Many of the members that joined the EU in 2004 and 2007 were among the lowest taxed – for example, in Romania, Lithuania, Latvia and Slovakia total taxes and social contributions amounted to less than 30 per cent of GDP. The corollary of this is that public expenditure as a proportion of GDP was also low in these countries.

Income distribution

The fact that the various components of income vary in importance for different household types, and that levels of earnings vary between individuals, results in an uneven

distribution of total income between households. The inequality is reduced to some extent by the deduction of taxes and social contributions and their redistribution to households in the form of social security benefits. For this reason, the analysis of income distribution is usually based on household disposable income. In the analysis of Households Below Average Income (HBAI) carried out by the Department for Work and Pensions (DWP), on which most of the tables and figures in this and the next section are based, payments of income tax, council tax (domestic rates in Northern Ireland) and employee national insurance contributions are deducted to obtain disposable income. For more details see Appendix, Part 5: Households Below Average Income (HBAI).

In the HBAI analysis, disposable income is presented both before and after the deduction of housing costs. It can be argued that the costs of housing at a given time may or may not reflect the true value of the housing that different households actually enjoy. For example, the housing costs of someone renting a property from a private landlord may be much higher than those for someone renting a local authority property of similar quality, for which the rent may be set without reference to a market rent. Equally, a retired person living in a property that they own outright may enjoy the same level of housing as their younger neighbour in an identical property owned with a mortgage, although their housing costs will be very different. Estimates are presented on both bases to take into account variations in housing costs that do not correspond to comparable variations in the quality of housing. Neither is given pre-eminence over the other. For more details, see Appendix, Part 5: Households Below Average Income (HBAI).

Figure 5.3 showed how the UK income distribution has evolved over the last three decades. The picture of the income distribution in 2005/06, summarised in Figure 5.13, shows considerable inequality. Each bar represents the number of people living in households with equivalised weekly disposable income in a particular £10 band (see analysing income distribution box on page 63 for definition of equivalisation). There is a greater concentration of people at the lower levels of weekly income and the distribution has a long tail at the upper end. The upper tail is in fact longer than shown: there were an estimated additional 2.5 million individuals living in households with disposable income greater than £1,000 per week who are not shown on the chart. The highest bar

represents nearly 1.5 million people with incomes of between £270 and £280 per week.

Research published by the Joseph Rowntree Foundation drawing on the British Social Attitudes Survey and other sources concludes that over the last 20 years, most people in Great Britain considered that the gap between those with high and low incomes is 'too large'. In 2004, 73 per cent of adults held this view. Although there is widespread acceptance that some occupations should be paid more than others, people think that the gap between high and low paid occupations is greater than it should be. This is not necessarily because they think that those on low incomes are underpaid, but that those on higher incomes are very overpaid. However, the research also found that far fewer people (32 per cent) explicitly support the principle of redistribution of income than think the income gap is too large. This could be because people do not feel particularly strongly about inequality or because they favour other kinds of policies rather than direct redistribution, but current evidence is unable to explain this.

Household disposable income differs considerably across the UK, and there are often greater income differences between local areas within regions than between regions. These differences often reflect differences in employment rates – see Chapter 4: Labour market, Table 4.6. In the absence of small area data on household income available from the population census or from surveys, the Office for National Statistics (ONS) has produced a set of model-based estimates for average household income in England and Wales based on Middle Super Output Areas. The methodology allows survey data to be combined with census and administrative data, to enable estimation at lower geographical levels such as Middle Super Output Areas. England and Wales can be divided into just under 7,200 such areas; for details see Appendix, Part 5: Model-based estimates of income. In Map 5.14 overleaf, the palest shaded areas are those in the bottom 12.5 per cent of the income distribution and the darkest shaded areas are those in the top 12.5 per cent of the distribution. Some of the areas with highest weekly household disposable incomes are in Greater London and the counties around London. For example, parts of Kensington and Chelsea, Croydon, St Albans, Surrey Heath and Epsom had average household disposable incomes of £544 per week and over in 2004/05, placing them in the top 12.5 per cent of the distribution. The areas with the lowest household incomes in 2004/05 were rather more widely spread geographically, with parts of Birmingham, Kirklees, Manchester, Leicester and Cardiff appearing in the bottom 12.5 per cent of the distribution. However, there can be considerable variations within a single local authority area. For example, there are areas within Tower Hamlets with average

Figure 5.13

Distribution of weekly household disposable income,[1] 2005/06

United Kingdom
Millions of individuals

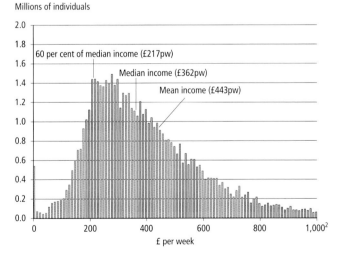

1 Equivalised household disposable income before deduction of housing costs (in £10 bands), using OECD equivalisation. See Appendix, Part 5: Households Below Average Income (HBAI), and Equivalisation scales.
2 There were also an additional 2.5 million individuals with income above £1,000 per week.

Source: Households Below Average Income, Department for Work and Pensions

Map 5.14

Average household disposable income:[1] by area,[2] 2004/05

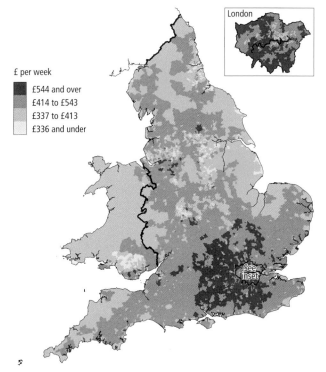

London

£ per week

- £544 and over
- £414 to £543
- £337 to £413
- £336 and under

See Inset

1 Equivalised household disposable income before deduction of housing costs.
2 Middle Layer Super Output Area. See Appendix, Part 5: Model-based estimates of income.

Source: Office for National Statistics

incomes within the top 12.5 per cent as well as areas within the bottom 12.5 per cent of the distribution. Tower Hamlets is also the area with the lowest working age employment rate – see Chapter 4: Labour market.

People in couple families under state retirement pension age and without children were nearly twice as likely as the population in the UK as a whole to be in the top 20 per cent of the distribution of disposable income in 2005/06 (Table 5.15). At the other end of the distribution, people under pension age living in single adult families with children were twice as likely as the population as a whole to be in the bottom fifth of the distribution, while only 3 per cent of such individuals were in the top fifth. Couple families with children and single people without children were fairly evenly spread throughout the distribution, whereas pensioner families, and in particular single pensioners, tended to be concentrated towards the lower end of the distribution.

The DWP's HBAI analysis provides an annual cross-sectional snapshot of the distribution of income based on the Family Resources Survey (FRS). The British Household Panel Survey complements this by providing longitudinal information about how the incomes of a fixed sample of individuals in Great Britain change from year to year. This makes it possible to track how people move through the income distribution over time, and to identify the factors associated with changes in their position in the distribution.

Around 40 per cent of individuals in the top quintile group of net equivalised household income in 1991 were also in that group in 2005, and a rather lower proportion, 34 per cent, were in the lowest quintile group in both years (Table 5.16). At the end of the 15-year period, over the whole of the distribution individuals were generally more likely to end up in the quintile group they started in than move into another quintile group. The exception was that people in the second to

Table 5.15

Distribution of household disposable income:[1] by family type, 2005/06

United Kingdom

Percentages

	Bottom fifth	Next fifth	Middle fifth	Next fifth	Top fifth	All (=100%) (millions)
Pensioner couple	21	26	22	17	13	7.4
Single pensioner	27	32	21	13	7	4.5
Under state pension age						
Couple with children	19	21	22	21	18	20.2
Couple without children	9	10	16	26	39	11.4
Single with children	40	30	19	8	3	5.1
Single without children	20	16	20	22	22	10.5
All individuals	20	20	20	20	20	59.1

1 Equivalised household disposable income before deduction of housing costs has been used to rank the individuals into quintile groups. See Appendix, Part 5: Households Below Average Income (HBAI), and Equivalisation scales.

Source: Households Below Average Income, Department for Work and Pensions

Table 5.16

Position of individuals in the income distribution[1] in 2005 in relation to their position in 1991

Great Britain   Percentages

| | 1991 income grouping | | | | |
	Bottom fifth	Next fifth	Middle fifth	Next fifth	Top fifth
2005 income grouping					
Bottom fifth	**34**	25	18	11	12
Next fifth	27	**23**	23	15	12
Middle fifth	19	22	**23**	22	14
Next fifth	12	18	20	**27**	22
Top fifth	8	12	16	25	**40**

1 Equivalised household disposable income before deduction of housing costs has been used for ranking the individuals. Income is equivalised using the McClements scale. See Appendix, Part 5: Households Below Average Income (HBAI), and Equivalisation scales.

Source: Department for Work and Pensions from British Household Panel Survey, Institute for Social and Economic Research

Table 5.17

Income mobility of sons born in 1970

Great Britain   Percentages

| | Parental average income quartile[1] | | | | |
	Bottom quarter	Next quarter	Next quarter	Top quarter	All parents
Son's earnings quartile aged 30 in 2000					
Bottom quarter	**37**	30	20	13	100
Next quarter	23	**30**	24	23	100
Next quarter	23	24	**29**	24	100
Top quarter	16	16	27	**40**	100
Total (all sons)	100	100	100	100	

1 Average of incomes measured when son aged 10 and 16.

Source: Centre for Economic Performance, from British Cohort Study 1970, Centre for Longitudinal Studies

bottom quintile group in 1991 were marginally more likely to be in the bottom quintile group in 2005. There was more movement in and out of the three middle quintile groups, simply because it is possible to move out of these groups through either an increase or a decrease in income. Movement out of the top group generally only occurs if income falls – an individual will remain in the group however great the increase in their income. The converse is true at the bottom of the distribution. Around one in eight of those in the bottom quintile group in 2005 had been in the top group in 1991, whereas a slightly smaller proportion moved from the bottom group to the top quintile group. This does not necessarily mean that the individual's income has changed to this extent, but that the total income of the household in which they live has changed. This can happen in a wide variety of ways, for example, a young person living with their parents in 1991 then setting up their own household might move from the top to the bottom quintile group. While the picture of income mobility is a complicated one, for the majority of individuals their position in 2005 in relation to 1991 – that is whether it was lower, higher or the same – was generally indicative of where they had spent most of the 15-year period.

Intergenerational income mobility takes a longer term view of how people move within the income distribution over the course of their lives. The degree of intergenerational mobility in society is seen by many as a measure of economic and social opportunity. It seeks to capture the extent to which a person's circumstances during childhood are reflected in their success,

or lack of it, in later life. The most intuitive way to measure the extent of intergenerational mobility is to see where children from the most or least affluent families end up in the earnings or income distribution as adults. This can be shown by a transition matrix similar to Table 5.16 but showing movements in the income distribution across a generation. Table 5.17 shows such a transition matrix for sons born in Great Britain in 1970. In this table, the income distribution is divided into quartile groups, or four equal sized groups of the population ranked according to income. In a fully mobile society, one-quarter of the children from each income group would end up in each quarter of the adult income distribution, so every cell would have the value 25. In the case of no mobility, all children would be in the same quartile group as their parents, and the lack of movement between quartile groups would be shown by values of 100 on the diagonal and zeros elsewhere.

For the cohort of sons born in 1970, 40 per cent of those born to parents in the top quartile group remained in the top quartile group as adults in 2000, whereas 13 per cent moved to the poorest quartile group. Likewise, far more of the least well-off quartile group remained in that group than would occur with perfect mobility – 37 per cent compared with 25 per cent. Further work by the same authors using comparable data on boys born in 1958 shows a higher level of intergenerational mobility than for the later cohort, indicating that intergenerational mobility has fallen. They find that part of the reason for the decline in mobility has been an increasing relationship between family income and educational attainment between the two cohorts. Although young people

5

from all income backgrounds were more likely to stay on in education at both age 16 and age 18 in the later cohort, the likelihood of those from the poorest backgrounds having completed a degree by age 23 scarcely changed compared with the earlier cohort. It therefore appears that the expansion in higher education has disproportionately benefited those from higher income families.

Low Income

Low income could be defined as being in the bottom quintile or decile group, but these definitions are not generally used because of their relative nature. It would mean that 20 or 10 per cent of the population would always be defined as poor. Other approaches generally involve fixing a threshold in monetary terms, below which a household is considered to be 'poor'. This threshold may be calculated in a variety of ways. In countries at a very low level of development it may be useful to cost the bare essentials to maintain human life and use this as the yardstick against which to measure low income. This 'basic needs' measure is of limited usefulness for a developed country such as the UK.

The approach generally used in more developed countries is to fix a low income threshold in terms of a fraction of the median income of the population. This threshold may then be fixed in real terms for a number of years, or it may be calculated in respect of the income distribution for each successive year. The Government's Opportunity for All (OfA) indicators use both approaches. The proportions of people living in households with incomes below various fractions of contemporary median income are monitored, and are referred to as those with relative low income. The proportions with incomes below various fractions of median income in 1998/99 (the reference year for which the threshold was set), known as those with absolute low income, are also monitored. A third OfA indicator measures the number of people with persistent low income, defined as being in a low income household in three out of the last four years. In addition, the Government has announced that to monitor progress against its target of halving the number of children in low income households by 2010 compared with 1998/99 and eradicating child poverty by 2020, there will be another measure that combines material deprivation and relative low income for families with children.

The low income threshold generally adopted in the UK, and used in the remainder of this section, is 60 per cent of contemporary equivalised median household disposable income before the deduction of housing costs, see Appendix, Part 5: Equivalisation scales. In 2005/06 this represented an income of £217 per week.

Figure 5.18

Proportion of people whose income is below various percentages of median household disposable income[1]

United Kingdom/Great Britain[2]
Percentages

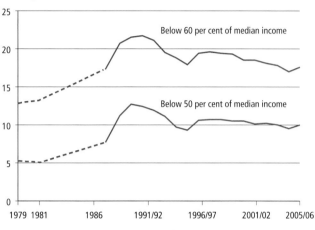

1 Contemporary household disposable income before deduction of housing costs, using OECD equivalisation scale. See Appendix, Part 5: Households Below Average Income (HBAI), and Equivalisation scales for variations in source and definition on which the time series is based.
2 Data for 1994/95 to 2001/02 for Great Britain only.

Source: Households Below Average Income, Department for Work and Pensions

In 1979, 13 per cent of the UK population were living in low income households (Figure 5.18). The proportion of people on low incomes rose rapidly during the 1980s to reach a plateau of around 21 to 22 per cent of the population in the late 1980s and early 1990s. The proportion showed small falls in most years since 1993/94 to reach 17 per cent in 2004/05, though in 2005/06 it was estimated to have risen slightly to 18 per cent of the population or 10.4 million people. This pattern is also reflected in the proportion of people with incomes less than 50 per cent of the median. Note that between 1994/95 and 1997/98 these figures exclude Northern Ireland, but this is estimated to have a minimal impact on the trends.

Although the overall risk of living in a low income household fell by 4 percentage points between 1990–91 and 2005/06 from 22 per cent to 18 per cent, different groups within the population experienced varying changes in risks. People of working age were at less risk of living in a low income household than either pensioners or children, and this risk varied little between 1990–91 and 2005/06 (Figure 5.19). The biggest reductions in risk have been experienced by pensioners: the proportion living in a low income household fell from 37 per cent in 1990–91 to 21 per cent in 2004/05 and 2005/06. The proportion of children living in low income households also fell over this period, from 27 per cent in 1990–91 to 21 per cent in 2004/05, the same risk as for

Figure 5.19

Individuals living in households below 60 per cent of median household disposable income[1]

United Kingdom/Great Britain[2]

Percentages

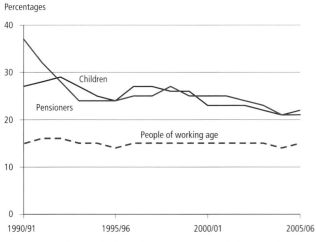

1 Equivalised household disposable income before deduction of housing costs, using OECD equivalisation scale. See Appendix, Part 5: Households Below Average Income (HBAI), and Equivalisation scales for variations in source and definition on which the time series is based.
2 Data for 1994/95 to 2001/02 for Great Britain only.

Source: Households Below Average Income, Department for Work and Pensions

pensioners, but rose slightly in 2005/06 to 22 per cent (or 2.8 million children).

Children were at greater than average risk of living in a low income family if they were living in a family with four or more children, if they were living in a lone-parent family, or if they were living in a family where the head of the household came from an ethnic minority group. However, the greatest risk factor is living in a workless family. Around two-thirds of children living in workless couple families and slightly more than one-half of those in workless lone-parent families in 2005/06 were living in households with below 60 per cent of median income (before deduction of housing costs). If housing costs are deducted, these proportions rise to around three-quarters for children in both workless couple and lone-parent families.

Low income may result in material deprivation – generally defined as wanting particular types of goods and services but being unable to afford to buy them. The extent of material deprivation among children in the UK is explored in Table 6.10 in Chapter 6: Expenditure.

For some people, such as students and those unemployed for a brief period, the experience of low income may be a relatively transient one, but for others it may be more permanent. The British Household Panel Survey (BHPS) provides longitudinal data that allow income mobility and the persistence of low income to be analysed. The definition of the Government's OfA

indicator for persistent low income is 'at least three years out of four below thresholds of 60 or 70 per cent of median income'. Between 1991–1994 and 2002–2005, the proportion of individuals experiencing persistent low income fell from 12 per cent to 9 per cent. The proportion of working-age adults experiencing persistent low income fell slightly, from 8 per cent during 1991–1994 to 6 per cent during 2002–2005, and the proportion of children fell substantially, from 20 per cent to 11 per cent. The proportion of pensioners experiencing persistent low income rose from 17 per cent in 1991–1994 to 21 per cent in 1998–2001, but has since fallen back to 15 per cent in 2002–2005.

Wealth

Wealth can be held in the form of financial assets, such as savings accounts or shares, which provide a flow of current income, or pension rights, which provide entitlement to a future income flow. These types of asset form financial wealth. Ownership of non-financial wealth may provide financial security even if it does not provide a current income flow; a house or a work of art, for example, could be sold to provide income if necessary. In this section the term 'wealth' includes both financial and non-financial assets. There is a further distinction sometimes made between marketable and non-marketable wealth. Marketable wealth comprises assets that can be sold and their value realised, whereas non-marketable wealth comprises mainly pension rights that often cannot be cashed in. Wealth may be accumulated either by the acquisition of new assets through saving or by inheritance, or by the increase in value of existing assets.

Aggregate data on the wealth of the household sector compiled in the UK National Accounts indicate that of total assets of around £8,270 billion in 2006, 45 per cent were held in the form of residential buildings (Table 5.20 overleaf). Even when account is taken of the loans outstanding on the purchase of housing, this form of wealth grew strongly between 1991 and 2006. This reflects the buoyant state of the housing market, as well as the continued growth in the number of owner-occupied dwellings (see Chapter 10: Housing, for further information).

The second most important element of household wealth is financial assets held in life assurance and pension funds, amounting to £2,110 billion in 2006. This element of household wealth grew strongly in real terms during the 1990s, as a result of increases in the contributions paid into occupational pension schemes as well as increased take-up of personal pensions. It fell by 11 per cent in real terms between 2001 and 2002, reflecting the fall in stock market values over this period, but recovered to reach its 2001 level in 2004, and has since grown strongly.

5

Table 5.20

Composition of the net wealth[1] of the household sector

United Kingdom

£ billion at 2006 prices[2]

	1991	2001	2003	2004	2005	2006
Non-financial assets						
Residential buildings	1,633	2,329	3,056	3,380	3,420	3,696
Other	480	540	663	713	726	772
Financial assets						
Life assurance and pension funds	881	1,722	1,645	1,722	1,980	2,110
Securities and shares	366	649	539	578	617	584
Currency and deposits	551	749	844	897	944	996
Other assets	93	102	103	110	111	112
Total assets	4,004	6,091	6,850	7,400	7,798	8,270
Financial liabilities						
Loans secured on dwellings	457	649	823	919	962	1,046
Other loans	122	175	197	218	226	232
Other liabilities	65	68	95	93	93	92
Total liabilities	644	892	1,115	1,230	1,281	1,370
Total net wealth	**3,360**	**5,199**	**5,735**	**6,170**	**6,517**	**6,900**

1 At end of each year. See Appendix, Part 5: Net wealth of the household sector.
2 Adjusted to 2006 prices using the expenditure deflator for the household sector. See Appendix, Part 5: Household income data sources.

Source: Office for National Statistics

Occupational, personal and stakeholder pensions are important determinants of where older people appear in the income distribution, and so the extent to which people of working age are making provision for their retirement is of considerable policy interest. In 2005/06 the Family Resources Survey (FRS) found that 56 per cent of all adult employees of working age in the UK had some non-state pension provision, compared with 34 per cent of the self-employed and only 3 per cent of other

Table 5.21

Savings: by economic status of family unit and amount, 2005/06

United Kingdom

Percentages

	No savings	Less than £1,500	£1,500 but less than £10,000	£10,000 but less than £20,000	£20,000 and more	All families (=100%) (thousands)
Self-employed	22	23	28	10	16	2,307
Single or couple, both in full-time work	31	26	26	8	9	9,010
Couple, one in full-time work, one in part-time work	20	24	28	11	16	2,923
Couple, one in full-time work, one not working	27	22	24	11	15	2,445
One or more in part-time work	42	23	17	6	12	3,262
Head or spouse aged 60 or over	25	16	26	11	21	8,523
Head or spouse unemployed	75	15	7	1	1	1,065
Head or spouse sick or disabled	71	17	7	2	3	2,116
Other family units	65	17	10	2	5	1,666
All families	35	21	23	8	13	33,317

Source: Family Resources Survey, Department for Work and Pensions

adults of working age (including the unemployed, those looking after the family/home and those who were sick or disabled). In each of these employment status groups, those aged from 35 to 59 were the most likely to have non-state pension provision, and overall men were more likely to have provision than women. However, among employees aged under 35, women were marginally more likely to have provision than men. Among employees, the most common form of provision was an occupational pension only, for which 45 per cent had provision. However, among the self-employed, 2 per cent had occupational pension provision only compared with 32 per cent with a personal or stakeholder pension.

The assets that people probably most closely identify with savings are securities and shares, and currency and deposits, being the most easily accessible forms of financial assets. These formed around one-fifth of total assets of the household sector in 2006. Data from the FRS based on individuals' estimates of their savings indicated that more than one-third of families in the UK had no savings at all in 2005/06 (Table 5.21). Savings patterns vary with economic status. Couples where one or both were aged 60 or over were the most likely to have substantial savings – more than one-fifth had savings of £20,000 or more. This reflects life cycle effects, older people will have been able to build up savings during their working lives. Households where the head or spouse was unemployed or sick/disabled were the most likely to have no savings.

The term 'financial exclusion' is sometimes used to describe people who do not use formal financial services at all. Data from the FRS indicate that in 2005/06, 3 per cent of individuals did not have any kind of bank account (including a Post Office account). This proportion rose to 6 per cent of individuals living in households with an income below 60 per cent of the median (before deduction of housing costs).

Figure 5.22

Reasons for saving, summer 2007

Great Britain
Percentages

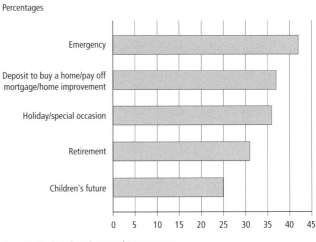

Source: National Savings and Investments

The National Savings and Investments Quarterly Savings Survey explores why people save, why they do not, and what stops them saving more. In summer 2007, around one-half of adults in Great Britain were saving regularly. Of all those with any savings (75 per cent), three in four were saving with no specific goal in mind. Of those who did have a specific goal, the most popular reason for saving was for an emergency (42 per cent) followed by a deposit to buy a home or for home improvements, or to pay off their mortgage (37 per cent) (Figure 5.22). Retirement as a savings goal was mentioned by 31 per cent of regular savers. The most common reasons people gave for not saving more were that they could not afford to do so (52 per cent) or that they did not feel that they needed to save more (22 per cent).

5

5

Chapter 6

Expenditure

- Between 1971 and 2006, the volume of expenditure by households in the UK increased by two and a half times. (Figure 6.1)

- Expenditure on communication (postal services, telephone equipment and services) in the UK in 2006 was more than nine times more in real terms than that in 1971. (Table 6.3)

- Total net lending to individuals by banks, building societies and other lenders in the UK doubled in real terms between 2000 and 2003 and remained high until 2007. (Figure 6.13)

- In 2006, 42 per cent of individuals in Great Britain had some form of unsecured debt, 19 per cent owed money on a credit card, 16 per cent on a personal loan and a further 9 per cent on a car loan. (Table 6.15)

- In England and Wales there were 106,700 individual insolvencies in 2007. This compared to 67,600 in 2005. (Figure 6.16)

- In the UK between 1996 and 2006, the consumer prices index for education (which includes university tuition fees and private school fees) increased by 77 per cent, while the index for clothing and footwear fell by 41 per cent. (Figure 6.18)

There have been substantial changes in the pattern of household expenditure over the last 35 years. Trends in household expenditure provide an insight into changes in consumer preferences, the growth in choices available to consumers and their increased purchasing power, standards of living and wider changes in society. There have also been developments in the way that purchases are made, for example the use of different methods of payment and credit.

Household and personal expenditure

In 2006 the volume of spending on goods and services in the UK was two and a half times that in 1971 (Figure 6.1). This increase in expenditure was made possible by the similar increase in real household incomes over the same period (see also Chapter 5: Income and wealth, Figure 5.1). The volume of household expenditure in the UK has increased every year since 1971, with the exception of 1974, 1980, 1981 and 1991. These years correspond closely to periods of recession in the UK economy.

Figure 6.1

Volume of domestic household expenditure[1]

United Kingdom

Index numbers (1971=100)

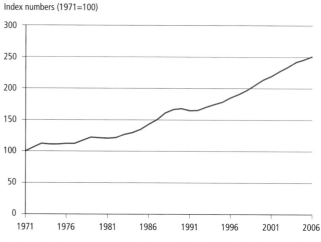

1 Chained volume measure. See Appendix, Part 6: Household expenditure. Final consumption expenditure in the UK by UK and foreign households.

Source: Office for National Statistics

Table 6.2

Household expenditure: by purpose[1]

United Kingdom

Percentages

	1971	1981	1991	2001	2006
Food and non-alcoholic drinks	21	17	12	9	9
Alcoholic drinks and tobacco	7	6	5	4	4
Clothing and footwear	9	7	6	6	6
Housing, water and fuel[2]	15	17	18	18	20
Household goods and services	7	7	6	6	6
Health	1	1	1	2	2
Transport	12	15	15	15	15
Communication[2]	1	2	2	2	2
Recreation and culture	9	9	10	12	12
Education	1	1	1	1	1
Restaurants and hotels[2]	10	11	12	11	12
Miscellaneous goods and services	7	7	11	11	11
Total domestic household expenditure	100	100	100	98	98
of which goods	65	61	53	49	48
of which services	35	40	47	49	51
UK tourist expenditure abroad	1	2	3	4	4
less Foreign tourist expenditure	2	2	2	2	2
All household expenditure[3] (=100%) (£ billions)	34	147	358	632	795

1 According to the Classification of Individual Consumption by Purpose (COICOP). See Appendix, Part 6: Household expenditure.
2 Housing water and fuel includes rent, imputed rent for owner occupiers, maintenance and repair of dwellings, and utilities. Excludes mortgage payments and council tax (domestic rates in Northern Ireland). Communication includes mobile phone equipment and services. Restaurants and hotels includes purchases of alcoholic drinks in pubs, restaurants and hotels.
3 Includes expenditure by UK households in the UK and abroad.

Source: Office for National Statistics

This rise in the volume of expenditure was accompanied by substantial changes in the way that households allocate expenditure to different goods and services. In 1971, 65 per cent of total household expenditure in the UK was spent on goods compared with 35 per cent on services (Table 6.2). However since 1971 the proportion of expenditure allocated to goods has fallen, while that allocated to services has increased. In 2001, expenditure on services exceeded that on goods for the first time, and by 2006 expenditure on goods was 48 per cent of total expenditure compared with 51 per cent on services. In 1971, food and non-alcoholic drinks was the largest category, accounting for 21 per cent of household expenditure. By 2006 this had fallen to 9 per cent. This is not to say that real expenditure on food and non-alcoholic drinks is falling, rather that expenditure on other goods and services is rising much more rapidly, so food and drink account for a falling proportion of expenditure. In 2006 housing, water and fuel was the largest category of expenditure, accounting for 20 per cent of total expenditure, whereas in 1971 it accounted for

15 per cent. Other categories showing a marked increase over the period were recreation and culture (rising from 9 to 12 per cent), transport (rising from 12 to 15 per cent), and restaurants and hotels (rising from 10 to 12 per cent). Among the categories for which the proportion of total spending fell between 1971 and 2006 were clothing and footwear, from 9 per cent to 6 per cent, and alcohol and tobacco, from 7 per cent to 4 per cent. The declining trend in adult cigarette smoking is described in Chapter 7: Health, Figure 7.13.

Changes in the level of consumption of goods and services are measured using volume indices. Volume indices are calculated by adjusting the total value of expenditure within each category, to account for the corresponding price changes. Between 1971 and 1991 the volume of consumption of services in the UK increased by 80 per cent while the consumption of goods increased more slowly, by 56 per cent (Table 6.3). This is consistent with the increasing proportion of expenditure allocated to services, which was described above.

Table 6.3

Volume of household expenditure:[1] by purpose

United Kingdom   Index numbers (1971=100)

	1971	1981	1991	2001	2006	£ billions (current prices) 2006
Food and non-alcoholic drinks	100	105	117	137	152	71
Alcoholic drinks and tobacco	100	99	92	88	89	29
Clothing and footwear	100	120	187	344	491	46
Housing, water and fuel[2]	100	117	139	152	160	159
Household goods and services	100	117	160	262	301	45
Health	100	125	182	188	212	13
Transport	100	128	181	246	271	116
Communication[2]	100	190	307	790	956	17
Recreation and culture	100	158	279	545	783	98
Education	100	160	199	255	226	11
Restaurants and hotels[2]	100	126	167	193	211	92
Miscellaneous goods and services	100	121	231	282	302	86
Total domestic household expenditure	100	121	165	220	251	783
of which goods	100	117	156	227	279	379
of which services	100	128	180	218	232	403
UK tourist expenditure abroad	100	193	298	668	763	31
less foreign tourist expenditure	100	152	187	210	252	19
All household expenditure[3]	100	121	167	227	259	795

1 Chained volume measure. See Appendix, Part 6: Household expenditure.
2 Housing water and fuel includes rent, imputed rent for owner occupiers, maintenance and repair of dwellings, and utilities. Excludes mortgage payments and council tax (domestic rates in Northern Ireland). Communication includes mobile phone equipment and services. Restaurants and hotels includes purchases of alcoholic drinks in pubs, restaurants and hotels.
3 Includes expenditure by UK households in the UK and abroad.

Source: Office for National Statistics

However after 1991, and particularly after 2001, the consumption of goods increased much more quickly than the consumption of services. Between 1991 and 2006 consumption of goods increased by 79 per cent, compared with an increase of just 29 per cent in the consumption of services. This is despite the proportion of expenditure allocated to goods continuing to fall slightly during this period. These seemingly conflicting patterns can be explained by the fact that since the mid-1990s the prices of goods have tended to increase more slowly than the prices of services. Indeed the prices of some goods have fallen (Figure 6.18 later in this chapter looks at consumer prices indices over this period). So while the balance of spending has continued to move from goods towards services, slower growth in the price of goods has enabled an increasing volume of goods to be purchased for a smaller proportion of total expenditure. Conversely, although an increasing proportion of expenditure has been spent on services, the overall increase in the price of those services means that the volume of consumption of services has increased more slowly.

The category of expenditure with the largest increase in the volume of consumption between 1971 and 2006 in the UK was communication which includes mobile phone equipment and services. Expenditure on communication in 2006 was more than nine times that in 1971, while expenditure on recreation and culture was around eight times that in 1971. Within the recreation and culture category, the volume of expenditure increased most rapidly on information processing equipment (which includes personal computers), photographic equipment, audio-visual and recording equipment, and games, toys and hobbies that include electronic and video games. The volume of spending by UK tourists abroad in 2006 was also around eight times that in 1971, while expenditure by foreign tourists in the UK increased by two and a half times.

The volume of expenditure on clothing and footwear increased five times between 1971 and 2006. This is despite the fact that the proportion of total expenditure allocated to this category declined. The volume of expenditure on food and non-alcoholic drinks increased by 52 per cent over the same period, while falling as a proportion of total expenditure. The only category showing a decline in the volume of spending over the period was alcohol and tobacco, (this was due to the decline in the volume of spending on tobacco in particular which fell by 53 per cent). This category only includes alcoholic drinks purchased for consumption at home – spending in pubs and bars is classified along with restaurants and hotels. However the volume of spending on alcohol for consumption at home increased by 136 per cent between 1971 and 2006, with increases in spending on wine (213 per cent), spirits (148 per cent) and beer (45 per cent).

Figure 6.4

Household expenditure[1] per head: by region, 2006

United Kingdom
Index numbers (UK=100)

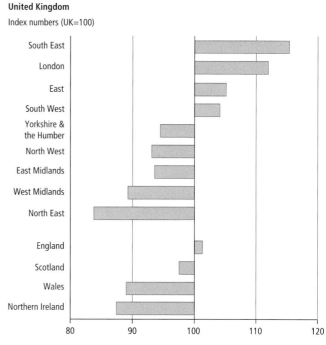

1 See Appendix, Part 6: Expenditure and Food Survey.
Source: Expenditure and Food Survey, Office for National Statistics

Levels of household expenditure vary across the regions of the UK. In 2006 household expenditure per head was highest in the South East where it was 15 per cent above the average for the UK (Figure 6.4). Expenditure in London was 12 per cent above average, while expenditure in the West Midlands and the North East were 11 per cent and 16 per cent below average respectively. Expenditure in Scotland was relatively close to the average for the UK, while in Wales and Northern Ireland it was lower by 11 per cent and 13 per cent respectively.

In addition to these regional variations there are also differences in household expenditure patterns between urban and rural areas. Urban areas are defined as settlements of 10,000 or more people. In rural areas average household expenditure per head was 12 per cent higher than in urban areas in 2006 (average incomes are also higher in rural areas).

Expenditure also varies according to the socio-economic group of the household reference person (see Appendix, Part 1: National Statistics Socio-economic Classification). In 2006, the average weekly expenditure in the UK was highest in households where the household reference person (HRP) was in the managerial and professional group (£676 per week) (Table 6.5). This compared with £418 for households where the HRP belonged to the routine and manual group and £323 for households in the never worked and long-term unemployed group.

Table 6.5

Household expenditure:[1] by socio-economic classification,[2] 2006

United Kingdom   £ per week

	Occupational groups				
	Managerial and professional	Intermediate	Routine and manual	Never worked[3] and long-term unemployed	All households[4]
Food and non-alcoholic drinks	56.70	49.49	45.99	38.05	46.89
Alcoholic drinks, tobacco and narcotics	12.86	12.69	13.11	8.79	11.12
Clothing and footwear	35.25	25.45	22.44	25.98	23.24
Housing (net),[5] fuel and power	56.04	51.83	50.03	63.51	47.56
Household goods and services	44.99	32.49	24.99	16.43	30.26
Health	7.32	4.31	4.52	1.37	5.87
Transport	100.81	70.18	52.49	41.76	62.03
Communication[6]	14.81	14.69	12.13	11.72	11.75
Recreation and culture	82.65	67.35	54.46	31.95	58.48
Education	15.84	5.24	2.58	15.85	7.22
Restaurants and hotels	59.44	41.48	35.51	28.65	37.88
Miscellaneous goods and services	53.61	39.87	33.04	16.91	36.01
Other expenditure items	136.07	98.74	66.74	22.15	77.59
Total expenditure (£ per week)	676.37	513.81	418.01	323.11	455.89

1 See Appendix, Part 6: Expenditure and Food Survey.
2 Of the household reference person. Excludes retired households. See Appendix, Part 1: National Statistics Socio-economic Classification (NS-SEC).
3 Includes households where the reference person is a student.
4 Includes retired households and others that are not classified.
5 Excludes mortgage interest payments and council tax (domestic rates in Northern Ireland) which are included in 'other expenditure items'. Also excludes imputed rent for owner occupiers.
6 Includes mobile phone equipment and services.

Source: Expenditure and Food Survey, Office for National Statistics

Some categories of expenditure varied less between socio-economic groups. These included expenditure on food and non-alcoholic drinks; alcohol, tobacco and narcotics; housing, fuel and power (which includes rent but not mortgage payments); and communication. In fact, there was no evidence of variation in expenditure on alcoholic drinks and tobacco between occupational groups. The categories of expenditure which varied most between socio-economic groups included household goods and services, health, transport, and education. Households in higher spending socio-economic groups, namely managerial and professional, and intermediate groups, tended to spend more on these items both per week and as a proportion of their income. There was a large variation in the 'other expenditure items' category, two-thirds of which is made up of other housing related costs, particularly mortgage interest payments and council tax. The managerial and professional group had the highest expenditure on this category. At £136 per week, this was double that spent by households in the routine and manual group, and six times that for the never worked and long-term unemployed group.

Households where the household reference person is a student are included in the never worked and long-term unemployed group. Although total expenditure by households in this group was low, they nevertheless had relatively high expenditure on: clothing and footwear; housing, fuel and power; communication; and education.

Differences in spending also exist between ethnic groups in the UK. Over the period 2003/04 to 2005/06 total expenditure per head was lower among households where the household reference person (HRP) defined themselves as either Asian, Black or Mixed, compared with households where the HRP was White. Average expenditure per head for households where the HRP was Asian was £125 per week, while for households in both the Black and Mixed groups, it was £142 per week (Table 6.6 overleaf). This compared with the average for all households of £182 per week, and an average of £187 per week for households where the HRP was White.

Some categories of expenditure varied broadly in line with these variations in total expenditure. For example, households

Table 6.6

Household expenditure per head: by ethnic group[1] of household reference person, 2003/04–2005/06

United Kingdom

£ per week

	White	Mixed	Asian	Black	Other	All households
Food and non-alcoholic drinks	19.30	15.40	12.70	13.50	14.70	18.80
Alcoholic drinks, tobacco and narcotics	5.10	3.70	1.10	1.70	1.70	4.80
Clothing and footwear	9.90	9.90	8.10	8.40	7.30	9.80
Housing (net),[2] fuel and power	17.40	17.90	15.60	21.40	21.30	17.40
Household goods and services	13.50	11.40	8.70	8.70	6.10	13.10
Health	2.30	1.90	1.10	1.30	0.50	2.20
Transport	26.30	15.30	17.40	18.80	30.60	25.60
Communication[2]	4.90	5.20	4.10	6.10	4.90	4.90
Recreation and culture	25.50	14.70	10.90	13.90	19.90	24.50
Education	2.40	2.00	4.50	3.20	4.10	2.60
Restaurants and hotels[2]	15.80	11.30	7.60	7.80	10.80	15.20
Miscellaneous goods and services	14.90	11.50	10.60	10.60	12.10	14.50
Other expenditure items	29.60	21.40	23.00	26.00	33.30	29.20
Total expenditure (£ per week)	186.80	141.70	125.30	141.60	167.30	182.50

1 See Appendix, Part 1: Classification of ethnic groups.
2 Housing water and fuel includes rent, imputed rent for owner occupiers, maintenance and repair of dwellings, and utilities. Excludes mortgage payments and council tax (domestic rates in Northern Ireland). Communication includes mobile phone equipment and services. Restaurants and hotels includes purchases of alcoholic drinks in pubs, restaurants and hotels.

Source: Expenditure and Food Survey, Office for National Statistics

where the HRP was Asian spent £13 per head per week on food and non-alcoholic drinks, while households where the HRP was Black spent £14 per week and households where the HRP was White spent £19 per week. Other categories of expenditure varied in a way which did not simply reflect variations in total expenditure but may be explained by other factors related to ethnicity. For example, expenditure on alcohol, tobacco and narcotics is much lower in households where the HRP is Asian, Black, or Other compared with households where the HRP is White (and much lower than could be explained just by the differences in total expenditure). Ethnic minority groups allocated lower proportions of their total expenditure to recreation and culture, and restaurants and hotels, compared to households where the HRP was White. However, higher proportions were allocated to education and communication among Black and other groups.

The Mixed, Black, and Other groups spent higher amounts on housing, fuel, and power (which includes rent but not mortgage payments), compared with households where the HRP was White. Households where the HRP was White spent more than other households on 'other expenditure items' (which includes mortgage interest payments). For minority groups in general, expenditure on these two categories which

include housing costs, tended to represent a higher proportion of their total expenditure.

In 2006, expenditure on food and drinks for consumption either at home or away from the home, represented 19 per cent of the total expenditure of UK households. An average of £46.90 per week was spent on food and non-alcoholic drink to be consumed at home, with £6.50 spent on alcoholic drinks to be consumed at home (Table 6.7). A further £31.90 per week was spent on catering services – food and drink (alcoholic and non-alcoholic) from restaurants, cafes, pubs, other food purchased for consumption outside the home, and take-aways.

The total expenditure by each household is likely to depend on that household's income. Separating households into income quintile groups reveals how household expenditure changes according to household income (see Chapter 5: Income and wealth, analysing income distribution box for more on income quintiles). For example in 2006, households in the top quintile or the top 'fifth' of the income distribution had a total expenditure 3.3 times greater than households in the bottom 'fifth'.

Expenditure on food and non-alcoholic drinks also changed according to income, although by a smaller amount –

Table 6.7

Household expenditure[1] on food, drink and catering services: by income quintile group,[2] 2006

United Kingdom

£ per week

	Bottom fifth	Next fifth	Middle fifth	Next fifth	Top fifth	All households	Ratio top/ bottom fifth
Food and drink for consumption at home[3]	38.30	46.30	55.00	61.30	65.80	53.40	1.7
Food and non-alcoholic drinks	35.30	41.90	48.50	52.90	55.80	46.90	1.6
Alcoholic drinks	3.00	4.40	6.60	8.40	10.00	6.50	3.3
Catering services	15.30	20.50	30.50	40.60	52.50	31.90	3.4
Restaurant and café meals	5.30	8.00	11.60	16.10	22.70	12.80	4.3
Alcoholic drinks (away from home)	3.60	4.40	8.30	12.10	13.50	8.40	3.8
Take-away meals eaten at home	2.60	3.30	4.00	4.80	4.70	3.90	1.8
Other take-away and snack food	2.90	3.20	3.90	4.80	6.20	4.20	2.1
Food from caterers and canteens	0.80	1.50	2.70	2.70	5.40	2.60	6.4
Total expenditure on food and drink	53.60	66.70	85.60	101.90	118.30	85.20	2.2
Total household expenditure (£ per week)	226.80	324.20	428.80	546.30	753.10	455.90	3.3

1 See Appendix, Part 6: Expenditure and Food Survey.
2 Households are ranked by equivalised gross income. See Chapter 5: Analysing income distribution box for an explanation of quintile groups.
3 Excludes take-away meals which are classified under catering services.

Source: Expenditure and Food Survey, Office for National Statistics

6

households in the top income group spent 1.6 times more on food and non-alcoholic drink compared to households in the bottom income group. For both alcohol for consumption at home and catering services, the gap between expenditure by the top and bottom income groups was greater, with households in the top income group spending more than three times the amount spent by households in the bottom group. The gap was also greater for expenditure on restaurant and café meals (4.3 times) and alcoholic drinks (consumed away from home) (3.8 times) than for expenditure on take-away meals eaten at home (1.8 times) and other take-away and snack food (2.1 times).

Diet plays an important role in supporting a healthy lifestyle, (see also Chapter 7: Health). In recent years, there has been increasing importance on eating more fresh fruit and vegetables and this has translated into changes in our expenditure patterns. Between 1974 and 2005/06, household purchases of fruit (measured in grams per person per week) in the UK increased by 77 per cent (Table 6.8). This increase was largely due to increases in purchases of stone fruit, soft fruit, and bananas. Fruit juice has increasingly become part of the national diet, with ten times more being purchased a week in 2005/06 compared to 1974. While total purchases of vegetables declined by 22 per cent, this was almost entirely due to the decline in purchases of fresh potatoes, down from

Table 6.8

Purchases of fruit and vegetables

United Kingdom

Grams per person per week

	1974	2005/06
Total vegetables	2,578	1,998
Fresh potatoes	1,318	587
Other fresh vegetables[1]	769	802
Processed potatoes	119	255
Other processed vegetables[2]	372	354
Total fruit	731	1,292
Total fresh fruit	515	856
Oranges and other citrus fruits	136	151
Apples and pears	229	226
Stone fruit	16	78
Soft fruit[3]	25	108
Bananas	84	225
Other fresh fruit[4]	25	68
Fruit juices (ml)	34	350
Other fruit products[5]	182	87

1 Includes fresh green vegetables.
2 Includes frozen vegetables but excludes processed potatoes.
3 Includes grapes.
4 Includes melons.
5 Includes tinned, dried and frozen fruit and products containing nuts.

Source: Department for Environment, Food and Rural Affairs

1.3 kg per person per week to 0.6 kg. There were increases in purchases of fresh vegetables other than potatoes, and in purchases of processed potatoes.

Income and expenditure patterns are reflected in both the ownership of goods, or in some cases, in the inability of families to afford some goods and services. The volume of expenditure on goods has increased rapidly in recent years, and one consequence of this has been that the ownership of new consumer durables has extended rapidly to a greater proportion of households. For example, during the last decade in the UK, there have been large increases in the ownership of mobile phones and home computers (Figure 6.9). The proportion of households with a mobile phone increased from 20 to 80 per cent between 1997/98 and 2006, while ownership of home computers increased from 29 per cent to 67 per cent. Ownership of microwave ovens, tumble dryers, and dishwashers has increased more slowly. Over 90 per cent of households now have microwave ovens, compared with 59 per cent for tumble dryers, and 38 per cent for dishwashers.

Of course, the choices that households make about how they spend their money are determined not only by preferences, but also by the ability to afford different items. Households who cannot afford to purchase goods and services which most households would regard as necessities can be deemed as experiencing material deprivation (this does not include households that decide they do not want these things). Material deprivation is an alternative non-monetary indicator of

Figure 6.9

Household ownership of selected consumer durables

United Kingdom

Percentages

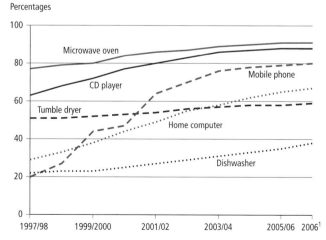

1 Figures for 2006 correspond to the calendar year, while the figures for earlier years correspond to financial years.

Source: Expenditure and Food Survey, Family Expenditure Survey, Office for National Statistics

Figure 6.10

Children lacking selected necessities through the inability of their families to afford them, 2005/06

United Kingdom

Percentages

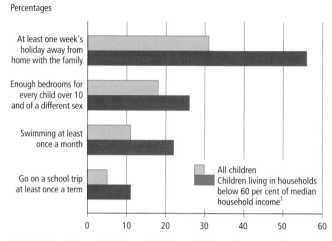

1 Equivalised household disposable income before deduction of housing costs, using OECD equivalisation scale. See Appendix, Part 5: Equivalisation scales.

Source: Households Below Average Income, Department for Work and Pensions

poverty. The Department for Work and Pension's publication, *Households Below Average Income* uses a list of 21 items commonly regarded as necessities to measure material deprivation for households with children.

It is clear that children in households which have incomes below the most commonly used poverty threshold (which is 60 per cent of median household income, see also Chapter 5: Income and wealth) are also more likely to go without these perceived necessities, because their family could not afford them. For example in 2005/06, 31 per cent of all children in the UK lacked at least one week's holiday away from home with the family because their families could not afford it (Figure 6.10). However, among children living in households with an income below 60 per cent of the median income this increased to 56 per cent. Similar patterns are observed with regard to being able to afford sufficient bedrooms for every child over 10 (of a different sex), going swimming at least once a month, and going on a school trip once a term.

Transactions and credit

The Retail sales index is a monthly measure of the turnover of retail businesses in Great Britain and is used as a key economic indicator. For most of the last 10 years, growth in the volume of retail sales has been relatively strong. Over this period, the average growth rate as measured by the seasonally adjusted index has been 4.2 per cent per year compared to an average of 3.3 per cent over the last 20 years. In 2005 growth fell to

Figure 6.11

Volume of retail sales[1]

Great Britain

Index numbers (2000=100)

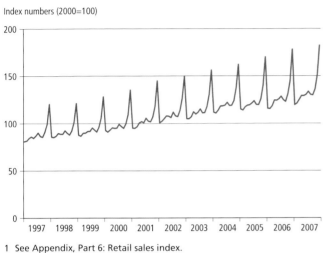

1 See Appendix, Part 6: Retail sales index.

Source: Office for National Statistics

Figure 6.12

Non-cash transactions:[1] by method of payment

United Kingdom

Billions

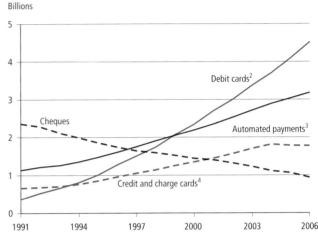

1 Figures are for payments by households. Cheque encashments and cash withdrawals from ATMs and branch counters using credit/charge and debit cards are not included. Based on data supplied by UK card issuers.
2 Visa Debit and Switch cards in all years; includes Electron cards from 1996 and Solo cards from 1997.
3 Includes direct debits, standing orders, direct credits and inter-branch automated items.
4 Visa, MasterCard, travel/entertainment cards and store cards.

Source: APACS – the UK Payments Association

1.8 per cent which was the lowest figure since 1995, although growth increased again in 2006 (to 3.1 per cent) and 2007 (to 4.3 per cent).

Retail sales are highly seasonal. The non-seasonally adjusted index shows how the volume of sales varies considerably over the course of the year and how sales increase sharply in the build up to Christmas (Figure 6.11). Comparing the non-seasonally adjusted index to the seasonally adjusted index provides a measure of the seasonal variation in retail sales. Since 1997 the seasonal effect on sales each November has been equivalent to an increase of 9 per cent in the volume of sales, while in December the seasonal effect has been 32 per cent.

Since 1991 there have also been changes in the way that transactions are carried out. Statistics from APACS (the UK payments association) show that the use of debit cards has continued to grow rapidly. Between 1991 and 2006 there was a thirteenfold increase in the number of payments by debit card in the UK (Figure 6.12). The number of automated payments, which include direct debits and standing orders, increased nearly threefold during the same period. The use of personal cheques has declined steadily and in 2006 the number of cheques written was less than half that in 1991. The volume of transactions using credit and charge cards, such as store cards, rose steadily from 1991 until 2004, but has fallen slightly since then. This was the first fall since 1991 and coincided with a fall in the amount of net consumer credit lending (see Figure 6.13).

Total net lending to individuals by banks, building societies and other lenders is a measure of the value of new loans less repayments over a given period. It is made up of lending secured against dwellings, and consumer credit. Between 1993 and 2000, net lending to individuals in the UK increased gradually and by the end of 2000 it had reached £16.6 billion per quarter (in 2006 prices, seasonally adjusted) (Figure 6.13).

Figure 6.13

Net lending to individuals[1]

United Kingdom

£ billion per quarter at 2006 prices[2]

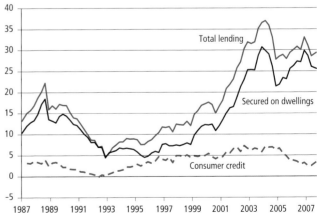

1 Lending secured on dwellings and consumer credit. Also includes lending to housing associations. Seasonally adjusted.
2 Adjusted to 2006 prices using the retail prices index. See Appendix, Part 6: Retail prices index.

Source: Bank of England

It then started to increase more rapidly, and reached £36.9 billion in the first quarter of 2004. While lending has not subsequently surpassed this level, it has remained high and in the third quarter of 2007 was £29.0 billion. Lending had reached a previous high of £22.2 billion in the third quarter of 1988 but fell during the recession of the early 1990s.

Lending secured on dwellings makes up the major part of total net lending. Changes in the amount of secured lending are influenced by changes in the level of housing market activity and house prices (see Chapter 10: Housing). Increased house prices not only require home buyers to borrow more money, but also encourage existing home owners to secure borrowing against their properties for purposes other than house purchase. The increase in secured lending after 2000 in the UK was driven by rapidly increasing house prices. The fall in secured lending from late 2004 to mid-2005, and the subsequent recovery, closely reflect the fall then subsequent recovery in both the number of housing market transactions and house price growth through this period.

Consumer credit which makes up the remainder of total net lending consists of credit card lending, overdrafts and non-secured loans and advances to individuals. This type of lending also fell to a low level during and after the recession of the early 1990s before increasing through the mid- and late-1990s. From 2002 until the start of 2005 consumer credit in the UK remained at around £6 billion per quarter (in 2006 prices). This high level of consumer credit lending ultimately led to high levels of individual insolvency and debt write-off (individual insolvencies are shown in Figure 6.16). As these consequences became increasingly apparent, lenders were forced to reduce consumer credit lending (and borrowers were forced to reduce borrowing), with the result that consumer credit fell rapidly during 2005 and by the third quarter of 2007 it had fallen to £3.3 billion, one-half of its level at the start of 2005.

The high level of total net lending, particularly after 2001, has seen the total amount of debt outstanding continue to increase. At the end of 1993 individuals in the UK owed a total of £574 billion. By the end of the third quarter of 2007, this had increased to £1,320 billion (all in 2006 prices).

Rising house prices have allowed some home owners to increase their secured borrowing against the increased value of their house (see also Chapter 10: Housing, Table 10.20 for uses of equity released). Secured loans which are not used for house purchase or home improvements can be used to increase consumption expenditure, pay off debts, or invest in financial assets. Figures from the Bank of England suggest that, in 2006, around 43 per cent of secured borrowing in the UK was used for purposes other than house purchase or home improvement.

Figure 6.14

Housing equity withdrawal[1] as a proportion of post-tax income

United Kingdom
Percentages

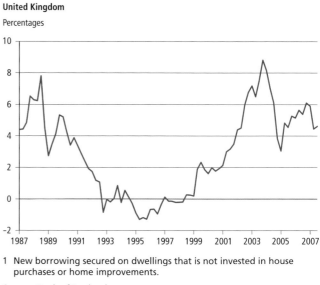

1 New borrowing secured on dwellings that is not invested in house purchases or home improvements.

Source: Bank of England

For these households, this borrowing represents a substantial supplement to their existing income. Between 2002 and 2006, for UK households as a whole, the amount of borrowing through housing equity withdrawal was equivalent to an additional 6 per cent of post-tax income (Figure 6.14). Borrowing through mortgage equity withdrawal also reached a similar level in the late 1980s, although as with other forms of lending it declined in the early 1990s before increasing again in the late 1990s. Housing equity withdrawal averaged below zero between 1993 and 1998 indicating that repayments outweighed new lending. The increase to almost 9 per cent in the final quarter of 2003, then the fall during 2004, and subsequent recovery in 2005, is more extreme than for net lending as a whole. This suggests that the level of housing equity withdrawal is more sensitive to changes in house prices and the housing market, than the level of secured lending for house purchases.

A wide variety of different forms of unsecured consumer credit are available. A survey conducted by the Office for National Statistics from August to September 2006 using the National Statistics Omnibus Survey on behalf of the Financial Services Authority, showed that just over 42 per cent of adults in Great Britain had some form of unsecured debt, and that the median amount owed was £3,000. The survey showed that 19 per cent of adults owed money on a credit card, 16 per cent on a personal loan and a further 9 per cent on a car loan (Table 6.15). The average amounts per adult outstanding for each of these forms of credit were also high: £2,280 for

Table 6.15

Proportion of adults with unsecured debt and amount outstanding: by type of debt, 2006[1]

Great Britain

	Adults with different types of unsecured debt (percentages)	Average amount outstanding (£)
Credit card	19	2,284
Personal loan	16	7,751
Car loan	9	5,769
Catalogue	6	220
Student loan company	5	6,973
Family & friends	3	2,875
Storecard	3	471
Social fund loan	2	484
Money lender	1	1,336
Store loan	1	1,201
Rent arrears	1	682

1 Data collected between August and September 2006.

Source: Financial Services Authority; Office for National Statistics

Figure 6.16

Individual insolvencies

England & Wales

Thousands

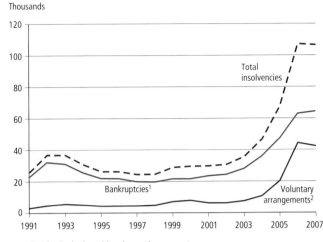

1 Individuals declared bankrupt by a court.
2 Individuals who make a voluntary agreement with their creditors. Includes Deeds of Arrangement, which enable debtors to come to an agreement with their creditors.

Source: Insolvency Service

credit cards; £7,750 for personal loans; and £5,770 for car loans. Some 5 per cent of individuals had a debt with the student loans company with an average outstanding debt of almost £7,000, while 3 per cent owed money to family and friends with an average debt of £2,875. Six per cent of individuals had debts having bought goods through catalogues, although the average amount outstanding was small.

The same survey showed that over 2 per cent of consumers with bills and credit commitments in Great Britain had fallen behind with some or many of those bills or commitments. Six per cent reported that they were keeping up but that it was a constant struggle, while 26 per cent reported that they were keeping up but struggled from time to time. Two-thirds of consumers with bills and credit commitments reported no difficulties.

High levels of borrowing have resulted in an increase in the number of individual insolvencies. These can occur when individuals are unable to meet their debt repayments. Some of the statutory insolvency instruments available to individuals experiencing financial difficulties include bankruptcy and individual voluntary arrangements (IVAs). An individual can be declared bankrupt when the court concludes that there is no likelihood of the debt being repaid. However, in some circumstances the courts encourage a voluntary arrangement to be set up between the debtor and the creditors. In England and Wales there were 106,700 individual insolvencies in 2007, and 107,300 in 2006 (both bankruptcies and IVAs)

(Figure 6.16). This compares with 67,600 in 2005, and 35,600 in 2003. The number of insolvencies in 2006 and 2007 is three times the number that occurred in both 1992 and 1993 when there was a higher level of insolvencies caused by the recession of the early 1990s. The Insolvency Service also provide information about the occupation of people declared bankrupt. In 2005, 36 per cent of bankruptcies involved people who had no occupation, while 29 per cent were employees, and 23 per cent were self-employed. It is clear that the recent increase in bankruptcies has primarily been among employees and those unemployed or with no occupation. Between 2002 and 2005, bankruptcies involving the self-employed increased by 22 per cent, compared with 131 per cent for bankruptcies involving employees, and 146 per cent for bankruptcies involving those unemployed or with no occupation.

The increasing number of insolvencies has forced banks to write-off increasing amounts of bad debt. Figures from the Bank of England show that in 2006 there were write-offs on lending to individuals of £6.75 billion. This had increased from £3.89 billion in 2004, and £1.42 billion in 1998 (all in 2006 prices). In 2006, unsecured lending accounted for 98 per cent of debt write-offs. Figures from the Department of Communities and Local Government show that the number of home repossessions and the number of mortgages in arrears also remained relatively low in 2005 and 2006. This suggests that it was primarily unsecured lending which led to the increase in individual insolvencies between 2002 and 2006.

Prices

The way that individuals and households choose to spend their money is affected by the price of goods and services. The retail prices index (RPI) measures the average monthly change in the prices of a variety of goods and services purchased by households, and is the most longstanding measure of inflation in the UK. The RPI is measured using a 'basket' of goods and services which is deemed to be representative of all the goods and services on which people typically spend their money.

The consumer prices index (CPI) is the main measure of inflation used within the Government's monetary policy framework and for international comparison. There are some differences between the RPI and CPI in terms of the items and population covered by these indices. For example, council tax and owner occupiers' housing costs (which includes mortgage interest payments, house depreciation and buildings insurance) are excluded from the CPI. The CPI inflation rate has usually been lower than the RPI rate.

Since 1993, inflation as measured by the RPI has tended to be lower and more stable than in the years before 1993 (Figure 6.17). In the mid-1970s and early 1980s in particular, there were periods when the rate of inflation exceeded 20 per cent per year. Since 1997 the Bank of England has had responsibility for setting interest rates to meet the Government's inflation target. Since December 2003 the target rate of inflation has been 2 per cent as measured by the CPI (from 1997 to 2003 the target was 2.5 per cent as measured by the RPI). During the period between February 1997 and

Figure 6.17

Consumer prices index[1] and retail prices index[2]

United Kingdom
Percentage change over 12 months

1 See Appendix, Part 6: Consumer prices index. Data for years prior to 1996 are estimates.
2 See Appendix, Part 6: Retail prices index.

Source: Office for National Statistics

Figure 6.18

Percentage change in consumer prices indices:[1] by purpose of expenditure, 1996–2006

United Kingdom
Percentages

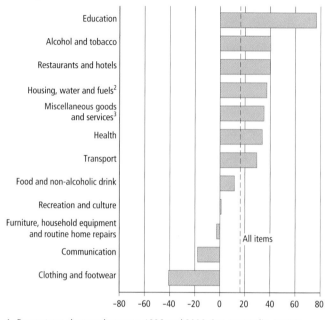

1 Percentage changes between 1996 and 2006. See Appendix, Part 6: Consumer prices index.
2 Includes rent but excludes mortgage interest payments.
3 Includes personal care, personal effects (e.g. jewellery and watches), social protection, insurance and financial services.

Source: Office for National Statistics

June 2005, the CPI was at, or below, 2 per cent. Between mid-2005 and the end of 2007, inflation tended to be slightly higher than before but, with the exception of March 2007 when it was 3.1 per cent, it remained within 1 per cent of the inflation target, and still low by historical standards.

While the overall rate of inflation has been low over the last 15 years, the prices for some categories of goods and services have increased much more than others. Figure 6.18 shows the percentage change between 1996 and 2006 in the consumer prices indices for the 12 major categories of consumption that constitute the CPI. Over this period the biggest percentage increase was for education costs, which include university tuition fees and private school fees, which increased by 77 per cent. There were also price increases for alcohol and tobacco; restaurants and hotels; housing, water and fuel; miscellaneous goods and services (which include personal care and financial services); and health. These items rose by at least twice as much as the all items index. There were two categories that decreased substantially in price, with the largest decreases being in clothing and footwear (down 41 per cent), followed by communication which includes postal and telephone services, mobile phone equipment and services, and

Internet subscription services (down 18 per cent). In general, the cost of services have tended to rise at a rate higher than the all items CPI, while goods have been more likely to increase at a lower rate or have fallen in price, with the exception of alcohol and tobacco.

While the items in the basket of goods and services used to measure consumer prices are subject to change over time, some items have been included for many years. This makes it possible to show how the prices of these individual items have changed over time. For example, between 1971 and 2006, the price of cigarettes in the UK increased by 18 times, and the price of a pint of beer by 17 times (Table 6.19). Part of this increase is due to increased duties levied on cigarettes and alcohol. The price of white fish fillets also increased 16 times over this period. The price of unleaded petrol has doubled since 1991, which is largely attributable to a combination of the rise in world market price and indirect tax, which includes fuel duty and value added tax (VAT) (see Chapter 12: Transport, Figure 12.15, for more on fuel prices). The price of tomatoes,

Table 6.19

Cost of selected items

United Kingdom						Pence
	1971	1981	1991	1996	2001	2006
500g back bacon[1]	37	142	235	293	343	377
White fish fillets, per kg	58	245	629	455	866	944
Eggs (large), per dozen	26	78	118	158	172	181
1 pint pasteurised milk[2]	5	19	32	36	36	35
250g cheddar cheese	13	58	86	115	128	142
800g white sliced bread	10	37	53	55	51	81
New potatoes,[3] loose per kg	13	31	34	56	87	80
Tomatoes, loose per kg	35	95	147	129	125	132
Mushrooms, loose per kg	60	211	290	335	262	246
Apples (dessert), per kg	22	55	120	112	116	122
Bananas, per kg	18	64	119	93	106	90
Packet of 20 cigarettes (filter tip)[4]	27	97	186	273	412	476
Pint of beer[5]	15	65	137	173	203	251
Whiskey (per nip)	..	..	95	123	148	180
Litre of unleaded petrol	..	..	45	57	76	91

1 In 1971 and 1981 the price is for unsmoked. In 1991 the price is an average of vacuum and not vacuum-packed.
2 Delivered milk included from 1996.
3 In season new potatoes prior to 1993.
4 Change from standard to king size in 1991.
5 Bottled until 1981 and draught lager after.

Source: Office for National Statistics

Figure 6.20

Comparative price levels[1] for household expenditure: EU comparison, 2006

Index numbers (UK=100)

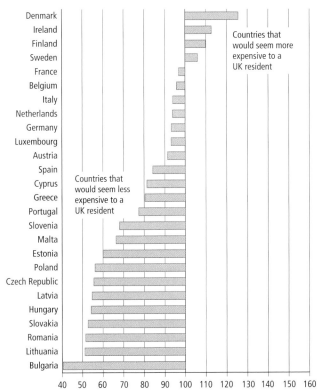

1 Price level indices for private consumption, defined as the ratio of purchasing power parities to exchange rates, provides a measure of the difference in price levels between countries. See Appendix, Part 6: Purchasing power parities.

Source: Office for National Statistics

mushrooms, and bananas all increased between 1971 and 1991, but then generally fell between 1991 and 2006.

The international spending power of sterling depends both on exchange rates, and on the ratios of prices between the UK and other countries which are measured by purchasing power parities. These can be used to calculate comparative price levels, which provide a measure of the difference in price levels between countries, and show which countries in the European Union would appear more expensive to a UK resident and which would appear cheaper (Figure 6.20). In 2006, a UK resident would have found prices in Denmark, Ireland, Finland and Sweden to be more expensive than the UK. Prices in Denmark were 26 per cent higher than in the UK. Prices in France, Italy and Germany were slightly cheaper than in the UK, while prices in the Eastern European countries were substantially cheaper. Prices in Bulgaria and Romania, who joined the EU at the start of 2007, were 40 per cent and 51 per cent of the level in the UK. Prices in the UK are approximately 11 per cent above the EU-27 average.

6

Chapter 7

Health

- In the UK in 2004, males could expect to live 62.3 years free from a limiting long-standing illness or a disability and females 63.9 years. (Table 7.2)

- In 2006 in Great Britain, 91 per cent of males and 89 per cent of females reported having good or fairly good health. (Table 7.3)

- Between 1971 and 2006, age-standardised death rates for circulatory diseases in the UK fell from 6,936 to 2,462 per million males and from 4,285 to 1,559 per million females. (Figure 7.4)

- Between 1994 and 2006 the proportion of men classified as obese in England increased from 14 per cent to 24 per cent, while the proportion for women rose from 17 per cent to 24 per cent. (Page 98)

- Between 1991 and 2006, death rates from alcohol-related causes in the UK rose from 9.1 to 18.3 per 100,000 men and from 5.0 to 8.8 per 100,000 for women. (Figure 7.12)

- In 2004 in Great Britain, the proportion of children aged 5 to 16 with a mental disorder was more than twice as high among those living in 'hard pressed' areas than those in areas populated by 'wealthy achievers'. (Figure 7.17)

DATA

Download data by clicking the online pdf

www.statistics.gov.uk/ socialtrends38

Over the past century there have been notable improvements in health in the UK. These can be attributed to improved nutrition, advances in medical science and technology, and the development of health services that are freely available to all. There are, however, some statistically significant health inequalities between different groups in society. Factors influencing these include income, and its effect on the quality of diet and housing that are affordable, and awareness of healthy lifestyles, which can impact on health problems linked to diet, levels of physical activity, smoking and drinking.

Key health indicators

Life expectancy is a widely used indicator of the state of the nation's health. There have been large improvements in expectancy of life at birth over the past century for both males and females. In 1901 males born in the UK could expect to live around 45 years and females to around 49 years (Figure 7.1). By 2006 life expectancy at birth had risen to 77 years for males and to 82 years for females. Since before the beginning of the 20th century, female life expectancy at birth has been consistently higher than that of males. The disparity was at its greatest in 1969, when females could expect to live on average 6.3 years longer than males born in the same year. Since then the gap has steadily narrowed, with this trend projected to continue until around 2014, when the difference is expected to level off at around 3.5 years. Life expectancy at birth is projected to continue to rise for both sexes, to reach more than 81 years for males and more than 84 years for females by 2021.

Figure 7.1

Expectation of life[1] at birth: by sex

United Kingdom
Years

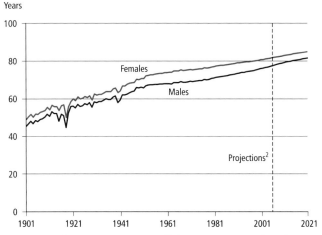

1 See Appendix, Part 7: Expectation of life. The average number of years
   a new-born baby would survive if he or she experienced age-specific
   mortality rates for that time period thoughout his or her life.
2 2006-based projections for 2007 to 2021.

Source: Government Actuary's Department, Office for National Statistics

Table 7.2

Life expectancy, healthy life expectancy and disability-free life expectancy:[1] by sex, 2004

United Kingdom   Years

	Males		Females	
	At birth	At age 65	At birth	At age 65
Life expectancy	76.6	16.6	81.0	19.4
Healthy life expectancy	67.9	12.5	70.3	14.5
Years spent in poor health	8.7	4.1	10.7	4.9
Disability-free life expectancy	62.3	9.9	63.9	10.7
Years spent with disability	14.3	6.7	17.1	8.7

1 See Appendix, Part 7: Expectation of life, and Healthy life expectancy
   and disability-free life expectancy.

Source: Government Actuary's Department; Office for National Statistics

In contrast to the long-term improvements seen in life expectancy at birth, it was not until the latter part of the 20th century that life expectancy for adults in the UK showed a continuous improvement. Since the early 1970s the increase in life expectancy among older adults has been particularly notable. Between 1971 and 2006 life expectancy for men aged 65 increased by 4.9 years, compared with an increase of 1.7 years between 1901 and 1971. This improvement can be linked to a rapid decline in death rates among men at these older ages (see Chapter 1: Population, Table 1.9).

Despite its use as a general indicator of the population's health, life expectancy takes no account of the quality of life and whether it is lived in good health, with disability or dependency. Summary health measures such as healthy life expectancy and disability-free life expectancy focus on the population's health-related quality of life. In the UK in 2004, the healthy life expectancy of males was 67.9 years at birth and 12.5 years at age 65. For females, the equivalent figures were 70.3 years and 14.5 years respectively (Table 7.2).

Disability-free life expectancy, defined as the expected number of years lived free from a limiting long-standing illness, is calculated using life expectancy and self-reported limiting long-standing illness data. Such conditions include arthritis, back pain, heart disease and mental disorders. There were similar patterns for males and females in terms of the number of years they could expect to live free from a limiting long-standing illness or a disability. In the UK in 2004, on average males could expect to live 62.3 years free from a limiting long-standing illness or a disability, and 9.9 years at age 65. For females the equivalent figures were 63.9 years at birth, and 10.7 years at age 65.

Within the UK in 2004, England had the highest life expectancy at birth of 76.9 years for men and the highest disability-free life expectancy at birth of 62.6 years for men. England also had the highest life expectancy at birth of 81.2 years for women and the highest disability-free life expectancy for women, of 64.2 years. The lowest life expectancy was in Scotland at 74.2 years for men and 79.3 years for women. The lowest disability-free life expectancy for men was in Northern Ireland at 59.7 years and for women, 60.3 years.

The proportion of males and females reporting good health in Great Britain in 2006 was similar in all age groups but between the ages of 16 and 24 the figures for males were 5 percentage points higher than those for females (Table 7.3). In total 68 per cent of males and 66 per cent of females reported good health in contrast to 9 per cent of males and 11 per cent of females who reported their health as not good. In Northern Ireland 67 per cent of males and 64 per cent of females reported good health. In the 75 years and over age group 31 per cent of males and 28 per cent of females reported good health.

Since the early 1970s, circulatory diseases (which include heart disease and stroke) have remained the most common cause of death among both males and females in the UK. However, they have also shown by far the greatest decline of the main diseases that cause death, particularly among males (Figure 7.4). In 1971, age-standardised death rates for circulatory diseases were 6,936 per million males and

Table 7.3

Self-reported general health:[1] by sex and age, 2006[2]

Great Britain				Percentages
	Good	Fairly good	Not good	All
Males				
0–15	85	12	2	100
16–24	83	14	3	100
25–44	74	20	6	100
45–64	58	28	14	100
65–74	44	36	19	100
75 and over	33	43	24	100
All ages	68	23	9	100
Females				
0–15	87	11	2	100
16–24	78	18	3	100
25–44	70	21	8	100
45–64	59	26	15	100
65–74	43	38	19	100
75 and over	33	39	28	100
All ages	66	23	11	100

1 See Appendix, Part 7: Self-reported illness.
2 See Appendix, Part 2: General Household Survey.

Source: General Household Survey (Longitudinal), Office for National Statistics

7

Figure 7.4

Mortality:[1] by sex and leading cause groups

United Kingdom[2]

Rates per million population

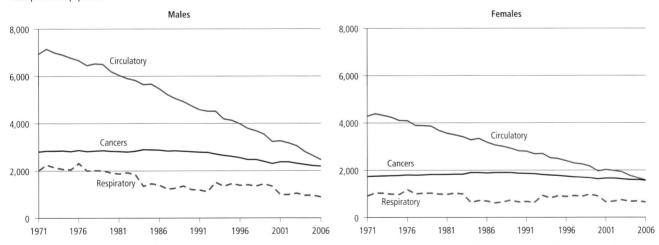

1 Data are for all ages and have been age-standardised using the European standard population. See Appendix, Part 7: Standardised rates, and International Classification of Diseases.
2 Data for 2000 are for England and Wales only.

Source: Office for National Statistics

4,285 per million females. By 2006 these rates had fallen to 2,462 per million for males and 1,559 per million for females, when the death rate for circulatory disease in females was lower than cancer for the first time.

Over the past 35 years cancers have been the second most common cause of death among men. The same was true for women until 2006 when cancers became the most common cause of death. Death rates from cancer peaked in 1984 for males at 2,899 per million, and by 2006 had fallen to 2,201 per million. Death rates from cancer for females are typically lower than those for males and peaked in 1989 at 1,905 per million, since when they have fallen gradually to 1,569 per million in 2006. These variations in mortality trends partly reflect differences in the types of cancer males and females are likely to experience, the risk factors associated with developing them and the relative survival rates for different cancers. The incidence and survival rates for the most common forms of cancer are examined later in this chapter.

The reduction in infant mortality (defined as deaths in the first year of life) was one of the factors contributing to an overall increase in life expectancy, particularly in the first half of the 20th century. In 1930, there were 60.0 deaths under the age of one, per 1,000 live births in England and Wales (Figure 7.5). In the years to the beginning of the Second World War, there was a gradual fall in the infant mortality rate to 50.6 in 1939. Although the rate fluctuated in the early 1940s, following the Second World War, there was a steady fall in the infant mortality rate from 46.0 per 1,000 live births in 1945 to half that at 23.1 per 1,000, 12 years later in 1957. This decline

Figure 7.5

Infant[1] and neonatal[2] mortality

England & Wales

Rates per 1,000 live births

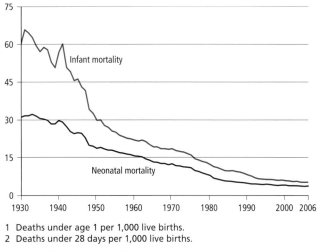

1 Deaths under age 1 per 1,000 live births.
2 Deaths under 28 days per 1,000 live births.

Source: Office for National Statistics

continued and in 2004, there were 5.0 deaths per 1,000 live births. The rate slightly increased to 5.1 in 2005, then declined to 5.0 deaths per 1,000 live births in 2006. The fall in infant mortality rates can be linked to improvements in diet and sanitation, better antenatal, postnatal and medical care, and the development of vaccines and immunisation programmes.

Neonatal mortality (defined as deaths in babies under 28 days) and perinatal mortality (defined as stillbirths and deaths to babies under seven days) rates followed similar historical trends to those for infant mortality. The neonatal mortality rate fell until 2001, when it levelled out at a rate of 3.6 deaths per 1,000. It fell again to 3.4 deaths per 1,000 births by 2005 before rising to 3.5 in 2006. Perinatal mortality fell until 2001 to a rate of 8.0 deaths per 1,000 and remained at this level until 2006 apart from a small rise in 2003 and 2004.

Despite the decline in infant mortality rates, notable socio-economic inequalities still exist. In England and Wales in 2005, the infant mortality rate among babies born inside marriage, whose fathers were in semi-routine occupations, was 6.1 per 1,000 live births. This was more than twice the infant mortality rate of 2.7 per 1,000 live births for those who were born inside marriage and whose fathers were in large employers and higher managerial occupations. For babies born outside marriage, where the birth was jointly registered by both parents, there was a similar pattern, with an infant mortality rate of 6.8 per 1,000 live births for babies whose fathers were in semi-routine occupations. This compared with a rate of 3.1 for those with fathers in large employers and higher managerial occupations.

Over the past 15 years there have been contrasting trends in the occurrence of the most commonly diagnosed childhood infections. A measles epidemic in 1994 in the UK had 23,500 notifications, almost twice the level of 1993. Since 1994, there has been a downward trend until 2005, when there were 2,330 notifications, before rising to 4,020 notifications in 2006 (Figure 7.6).

In 2005 there was a mumps epidemic, with 66,500 notifications in the UK. More than 80 per cent of notifications were in people aged 15 and over. The increase in this age group largely reflects lower immunity rates among older teenagers and young adults who were born before the introduction of the measles, mumps, rubella (MMR) triple vaccine in the UK in 1988. Coverage levels of 90 per cent for MMR were achieved by the early 1990s, but in recent years concerns over the safety of the vaccine have led to a fall in uptake. The uptake rate was particularly low in London with only 75 per cent of children immunised by their second birthday in 2006/07 compared to 89 per cent in the North East of England.

Figure 7.6

Notifications of measles, mumps and rubella

United Kingdom
Thousands

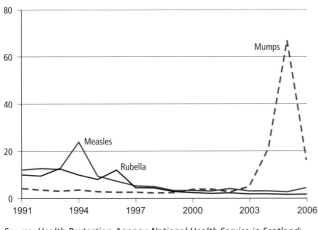

Source: Health Protection Agency; National Health Service in Scotland; Communicable Disease Surveillance Centre (Northern Ireland)

Rubella (also referred to as German measles), like measles, often occurs in epidemics in populations where vaccination has not been in use. The last epidemic occurred in 1996, when there were slightly less than 12,000 notifications in the UK. Since 2000 the annual number of notifications has been between 1,300 and 2,100. The disease is rarely serious except in pregnant women, where it may lead to abnormalities in unborn babies.

The number of reported cases of tuberculosis (TB) has been increasing steadily since the late 1980s. In 2006, more than 8,000 cases were reported in England and Wales, around 40 per cent more than in 1999 (Figure 7.7). Since 2001 the notification rate among people who were born in the UK remained very low,

Figure 7.7

Tuberculosis rates: by place of birth

England & Wales
Rates per 100,000 population

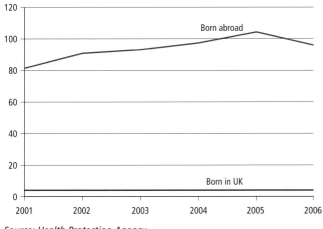

Source: Health Protection Agency

at around 4 per 100,000 population of England and Wales. The rate among those born abroad was much higher.

Between 2001 and 2006 there was an overall increase in the TB rate among those born abroad, from 81 to 96 per 100,000 population in England and Wales. The increase over this period was largely in specific groups and areas. In 2006, 42 per cent of reported cases in England and Wales were in London. Overall, almost 40 per cent of cases were among people from an Indian, Pakistani or Bangladeshi ethnic group.

Diet and obesity

Diet has an important influence on weight and general health. The Department of Health recommends that a healthy diet should include at least five portions a day of a variety of fruit and vegetables (excluding potatoes). In 2006, 28 per cent of men and 32 per cent of women in England met this target (Table 7.8). Increased intake of fruit and vegetables is associated with decreasing the risk of developing various diseases and in

Table 7.8

Daily portions of fruit and vegetables consumed: by sex and age, 2006

England   Percentages

| | Number of portions per day | | | | |
	None	Above 0 but less than 5	5 or more	All	Average daily portions
Men					
16–24	12	69	19	100	3.0
25–34	7	67	27	100	3.7
35–44	9	62	29	100	3.5
45–54	6	64	30	100	3.7
55–64	5	64	32	100	3.9
65–74	3	66	31	100	4.0
75 and over	3	67	29	100	3.8
All aged 16 and over	7	65	28	100	3.6
Women					
16–24	8	70	22	100	3.3
25–34	5	64	31	100	3.9
35–44	6	61	33	100	4.0
45–54	4	61	35	100	4.2
55–64	2	58	39	100	4.5
65–74	2	64	33	100	4.1
75 and over	3	73	25	100	3.6
All aged 16 and over	5	64	32	100	3.9

Source: Health Survey for England, The Information Centre for health and social care

2006, the proportion of adults eating five or more portions a day generally increased with age up to the age of 64. Among men the proportion peaked at 32 per cent among those aged 55 to 64. Among women those aged 55 to 64 were the most likely to consume five or more portions, at 39 per cent. Young men and women aged 16 to 24 were by far the least likely group to consume the recommended daily portions of fruit and vegetables and were also the most likely to consume none at all. In 2006, 19 per cent of men and 22 per cent of women in this age group reported consuming five or more portions of fruit and vegetables on a daily basis, while 12 per cent of men and 8 per cent of women ate none at all.

In 2006, 19 per cent of boys and 22 per cent of girls aged 5 to 15 in England reported eating at least five portions of fruit and vegetables (excluding potatoes) on a daily basis. These proportions were notably higher than in 2004 (13 per cent of boys and 12 per cent of girls).

Access to a healthy diet is partly linked to affordability. In 2005/06 those living in UK households in the top one-fifth of the income distribution consumed more fresh fruit and vegetables (excluding potatoes) on a weekly basis than those in lower income groups (Figure 7.9). Households in the top quintile group (see Chapter 5: Income and wealth, analysing income distribution box) consumed an average of 857 grams of fresh vegetables and 943 grams of fresh fruit per person per week. In contrast,

households in the bottom quintile group consumed 742 grams of fresh vegetables and 828 grams of fresh fruit per person per week. Those in the middle fifth quintile group, on average, consumed more processed potatoes and potato products, and processed vegetables than any other quintile group.

Diets that are high in fat and low in fresh fruit and vegetables can contribute to a person being overweight or obese. Obesity is linked to heart disease, diabetes and premature death. The body mass index (BMI) is a common measure for assessing an individual's weight relative to their height, and a BMI score of 30 kg/m^2 or more is taken as the definition of obesity (see Appendix, Part 7: Body mass index). In recent years the proportion of the adult population in England who are obese has increased. Between 1994 and 2006 the proportion of men aged 16 and over who were classified as obese increased from 14 per cent to 24 per cent, while among women the proportion rose from 17 per cent to 24 per cent. In addition, a further 43 per cent of men and 32 per cent of women were classified as overweight (BMI score of 25 kg/m^2 to less than 30 kg/m^2). In 2006, the proportion of the adult population classified as obese or overweight was 67 per cent and 56 per cent of men and women respectively (Figure 7.10).

There is also concern over the increasing proportion of children who are obese or overweight. Based on the UK 1990 national BMI percentiles classification, between 1995 and 2006, the proportion of boys aged 2 to 15 in England who were

Figure 7.9

Consumption of fruit and vegetables in the home: by income grouping[1] of household, 2005/06

United Kingdom

Grams per person per week

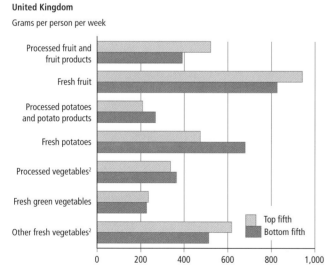

1 Gross weekly income has been used to rank the households into quintile groups. See Chapter 5: Income and wealth, analysing income distribution box for more on quintiles.
2 Excluding potatoes.

Source: Expenditure and Food Survey, Office for National Statistics; Department for Environment, Food and Rural Affairs

Figure 7.10

Proportion of adults and children[1] who are obese or overweight:[2] by sex

England

Percentages

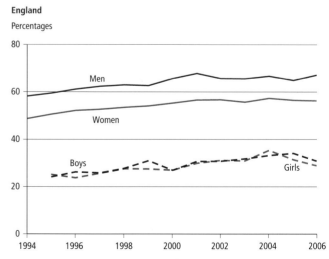

1 Adults aged 16 years and over, children aged 2 to 15 years.
2 Using the body mass index (BMI) for people aged 16 and over and the 1990 UK national body mass index percentile classification for those aged 2 to 15. See Appendix, Part 7: Body mass index.

Source: Health Survey for England, The Information Centre for health and social care

classified as obese increased from 11 per cent to 17 per cent. Among girls in this age group the proportion rose from 12 per cent to 15 per cent, although there was some fluctuation between years. Among girls aged 2 to 15, the proportion who were obese decreased between 2005 and 2006, from 18 per cent to 15 per cent. Future years' data will show whether this is part of a downward trend. There was no significant change among boys over this period. In 2006, 13 per cent of boys and 14 per cent of girls aged 2 to 15 in England were classified as overweight.

Alcohol and smoking

Excessive alcohol consumption can lead to an increased likelihood of developing health problems such as high blood pressure, cancer and cirrhosis of the liver. The Department of Health advises that consumption of three to four units of alcohol a day for men and two to three units a day for women should not lead to significant health risks. Consistently drinking more than these levels is not advised because of the associated health risks. By the end of 2008 the Government expects all alcoholic drinks labels to include alcohol unit information.

In 2006, 40 per cent of men and 33 per cent of women in Great Britain reported exceeding the recommended amount of alcohol on at least one day during the week before interview (Table 7.11). People aged 25 to 44 were more likely (44 per cent) to exceed the recommended daily amount compared to people aged 65 and over who were least likely to exceed the recommended daily amount (17 per cent). Men aged 25 to 44 were the most likely of all to binge drink (defined as the consumption of twice the recommended daily amount). In 2006, 31 per cent had done so on at least one day in the previous week compared with 7 per cent of men aged 65 years and over.

In 2006 there was little variation by socio-economic group (see Appendix, Part 1: National Statistics Socio-economic Classification (NS-SEC)) of the household reference person (see Appendix, Part 7: Household reference persons) in the proportion of men who consumed more than the recommended levels of alcohol on at least one day in the week before interview. In contrast among women, those in large employer and higher managerial households were the most likely to exceed the recommended limits, with 47 per cent having done so on at least one day in the previous week. This compared with 24 per cent of women where the household reference person was in the routine socio-economic group.

In general, the higher the level of gross weekly household income, the more likely men and women were to drink alcohol in the previous week and to exceed the daily benchmarks.

Table 7.11

Adults' daily alcohol consumption:[1] by sex and age, 2006[2]

Great Britain   Percentages

	16–24	25–44	45–64	65 and over	All aged 16 and over
Men					
4 units or less[3]					
Drank nothing in previous week	40	27	24	33	29
Up to 4 units	18	25	33	46	31
More than 4 units[3]					
More than 4 units and up to 8 units	12	17	21	14	17
More than 8 units	30	31	21	7	23
	100	100	100	100	100
Women					
3 units or less[3]					
Drank nothing in previous week	47	40	40	56	44
Up to 3 units	14	20	25	30	23
More than 3 units[3]					
More than 3 units and up to 6 units	14	19	23	12	18
More than 6 units	25	21	12	2	15
	100	100	100	100	100

1 On at least one day in the previous week. See Appendix, Part 7: Alcohol consumption.
2 Figures obtained from converting volume of alcohol drunk to number of alcohol units drunk.
3 Department of Health guidelines recommend men should not regularly drink more than 3 to 4 units of alcohol per day, and women should not regularly drink more than 2 to 3 units of alcohol per day.

Source: General Household Survey (Longitudinal), Office for National Statistics

In 2006, 51 per cent of men in households with a gross weekly income of £1,000 or more drank more than four units on at least one day in the previous week, compared with 32 per cent of men in households with a gross weekly income of less than £200. There was a similar pattern for women, with 47 per cent of those with a gross weekly income of £1,000 or more per week and 20 per cent with a gross weekly income of less than £200 drinking more than three units on at least one day in the previous week.

The number of alcohol-related deaths in the UK was 4,144 in 1991 and 8,758 in 2006. Death rates from alcohol-related causes were much higher among men than women and the

7

Figure 7.12

Death rates[1] from alcohol-related causes:[2] by sex

United Kingdom

Rates per 100,000 population

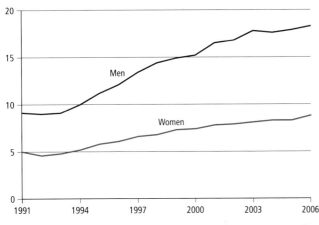

1 Age-standardised to the European standard population. See Appendix, Part 7: Standardised rates. Rates from 2001 are not directly comparable with those for earlier years because of the change from ICD-9 to ICD-10. See Appendix, Part 7: International Classification of Diseases.
2 See Appendix, Part 7: Alcohol-related causes of death.

Source: Office for National Statistics

gap between the sexes has widened in recent years (Figure 7.12). In 2006 the male death rate was 18.3 per 100,000, more than twice the rate of 8.8 per 100,000 for women. The alcohol-related death rates among men increased in all age groups between 1991 and 2006, and in 2006 were highest among those aged 55 to 74, at 44.6 per 100,000. There were similar patterns among women with the highest death rate in 2006 being among those aged 55 to 74, at 21.1 per 100,000.

There are large variations in alcohol-related death rates between countries and regions of the UK. Between 1991–93 and 2002–2004, Scotland had the highest rates for men and women in all age groups, while Yorkshire and the Humber and the East Midlands had the lowest rates for males and females. Alcohol-related death rates in the South East, South West and East of England were also low for females.

Across the UK during the period 1999–2003, alcohol-related death rates were highest among those living in the most deprived areas (wards ranked from least to most deprived using the Carstairs Index – see Appendix, Part 7: Area deprivation). Among women, alcohol-related death rates for those living in the most deprived areas were more than three times higher than for those living in the least deprived areas, rising from 3.7 deaths per 100,000 in the areas in which the 5 per cent least deprived areas fall to 11.3 per 100,000 in the areas in which the 5 per cent most deprived areas fall. For men the relationship was even stronger. The alcohol-related death rate for men living in the 5 per cent most deprived areas was more

than five times higher than the rate for those living in the 5 per cent least deprived areas, 31.9 deaths per 100,000 compared with 6.2 deaths per 100,000.

Over the past 32 years there was a substantial decline in the proportion of adults aged 16 and over in Great Britain who smoked cigarettes. Smoking is related to a range of health problems, including lung cancer, heart disease, stroke, chronic bronchitis and emphysema. In 1974, 51 per cent of men aged 16 and over and 41 per cent of women were smokers. By 2006, 23 per cent of men and 21 per cent of women were smokers (Figure 7.13). Among both men and women much of the decline occurred in the 1970s and early 1980s, after which the rate of decline slowed. The reduction in the difference between the proportion of men and women who smoke partly reflects different cohort patterns for smoking, as smoking became common among men several decades before it did among women.

Since the early 1990s the prevalence of cigarette smoking has been higher among those aged 20 to 24 than among those in other age groups in Great Britain. In 2006, 33 per cent of men and 29 per cent of women in this age group were smokers compared to 13 per cent of men aged 60 and over and 12 per cent of women aged 60 and over who smoked.

Smoking prevalence varies markedly by socio-economic group. In 2006, 31 per cent of men and 28 per cent women in routine

Figure 7.13

Prevalence of adult[1] cigarette smoking:[2] by sex

Great Britain

Percentages

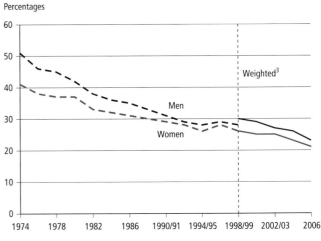

1 People aged 16 and over.
2 From 1988 data are for financial years. Between 1974 and 2000/01 the surveys were run every two years. See Appendix, Part 2: General Household Survey.
3 From 1998/99 data are weighted to compensate for nonresponse and to match known population distributions. Weighted and unweighted data for 1998/99 are shown for comparison.

Source: General Household Survey (Longitudinal), Office for National Statistics

Figure 7.14

Main reasons for wanting to stop smoking[1]

Great Britain

Percentages[2]

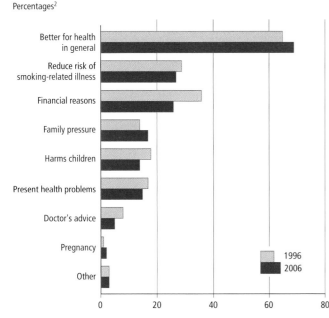

1 Smokers who want to stop smoking.
2 Percentages do not add up to 100 per cent as respondents could give more than one answer.

Source: Omnibus Survey, Office for National Statistics

and manual occupation households in Great Britain were smokers, compared with 17 per cent of men and 14 per cent of women in managerial and professional households. The Government target, set out in the *NHS Cancer Plan* of 2000,

is to reduce the proportion of smokers in manual occupation groups to 26 per cent by 2010.

To meet government targets for reducing the prevalence of cigarette smoking, people have to be discouraged from starting to smoke and people who smoke have to be encouraged to stop. A survey asking smokers their main reasons for wanting to quit smoking found the most common reason in Great Britain in 2006 was for better general health (69 per cent) (Figure 7.14). This compared with 65 per cent who gave this reason in 1996. The next most common reason for wanting to stop smoking in 2006 was to reduce the risk of smoking-related illness (27 per cent). This was, however, a lower proportion than in 1996 when 29 per cent gave this as a reason to quit. Financial reasons were the main reason for 36 per cent of smokers giving up in 1996; by 2006 this had fallen to 26 per cent.

Cancer

Around one-third of the population develop cancer at some time in their lives and in its various forms. Trends in lung cancer incidence are strongly linked to those for cigarette smoking, which is by far the greatest single risk factor for the disease. The incidence of lung cancer has fallen sharply in men since the early 1990s, mainly as a result of the decline in cigarette smoking (see Figure 7.13). In 1993 the age-standardised lung cancer incidence rate for men in the UK was 87 per 100,000 (Figure 7.15). By 2004, this had fallen by 28 per cent to 63 per 100,000. Lung cancer incidence rates among women are far

Figure 7.15

Standardised incidence rates[1] of major cancers: by sex

United Kingdom

Rates per 100,000 population

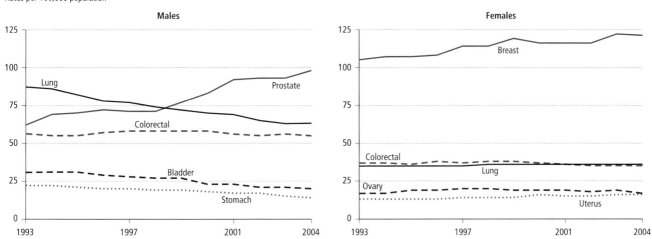

1 Age-standardised to the European standard population. See Appendix, Part 7: European standard population, Standardised rates, and International Classification of Diseases.

Source: Office for National Statistics

lower, largely as a consequence of a historically lower incidence of smoking among women.

The incidence of both prostate cancer among men and breast cancer among women has risen considerably over the past ten years and these are the most commonly diagnosed cancers for men and women respectively. The incidence rate for prostate cancer rose from 62 per 100,000 men in 1993 to 98 per 100,000 in 2004. In 1999 prostate cancer overtook lung cancer as the most commonly diagnosed cancer among men. Although there is no NHS screening programme for prostate cancer, the increase in incidence rates is mainly as a result of the large increase in the number of men presenting for individual screening using the PSA (prostate-specific antigen) test. This has increased the likelihood of early diagnosis.

Over the past ten years breast cancer has been the most commonly diagnosed form of cancer among women. In 1993 the incidence rate was 105 per 100,000 women. By 2004 this had risen to 121 per 100,000. The increase in the incidence of

breast cancer is partly the result of the introduction of the NHS breast cancer screening programme between 1988 and 1994, which raised awareness of the condition and symptoms. This led to a large number of cases being diagnosed earlier than they may otherwise have been.

Cancer patient survival is a key indicator of the effectiveness of cancer control in the population. Survival rates from lung cancer are low compared with the other most common cancers. For those diagnosed with lung cancer in England in the period 1999–2003 the five-year survival rate (adjusted for overall levels of mortality from other causes in the general population) for men was 6.5 per cent and for women, 7.6 per cent (Table 7.16). In contrast, five-year survival rates for colon cancer were around 49.6 per cent for men and 50.8 per cent for women. Survival rates for types of cancer where some form of screening is available were even higher. The five-year survival rate was 74.4 per cent for prostate cancer and 81.0 per cent for female breast cancer.

Mental health

In recent years there has been an increasing interest in the mental health problems experienced by children and young people. In 2004, 10 per cent of 5 to 16-year-olds living in private households in Great Britain had a clinically diagnosed mental disorder. These included: 4 per cent with an emotional disorder, 6 per cent with a conduct disorder, 2 per cent with a hyperkinetic disorder (characterised by hyperactive, impulsive or inattentive behaviour) and 1 per cent with a less common disorder (including autism, tics and eating disorders), however children can suffer multiple disorders. Boys in this age group were more likely to have some form of mental disorder (12 per cent) than girls (8 per cent).

The association between social disadvantage and mental disorder is well documented. Analysis by ACORN (see Appendix, Part 7: ACORN classification), which combines geographic and demographic characteristics to distinguish different types of people in different areas of Great Britain, showed that children living in areas classed as 'hard pressed' were the most likely to be assessed as having a mental disorder. In 2004, among children aged 5 to 16, 17 per cent of boys and 12 per cent of girls living in a hard pressed area had some type of mental disorder (Figure 7.17). Those living in 'wealthy achievers' areas were the least likely of all children to experience any type of mental disorder, at 7 per cent of boys and 5 per cent of girls. This trend was evident for the three main types of disorder among both boys and girls, and for both younger and older children.

In 2000 (the latest year for which data are available), about one in six adults (164 cases per 1,000 adults) aged 16 to 74

Table 7.16

Five year relative survival rates for major cancers: by sex 1999–2003[1]

England

	Survival rate (percentages)	Number of cases
Males[2]		
Prostate	74.4	124,088
Bladder	61.7	31,755
Colon	49.6	42,247
Stomach	13.3	23,033
Oesophagus	9.1	18,279
Lung	6.5	82,787
Females[2]		
Breast	81.0	170,664
Cervix	63.0	12,024
Bladder	53.2	12,434
Colon	50.8	40,633
Stomach	15.9	12,308
Oesophagus	12.0	10,897
Lung	7.6[3]	53,399

1 Diagnosed during 1999-2003. See Appendix, Part 7: Relative survival rates.
2 Aged 15 to 99 years. Data have been age-standardised using the European standard population. See Appendix, Part 7: Standardised rates, and European standard population.
3 Not possible to produce an age-standardised five-year survival rate for lung cancer in women; this figure refers to the unstandardised survival estimate.

Source: Office for National Statistics

Figure 7.17

Prevalence of mental disorders[1] among children:[2] by sex and ACORN classification,[3] 2004

Great Britain
Percentages

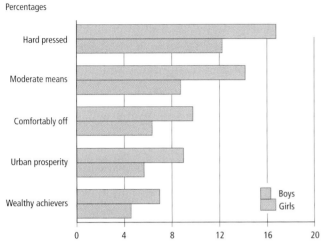

1 See Appendix, Part 7: Mental disorders.
2 Aged 5 to 16 years and living in private households.
3 See Appendix, Part 7: ACORN classification.

Source: Mental Health of Children and Young People Survey, Office for National Statistics

living in private households in Great Britain reported experiencing symptoms of a neurotic disorder ranging from the most common 'mixed anxiety and depressive disorder' to the less common 'phobia', in the seven days before interview for the Psychiatric Morbidity Survey. More women than men experienced neurotic disorder symptoms with the exception of

panic disorder for which rates were the same for men and women at 7 cases per 1,000.

Mental illness is a risk factor for suicide. Trends in suicide rates have varied by age group and sex in the UK over the last 35 years (Figure 7.18). Until 1988, men aged 65 and over had the highest suicide rates. In 1986 the suicide rate among men aged 65 and over peaked at 26.3 per 100,000 population and then fell, to 13.0 per 100,000 in 2006. In contrast, suicide rates for younger men rose over the period, in particular for those aged 25 to 44, for whom the suicide rate almost doubled from 13.6 per 100,000 in 1971 to a peak of 26.9 per 100,000 in 1998. The suicide rate among men in this age group has since declined, but in 2006 remained the highest of all age groups and of both sexes, at 21.3 per 100,000.

There is a clear difference in suicide rates between men and women. In 2006 the age-standardised rate for all men aged 15 and over in the UK was 17.4 per 100,000, three times that of women, at 5.3 per 100,000. Among women aged 45 and over, suicide rates more than halved between 1981 and 2006. For younger women the rates have remained fairly stable since the mid-1980s.

Analysis of data for England and Wales for the period 1999 to 2003 show suicide rates are highest in the most deprived areas (see Appendix, Part 7: Area deprivation). Among men aged 15 and over, the suicide rate for those living in the most deprived areas was 25.4 per 100,000, more than twice the rate of those in the least deprived areas (11.9 per 100,000).

7

Figure 7.18

Suicide rates:[1] by sex and age

United Kingdom
Rates per 100,000 population

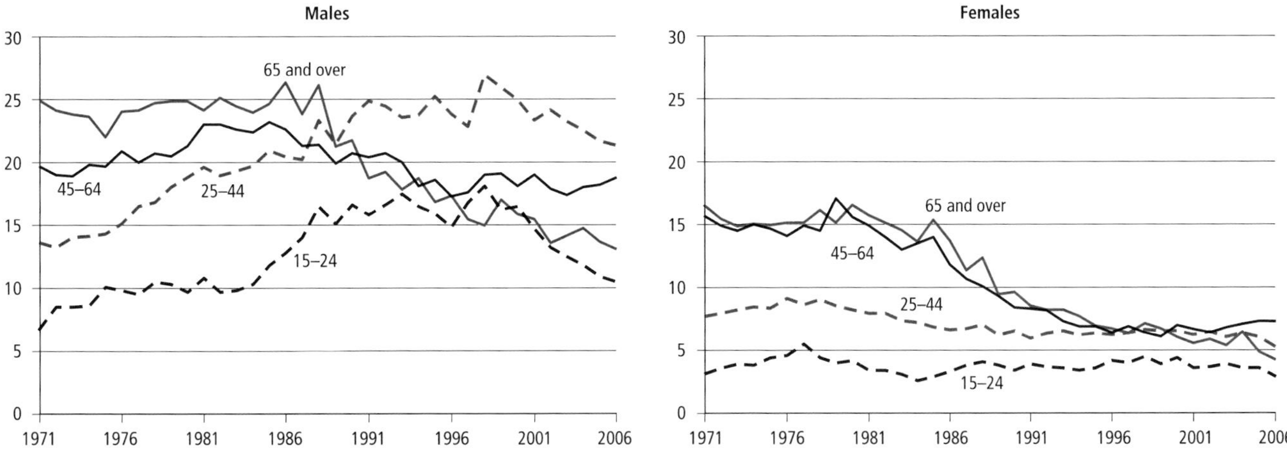

Males

30

25   65 and over

20

45–64   25–44

15

15–24

10

5

0
1971   1976   1981   1986   1991   1996   2001   2006

Females

30

25

20

65 and over

15   45–64

25–44

10

15–24

5

0
1971   1976   1981   1986   1991   1996   2001   2006

1 Includes deaths with a verdict of undetermined intent (open verdicts). Rates from 2002 are coded to ICD-10. See Appendix, Part 7: International Classification of Diseases. Rates are age-standardised to the European standard population. See Appendix, Part 7: Standardised rates, and European standard population.

Source: Office for National Statistics; General Register Office for Scotland; Northern Ireland Statistics and Research Agency

Although suicide rates among women were much lower than rates among men in all areas, the rate for women in the most deprived areas was more than twice that of women in the least deprived areas, at 7.4 per 100,000 compared with 3.6 per 100,000.

Sexual health

Since the late 1990s the increase in notifications of sexually transmitted diseases, especially among young people, has become a major public health concern across the UK. People who have unprotected sex and multiple sexual partners are at the greatest risk of contracting a sexually transmitted infection. In Great Britain during 2006/07 men between the ages of 20 and 49 were more likely than women to have had more than one sexual partner in the previous year (Table 7.19). Among both sexes, multiple sexual partnerships were most common among those below the age of 25. Men aged 20 to 24 were the most likely of all men under 50 to report having had more than one sexual partner in the previous year and men aged 16 to 19 were the most likely to have had none. Women aged 16 to 19 were the most likely of all women under 50 to report having more than one sexual partner in the previous year and also most likely to have had none.

For both men and women, the number that have had only one partner increases with age up to 44 years in women and up to

Table 7.19

Number of sexual partners[1] in the previous year: by sex and age, 2006/07

Great Britain   Percentages

	16–19	20–24	25–34	35–44	45–49
Men					
No partners	44	7	7	9	12
1 partner	27	48	77	83	83
2 or 3 partners	22	30	12	5	4
4 or more partners	7	14	5	4	1
All aged 16–49	100	100	100	100	100
Women					
No partners	34	6	7	9	16
1 partner	35	74	83	86	83
2 or 3 partners	23	17	8	3	1
4 or more partners	8	3	2	1	-
All aged 16–49	100	100	100	100	100

1 Self-reported in the 12 months prior to interview.

Source: Omnibus Survey, Office for National Statistics

Table 7.20

Reasons for using a condom:[1] by sex and age, 2006/07

Great Britain   Percentages

	16–24	25–34	35–49[2]
Men			
Prevent pregnancy	28	55	64
Prevent infection	4	4	8
Both reasons	67	38	27
Other reason	1	4	2
All aged 16–49	100	100	100
Women			
Prevent pregnancy	22	50	66
Prevent infection	11	6	7
Both reasons	63	41	23
Other reason	4	4	4
All aged 16–49	100	100	100

1 People currently in a sexual relationship or had one in last 12 months and had used a male condom in last 12 months.
2 Figures for 45 to 49 age group are merged with 35 to 44 age group due to inadequate sample size yielding unreliable figures.

Source: Omnibus Survey, Office for National Statistics

49 years in men, though for men, numbers are similar in both the 35 to 44 and 45 to 49 age groups. In both men and women the number with no partner falls rapidly after the age of 19 years. This in part reflects marital status among the older age groups. In 2006/07, 94 per cent of married or cohabiting men aged 16 to 69 and 97 per cent of married or cohabiting women aged 16 to 49 reported having only one sexual partner in the previous year.

For people who have multiple sexual partnerships, condom use can help reduce the risk of contracting sexually transmitted diseases. In 2006/07 in Great Britain, 85 per cent of men aged 16 to 69 and 77 per cent of women aged 16 to 49 who had more than one sexual partner in the previous year used a condom. This compared with 36 per cent of men and 45 per cent of women who had one partner. People's reasons for using a condom vary by age and whether or not they have multiple partners. In 2006/07, 67 per cent of men and 63 per cent of women aged 16 to 24 reported using a condom both to prevent infection and for contraceptive purposes (Table 7.20). Most people aged 25 and over used condoms only as a form of contraceptive, which reflects the likelihood that older people are in a monogamous relationship (see Table 7.19).

Map 7.21

Diagnoses of genital chlamydia: by sex and region,[1] 2006

Males

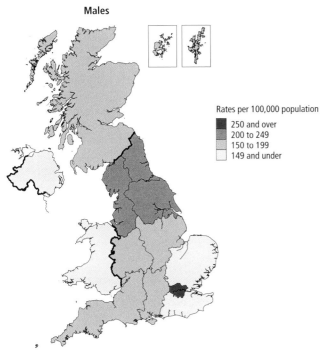

Rates per 100,000 population

- 250 and over
- 200 to 249
- 150 to 199
- 149 and under

Females

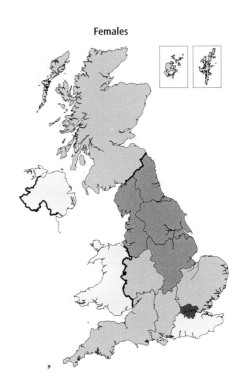

1 Regions in England are divided into the 10 Strategic Health Authorities.

Source: Health Protection Agency

Sexually transmitted infections (STIs), including HIV infection, are the most prevalent infectious disease problem in the UK. In 2006 around 621,312 diagnoses were made in genito-urinary medicine (GUM) clinics in the UK. Genital chlamydia was the most common STI diagnosed at 113,585 diagnoses in 2006.

Rates of diagnoses varied across the UK. London had the highest rates of genital chlamydial infections for both men and women in 2006, at 285 per 100,000 for men and 265 per 100,000 for women (Map 7.21). In the East Midlands, East of England, South Central and Yorkshire and the Humber, rates were higher among women than men. Northern Ireland had the lowest rates in the UK for both men and women, at less than 120 per 100,000. Wales had a rate of 125 per 100,000 for men and 127 per 100,000 for women and Scotland had a rate of 177 per 100,000 for men and 163 per 100,000 for women.

In 2006 uncomplicated gonorrhoea was the second most common bacterial STI diagnosed in GUM clinics in the UK. In contrast to genital chlamydia there has been a gradual decline in the number of diagnoses since 2003, and between 2005 and 2006, there was a 1.3 per cent decrease to 19,000. The highest rates of diagnoses in 2006 were in men aged 20 to 24 (188 per 100,000) and in women aged 16 to 19 (128 per 100,000). Men accounted for 72 per cent of the overall

diagnoses, with one-third of these occurring in men who have sex with men.

By the end of 2006, an estimated 73,000 people of all ages were living with HIV in the UK. Of these individuals approximately one-third remain undiagnosed. In 2006, 7,800 new HIV cases were diagnosed. The annual number of newly diagnosed persons has increased by 182 per cent between 1997 and 2006.

An estimated 4,700 men and 3,100 women were newly diagnosed with HIV in the UK in 2006 (see Appendix, Part 7: New HIV diagnoses database). HIV infections acquired heterosexually accounted for much of the rapid rise in the number of new HIV diagnoses in both men and women (4,750 in 2006 compared with 1,020 in 1997) although there was also an increase in the number of diagnoses among men who have sex with men, 2,700 in 2006 compared with 1,410 in 1997 (Figure 7.22 overleaf). Since 1999 the numbers of new HIV diagnoses among heterosexuals have outnumbered those among men who have sex with men. However, the 2,700 new diagnoses of HIV infection among men who have sex with men reported in 2006 was the highest ever, partly reflecting increased testing. Approximately three-fifths of newly diagnosed persons in 2006 who acquired their infection in the UK were heterosexual.

Figure 7.22

New HIV diagnoses[1] by year and route of transmission

United Kingdom

Thousands

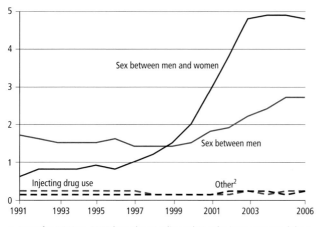

1 Data for 2003 to 2006 have been adjusted to take into account delays between diagnoses and reporting. See Appendix, Part 7: New HIV diagnoses database.
2 Other routes of infection include children infected through mother to child transmission, those infected through the receipt of blood or blood products, and routes of transmission not yet ascertained.

Source: Health Protection Agency

Of the estimated total number of new diagnoses in the UK in 2006, 3,650 were Black African (most of who were infected abroad) and 3,250 were White. African born men and women accounted for 35 per cent of the total number of adults living with HIV in 2006, with 31 per cent of those unaware of their infection. Of all heterosexually acquired HIV infections African born men and women accounted for 68 per cent of the total, with 61 per cent of those unaware of their infection.

HIV can also be acquired through injecting drugs. The number of diagnoses with drug injection being the most likely source of infection has remained relatively low in recent years, with 190 diagnoses in 2006. A small number of infections acquired by other routes such as blood transfusions (all acquired abroad) have remained low and constant over the last decade.

7

Chapter 8

Social protection

- In 2006/07, social security benefit expenditure in the UK was £134 billion, over twice the amount in 1978/79, in real terms. (Figure 8.1)

- In 2005/06 local authorities in England spent £19.3 billion on personal social services, 43 per cent was directed at older people and 25 per cent was directed at children and families. (Figure 8.4)

- The top 500 fundraising charities in the UK spent more than £3 billion on social protection in 2005/06. Children's charities spent the most at £669 million. (Figure 8.6)

- In 2006, 82 per cent of people questioned in Great Britain believed that waiting times for appointments with hospital consultants were in need of a lot of or some improvement. (Table 8.14)

- In 2005/06, 39 per cent of single male and 46 per cent of single female pensioners in the UK received income-related benefits compared with 21 per cent of pensioner couples. (Table 8.16)

- At March 2006 there were 32,100 children on child protection registers in the UK. Nearly half of all cases were due to neglect. (Table 8.20)

Social protection describes the help given to those who are in need or are at risk of hardship for reasons such as illness, low income, family circumstances or age. Central government, local authorities and private bodies (such as voluntary organisations) all provide help and support. Help may be provided through direct cash payments such as social security benefits or pensions; payments in kind such as free prescriptions; or the provision of services, for example through the National Health Service (NHS) (see Appendix, Part 8: Expenditure on social protection benefits). Unpaid care, such as that provided by family members, also plays a part. Social protection policies can also be used to reduce poverty and wealth gaps through the provision of services and means tested benefits and payments such as tax credits to low earners and assistance with childcare.

Expenditure

The Department for Work and Pensions (DWP) in Great Britain and the Department for Social Development in Northern Ireland are responsible for managing social security benefits, for example the state retirement pension, disability allowance, income support and pension credit. After allowing for inflation, social security benefit expenditure in the UK more than doubled from £66 billion in 1978/79 to £134 billion in 2006/07 (Figure 8.1). Spending on social security benefits can be influenced by the economic cycle, demographic changes and government policies. After falling between 1986/87 and 1989/90, there was a rapid increase in spending on social security benefits, rising to £117 billion in 1993/94 reflecting increases in the number of people who were unemployed or

economically inactive (see Glossary in Chapter 4: Labour market, page 47). Since 1994/95 the increase in social protection expenditure has been more gradual, this may be a result of a fall in unemployment and associated benefits and increases in expenditure on benefits aimed specifically at pensioners and children.

Of the £134 billion UK benefit expenditure in 2006/07, more than £119 billion was managed by the DWP in Great Britain. The majority of this (59 per cent) was for people of state pension age (age 65 and over for men and 60 and over for women), 26 per cent was directed at people of working age, 13 per cent was directed at those with disabilities and 2 per cent was for children. Expenditure directed at children comprises benefits provided to adults with responsibility for children. These include income support, disability allowances, housing and council tax benefits but exclude child benefit payments. Child benefit payments are administered and paid by HM Revenue and Customs (HMRC) and totalled £10.1 billion in the UK in 2006/07. In addition to benefits, financial assistance has also been provided by HMRC since 1999/2000 in the form of tax credits. Expenditure on tax credits reached £18.7 billion in 2006/07 and £1 billion was paid in war pensions by the Veterans Agency. In Northern Ireland, the Department for Social Development spent nearly £4 billion on pensions and income-related pension credit; contributory and disability benefits; job seekers allowance and income support; and social fund payments such as winter fuel payments. Of the £4 billion, £432m was spent on housing benefits and assistance with domestic rates. Around half (47 per cent) of the remaining £3.5 billion was directed at those over pension age, 28 per cent was directed at those of working age and 25 per cent was directed at those with disabilities and carers.

Information about expenditure on social protection within the EU is collated by Eurostat as part of the European System of integrated Social Protection Statistics (ESSPROS). The main components of expenditure on social protection benefits which protect people against common sources of hardship include: government expenditure on benefits, social services, health services and personal social services; sick pay paid by employers; and payments made from occupational and personal pension schemes.

Total UK expenditure on social protection as defined by ESSPROS in 2005/06 was £325 billion. This was equivalent to 26 per cent of gross domestic product (GDP) at market prices or around £5,400 per person, however, social protection is not spread evenly over the whole population. Expenditure on benefits for old age and 'survivors' (defined as those whose entitlement derives from their relationship to a deceased

Figure 8.1

Social security benefit expenditure in real terms[1]

United Kingdom
£ billion at 2006/07 prices

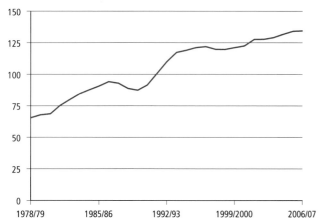

1 Adjusted to 2006/07 prices using the GDP market prices deflator (third quarter 2007).

Source: Department for Work and Pensions; HM Revenue and Customs; Veterans Agency; Department for Social Development, Northern Ireland

8

Figure 8.2

Expenditure on social protection benefits in real terms:[1] by function

United Kingdom

£ billion at 2005/06 prices

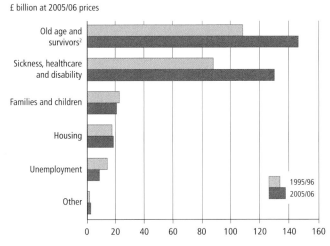

1 Adjusted to 2005/06 prices using the GDP market prices deflator.
2 Survivors are those whose entitlement derives from their relationship to a deceased person (for example, widows, widowers and orphans).

Source: Office for National Statistics

person, for example, widows, widowers and orphans) accounted for 45 per cent of the UK total (Figure 8.2). Spending on sickness, healthcare and disability accounted for 40 per cent, and that on families and children accounted for 6 per cent. In real terms, after allowing for inflation, there was a 30 per cent rise in total social protection expenditure between 1995/96 and 2005/06. Over this period, expenditure on sickness, healthcare and disability increased by 48 per cent and spending on benefits for old age and survivors increased by 36 per cent. Included within expenditure on old age and survivors are payments for disability and income support. These payments are included in this category because old age or survivors status is the primary reason for the expenditure. Expenditure on families and children showed an 8 per cent decrease to £20 billion, although it remained above that of housing, unemployment and other expenditure. Spending on unemployment showed a steady decline over the period from £13.9 billion to £8.4 billion, with the exception of 2001/02 when it rose to £10.4 billion before falling again to £8.2 billion the following year.

In order for meaningful comparisons to be made across the countries in the EU, levels of expenditure can be adjusted to take account of differences in the level of prices for goods and services within each country. The adjustments are made using 'purchasing power parities' (PPPs) which are currency conversion rates that convert economic indicators, expressed in national currencies, to a common artificial currency called the purchasing power standard (PPS). The PPS takes account of price level differences and allows comparisons to be made

between the relative price or expenditure differences between countries. Reasons for differences lie in variations in social protection systems, demographic structures, unemployment rates or other social, institutional and economic factors.

In 2004 UK spending on social protection was equivalent to PPS 7,000 per person, above the EU-25 average of PPS 6,200 per person (Figure 8.3). Among the EU-25 member states, Luxembourg spent the most when expressed as per head of the resident population, at PPS 12,200. However, a large proportion of benefits in Luxembourg are paid to citizens living outside the country (primarily on healthcare, pensions and family allowances) which inflates the per head figure. Sweden and Denmark spent the next highest on social protection at PPS 8,800 and PPS 8,500 per head respectively. Of the EU-15 member states, Spain and Portugal spent the least, at around PPS 4,400 and PPS 4,100 per head. Of the ten countries that joined the EU in May 2004, Slovenia spent the most on social protection per head, at PPS 4,400, while Latvia spent the least, at PPS 1,200.

Figure 8.3

Expenditure[1] on social protection per head: EU-25 comparison, 2004

PPS thousand per head

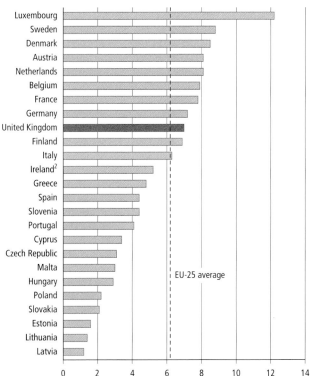

1 Before deduction of tax, where applicable. Tax credits are generally excluded. Figures are purchasing power standard per inhabitant. Includes administrative and other expenditure incurred by social protection schemes. See Appendix, Part 6: Purchasing Power Parities.
2 Excludes funded occupational pension schemes for private sector employees.

Source: Eurostat

Figure 8.4

Local authority personal social services expenditure:[1] by recipient group, 2005/06

England

Percentages

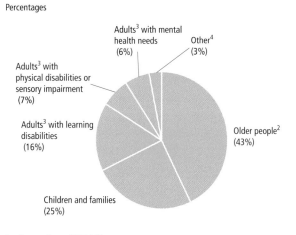

Total expenditure: £19.3 billion

1 All figures include overhead costs. Expenditure excludes capital charges, income from joint arrangements and other income.
2 Aged 65 and over including older mentally ill.
3 Adults aged under 65.
4 Includes expenditure on asylum seekers and overall service strategy.

Source: The Information Centre for health and social care

In 2005/06 local authorities in England spent £19.3 billion on personal social services (Figure 8.4). This includes expenditure on home help and home care, looked after children, children on child protection registers and foster care. Nearly £8.4 billion was spent on older people (those aged 65 and over), the largest single portion at 43 per cent. Spending on children and families accounted for 25 per cent of total personal social services expenditure at £4.8 billion. Combined spending on adults under 65 with learning difficulties, physical disabilities or mental health needs accounted for 29 per cent (£5.5 billion). Total expenditure on personal social services increased by 6 per cent in cash terms compared with 2004/05, with expenditure on adults with physical disabilities showing the largest increase (10 per cent) over the period.

The British Social Attitudes Survey includes questions on attitudes towards various aspects of welfare expenditure. In 2006 more than one-third (36 per cent) of adults aged 18 and over in Great Britain thought that the government should spend more money on welfare benefits for the poor, even if this led to higher taxes (Table 8.5). Those employed in semi-routine and routine occupations, traditionally the lower paying occupations, were most in favour (40 per cent). Employers in small organisations or those working on their own account were least in favour and were the only group where a smaller proportion agreed than disagreed (30 per cent and 38 per cent respectively). This group also contained the highest

Table 8.5

Attitudes towards extra spending on social benefits, 2006[1]

Great Britain

Percentages

	Agree	Neither agree nor disagree	Disagree
Managerial & professional occupations	35	30	35
Intermediate occupations	31	39	30
Employers in small organisations; own account work	30	32	38
Lower supervisory & technical occupations	38	39	23
Semi-routine & routine occupations	40	35	25
Total[2]	36	35	30

1 Respondents aged 18 and over were asked 'Please tick a box to show how much you agree or disagree that the government should spend more money on welfare benefits for the poor, even if it leads to higher taxes.' Excludes those who responded 'don't know' or did not answer.
2 Includes 'never had job' and 'not classifiable'.

Source: British Social Attitudes Survey, National Centre for Social Research

Figure 8.6

Expenditure on social protection by the top 500 charities:[1] by category,[2] 2005/06

United Kingdom

£ million

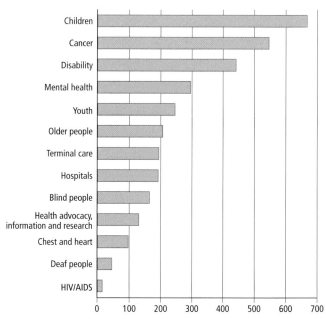

1 Charities Aid Foundation top 500 fundraising charities. Direct charitable expenditure.
2 Category, also known as cause, is self-classified by charity.

Source: Charity Trends 2007, Charities Aid Foundation

proportion of all groups of those who disagreed with the question.

Charities are another source of social protection assistance in the UK, although this assistance is not counted in ESSPROS and is small compared with total social protection expenditure. The top 500 fundraising charities in the UK, based on voluntary donated income generated during the year, spent nearly £3.3 billion on social protection in 2005/06, an increase of 7.6 per cent (£231 million) from 2004/05. Of these, children's charities spent the most on social protection (£669 million, or 21 per cent of the total), followed by cancer related charities (£547 million) and those for people with disabilities (£443 million) (Figure 8.6) (see also Chapter 13: Lifestyles and social participation, Figure 13.17).

Carers and caring

The *Community Care Reforms Act* was introduced in 1993 to enable more people to continue to live in their own homes as independently as possible. Services are offered by the local authority and may involve routine household tasks within or outside the home, personal care of the client or respite care in support of the client's regular carers. Local authority home care services assist people – principally those with physical disabilities (including frailty associated with ageing), dementia, mental health problems and learning difficulties – to continue living in their own home and to function as independently as possible. The number of home help hours purchased or provided by local authorities in England increased between 1993 and 2006 (Figure 8.7). In September 2006, local authorities provided or purchased 3.7 million hours of home care services during the survey week, compared with 3.6 million hours in September 2005 and 2.5 million hours in September 1996, an increase of almost 50 per cent over the decade to 2006.

There has also been a gradual change in the way in which these services are sourced. In 1996 the majority of home help contact hours in England were directly provided by local authorities (64 per cent); in 2006 this had fallen to 25 per cent. Instead, an increasing number of hours of care have been purchased from the independent sector (both private and voluntary), rising more than threefold over the decade, from 0.9 million in 1996 to 2.8 million in 2006 when it was the main source of provision. Of households where some form of home help or home care contact is provided, the proportion receiving more than five hours of home help or home care contact and six or more visits per week, has increased steadily from 21 per cent in 1995 to 50 per cent in 2006. This reflects an increased focus by councils on raising the number and intensity of home care visits. The number of households

Figure 8.7

Number of contact hours of home help and home care:[1] by provider

England

Millions

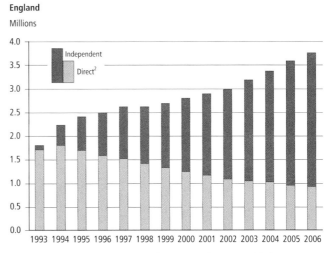

1 During a survey week in September. Contact hours provided or purchased by local authorities. Households receiving home care purchased with a direct payment are excluded.
2 Directly provided by local authorities.

Source: The Information Centre for health and social care

receiving low intensity care (two hours or less of home help or home care and one visit per week) as a proportion of all households receiving care has fallen from 32 per cent in 1995 to 12 per cent in 2006. Of those receiving intensive home care, 75 per cent were aged 65 and over. Of the remainder, in the 18 to 64 age group, people with physical disabilities (12 per cent) and people with learning disabilities (10 per cent) were the next largest client groups.

The Information Centre for health and social care conducts regular user experience surveys into the services received in England. In 2005/06 clients aged 65 and over receiving home care services were asked how satisfied they were with the level of care they received. The combined proportion of those who were either extremely satisfied or very satisfied was 59 per cent compared to 57 per cent when the same survey was carried out in 2002/03. More than one-third (35 per cent) stated that they were very satisfied in 2005/06, while around one-quarter (24 per cent) were extremely satisfied (Table 8.8 overleaf). Of those responding 3 per cent expressed dissatisfaction while 38 per cent were either quite satisfied or neither satisfied nor dissatisfied. In the same survey, around two-thirds (65 per cent) of clients felt their care worker always did what they wanted and more than one-quarter (27 per cent) nearly always did, while 1 per cent felt their care worker never did what they wanted. Asked whether they felt their care worker came at a time that suited them, the majority (86 per cent) felt that they always or usually did so, compared with 89 per cent in 2002/03.

8

Table 8.8

Older people's[1] satisfaction with level of home care, 2005/06

England		Percentages
	2002/03	2005/06
Extremely satisfied	25	24
Very satisfied	32	35
Quite satisfied	31	32
Neither	6	6
Quite dissatisfied	3	2
Very dissatisfied	1	1
Extremely dissatisfied	1	1

1 Aged 65 and over.

Source: The Information Centre for health and social care; Department of Health

A study by the University of Leeds carried out on behalf of Carers UK, which looked at calculating the value of unpaid care estimated that carers, both registered and unregistered carried out £87 billion worth of economic activity in the UK in 2005/06. In England in 2005/06 there were 284,000 people registered as providing care and of these, half received support services including breaks and other assistance to help them in their caring duties (Table 8.9). Councils provide support services to carers to assist them in their caring role and help to maintain their own health and well-being. These support services include breaks for the carer, emotional support, driving lessons, moving and handling classes, and access to training for the carer. Although there was almost an even split between carers receiving support services and those receiving information and advice, there were large differences between carer groups.

Table 8.9

Number of carers receiving services: by client type of the person cared for, 2005/06[1]

England			Thousands
	Support services	Information only	All carers
Physical disability	95	110	205
Mental health	23	18	41
Learning disability	16	10	26
Vulnerable people	6	3	9
Substance misuse	2	1	2
All client groups	142	142	284

1 Services supplied by local authorities.

Source: The Information Centre for health and social care

Carers with responsibility for people with problems relating to substance misuse were more likely than carers in any other group to receive support services other than information only (79 per cent), followed by those caring for vulnerable people (67 per cent). This may reflect the fact that these were the two smallest groups of carers, constituting 4 per cent of all carers between them. The largest group, with 72 per cent of all carers comprised those caring for people with physical disabilities. Just under half of the carers in this group (46 per cent) received support services and the remainder received information only. This was the only group of carers where more received information and advice than received support services and help. However, the number of those caring for people with physical disabilities and receiving support services (95,000) was more than twice the total number of carers of people in the mental health category (41,000) receiving any kind of support.

Sick and disabled people

The Government provides a number of financial benefits for sick and disabled people. Disability living allowance (DLA) is a benefit for people who are disabled, have personal care needs, mobility needs, or both, and who are aged under 65. Attendance allowance (AA) is paid to people who become ill or disabled on or after their 65th birthday and because of the extent or severity of their physical or mental condition, need someone to help with their personal care. In 2006/07 there were 4.4 million people in receipt of DLA and/or AA in Great Britain, compared with 4.0 million in 2003/04. This increase reflects changes in entitlement conditions for benefits, demographic changes and increased take-up.

In 2006/07, 2.9 million people in Great Britain were in receipt of DLA and 1.5 million received AA (Table 8.10). Both these figures have increased steadily since 2003/04 by around 10 per cent. The most common condition suffered by people receiving the allowances, was arthritis; 502,000 sufferers received DLA and 477,000 received AA. Other common conditions for recipients of DLA included 'other mental health causes' such as psychosis and dementia, learning difficulties and back ailments. Common conditions for people receiving AA included frailty, heart disease and mental health causes. There were around twice as many women as men in receipt of AA, while receipt of DLA was evenly split.

Incapacity benefit (IB) and severe disablement allowance (SDA) are benefits for people of working age who are unable to work because of illness and/or disability, and can be claimed in addition to other benefits. The number of people receiving IB or SDA or those benefits they replaced, such as sickness benefit

Table 8.10

Recipients of selected benefits for sick and disabled people[1]

Great Britain

Thousands

	2003/04	2004/05	2005/06	2006/07
Incapacity Benefit				
Incapacity benefit only	829	818	777	737
Severe disability allowance[1]	309	296	283	271
Incapacity benefit and disability living allowance	518	526	532	535
Incapacity benefit and income support	673	645	625	614
Incapacity benefit, income support and disability living allowance	448	467	480	496
Incapacity and other benefits[2]	2,819	2,800	2,747	2,704
Income support only	876	840	824	828
Attendance allowance/ disability living allowance[3]	3,989	4,124	4,246	4,365
Attendance allowance[4]	1,364	1,411	1,461	1,504
Disability living allowance[4]	2,625	2,713	2,786	2,861

1 See Appendix, Part 8: Expenditure on social protection benefits. At February each year.
2 Includes other benefit combinations not listed here.
3 People receiving both Attendance Allowance and Disability Living Allowance are counted twice.
4 Includes those in receipt of an allowance but excludes those where payment is currently suspended (for example, because of a stay in hospital).

Source: Work and Pensions Longitudinal Study, Department for Work and Pensions

and invalidity benefit, has fallen steadily between 2003/04 and 2006/07 from 2.8 million claimants to 2.7 million. While the overall trend for IB and IB plus other benefits has fallen some categories have seen small increases. Numbers for those in receipt of IB and DLA have increased by 17,000 to 535,000 between 2003/04 and 2006/07 and those claiming IB, DLA and income support have increased by 48,000 to 496,000 over the same period.

Income support is a means tested benefit payable to people of working age on low incomes and may be paid on top of other benefits or income. Between 2003/04 and 2006/07, there was a decline in the number claiming income support only of 48,000 (5 per cent).

In addition to financial assistance, people who are sick and disabled are provided with a range of health services through the National Health Service (NHS). Primary care services include those provided by general medical practitioners (GPs), dental

practitioners and opticians, and by the NHS Direct telephone, website and digital TV service in England and Wales and NHS 24 in Scotland. Secondary care services, such as NHS hospitals, provide acute and specialist services to treat conditions that normally cannot be dealt with by primary care services.

The NHS is increasingly using technology in patient care. NHS Direct, the telephone helpline launched in England and Wales in 1998, provides access to health advice and information. In 2007 the service handled more than 22,000 calls a day, or more than 8 million calls a year. The NHS Direct Online website provides evidence-based health information. Since its launch in December 1999 usage has increased steadily year on year. In 2001/02 the average number of visits per month to the website was 169,000. By 2006/07 this had risen to 1.75 million visits. This may in part be due to increased access to the Internet; in 2002, 11 million homes had access to the Internet, by 2007 this had risen to 14.9 million (see also Chapter 13: Lifestyles and social participation, Table 13.4). The most popular section of the website, attracting 272,000 visits in September 2007, was the health encyclopaedia and the most searched for topics were diabetes, irritable bowel syndrome, back pain and pregnancy. The second most popular section of the website, with 268,000 visits, was the self-help guide. This takes visitors through a series of questions and answers about health issues and offers advice on what to do for the best. Versions of the service have also been launched in Wales and Scotland. NHS Direct Interactive is another service, available via satellite or Freeview to more than 17 million homes with access to a digital television service, or 68 per cent of all homes with a television (see also Chapter 13: Lifestyles and social participation, Figure 13.2).

In 2006 more than 1.2 million full-time equivalent staff were employed in NHS hospital and community health services in the UK, offering secondary care. Around 500,000 of these were nursing, midwifery and health visiting staff; 105,000 were medical and dental staff; and 620,000 were other non-medical staff, such as therapists, administrative support, management and infrastructure support. A further 279,000 people were employed in personal social services such as home carers, residential care staff, social workers and administrative support. The number of full-time equivalent staff throughout health and personal social services has remained broadly the same in 2005 and 2006 in the UK. England recorded a small decrease in numbers, while Northern Ireland, Wales and Scotland recorded small increases.

At September 2006 there were more than 40,000 GPs in the UK compared with more than 35,000 in September 2000,

8

Table 8.11

NHS general, dental and ophthalmic practitioners[1]

United Kingdom   Thousands

	2000	2003	2006
GPs[2]	35.2	37.2	40.2
Dental practitioners[3]	21.9	23.1	25.3
Opthalmic practitioners[4]	10.1	10.5	10.9

1 At 30 September. Dental and ophthalmic data for 2006 for England as
   at 31 March 2007.
2 Excludes registrars and retainers. See Appendix, Part 8: General
   practitioners.
3 Dental practitioners include principals, assistants and vocational
   dental practitioners. Salaried dentists, hospital dental services and
   community dental services are excluded.
4 Optometrists and ophthalmic medical practitioners contracted to
   perform NHS sight tests.

*Source: The Information Centre for health and social care; Welsh
Assembly Government; NHS in Scotland; Central Services Agency,
Northern Ireland*

an increase of 14 per cent (Table 8.11). Over the same period
the number of NHS dental practitioners increased from
around 22,000 to just over 25,000, an increase of almost
16 per cent, and the number of ophthalmic practitioners
increased from 10,000 to 11,000, a 7 per cent increase.
Average GP patient lists decreased during this period, with
England showing the largest decrease in list size, from an
average 1,795 in 2000 to 1,610 in 2006. Northern Ireland
showed the smallest decrease, from an average 1,673 in 2000
to 1,631 in 2006. Each of the countries within the UK
experienced a fall in registrations with dentists over the same
period, with Scotland recording the largest fall, from an
average 1,305 in 2000 to 1,062 in 2006.

An out-patient is a person who is seen by a hospital
consultant for treatment or advice but who is non-resident at
the hospital. In 2006 in Great Britain, 13 per cent of males and
15 per cent of females reported visiting an out-patient or
casualty department at least once in the preceding three
months, when questioned as part of the General Household
Survey. For females, with the exception of girls aged
under five, the likelihood of having been an out-patient
generally increased with age (Figure 8.12). Females aged
between 5 and 15 were least likely to have been out-patients
and those aged 75 and over most likely. In contrast among
males, those in the 16 to 44 age group were least likely to
have been out-patients followed by those in the 5 to 15
category. Men aged 45 to 64 were as likely as boys aged
under 5 to be an out-patient. Once men are aged 65 and older,
the instance of becoming an out-patient continues to increase
with age.

Figure 8.12

Out-patient or casualty department attendance:[1] by sex and age, 2006[2]

Great Britain

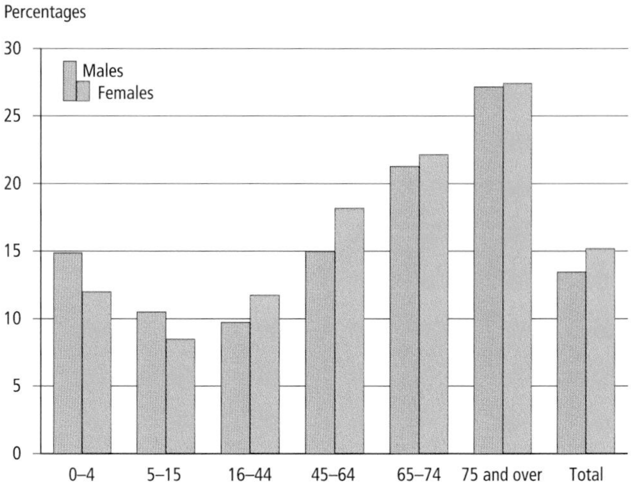

Percentages

1 In the three months before interview.
2 See Appendix, Part 2: General Household Survey.

*Source: General Household Survey (Longitudinal), Office for National
Statistics*

An in-patient is a person who is admitted to hospital and
spends at least one night there. In the UK between 1991/92
and 2005/06, the number of finished consultant episodes
(those where the patient has completed a period of care
under one consultant which included a stay in hospital)
classified as 'acute' doubled to reach almost 14 million while
the number of in-patient episodes per bed more than doubled
from 51.4 to 108.7 (Table 8.13).

The number of finished consultant episodes for the mentally ill
has fallen in recent years and in 2005/06 was 34 per cent
lower than in 1991/92. The number of in-patient episodes per
bed remained steady between 1991/92 and 2005/06,
recording a small rise from 4.5 to 5.2. Over the same period
the number of in-patient episodes per bed for people with
learning disabilities doubled from 2.4 to 5.1.

The British Social Attitudes Survey includes questions on
attitudes towards various aspects of NHS care and provides
insights into the general public's views on services. Satisfaction
levels with NHS hospitals were generally higher in 2006 than in
2004. In 2006, 61 per cent of adults in Great Britain aged
18 and over felt that waiting times for ambulances after 999 calls
were satisfactory or very good, based on their own experience
or from what they had heard (Table 8.14). This was an increase
of 6 percentage points from 2004. Opinions regarding the
general condition of hospital buildings were also higher than
in 2004, 45 per cent believing them to be satisfactory or very
good, compared with 37 per cent in 2004. There was little

Table 8.13

NHS in-patient activity for sick and disabled people[1]

United Kingdom

	1991/92	2001/02	2002/03	2003/04	2004/05	2005/06
Acute[2]						
Finished consultant episodes (thousands)	6,974	12,170	12,476	12,877	13,209	13,959
In-patient episodes per available bed (numbers)	51.4	94.6	96.9	99.0	101.8	108.7
Mean duration of stay (days)	6.0	3.5	3.5	3.5	3.3	3.1
Mentally ill						
Finished consultant episodes (thousands)	281	259	255	238	232	185
In-patient episodes per available bed (numbers)	4.5	6.6	6.5	6.2	6.2	5.2
Mean duration of stay[3] (days)	114.8	34.2	34.2	40.7	42.5	50.1
People with learning disabilities						
Finished consultant episodes (thousands)	62	41	42	34	31	25
In-patient episodes per available bed (numbers)	2.4	5.7	6.8	5.4	5.7	5.1
Mean duration of stay[3] (days)	544.0	105.8	94.6	53.0	71.7	101.6

1 See Appendix, Part 8: In-patient activity. Data for England for patients in acute category have been revised from 2001/02 onwards.
2 General patients on wards, excluding elderly, maternity and neonatal cots in maternity units.
3 Scotland data unavailable from 2001/02 onwards.

Source: The Information Centre for health and social care; Welsh Assembly Government; NHS in Scotland; Department of Health, Social Services and Public Safety, Northern Ireland

Table 8.14

Satisfaction with NHS hospitals and GPs in their area, 2006[1]

Great Britain   Percentages

	In need of a lot of improvement	In need of some improvement	Satisfactory	Very good
Hospital Services				
Waiting times for ambulance after 999 call	8	31	49	12
General conditions of hospital buildings	19	36	38	7
Waiting area for out-patients	12	34	50	4
Waiting areas in A&E	20	36	40	4
Waiting times for seeing doctor in A&E	35	44	19	2
Waiting time for appointments with hospital consultants	41	41	17	2
Waiting times in out-patient departments	20	50	28	1
Hospital waiting lists for non-emergency operations	33	45	21	1
GP services				
Waiting areas at GP surgeries	5	16	64	14
GP appointment system	15	34	39	11
Amount of time GP gives to each patient	11	25	52	12

1 Respondents aged 18 and over were asked 'From what you know or have heard, please tick a box for each of the items below to show whether you think the National Health Service in your area is, on the whole, satisfactory or in need of improvement.' Excludes those who responded 'don't know' or did not answer.

Source: British Social Attitudes Survey, National Centre for Social Research

8

change in opinions on waiting times for appointments with hospital consultants and waiting times to see a doctor in accident and emergency where 82 per cent and 79 per cent respectively felt they were in need of a lot or some improvement. Hospital waiting lists for non-emergency operations were felt to be the next in need of improvement at 78 per cent, unchanged from 2004. Opinions regarding GP services in 2006 were similar to 2004. Those saying that GP waiting areas and amount of time given to each patient by GPs were either satisfactory or very good were both similar to 2004, at 78 per cent and 64 per cent respectively. The proportion expressing the same opinion of GP appointment systems remained unchanged at 50 per cent.

Older people

In the UK, much of central government expenditure on social protection for older people is through payment of the state retirement pension. Nearly everyone over state pension age (age 65 for men and 60 for women) receives this pension. Some also receive income-related state benefits, such as council tax or housing benefit. However, there is an increasing emphasis on people making their own provision for retirement, and this can be through an occupational, personal or stakeholder pension (see also Chapter 5: Income and wealth, Table 5.8).

In 2005/06, 55 per cent of single male pensioners in the UK had an occupational pension in addition to the state pension, compared with 49 per cent of single female pensioners and 56 per cent of pensioner couples (Table 8.15). Much smaller proportions of pensioners had a personal pension as well as the state pension, 9 per cent of single male pensioners and 3 per cent of single female pensioners. The lower percentages for women may be in part because women traditionally have lower employment rates than men (see also Chapter 4: Labour market, Figure 4.4) and were also less likely to have been in pensionable jobs. Women were also less likely to have been self-employed and therefore to have had a personal pension.

The state retirement pension in the UK at April 2007 was £87.30 per week, based on a claimant's own, or late partner's, National Insurance (NI) contributions. Women who have not worked or do not have sufficient NI contributions of their own can claim a pension of £52.30 based upon their husband's NI contributions. There is also a range of state benefits available for older people in the UK including pension credit, which replaced the minimum income guarantee in 2003. Pension credit provided a minimum income of £119.05 a week for single pensioners and £181.70 for pensioner couples in 2007/08. In addition, it provided a means tested income top up for those saving towards retirement where either a single person, or one or both of the partners in a couple, was aged over 65. Single pensioners entitled to the top up can receive an additional £19.05 a week, and pensioner couples could be entitled to an additional £25.26.

Single pensioners are more likely than pensioner couples to receive any type of income-related benefit. In 2005/06,

Table 8.15

Pension receipt: by type of pensioner unit,[1] 2005/06

United Kingdom

Percentages

	Pensioner couples	Single male pensioners	Single female pensioners	All pensioners
State retirement pension[2]/minimum income guarantee/pension credit only	21	31	43	32
Plus				
Occupational, but not personal pension[3]	56	55	49	53
Personal, but not occupational pension[3]	10	9	3	7
Both occupational and personal pension[3]	8	3	2	5
Other combinations, no retirement pension/ minimum income guarantee/pension credit	2	0	1	1
None	3	2	2	2
All people	100	100	100	100

1 A pensioner unit is defined as either a single person over state pension age (65 for men, 60 for women), or a couple where one or more is over state pension age.
2 Includes receipt of other contributory benefits. See Appendix, Part 8: Pension schemes.
3 Occupational and personal pensions include survivor's benefits.

Source: Pensioners' Incomes Series, Department for Work and Pensions

Table 8.16

Receipt of selected social security benefits among pensioners: by type of benefit unit,[1] 2005/06

United Kingdom   Percentages

	Single		Couple
	Men	Women	Couple
Income-related			
Council tax benefit	34	40	18
Income support/minimum income guarantee/pension credit	22	31	13
Housing benefit	23	24	9
Any income-related benefit[2]	39	46	21
Non-income-related[3]			
Incapacity or disablement benefits[4]	19	23	26
Any non-income related benefits[2]	97	97	100
Any benefit[2]	99	99	100

1 Pensioner benefit units. See Appendix, Part 8: Benefit units.
2 Includes benefits not listed here. Components do not add up to the total as each benefit unit may receive more than one benefit.
3 Includes state retirement pension.
4 Includes incapacity benefit, disability living allowance (care and mobility components), severe disablement allowance, industrial injuries disability benefit, war disablement pension and attendance allowance.

Source: Family Resources Survey, Department for Work and Pensions

39 per cent of single male pensioners and 46 per cent of single female pensioners in the UK received income-related benefits, compared with 21 per cent of pensioner couples (Table 8.16). Among single pensioners, a greater proportion of women than men were in receipt of income support or pension credit (31 per cent compared with 22 per cent). For pensioner couples the proportion was lower, at 13 per cent. Compared with 2004/05, these proportions remained steady, with single female pensioners and pensioner couples both showing a 1 per cent increase in 2005/06 while single male pensioners remained the same. Between one-fifth and one-quarter of pensioners received disability-related benefits, whether single or in a couple. Again, there was little change between 2004/05 and 2005/06.

Families and children

The Government provides a number of benefits for families with children in the UK. They include income-related benefits paid to low income families such as housing and council tax benefit and income support; and non-income-related benefits such as child benefit and incapacity or disablement benefits. In 2005/06, 90 per cent of lone parents with dependent

children in the UK and 57 per cent of couples with children received income-related benefits. Among lone parents with dependent children, 69 per cent received working families tax credit or income support compared with 13 per cent of couples with dependent children (Table 8.17). This may reflect the employment status of lone mothers, who head the majority of lone-parent families and are less likely to be employed than mothers with a partner. According to the 2005 Families and Children Study (FACS 2005) 42 per cent of lone mothers did not work compared with 28 per cent of mothers with a partner. The study showed that the employment gap between lone-mother families and couples has reduced since FACS 2004 when the number of lone mothers not in work was 48 per cent while the figures for mothers with a partner are unchanged.

Childcare can be provided informally by grandparents and other relatives, older children, partners, ex-partners and friends. In 2005, more than one-third, (37 per cent) of all families in Great Britain where the mother was in work relied on informal childcare. The most common source, for both couples and lone parents, was grandparents (29 per cent and 33 per cent respectively). Other relatives provided childcare for

Table 8.17

Receipt of selected social security benefits among families: by type of benefit unit,[1] 2005/06

United Kingdom   Percentages

	Lone parent with dependent children	Couple with dependent children
Income-related		
Council tax benefit	46	7
Housing benefit	44	6
Working families tax credit, income support or pension credit	69	13
Jobseeker's allowance	1	2
Any income-related benefit	90	57
Non-income related		
Child benefit	97	97
Incapacity or disablement benefits[2]	9	8
Any non-income related benefits	97	97
Any benefit or tax credit[3]	98	97

1 Families below pension age. See Appendix, Part 8: Benefit units.
2 Incapacity benefit, disability living allowance (care and mobility components), severe disablement allowance, industrial injuries disability benefit, war disablement pension, attendance allowance and disabled persons tax credit.
3 Includes all benefits not listed here. Components do not add up to the total as each benefit unit may receive more than one benefit.

Source: Family Resources Survey, Department for Work and Pensions

Table 8.18

Childcare arrangements for children with working mothers: by family characteristics, 2005

Great Britain

Percentages[1]

	Formal childcare[2]	Informal childcare[3]	Childcare not required
Family type			
Lone parent	26	45	41
Couple	28	36	49
Family type working status			
Lone parent: 1 to 15 hours	11	41	53
Lone parent: 16 hours and above	28	46	40
Couple – both: 16 hours and above	31	38	45
Couple – one only: 16 hours and above	19	28	61
Age of child			
0–4 years	48	47	27
5–10 years	25	42	45
11–15 years	4	20	77

1 Percentages do not add up to 100 per cent as respondents could give more than one answer.
2 Includes nurseries/crèches, nursery schools, playgroups, registered childminders, after school clubs/breakfast clubs, and holiday play schemes.
3 Provided by the main respondent's partners/ex-partners, parents/parents-in-law, other relatives and friends, and older children.

Source: Families and Children Study, Department for Work and Pensions

6 per cent of both couples and lone parents. Lone parents were more likely to rely on ex-partners for childcare (13 per cent) than couples (1 per cent).

As children get older, use of formal childcare in Great Britain decreases. In 2005 nearly one-half (48 per cent) of children under five whose mothers worked were looked after under formal childcare arrangements (Table 8.18). This fell to one-quarter (25 per cent) for children aged five to ten, when children are of primary school age, and decreased further when they reached secondary education age. Around seven in ten children aged under five with working mothers in Great Britain received some form of childcare in 2005. Use of informal childcare decreases more slowly with age than use of formal childcare, with around four in ten children between the ages of five and ten and around two in ten children between ages eleven and fifteen receiving this form of childcare.

The hours per week that parents work may determine or be determined by the type of childcare used. In 2005 in Great Britain, one-quarter of working lone mothers used formal childcare and around half used informal childcare. For couples where only one parent worked 16 or more hours a week, around one-fifth used formal childcare. This may be because the other parent was at home looking after the child. Formal types of childcare were less likely than informal types to be used when one or more parents worked less than 16 hours

per week. Parental perceptions of the affordability of local childcare provision varied between lone parents and couples. In the FACS 2005, 28 per cent of lone parents in Great Britain described their local childcare provisions as 'not at all affordable' compared with nearly one-quarter (23 per cent) of couples. A further 35 per cent of lone parents found the provisions 'fairly affordable' compared with 44 per cent of couples. Couples where both worked 16 hours or more per week were more likely than those where either partner worked between 1 and 15 hours to consider local childcare to be 'fairly affordable' – 47 per cent compared with 42 per cent. Most parents rated the quality of childcare in their local area as either very or fairly good, 59 per cent of couples and 51 per cent of lone parents; 2 per cent of couples and 5 per cent of lone parents felt that the quality was fairly or very poor. Around one in ten parents said the childcare was neither good nor poor; 9 per cent of couples and 12 per cent of lone parents. The remainder, 29 per cent of couples and 33 per cent of lone parents answered don't know.

Childcare is essential in supporting parents to take up or return to employment. There is a government target to increase the take-up of formal childcare places by lower-income families in England, to 735,000 by 2008 from 615,000 in 2005. Childcare can be provided by formal paid sources such as nurseries and crèches; nursery schools and playgroups; registered childminders; after school and breakfast clubs or holiday play

Table 8.19

Registered childcare places,[1] 2006

England & Wales		Thousands
	Providers	Places
Childminders	73.6	333.7
Full day care	14.1	608.2
Out of school day care	11.4	394.5
Sessional day care	10.2	247.4
Crèche day care	2.8	48.4
All	112.1	1,632.2

1 See Appendix, Part 8: Registered childcare places.

Source: OFSTED; Welsh Assembly Government

schemes. Across the UK parents can receive financial support from the Government if they use these services, as long as the service providers are registered and approved. In 2006 there were around 112,000 providers offering 1.6 million registered places in England and Wales (Table 8.19). Two-thirds (66 per cent) of the providers of services were childminders, offering 20 per cent of places, an average of 5 places per provider. The second largest were full-day care providers (13 per cent of providers). This group provided the greatest proportion of places (37 per cent). This is perhaps unsurprising as full-day care providers offer the largest average number of places at 43 places per provider offering childcare services. Crèche day-care was the smallest sector, both in terms of providers and places (2 per cent and 3 per cent respectively). Again this is in part because of the average number of places (17), the next smallest after childminders.

The 2005 FACS showed that families with children of young ages were most likely of all families with children to receive financial help from relatives. Of families where the youngest child was under 5, 43 per cent reported that they received financial help from their families. Families where the youngest child was in their late teens (aged 16 to 18) were least likely to receive financial help from their families (19 per cent). Such help included being given or loaned money, or receiving financial help towards bills, clothing, holidays or other items. Lone parents working up to 15 hours per week were the most likely of all types of family to receive financial help from relatives

Table 8.20

Number of children and young persons on the child protection register: by category of abuse, 2005/06[1]

United Kingdom[2]			Thousands
	Boys	Girls	Total
Neglect	6.6	6.1	14.3
Emotional abuse	3.3	3.1	7.0
Physical abuse	2.1	1.9	4.9
Sexual abuse	1.0	1.4	2.9
Multiple/not specified	1.4	1.4	3.1
Total number of children	14.3	13.9	32.1

1 At 31 March. Children and young persons under the age of 18.
2 Breakdown by sex: England and Wales only.

Source: Department for Children, Schools and Families; Welsh Assembly Government; Scottish Government; Department of Health, Social Services and Public Safety, Northern Ireland

(60 per cent). Lone parent families were more likely than couples to receive financial help from their family, 52 per cent received such help compared with 29 per cent of couples. The largest source of help for both groups was relatives buying clothes for the parent or children, 32 per cent of lone parents and 15 per cent of couples received such help. Asked whether money runs out before the end of the month/week, twice as many couples (38 per cent) reported that they 'never' ran out of money than single parents (19 per cent); additionally lone parents were three times more likely than couples to 'always' run out of money, 6 per cent compared with 19 per cent.

Children may be placed on a local authority child protection register if a social services department considers they are at continuing risk of significant harm. At March 2006, 32,100 children were on child protection registers in the UK (Table 8.20). Neglect was the most common reason to be placed on the register, accounting for over 44 per cent of all cases. Emotional abuse was the second most common reason, accounting for 22 per cent of all cases. A breakdown by sex is available for England and Wales only and there were around 400 more boys than girls on the register, with boys outnumbering girls in three of the four specified categories. The exception was sexual abuse, with 10 per cent of girls falling into this category compared with 7 per cent of boys.

8

8

Chapter 9

Crime and justice

- The 2006/07 British Crime Survey (BCS) showed that 11.3 million crimes were committed against adults living in private households living in England and Wales. (Figure 9.1)

- In 2006/07, around one-third of crime recorded by the police in Great Britain was theft and handling stolen goods. The most common recorded crime in Northern Ireland was criminal damage (30 per cent). (Figure 9.2)

- Vandalism accounted for more than one-quarter of BCS crime in 2006/07 and was the only offence group with a significant increase in offences (10 per cent) since 2005/06. (Page 122)

- Between 2000 and 2004/05, the proportion worried about violent crime in England and Wales fell from 24 to 17 per cent, but has since begun to rise. (Figure 9.9)

- In England and Wales 55 per cent of adult offenders released from prison or starting community service in the first quarter of 2004 re-offended within two years and were subsequently reconvicted. (Page 132)

- The 2006/07 BCS showed that 79 per cent of the public are confident that the CJS respects the rights of the accused, while only 25 per cent are confident that it is effective in dealing with young people. (Table 9.20)

Many people are affected by crime, either through suffering or loss or through changes in actual and perceived levels of crime affecting their daily routines. Dealing with crime and associated problems is an ever-present concern for society and the Government. There are two main sources of statistics on levels of crime: household population surveys of crime, and police recorded crime (see Measures of crime box).

Crime levels

This chapter discusses both the incidence and prevalence of crime, (see also Appendix, Part 9: Prevalence rates and incidence rates). The incidence of crime, defined as the number of crimes experienced is reported in this section. The prevalence of crime, or percentage who were victims, is covered in the Offences and victims section later in the chapter. The 2006/07 British Crime Survey (BCS) estimated that 11.3 million crimes were committed against adults living in private households in England and Wales (Figure 9.1). The number of crimes

Figure 9.1

British Crime Survey offences[1]

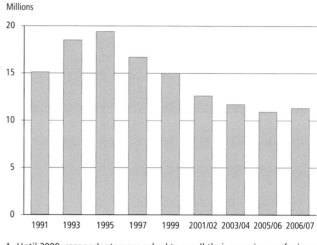

England & Wales

Millions

1 Until 2000, respondents were asked to recall their experience of crime in the previous calendar year. From 2001/02 the British Crime Survey became a continuous survey and the recall period was changed to the 12 months before interview.

Source: British Crime Survey, Home Office

Measures of crime

There are two main measures of the extent of crime in the UK: surveys of the public, and crime recorded by the police. The British Crime Survey (BCS) interviews adults aged 16 and over who are living in private households in England and Wales. The Scottish Crime and Victimisation Survey (SCVS) and the Northern Ireland Crime Survey (NICS) interview adults aged 16 and over. In some ways the BCS, the SCVS and the NICS give a better measure of many types of crime than police recorded crime statistics. These surveys show the large number of offences that are not reported to the police and also give a more reliable picture of trends, as they are not affected by changes in levels of reporting to the police or by variations in police recording practice (see Appendix, Part 9: Types of offences in England and Wales, and in Northern Ireland).

Recorded crime data covers those offences reported to and recorded by the police. The National Crime Recording Standard (NCRS) (introduced in England and Wales in 2002) and the Scottish Crime Recording Standard (SCRS) (introduced in 2004) were implemented with the aim of taking a more victim-centred approach and providing consistency between police forces (see Appendix, Part 9: National Crime Recording Standard).

Police recorded crime and survey measured crime have different coverage. Unlike crime data recorded by the police, the surveys are restricted to crimes against adults living in private households and their property and do not include some types of crime (for example, fraud, murder and victimless crimes such as drug use, where there is not a direct victim).

See also Appendix, Part 9: Availability and comparability of data from constituent countries.

estimated by the BCS rose steadily throughout the 1980s and early 1990s, peaking in 1995. There followed a steady decline up until 2004/05, since when the level of crime measured by the BCS has remained broadly stable. The Scottish Crime and Victimisation Survey (SCVS) estimated that around 1.1 million crimes were committed against adults in private households in the 12 months before interview in 2005/06, an increase from 900,000 in 2003/04. The Northern Ireland Crime Survey (NICS) estimated that 180,000 crimes were committed against adults living in private households in the 12 months before interview in 2006/07. This was a decrease from the 220,000 crimes identified in the 2005 NICS.

According to the 2006/07 BCS around 54 per cent of all BCS offences involved some kind of acquisitive crime, which covers crime where items are stolen (including burglary, theft or attempted theft and vehicle related theft). Vehicle related theft (including theft of and from vehicles, but not including bicycles) was the most common acquisitive crime (1.7 million) and accounted for 15 per cent of all BCS crime. This represented a fall of 61 per cent in the number of vehicle related thefts since 1995. Vandalism accounted for more than one-quarter of all BCS crime in 2006/07 and was the only offence group to see a statistically significant increase in the number of incidents since 2005/06, at 10 per cent. In particular vehicle vandalism which constituted 17 per cent of all crime as measured by the 2006/07 BCS (1.9 million offences), had increased by 12 per cent from the 1.7 million offences estimated in the 2005/06 BCS. Violent incidents accounted for more than one-fifth of all crimes measured by the 2006/07 BCS. However, there has been a 41 per cent decrease in violent offences since 1995.

Of the victims interviewed by the BCS in 2006/07, 59 per cent said the crime had not been reported to, or known about by, the police. This lack of reporting is the main reason why BCS estimates of crime (see Appendix, Part 9: Comparable crimes) are higher than the actual recorded crime figures. Victims gave a variety of reasons for not reporting a crime to the police. The most common reason for victims of all types of crime was that they felt the crime was too trivial, there was no loss or they believed the police would not or could not do much about it (71 per cent). For violent crimes more than one-third (34 per cent) of victims felt that it was a private matter and did not want to involve the police.

In 2006/07 there were around 6 million crimes recorded by the police in the UK (Table 9.2). Nearly three-quarters (73 per cent) of recorded crimes in England and Wales were property crimes, including offences against vehicles, other theft, criminal damage, burglary and fraud and forgery. Violence against the person accounted for almost one-fifth of all recorded crime in

Table 9.2

Crimes recorded by the police: by type of offence,[1] 2006/07

United Kingdom   Percentages

	England & Wales	Scotland	Northern Ireland
Theft and handling stolen goods	36	33	23
Theft from vehicles	9	5	3
Theft of vehicles	4	4	3
Criminal damage	22	31	30
Violence against the person[2]	19	3	26
Burglary	11	7	10
Fraud and forgery	4	3	4
Drugs offences	4	10	2
Robbery	2	1	1
Sexual offences	1	1	1
Other offences[3]	1	11	3
All notifiable offences (=100%) (thousands)	5,428	419	121

1 See Appendix, Part 9: Types of offences in England and Wales, and in Northern Ireland, and Availability and comparability of data from constituent countries.
2 Data for Scotland are serious assaults only. Those for England and Wales, and Northern Ireland are all assaults including those that cause no physical injury.
3 Northern Ireland includes 'offences against the state'. Scotland excludes 'offending while on bail'.

Source: Home Office; Scottish Government; Police Service of Northern Ireland

England and Wales, the same proportion as in 2005/06. Following the introduction of the National Crime Recording Standard (NCRS) in 2002 (see Appendix, Part 9: National Crime Recording Standard) there was an overall increase in the number of crimes recorded that year, with minor crimes (including criminal damage, minor theft and assault without injury) being the most affected. The introduction of the Scottish Crime Recording Standard (SCRS) in April 2004 resulted in similar increases in the number of minor crimes recorded in Scotland.

The definition of crime in Northern Ireland is broadly comparable with that used in England and Wales. There were 121,000 crimes recorded by the police in Northern Ireland 2006/07, around two-thirds of which were property crimes. Around one-quarter (26 per cent) of recorded crime in Northern Ireland involved violence against the person.

In Scotland the term 'crime' is reserved for the more serious offences (broadly equivalent to 'indictable' and 'triable-either-way' offences in England and Wales) while less serious crimes are called 'offences' (see Appendix, Part 9: Availability and comparability of data from constituent countries). In 2006/07 there were 419,000 crimes recorded by the police in Scotland of which around one-third were theft and handling stolen goods (33 per cent) and criminal damage (31 per cent). Drug offences were the third most common recorded crime (10 per cent) in Scotland (Table 9.2).

In 2006/07 London had the highest total recorded crime rate of all the regions in England and Wales, at 124 offences per 1,000 population, but also had the largest fall in total recorded crime compared with 2005/06, at 6 per cent. The region with the lowest recorded crime rate was the East of England, at 83 offences per 1,000 population. The South East and the South West regions in England, and Wales were the only areas not to see a decrease in the total recorded crime rate since 2005/06. There were also regional variations by type of crime. London had the highest rates of recorded violence (24 offences per 1,000 population) and other theft (32 offences per 1,000 population). However the rate for London is not strictly comparable with other regions which have a better measure of victimisation risk, because a large number of the crimes in London are committed against non-residents (for example commuters and tourists). The North East and North West had the highest rates for recorded criminal damage (at 28 offences per 1,000 population in both regions).

Offences and victims

The 2006/07 British Crime Survey showed that almost one-fifth (19 per cent) of households in England and Wales had been

9

victims of household crime in the 12 months before interview and 7 per cent of adults had been victims of personal crime.

The 2005/06 Scottish Crime and Victimisation Survey (SCVS) estimated that 16 per cent of households had been victims of household crime in the previous 12 months and 7 per cent had been victims of personal crime. The 2006/07 Northern Ireland Crime Survey (NICS) estimated that 11 per cent of households in Northern Ireland had experienced household crime and 4 per cent experienced personal crime in the previous 12 months. As in England and Wales, vandalism and vehicle theft were the most common crimes recorded by surveys in both Scotland and Northern Ireland.

The 2006/07 BCS found that 3 per cent of households in England and Wales had been victims of domestic burglary during the previous year. Between the 1995 and 2006/07 surveys the number of burglary offences measured by the BCS has declined by 59 per cent from 1.8 million offences to 726,000. Most of this fall took place between the 1995 and 2004/05 BCS, with the number of burglaries being relatively stable ever since (Table 9.3).

Domestic burglary offences can be split into those with entry and those with no entry (attempted burglaries), or into those with loss and those with no loss. In 2006/07 there were

Table 9.3

Domestic burglary:[1,2] by type

England & Wales

Thousands

	Burglary		Burglary		All burglary
	With entry	No entry	With loss	No loss	
1981	474	276	373	376	749
1991	869	511	712	668	1,380
1995	998	772	791	979	1,770
1997	852	768	651	970	1,621
1999	767	523	551	739	1,290
2001/02	552	416	396	573	969
2002/03	561	412	407	566	973
2003/04	533	410	417	526	943
2004/05	469	287	327	429	756
2005/06	440	293	315	418	733
2006/07	425	301	310	417	726

1 Burglary with entry plus burglary with no entry add up to all burglary. Burglary with loss plus burglary with no loss also add up to all burglary.
2 Until 2000, respondents were asked to recall their experience of crime in the previous calendar year. From 2001/02 the British Crime Survey became a continuous survey and the recall period was changed to the 12 months before interview.

Source: British Crime Survey, Home Office

Figure 9.4

Mobile phone theft: by circumstance of how the phone was stolen, 2005/06

England & Wales

Percentages

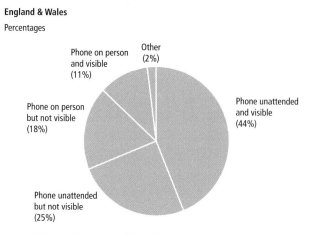

Source: British Crime Survey, Home Office

425,000 burglaries in England and Wales involving entry, a fall of 59 per cent since 1995. This includes all burglaries where a building (including any connecting outhouse or garage) was successfully entered, regardless of whether anything was stolen or not. Domestic burglaries were more likely to result in no loss than in anything being taken with 417,000 burglaries (including attempted burglaries) in 2006/07 having no loss, compared with 310,000 where something was successfully stolen.

In 2006 the Expenditure and Food Survey (EFS) reported that 80 per cent of households own one or more mobile phones, an increase from 27 per cent in 1998/99. Ownership is particularly prevalent among those households in the highest ten per cent income group (92 per cent) and among those households with one man, one woman and one child (90 per cent). The large increase in mobile phone ownership between 1998/99 and 2005/06 has also meant an increase in their being a target of theft, something which the police, the Government and industry are trying to tackle.

In 2006/07 the BCS reported that 4 per cent of households in England and Wales that owned a mobile phone had a mobile phone stolen in the last year. Less than one-half of these reported the theft to the police. The proportion experiencing mobile phone theft in the BCS has remained relatively stable since the BCS first started collecting specific details about mobile phones in 2002/03. According to the 2005/06 BCS the most common circumstance in which mobile phones were stolen was when they were left unattended and visible (44 per cent of all mobile phone thefts) (Figure 9.4). A further 25 per cent were stolen while the phone was left unattended although not visible. Nearly three in ten (29 per cent) of all stolen mobile phones were taken while on the owner's person,

Figure 9.5

Violent crimes:[1] by type[2]

England & Wales

Millions

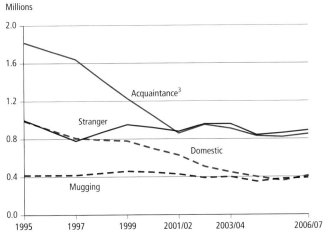

1   Until 2000, respondents were asked to recall their experience of crime in the previous calendar year. From 2001/02 the British Crime Survey (BCS) became a continuous survey and the recall period was changed to the 12 months before interview.
2   In the BCS violence consists of wounding, assaults with minor injury, assaults with no injury and robbery. It is divided into four types based on the relationship between the victim and suspect. See Appendix, Part 9: Violent crime.
3   Assaults in which the victim knew one or more of the offenders, at least by sight.

Source: British Crime Survey, Home Office

for example while being held in a pocket or bag or carried in the person's hand.

Between the 1995 and 2006/07 surveys, the BCS showed a 41 per cent decrease in the number of all violent crimes (see Appendix, Part 9: Violent crime) experienced by adults in England and Wales, from 4.2 million to 2.5 million. However, findings from the last three years of the survey (2004/05, 2005/06 and 2006/07) have shown the number of violent crimes has remained stable.

While the number of incidents for all types of violent crime has decreased between 1995 and 2006/07 the distribution of the different types has changed over this period. The proportions of violent crimes categorised as domestic violence and acquaintance violence decreased between 1995 and 2006/07 (Figure 9.5), from 23 per cent to 16 per cent for domestic violence and from 43 per cent to 33 per cent for acquaintance violence. Over the same period the proportion of violent incidents committed by strangers in England and Wales increased from around one-quarter (24 per cent) of all violent incidents in 1995 to more than one-third (36 per cent) in 2006/07 and the proportion of muggings increased from 10 per cent to 16 per cent.

Taking violent crimes overall, men are more likely than women to be victims though this varies by type of violence. According

to the 2006/07 BCS, 62 per cent of violent crimes were experienced by men. In particular, three-quarters (76 per cent) of victims of violence perpetrated by a stranger and over two-thirds (68 per cent) of victims of acquaintance violence were male. However, more women were victims of domestic violence with the 2006/07 BCS estimating 312,000 female victims compared with 93,000 male victims. Thus around three-quarters (77 per cent) of victims of domestic violence were women.

According to the 2006/07 BCS, around half (51 per cent) of the victims of violent crime sustained some type of injury. Victims of domestic violence were the most likely to report some kind of injury (68 per cent) followed by victims of stranger violence (48 per cent). Less than one-third of mugging victims sustained an injury.

The most common type of injuries among victims of violent crimes in England and Wales in 2006/07 include minor bruising and/or a black eye (30 per cent), severe bruising (16 per cent), cuts (15 per cent) and scratches (12 per cent). Victims of domestic violence were the most likely to report injuries with 40 per cent having suffered minor bruising and 27 per cent severe bruising. Around one-third of the victims of stranger violence and acquaintance violence also reported suffering minor bruising (32 per cent and 29 per cent respectively). Six per cent of domestic violence victims had suffered concussion or loss of consciousness and 3 per cent of both domestic violence and mugging victims had experienced broken bones.

Intimate violence includes domestic violence by a person's current or former partner or any family member, sexual assault and stalking. In the BCS respondents are asked about incidents of intimate violence experienced in the year before interview as well as since their 16th birthday. According to the 2005/06 BCS more than 6,700 respondents had experienced intimate violence in England and Wales in the previous year. Proportions of women experiencing intimate violence were higher than those for men for all types of violence (Figure 9.6 overleaf).

For both men and women, stalking was the most commonly experienced form of intimate violence in England and Wales; 9 per cent of women and 7 per cent of men experienced this in the last year. Around one in 20 respondents (6 per cent of women and 5 per cent of men) experienced any partner abuse (including non-sexual abuse, sexual assault and stalking by a partner). A similar proportion of men and women experienced non-sexual partner abuse in the previous year (including non-physical abuse, such as being prevented from having money or friends, or belittling, as well as threats and use of physical force). Women were more likely than men to be victims of sexual

9

Figure 9.6

Prevalence of intimate violence:[1] by type of violence, 2005/06

England & Wales

Percentages

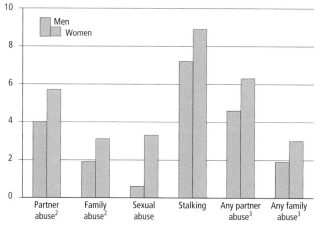

1 Victim of intimate violence in the previous 12 months. See Appendix, Part 9: Intimate violence.
2 Any non-sexual, emotional or financial abuse, threats or physical force by a current or former partner (partner abuse) or a family member other than a partner (family abuse).
3 Any partner abuse includes abuse, sexual assault and stalking by a partner. Any family abuse includes abuse, sexual assault and stalking by a family member.

Source: British Crime Survey, Home Office

assault (by any person including a partner or family member) in the previous year, 3 per cent compared with 1 per cent.

According to the 2005/06 BCS nearly three in ten women (29 per cent) and almost two in ten (18 per cent) men had experienced one or more forms of partner abuse since the age of 16. The greatest difference between the sexes for intimate violence since this age was for sexual assault, where almost one-quarter of all women (24 per cent) had such experience, including partner sexual abuse and less serious sexual assault, compared with 4 per cent of men.

For women who had experienced a serious sexual assault since the age of 16, the most common perpetrator was their partner (54 per cent), including current or previous partner or spouse. For men who had experience of sexual assault the most common offender was another person known to them (58 per cent) which includes friends, neighbours, a date or other acquaintances.

The likelihood of being a victim of crime is affected by, among other things, the level of deprivation in an area, with people living in deprived areas generally being more likely to be a victim of crime than those in less deprived areas (see Appendix, Part 9: Indices of Deprivation 2004). The 2006/07 BCS found that 10 per cent of households in the most deprived 20 per cent of areas in England were victims of vehicle theft,

Table 9.7

Households falling victim to crime:[1] by type of area,[2] 2006/07

England

Percentages

	All burglary	Vehicle-related theft[3]	Theft from the person	Criminal damage	All violence
Least deprived 20%	2	6	1	7	3
Next 20%	2	6	1	7	2
Middle 20%	3	7	1	8	3
Next 20%	3	9	2	9	4
Most deprived 20%	4	10	2	9	5
All areas	3	7	1	8	4

1 Proportion of households falling victim once or more to each crime.
2 See Appendix, Part 9: Indices of Deprivation 2004.
3 Vehicle owning households.

Source: British Crime Survey, Home Office

5 per cent were victims of violent crime, and 4 per cent were victims of burglary (Table 9.7). This compared with 6 per cent of households in the least deprived 20 per cent of areas being victims of vehicle theft, 3 per cent being victims of violent crime and 2 per cent being victims of burglary.

Being a victim of crime can be traumatic and the impact can vary depending on the type of offence and the circumstances under which it occurs. The impact can be worse where a person is repeatedly victimised. In the BCS, repeat victimisation is defined as being a victim of the same offence or group of offences more than once within the same year. Repeat victimisation accounts for the disparity found between incidence of crime (total numbers of offences per head of population) and prevalence rates (proportion of households being a victim once or more). The higher the level of repeat victimisation, the more these two rates differ.

According to the 2006/07 BCS, vandalism was the offence with the highest level of repeat victimisation in England and Wales, with 32 per cent of vandalism victims experiencing this crime more than once in the previous year (Figure 9.8). Assault, either with no injury (28 per cent) or with minor injury (24 per cent), had the next highest levels of repeat victimisation. Victims of theft from the person were least likely to experience repeat victimisation (7 per cent).

Levels of repeat victimisation for vandalism have remained relatively stable since the BCS began in 1981. Those for burglary have continued to decline since their peak in 1999 (20 per cent) and are now back at their lowest level since 1981. In 2006/07, 13 per cent of burglary victims were repeat victims.

Figure 9.8

Repeat victimisation[1] in the past 12 months: by type of offence, 2006/07

England & Wales
Percentages

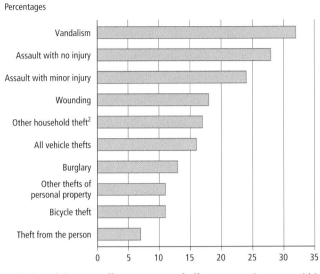

1 Victims of the same offence or group of offences more than once within the same 12 months.
2 Excludes burglary. Includes theft from both inside and outside a dwelling and from garages, sheds and outbuildings not directly linked to the dwelling.

Source: British Crime Survey, Home Office

Worry about crime

The 2006/07 British Crime Survey (BCS) estimated that 24 per cent of households were victims of crime at least once in the previous year. The proportion of adult victims of crime has continued to decrease since the peak of 40 per cent in 1995. Over the last ten years there has been a decrease of 33 per cent in the incidence of all household crime and a decrease of 32 per cent in the incidence of all personal crime in England and Wales (see Appendix, Part 9: Prevalence rates and incidence rates).

At the same time, two-thirds (65 per cent) of adults living in private households in England and Wales in 2006/07 believed that there was more crime in the country as a whole and 41 per cent believed there was more crime in their local area than in the previous two years. Since 2004/05 the proportions of people who reported that they worried about violent crime and burglary have increased by 1 percentage point (Figure 9.9). Worry about both these crimes has declined since 2000, from 24 to 17 per cent for violent crime and from 19 per cent to 13 per cent for burglary. Worry about car crime has also fallen over the period from 21 per cent in 2000 but has has remained relatively stable since 2004/05, when it was 13 per cent.

In Northern Ireland the proportion of people fairly or very worried about violent crime deceased from 24 per cent in

Figure 9.9

Trends in worry about crime[1,2]

England & Wales
Percentages

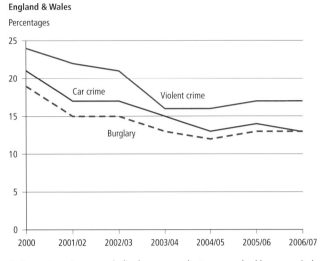

1 Percentage 'very worried' when respondents were asked how worried they were about the different types of crime.
2 Before 2001/02, respondents were asked to recall their experience of crime in the previous calendar year. From 2001/02 the British Crime Survey became a continuous survey and the recall period was changed to the 12 months before interview.

Source: British Crime Survey, Home Office

2003/04 to 22 per cent in 2006/07. Over the same period the proportion worried about burglary fell from 21 to 17 per cent and those worried about car crime, restricted to those who own, or have access to, a car, fell from 20 to 15 per cent.

In 2005/06 the BCS included questions on credit card crime and identity theft for the first time. It found that around one-fifth (19 per cent) of respondents in England and Wales were 'very worried' about credit card crime and a further 38 per cent were 'fairly worried'. This is set against the 2006/07 BCS finding that 4 per cent of plastic card users had been victims of fraud within the past 12 months.

The *Crime and Disorder Act (1998)* defined anti-social behaviour (ASB) as 'acting in a manner that caused or was likely to cause harassment, alarm or distress to one or more persons not of the same household (as the defendant)' (see Appendix, Part 9: Anti-social behaviour indicators). In the 2006/07 BCS, respondents were asked to identify the anti-social behaviours that they perceived as being a problem in their area from a list of seven behaviour strands. Almost one-fifth (18 per cent) of adults in England in Wales perceived there to be a high level of anti-social behaviour in their area, according to the overall ASB measure made up from the seven strands (Table 9.10 overleaf). This has remained relatively stable since 2001/02, the first year for which this measure is available.

Teenagers hanging around the streets, and litter were the most commonly perceived forms of anti-social behaviour in 2006/07,

9

Table 9.10

Anti-social behaviour indicators[1,2]

England & Wales   Percentages

	1992	1996	2000	2001/02	2002/03	2003/04	2004/05	2005/06	2006/07
Teenagers hanging around on the streets	20	24	32	32	33	27	31	32	33
Rubbish or litter lying around	30	26	30	32	33	29	30	30	31
People using or dealing drugs	14	21	33	31	32	25	26	27	28
Vandalism, graffiti and other deliberate damage to property	26	24	32	34	35	28	28	29	28
People being drunk or rowdy in public places	-	-	-	22	23	19	22	24	26
Noisy neighbours or loud parties	8	8	9	10	10	9	9	10	11
Abandoned or burnt-out cars[3]	-	-	14	20	25	15	12	10	9
High level of perceived anti-social behaviour[4]	-	-	-	19	21	16	17	17	18
Total (=100%)[5] (thousands)	10	8	10	33	37	38	45	48	47

1 Until 2000, respondents were asked to recall their experience of crime in the previous calendar year. From 2001/02 the British Crime Survey became a continuous survey and the recall period was changed to the 12 months before interview.
2 People saying anti-social behaviour is a 'very/fairly big problem' in their area. See Appendix, Part 9: Anti-social behaviour indicators.
3 Question only asked of one-quarter of the sample in 2001/02 and 2002/03.
4 This measure is derived from responses to the seven individual anti-social behaviour strands reported in the table.
5 Percentages do not add up to 100 per cent as respondents could give more than one answer.

Source: British Crime Survey, Home Office

with around one-third of people perceiving high levels of these behaviours (33 per cent and 31 per cent respectively). Between 2003/04 and 2006/07 the proportion of people perceiving drunk and rowdy behaviour in the street as a fairly or very big problem in their area increased by 7 percentage points and the proportion perceiving teenagers hanging around the street increased by 6 percentage points.

In Northern Ireland in 2005, 17 per cent of people perceived a high level of anti-social behaviour, according to the Northern Ireland Crime Survey (NICS). More than one-quarter of these saw teenagers hanging around (29 per cent), people using or dealing drugs (28 per cent), litter (28 per cent) and people being drunk or rowdy in public (25 per cent) as a problem in their area. In Scotland in 2005/06, 48 per cent of people perceived there to be a high level of anti-social behaviour in their area with drug dealing being a particular concern (50 per cent).

Householders and vehicle owners employ a variety of security measures to help combat perceived and actual crime. The use of devices such as security chains on doors, burglar alarms and sensor or timer lighting can have a positive effect on crime reduction because they act as deterrents as well as making it more difficult for a potential offender to succeed in an attempt at crime. In 2006/07, eight in ten households in England and Wales (including victims of burglary) had window locks on their property and more than seven in ten had a double lock or deadlock on their doors (Table 9.11). In contrast, four in ten households that had been victims of burglary in the last year

Table 9.11

Ownership of home and vehicle security devices, 2006/07

England & Wales   Percentages

	Ownership of each security device	
	Victims of burglary/vehicle theft	All households whether victim or not
Home		
Window locks	42	79
Double/deadlocks	40	75
Outdoor sensor/timer lights	18	40
Security chains on door	19	32
Burglar alarm	25	29
Indoor sensor/timer lights	10	24
Window bar/grilles	4	3
Vehicle		
Central locking	72	88
Any immobiliser[1]	63	78
Electronic	53	69
Mechanical	29	33
Car alarm	41	63
Window security etching	50	52
Tracking device	3	3

1 Data do not sum to the total of electronic and mechanical because households could have more than one car or van or use more than one device.

Source: British Crime Survey, Home Office

had these security devices (42 per cent and 40 per cent respectively). Ownership of both indoor and outdoor sensor or timer lights among all households was more than double that for those households that had been victims of burglary, suggesting that their presence may have a preventative effect. However, the proportion of households owning a burglar alarm was similar for all households and burglary victims (29 per cent compared with 25 per cent).

Security devices are also used to prevent car crimes. Almost nine in ten of all vehicle owners (including victims of theft) had a central locking system compared with around seven in ten victims of vehicle theft (88 per cent compared with 72 per cent). More than three-fifths (63 per cent) of all vehicle owners had a car alarm installed compared with around two-fifths (41 per cent) of vehicle theft victims.

Offenders

In 2006, 1.42 million offenders were sentenced for indictable and summary offences in England and Wales (see Appendix, Part 9: Types of offences in England and Wales), 4 per cent less than in 2005. Most of the offenders were male (80 per cent) and of these 7 per cent were aged under 18.

In 2006 in England and Wales, 6.1 per cent of all 17-year-old men were found guilty of, or cautioned for, one or more indictable offences, the highest rate for any age group and more than four times the corresponding rate for women (Figure 9.12). As young men and women entered their 20s the

proportion of offenders started to decline. Less than 1 per cent of men in each age group over the age of 45, and of women over the age of 20 were found guilty of, or cautioned for, an indictable offence in 2006.

In Northern Ireland, 7,100 offenders were found guilty of, or cautioned for, indictable offences in 2005. Of these, 87 per cent were male. Young men aged 18 were the most likely offenders with 4 per cent of all 18-year-old men being found guilty of, or cautioned for, an indictable offence. The proportion of offenders remained at around 3 per cent until age 22 when it began to decline. The proportion of women who were offenders was less than one-half of 1 per cent for all age groups.

The indictable offences for which people were found guilty of, or were cautioned for, were similar for men and women in England and Wales in 2006. For men, the most common indictable offence was theft or handling stolen goods (Figure 9.13), accounting for almost one-third (30 per cent of all male offences). This was also the most common offence for women with half (50 per cent) sentenced for this. For both men and women the next most common offences were violence against the person (20 per cent for men and 18 per cent for women) and other offences, which included fraud and forgery and indictable motoring offences (18 per cent of men and

Figure 9.12

Offenders[1] as a percentage of the population: by sex and age,[2] 2006

England & Wales
Percentages

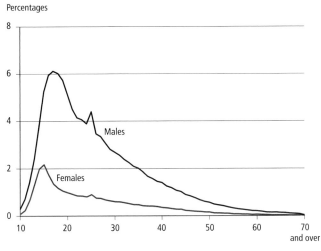

1 People found guilty of, or cautioned for, indictable offences.
2 Age 25 includes a number of offenders for whom age is unknown.

Source: Office for Criminal Justice Reform, Ministry of Justice

Figure 9.13

Offenders found guilty of, or cautioned for, indictable offences:[1] by sex and type of offence, 2006

England & Wales
Thousands

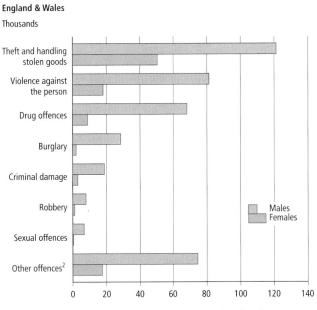

1 See Appendix, Part 9: Types of offences in England and Wales.
2 Includes fraud and forgery and indictable motoring offences.

Source: Office for Criminal Justice Reform, Ministry of Justice

Table 9.14

Offenders sentenced for indictable offences: by type of offence[1] and type of sentence,[2] 2006

England & Wales

Percentages

	Discharge	Fine	Community sentence	Fully suspended sentence	Immediate custody	Other	All sentenced (=100%) (thousands)
Theft and handling stolen goods	20	13	37	6	20	4	98.6
Drug offences	17	34	23	5	19	2	39.5
Violence against the person	7	5	41	13	29	4	41.9
Burglary	4	2	44	8	41	2	22.7
Fraud and forgery	16	13	36	9	24	2	18.3
Criminal damage	21	11	48	3	10	6	12.5
Motoring	3	26	28	13	28	1	6.1
Robbery	-	-	35	4	59	1	8.2
Sexual offences	3	3	27	6	57	3	4.9
Other offences	8	34	22	5	19	11	50.0
All indictable offences	13	17	34	7	24	4	302.5

1 See Appendix, Part 9: Types of offences in England and Wales.
2 See Appendix, Part 9: Sentences and orders.

Source: Home Office

17 per cent of women). While these three offences accounted for the majority of female offences, a further 17 per cent of men were found guilty of, or cautioned for, drugs offences.

The most common offence in 2005 for men found guilty of, or cautioned for indictable offences in Northern Ireland (29 per cent) was violence against the person accounting for 1,800 offences, followed by theft and handling stolen goods (23 per cent). For women, around 40 per cent of offenders were found guilty of, or cautioned for, theft and handling stolen goods accounting for 400 offences.

Of the 507,000 offenders found guilty of, or cautioned for, indictable offences in England and Wales in 2006, three-fifths (60 per cent) were sentenced. The type of sentence given depends on the offence committed and other factors that may be applied on a case by case basis (see Appendix, Part 9: Sentences and orders). The most common sentence for indictable offences in 2006 was a community sentence, given to 34 per cent of offenders, although drugs offenders were most commonly fined along with those convicted of 'other indictable offences' (34 per cent each) (Table 9.14). Around three-fifths of those found guilty of robbery and sexual offences were sentenced to immediate custody (59 per cent and 57 per cent respectively). Motoring offences vary in severity and this is reflected in the variety of sentences given. Under one-third of offenders were sentenced to immediate

custody (28 per cent), while 28 per cent received a community sentence and a further 26 per cent were fined.

In Northern Ireland 7,100 offenders were sentenced for indictable offences in 2005. A fine was the most common sentence for all offences apart from burglary, for which 25 per cent received a community sentence; and robbery and sexual offences, where the most common sentence for both was immediate custody (87 per cent and 47 per cent respectively).

Prisons and probation

Prison is the usual destination for offenders given custodial sentences or those who break the terms of their non-custodial sentence. The prison population (those held in prison or police cells, see Appendix, Part 9: Prison population for more details) in Great Britain was relatively stable in the 1980s and early 1990s but in the mid-1990s the population began to increase (Figure 9.15). The largest increase, 10 per cent, occurred between 1996 and 1997. Apart from a decrease of 1 per cent in 1999, the prison population has continued to increase every year since 1980 and in 2007 reached 87,000, 82 per cent higher than that in 1980 and 2 per cent higher than in 2006. Although this general pattern is true for all constituent countries of Great Britain, the prison population in Scotland remained relatively stable between 2004 and 2006 with only small year on year increases.

Figure 9.15

Average prison[1] population

Great Britain
Thousands

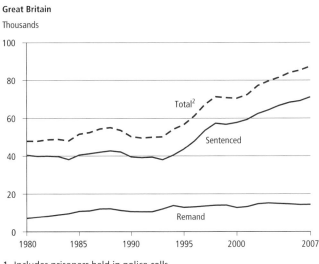

1 Includes prisoners held in police cells.
2 Includes non-criminal prisoners (for example, those held under the 1971 Immigration Act).

Source: Ministry of Justice; Scottish Government

Northern Ireland's prison population fell during the 1980s and 1990s to a low of 900 in 2001. One reason for the decrease in the late 1990s was the implementation of the *Northern Ireland (Sentences) Act 1998*, arising from the Belfast Agreement (Good Friday Agreement), which resulted in the release of a number of prisoners between 1998 and 2000. However, the prison population in Northern Ireland has increased progressively since that time and was around 40 per cent higher in 2006 than in 2002, at 1,400 prisoners.

Since 1980 the average number of sentenced prisoners in Great Britain has increased by 76 per cent (from 40,000 to 71,000). The number of remand prisoners has doubled (from 7,000 to 14,000). As well as an increase in custodial sentences, there has been an increase in the use of suspended sentences in England and Wales between 1993 and 2006. In 1993, 3 per cent of all offenders sentenced for indictable offences at Crown Court were given fully suspended sentences compared with 14 per cent in 2006.

Rising prison populations have led to concerns that prisons are reaching full capacity. In England and Wales between June 2006 and June 2007, there was a 2 per cent increase in the population in custody, including prisons, police cells under Operation Safeguard (the housing of inmates in police cells to reduce pressure on prisons), secure training centres and secure children's homes. The remand population in prison (including recalls but excluding fine defaulters) decreased by 2 per cent to 12,800 in June 2007 compared with June 2006. The sentenced prison population increased by 3 per cent from a year earlier.

Over the same period the population of all prisoners in Northern Ireland decreased by 1 per cent. In Scotland, between June 2005 and June 2006, there were increases in the prison population for both men (6 per cent) and women (14 per cent).

The increased prison population in England and Wales may be a result of the rise in the use of longer prison sentences. Between 1997 and 2006 the population serving a sentence of four years or more (both including and excluding indeterminate sentences) has increased at a faster rate than the population serving short term sentences of less than 12 months. The number of female prisoners in England and Wales serving a sentence of four years or more (including life and IPP, see Appendix, Part 9: Sentences and orders, and Prison population) more than doubled from over 700 in 1997 to around 1,500 in 2006, while the number of male prisoners serving sentences of 4 years or more (including life and IPP) increased by one-half (49 per cent), from 20,700 in 1997 to 30,800 in 2006.

The trend in Scotland followed that for England and Wales with the number of male prisoners serving sentences of four or more years (including life sentences) having increased by 22 per cent between 1997 and 2006, to 2,600. In Northern Ireland, there has been a decrease in the average sentence length for prisoners. The proportion of prisoners serving sentences of four or more years (including life sentences) decreased from 57 per cent to 48 per cent between 1997 and 2006. In contrast the proportion serving sentences of less than 12 months increased from 18 per cent to 21 per cent.

In 2006, 86 per cent of the prison population in England and Wales were British nationals and of these, 81 per cent were White (Table 9.16). This is the lowest proportion of white

Table 9.16

Prison population[1] of British nationals: by sex and ethnic group,[2] 2006

England & Wales

Percentages

	Males	Females	All
White	80.8	82.7	80.9
Mixed	2.7	4.1	2.8
Asian or Asian British	4.9	2.0	4.8
Black or Black British	10.6	10.0	10.6
Chinese or Other ethnic group	0.2	0.4	0.2
Total (=100%) (thousands)	62.7	3.4	66.2

1 Excludes prisoners held in police cells.
2 See Appendix, Part 1: Classification of ethnic groups.

Source: Ministry of Justice

prisoners recorded since 1996, when 86 per cent of British nationals in prison establishments were White. In 2006, 11 per cent of British nationals in prison establishments in England and Wales were Black or Black British and 5 per cent were Asian or Asian British. In Scotland 98 per cent of the British national prison population in 2006 were White, a proportion that has remained unchanged since 2004.

Release On Temporary Licence (ROTL) allows sentenced prisoners to be released temporarily from the establishment in which they are held. The main reasons for ROTL in 2005 are on compassionate grounds (to visit dying loved ones or for marriage or funeral attendance), to help the prisoners improve their chances of resettlement (for example job and housing interviews), to allow participation in education or community service (facility release) or for official visits such as court appearances. In 2005, 405,000 prisoners in England and Wales were released temporarily on licence, two-thirds (272,000) of which were facility licences while 13,000 prisoners were granted release on temporary licence on compassionate grounds (Figure 9.17).

Re-offenders are defined as offenders who are released from prison or those who have started a community sentence and who re-offended during a two year follow up period and who were subsequently convicted in court (see Appendix, Part 9: Re-offenders). More than one-half (55 per cent) of adult offenders released from prison or from starting a community sentence in England and Wales in the first quarter of 2004

Figure 9.17

Number of releases on temporary licence: by type of licence

England & Wales
Thousands

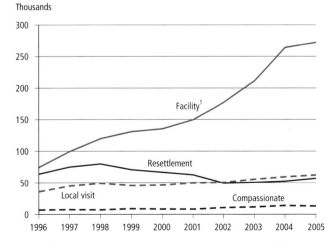

1 Available for prisoners who have served at least a quarter of their sentence. Release can be granted to participate in employment or community work, further education and job or housing interviews.

Source: Ministry of Justice

Figure 9.18

Prisoners reconvicted[1] within two years: by offence category

England & Wales
Percentages

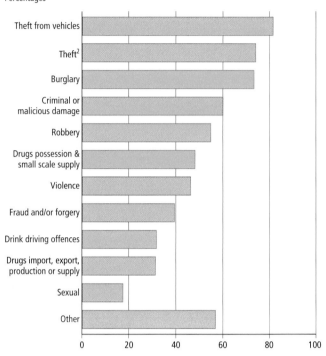

1 Includes offenders (aged 18 and over on date of release) who were released from prison or had started a community sentence in the first quarter of 2004, who re-offended during a two year follow up period and who were subsequently convicted in court. See Appendix, Part 9: Sentences and orders.
2 Includes theft and handling of stolen goods and theft of vehicles but excludes theft from vehicles.

Source: Ministry of Justice

re-offended within two years. On the whole offenders do not specialise in a particular crime and therefore the majority re-offending will not be reconvicted in the same category as the original offence. The original, or index, offences with the highest re-offending rates were theft from vehicles (82 per cent), theft (74 per cent) and burglary (73 per cent) (Figure 9.18). Men were more likely than women to re-offend for all types of offence, but the number of female offenders that re-offended is very small, making it difficult to make comparisons between the sexes.

Police and the civil justice system

A large share of expenditure on the criminal justice system (CJS) has traditionally been spent on the police service (52 per cent in England and Wales in 2003/04). In 2006/07 there were 158,600 full-time equivalent police officers in Great Britain, of which 121,900 were constables, 24,000 were sergeants and 12,300 were inspector or a higher rank (Table 9.19). In addition, there were 13,500 police community

Table 9.19

Police officer strength:[1] by rank and sex, 2006/07

Great Britain   Numbers

	Males	Females	All
ACPO[2] ranks	217	30	247
Chief superintendent/ superintendent	1,592	170	1,762
Chief inspector	1,929	255	2,184
Inspector	7,043	1,024	8,067
Sergeant	20,802	3,646	24,447
Constable	90,302	31,599	121,902
All ranks	121,884	36,724	158,608
Police staff	32,471	49,792	82,263
Police community support officers[3]	7,706	5,791	13,497
Traffic wardens[4]	625	406	1,031
Designated officers[3]	960	657	1,617
Total police strength	163,646	93,370	257,016
Special constabulary[3]	9,327	4,694	14,021

1 At 31 March 2007. Full-time equivalent figures rounded to the nearest whole number. Includes staff on secondment to NCOs (Non-commissioned officer in the armed forces), central services, and staff on career breaks or maternity/paternity leave. See Appendix, Part 9: Police.
2 Police officers who hold the rank of Chief Constable, Deputy Chief Constable or Assistant Chief Constable, or their equivalent.
3 England and Wales only as these are not available for Scotland. Headcounts for special constabulary.
4 Excludes local authority traffic wardens.

Source: Home Office; Scottish Government

support officers and 14,000 special constables in England and Wales in 2006/07 (see Appendix, Part 9: Police). Of all police officer staff in 2006/07 less than one-quarter (23 per cent) were female. The only rank where women accounted for a

higher proportion than this was that of constable (26 per cent). Around 9 per cent of male officers were of the rank of inspector and above compared with 4 per cent of female officers.

The 2006/07 British Crime Survey (BCS) reported that 51 per cent of people thought that the police in their area did an excellent or good job. Of those who were victims of crimes known to the police, 58 per cent were very or fairly satisfied with the way the police handled the matter.

The 2006/07 BCS asked people in England and Wales how confident they were with various aspects of the CJS. People were confident that the CJS respects the rights of people accused of committing a crime, with nearly eight in ten (79 per cent) being very or fairly confident that the CJS respects the rights of these people and treats them fairly (Table 9.20). There was less confidence in the effectiveness of the CJS in dealing with young people accused of crime, protecting the public and dealing with victims. Three-quarters (75 per cent) of people were not very or not at all confident in the effectiveness of the CJS in dealing with young people accused of crime and around two-thirds lacked confidence in the effectiveness of the CJS in meeting the needs of victims (67 per cent) or in reducing crime (63 per cent).

The level of confidence in the Northern Ireland CJS was similar to that in England in Wales, although respondents of the 2006/07 Northern Ireland Crime Survey (NICS) were more confident in the effectiveness of the CJS in dealing with young people accused of crime, with 27 per cent being fairly confident and 16 per cent being not at all confident.

Trial by jury is usually employed in serious criminal cases such as murder, rape, assault, burglary or fraud, which take place in the Crown Courts (see Appendix, Part 9: Courts system in England and Wales). In 2006/07, 393,900 jury summons were issued in

9

Table 9.20

Confidence in the criminal justice system, 2006/07

England & Wales   Percentages

	Very	Fairly	Not very	Not at all
Effective in dealing with young people accused of crime	2	23	53	22
Meets the needs of victims	3	31	47	20
Effective in reducing crime	3	34	49	14
Deals with cases promptly and efficiently	4	36	46	15
Effective in bringing people to justice	4	38	43	16
Respects the rights of people accused of committing a crime and treats them fairly	19	60	17	4

Source: British Crime Survey, Home Office

Table 9.21

Jury summons for Crown and Civil Courts[1]

England & Wales

Numbers[2]

	2002/03	2003/04	2004/05	2005/06	2006/07
Total number of summons issued	486,890	446,720	409,810	391,020	393,880
Total number of jurors who served	197,340	179,400	186,020	185,370	181,100
Deferred to serve at a later date	74,470	63,270	70,980	73,260	71,730
Refused deferral	296	366	268	263	162
Excused by right having served in past 2 years	29,250	27,290	8,640	4,390	4,410
Excused for other reasons[3]	134,120	107,330	97,810	94,170	97,460
Refused excusal	2,010	4,240	3,960	3,220	1,840
Disqualified – residency, mental disorders, criminality	101,710	95,870	82,510	79,770	87,260
Disqualified – aged over 70 at selection	59,010	57,080	53,110	50,700	54,170
Disqualified – failed police national computer (PNC) check	151	133	169	179	190
Failed to reply to summons	47,990	49,180	41,940	39,140	38,360
Summons undelivered	23,620	21,110	18,210	15,820	18,950
Postponed by Jury Central Summoning Bureau	12,300	8,270	12,940	9,120	5,640

1 See Appendix, Part 9: Courts system in England and Wales.
2 Numbers do not add up to the sum total as the data are taken over a rolling 12 month period and carry over juror details from month to month in deferral maintenance.
3 Including childcare, work commitments, medical, language difficulty, student, moved from area, travel difficulties, financial hardship.

Source: HM Courts Service

England and Wales and 181,100 jurors served (Table 9.21). Of the summons issued, one-quarter (97,500) of potential jurors were excused for reasons including childcare problems, medical reasons and language difficulties. In addition, more than one-fifth (87,300) of potential jurors were disqualified because of residency issues, mental disorders or criminality. The number excused decreased by 38 per cent between 2002/03 and 2006/07, while the number disqualified for failing the police national computer check (PNC) increased by over one-quarter (26 per cent).

Chapter 10

Housing

- Between 1971 and 2006 the number of dwellings in Great Britain rose from 18.8 to 25.7 million, while the number of households rose from 18.6 to 24.3 million. (Page 136)

- In 2005, 9 per cent of all new dwellings in England were built in flood risk areas and 80 per cent of the land used had been previously developed. (Page 137)

- In 2006/07, 47 per cent of new dwellings completed in England were flats, compared with 16 per cent in 1996/97 and 26 per cent in 1991/92. (Table 10.3)

- Between 1981 and 2006, the number of owner-occupied dwellings in the UK increased by 49 per cent to reach 18.5 million. (Figure 10.4)

- In 2006/07, 89 per cent of owner-occupiers in England were satisfied with their area compared with 80 per cent of those renting from the social sector. (Page 144)

- In 2006, 37 per cent of dwellings bought in the UK cost more than £200,000 while 15 per cent cost less than £100,000. (Figure 10.16)

DATA

Download data by clicking the online pdf

www.statistics.gov.uk/socialtrends38

Where and how a person lives is strongly influenced by a range of socio-economic and demographic factors, including income, employment and type and size of household. In recent years increasing house prices have made purchasing a home less affordable, particularly for first time buyers. In 2006 the average dwelling price in the UK was over three and a half times the average income for first time buyers compared with two and a half times in 1996. These factors all have an effect on a person's living conditions, including their tenure, the type and condition of their home and their satisfaction with the area in which they live.

Housing stock and housebuilding

Since the early 1950s the number of dwellings in Great Britain has nearly doubled from 13.8 million in 1951 to 25.7 million in 2006. The rise in housing stock reflects a greater demand for homes caused by the increase in the population (see Chapter 1: Population) and more particularly, a trend towards smaller households that has emerged since the 1970s (see Appendix, Part 2: Households). Between 1971 and 2006 the number of dwellings in Great Britain rose by 37 per cent, from 18.8 million to 25.7 million. During the same period the number of households increased by 31 per cent from 18.6 million to 24.3 million (see also Chapter 2: Households and families, Table 2.1), whereas the population increased by 9 per cent.

The damage caused to the nation's housing stock during the Second World War led to the provision of new housing being a post-war government priority. In the early post-war years local authorities undertook the majority of housing construction. During the mid-1950s, private enterprise housebuilding increased dramatically and has been the dominant sector for new housebuilding since 1959. Housebuilding completions in the UK, which include houses, bungalows and flats (see Appendix, Part 10: Housebuilding completions), peaked in 1968 when 426,000 dwellings were completed. More than one-half (53 per cent) of these were built by private enterprise and 47 per cent were built by the social sector, primarily local authorities but also including registered social landlords (RSLs) (See Appendix, Part 10: Public and private sectors) (Figure 10.1). Since the 1990s registered social landlords – predominantly housing associations – have dominated building in the social sector, accounting for 99 per cent of social sector completions in 2006/07. In the housebuilding sector as a whole, there were 218,000 completions in 2006/07, 88 per cent of which were by the private enterprise sector.

The number of housebuilding completions in England has been rising year-on-year since 2001/02. In 2006/07, 167,600 new homes were completed in England, 29 per cent more than in

Figure 10.1

Housebuilding completions:[1,2] by sector

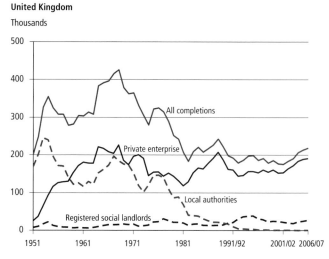

United Kingdom

Thousands

1 See Appendix, Part 10: Housebuilding completions, Public and private sectors, and Dwelling stock.
2 From 1990/91 data are for financial years.

Source: Communities and Local Government; Welsh Assembly Government; Scottish Government; Department for Social Development, Northern Ireland

2001/02. Over this period the number of new homes completed in each region of England increased. This was particularly evident in London, where the number increased by 58 per cent to 22,000 and in the East of England, where the number completed in 2006/07 was 23,000, 45 per cent higher than in 2001/02.

There is an increasing focus by the Government on recycling the land used for housebuilding, both to maximise the number of homes available and to help make them affordable. The Government's target for England published in 2000 is that by 2008, 60 per cent of new dwellings should be built on previously developed land (brownfield sites) or through conversions of existing buildings. This target was reached in 2001 when 61 per cent of new dwellings were built on previously developed land, mainly excluding conversions. This proportion continued to increase until 2005 (74 per cent) but fell in 2006 with 71 per cent of dwellings built on brownfield sites.

On a comparable basis that excludes conversions, there were wide regional variations in the increase in the proportion of new homes built on previously developed land in England between 1996 and 2006. East Midlands had the largest increase (73 per cent) in the proportion of new homes built on previously developed land from 37 per cent in 1996 to 64 per cent in 2006. The proportion of new homes built on previously developed land in the South West and West Midlands also increased by more than 50 per cent (66 per cent and 54 per cent respectively) (Figure 10.2). Regions with the

Figure 10.2

New dwellings built on previously developed land:[1] by region

England

Percentages

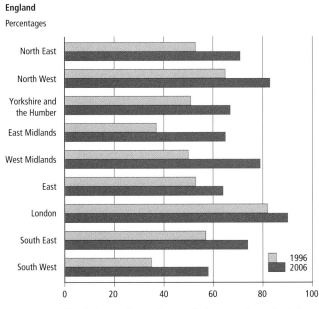

1 As reported by Ordnance Survey. Data exclude conversions of existing buildings.

Source: Communities and Local Government

Table 10.3

Housebuilding completions: by number of bedrooms

England   Percentages

	1991/92	1996/97	2001/02	2005/06	2006/07
Houses					
1 bedroom	4	1	-	-	-
2 bedrooms	22	21	11	8	8
3 bedrooms	28	36	28	26	25
4 or more bedrooms	20	26	37	20	20
All houses	74	84	77	54	53
Flats					
1 bedroom	15	7	6	10	11
2 bedrooms	10	8	15	35	35
3 bedrooms	1	1	1	1	1
4 or more bedrooms	-	-	-	-	-
All flats	26	16	23	46	47
All houses and flats (=100%) (thousands)	155	146	130	163	167

Source: Communities and Local Government

smallest increases since 1996 were London (7 per cent) and the East of England (19 per cent). The small increase in London could be explained by the fact that it had the highest proportion of the English regions of new dwellings built on previously developed land (excluding conversions) in 2006, at 90 per cent, thereby limiting opportunities for any new housebuilding in the region. Across England as a whole, there was a 4 per cent decrease in the proportion of new homes built on previously developed land between 2005 and 2006. In Scotland 44 per cent (8,972) of new dwellings were built on previously developed land in 2006, a 7 per cent increase since 2005 although a further 14 per cent were built on land that was of unknown previous use.

In 2005, 6 per cent of all land used for residential building in England was within a flood risk area (see also Chapter 11: Environment). Almost one in ten (9 per cent) of all new dwellings were built in flood risk areas and around 80 per cent of the land used for these new dwellings had been previously developed.

The density of new homes has also increased. In 2006 new dwellings in England were built at an average of 41 per hectare, compared with 40 per hectare in 2005 and 24 per hectare in 1995. At 80 dwellings per hectare, the density of new dwellings in London was higher than in any other English region in 2006. The East of England and the East Midlands had the lowest density of newly built homes, each with 34 per hectare.

The increase in the density of new dwellings constructed over the past ten years reflects changes in the type and size of homes, with a shift in the proportion built that are flats. Between 1996/97 and 2006/07 the proportion of new builds that were houses (including bungalows) has decreased (from 84 to 53 per cent) and the proportion of flats has increased (from 16 to 47 per cent) (Table 10.3). There was a similar shift in Wales, where 31 per cent of new dwellings in 2006/07 were flats compared with 9 per cent in 1996/97. As the proportion of newly built dwellings that are flats increased in England, the average number of bedrooms per new dwelling decreased. In 1996/97, 62 per cent of all newly built homes (houses and flats) had three or more bedrooms and 29 per cent had two. By 2006/07, the proportion of newly built homes with three or more bedrooms had fallen to 47 per cent, while the proportion of those with two bedrooms had risen to 42 per cent.

The recent trend of building smaller homes can be linked to the increasing numbers of one and two-person households and government initiatives to increase the supply and affordability of homes in areas of high demand (see Appendix, Part 10: Housing Green Paper).

Tenure and accommodation

One of the most notable housing trends in the UK since the early 1980s is the increase in owner occupation. Between 1981

10

Figure 10.4

Stock of dwellings:[1] by tenure

United Kingdom

Millions

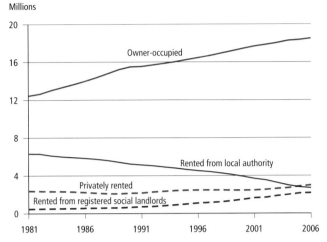

1 See Appendix, Part 10: Dwelling stock, and Tenure. Data for England and Wales are at 31 March, and for Scotland and Northern Ireland data are at 31 December the previous year, except for 1991, where census figures are used.

Source: Communities and Local Government; Welsh Assembly Government; Scottish Government; Department of the Environment, Northern Ireland

and 2006 the number of owner-occupied dwellings increased by 49 per cent to reach 18.5 million (Figure 10.4). Over the same period the number of homes rented from local authorities (LAs) fell by 57 per cent to 2.7 million. This decline is partly explained by the increase in owner occupancy, but also by the steadily growing number of homes rented from registered social landlords (RSLs) since the early 1990s. A large number of local authority dwellings have been transferred to RSLs (82 per cent of all local authority sales in 2006/07) under large scale voluntary transfer (LSVT) arrangements (see Appendix, Part 10: Sales and transfers of local authority dwellings) explaining much of the change in the proportion renting from LAs to RSLs. By 2006, 2.2 million homes were rented from RSLs compared with 0.5 million in 1981. The number of dwellings rented privately has been growing steadily in recent years, increasing from around 2.5 million in 2001 to 3 million in 2006.

The growth in the number of owner-occupied dwellings in Great Britain was helped by a number of schemes to increase low-cost home ownership. Since the early 1980s, those renting from local authorities with secure tenancies of at least two years' standing have been entitled to purchase their home. This scheme, known as 'right to buy', was particularly popular during the 1980s, following a period of stabilisation in the housing market and changes in legislation that enabled more tenants to buy. There was a peak of 167,000 sales in 1982/83. In 2006/07 there were just under 17,000 sales of right to buy

properties, a decrease of 37 per cent on the previous year and the lowest number since the scheme was introduced. Some of this decline could be explained by changes to the eligibility rules in January 2005 under the *Housing Act 2004* which means new tenants cannot buy until they have been resident for five years instead of the previous two. In Northern Ireland in 2006 there were around 2,500 sales of right to buy properties, a decrease of 17 per cent on the previous year.

Another scheme to increase low-cost home ownership in Great Britain is shared ownership. A number of schemes are available to key workers, existing social sector tenants and those in priority housing need, enabling them to buy a share of a property from an RSL and pay rent on the remaining share. Since the late 1990s large scale voluntary transfers have been the main contributors to the transfer of ownership from local authorities to other owners, mainly housing associations (see Appendix, Part 10: Sales and transfers of local authority dwellings).

Within Great Britain, tenure varies by socio-economic status (see Appendix, Part 1: National Statistics Socio-economic Classification). In 2006, 59 per cent of households with a reference person (see Appendix, Part 7: Household reference person) who was economically active were buying their home with a mortgage and 17 per cent owned their home outright (Table 10.5). Households with a reference person in the large employers and higher managerial group were the most likely to own their home with a mortgage (77 per cent). Retired households were the most likely to own their home outright (68 per cent), reflecting the long period of time it usually takes to repay a mortgage.

Those households where the reference person was in a routine and semi-routine occupation, those who have never worked and long-term unemployed households were the least likely of all groups to be owner-occupiers and the most likely to rent from the social sector. This was particularly notable among those who had never worked or were long-term unemployed, with 12 per cent owning their home outright and 73 per cent renting from the social sector. The proportions of households renting privately varied little across the socio-economic groups. The picture is similar in Northern Ireland. According to the 2006 Continuous Household Survey (CHS), around three-fifths (57 per cent) of all economically active people in Northern Ireland own their homes with a mortgage and around one-fifth (21 per cent) own them outright. Among those who were economically inactive, over one-quarter (28 per cent) rented their homes from the social sector.

Tenure varies markedly according to the type of household. In 2006 in Great Britain, lone-parent households with dependent

Table 10.5

Socio-economic classification:[1] by tenure,[2] 2006[3]

Great Britain   Percentages

	Owned outright	Owned with mortgage	Rented from social sector	Rented privately[4]	All tenures
Economically active					
Large employers and higher managerial occupations	14	77	2	6	100
Higher professional occupations	20	65	1	14	100
Lower managerial and professional occupations	14	68	6	12	100
Intermediate occupations	17	59	13	11	100
Small employers and own account workers	26	54	7	13	100
Lower supervisory and technical occupations	14	62	13	11	100
Semi-routine occupations	17	38	30	16	100
Routine occupations	16	43	27	14	100
Never worked and long-term unemployed	12	2	73	13	100
All economically active	17	59	12	12	100
Economically inactive					
Retired[5]	68	6	23	4	100
Other	16	12	59	13	100
All economically inactive	54	7	33	6	100
All socio-economic groups	32	40	20	10	100

1 Based on the current or last job of the household reference person. See Appendix, Part 1: National Statistics Socio-economic Classification (NS-SEC), and Appendix, Part 7: Household reference person.
2 See Appendix, Part 10: Tenure
3 See Appendix, Part 2: General Household Survey.
4 Includes rent-free accommodation.
5 Respondents who said they had retired from paid employment.

Source: General Household Survey (Longitudinal), Office for National Statistics

children were more likely than any other type of household to rent property rather than own it. Around two-thirds (66 per cent) of lone-parent households with dependent children rented their home, mostly from social sector landlords (RSLs or local authorities), while around one-third (34 per cent) lived in owner-occupied accommodation. In contrast, four-fifths (80 per cent) of couple households with dependent children were owner-occupiers and around 12 per cent rented from the social sector. In Northern Ireland the proportion of household types in each tenure group was very similar to those in Great Britain in 2006 with just under two-thirds (63 per cent) of lone-parent families with dependent children living in rented housing and just over one-third (37 per cent) owning their home, either outright or with a mortgage. Almost nine in ten couple households with dependent children (87 per cent) were owner-occupiers.

In 2006, 81 per cent of households in Great Britain lived in a house or bungalow, whether it was detached, semi-detached or terraced, regardless of tenure (Table 10.6 overleaf).

Semi-detached houses and terraced houses were the most common type of dwelling, lived in by 30 per cent and 28 per cent of all households, respectively. The type of accommodation varies by tenure. Owner-occupiers were more likely than social renters to live in houses, particularly in detached or semi-detached properties. In contrast, social renters were around six times more likely than owner-occupiers to live in a purpose-built flat.

In Northern Ireland, 94 per cent of households lived in a house or bungalow while 6 per cent lived in a flat in 2006. Houses were the most common type of dwelling for all tenures but among those renting from housing associations or other registered social landlords (RSLs) around two-thirds lived in houses (64 per cent) compared with at least 80 per cent in all other tenure groups.

The type of home that people live in often reflects the size and type of their household and what they can afford or are provided with. Among households with dependent children in Great Britain, couples were more likely than lone parents to live in a house or bungalow (93 per cent and 76 per cent

10

Table 10.6

Tenure: by type of accommodation, 2006[1]

Great Britain

Percentages

	House or bungalow			Flat or maisonette		All dwellings[3]
	Detached	Semi-detached	Terraced	Purpose-built	Other[2]	
Owner-occupied						
Owned outright	36	34	21	7	2	100
Owned with mortgage	27	34	31	7	2	100
All owner-occupied	31	34	27	7	2	100
Rented privately[4]						
Unfurnished	14	24	34	16	13	100
Furnished	8	13	29	30	20	100
All privately rented	12	21	32	20	15	100
Rented from social sector						
Local Authority	1	24	28	45	1	100
Housing association[5]	1	19	34	41	5	100
All rented from social sector	1	22	30	43	3	100
All tenures	23	30	28	15	3	100

1 See Appendix, Part 2: General Household Survey.
2 Includes converted flats, part of a house and rooms.
3 Includes other type of accommodation, such as mobile homes.
4 Rented privately includes rent-free accommodation. Furnished includes partly furnished.
5 Since 1996, housing associations are more correctly described as registered social landlords (RSLs).

Source: General Household Survey (Longitudinal), Office for National Statistics

respectively). The most common type of housing lived in by couples with dependent children were semi-detached houses (35 per cent). More than one-quarter (30 per cent) of couples with dependent children lived in terraced houses compared with 39 per cent of lone parents with dependent children. Lone parents with dependent children were more than three times as likely as couples with dependent children to live in a purpose-built flat or maisonette (15 per cent compared with 7 per cent). One-person households were far more likely than family households to live in a flat. In 2006, 34 per cent of one person households lived in a flat compared with 12 per cent of family households. Among those under state pension age (65 for men, 60 for women), 39 per cent lived in either a purpose-built or a converted flat, compared with 29 per cent of those over state pension age. In Northern Ireland in 2006 houses were the most common type of dwelling for all household types but one-person households under pensionable age were the most likely to live in a flat (21 per cent).

Homelessness

The homeless are among the poorest and most disadvantaged members of society. During 2006/07, 73,000 households in

England were accepted as homeless and in priority need. This was 22 per cent less than in 2005/06. The most common need category of households accepted as being in priority need was households with dependent children (55 per cent), and a further 12 per cent were households that included a pregnant woman. Around one-third (32 per cent) of the acceptances in 2006/07 were households where applicants were vulnerable for reasons including mental illness, domestic violence, physical disability, old age or those leaving care, custody or the armed forces. Wales and Scotland had a larger proportion than England of priority need acceptances that were vulnerable households (47 per cent and 66 per cent respectively) although in Scotland vulnerable households include more categories than the other countries, which may explain some of the difference.

Among households accepted as homeless by local authorities in England in 2006/07, the most common reason (37 per cent) was that parents, relatives or friends were no longer able or willing to accommodate them (Figure 10.7). This reason has accounted for the largest number of homeless households since 1997/98 with variations over the period reflecting the overall pattern of homelessness in England. A similar proportion of households became homeless following the

Figure 10.7

Households accepted as homeless by local authorities: by main reason for loss of last settled home[1]

England

Percentages

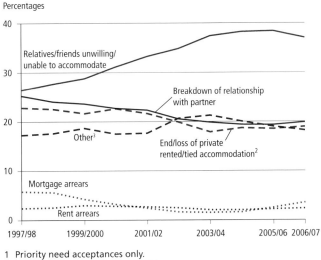

1 Priority need acceptances only.
2 Mainly the ending of an assured tenancy.
3 Includes households leaving an institution (such as hospital, prison or a residential home), and those returning from abroad, sleeping rough or in hostels, or made homeless by an emergency such as fire or flooding.

Source: Communities and Local Government

breakdown of a relationship, the loss of an assured tenancy, or 'other' reasons such as leaving an institution, around 20 per cent for each group in 2006/07. Around two-thirds of households that became homeless as a result of the breakdown of a relationship were because the relationship involved violence. The proportion of households made homeless because of mortgage arrears doubled from 2 per cent in 2003/04 to 4 per cent in 2006/07. However, the proportion made homeless for this reason is still well below the peak of 9 per cent in 1992/93.

In Scotland and Wales the reasons for households being accepted as homeless were very similar to England. In Scotland 35 per cent of households were made homeless because relatives or friends were unable to accommodate them and 25 per cent because of a relationship breakdown. In Wales the proportions made homeless for these reasons were 31 per cent and 21 per cent respectively. In Northern Ireland, around one in five households were accepted as homeless because friends or relatives were unable or unwilling to accommodate them (21 per cent) and one in six were accepted because of a relationship breakdown (17 per cent). In 2006/07 mortgage arrears accounted for 3 per cent of households becoming homeless in Wales and 1 per cent in both Scotland and Northern Ireland.

There were 87,000 households in temporary accommodation in England at the end of 2006/07, having fallen from a peak of

101,000 in 2004/05. This decrease is mainly the result of local authorities providing settled housing for those in temporary accommodation with support from both housing association partners and the private rented sector, along with fewer new cases of homelessness (see Figure 10.7). At the end of 2006/07 more than one-half (52 per cent) of the households living in temporary accommodation in England lived in self-contained properties leased in the private sector (46,000 households) and a further 21 per cent (18,000 households) were accommodated in self-contained social housing let on a temporary basis (Figure 10.8). Under the *Homelessness (Suitability of Accommodation) (England) Order 2003*, local authorities can no longer place families with children in bed and breakfast (B&B) accommodation for longer than six weeks. Between March 2003 and March 2007 the total number of homeless households living in B&B hotels fell by 65 per cent to 4,000. Over the same period, homeless households living in self-contained property leased from the private sector increased by 61 per cent to 46,000 (see also Tenure and accommodation section above).

In Scotland there was an overall increase of 10 per cent in the number of households in temporary accommodation between 2005/06 and 2006/07, from 8,300 to 9,200, with increases for all of the accommodation types. In Wales the total number of

Figure 10.8

Homeless households in temporary accommodation[1]

England

Thousands

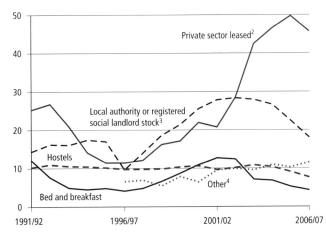

1 Excludes 'homeless at home' cases. See Appendix, Part 10: Homeless at home. Data are as at 31 March, and include households awaiting the outcome of homeless enquiries.
2 Prior to 1996/97, includes those accommodated directly with a private sector landlord.
3 Prior to 1996/97, includes all 'Other' types of accommodation.
4 From 1996/97, includes mobile homes (such as caravans and portacabins) or being accommodated directly with a private sector landlord.

Source: Communities and Local Government

10

households in temporary accommodation decreased by 8 per cent to 3,100 over this period.

Housing condition and satisfaction with area

To be considered 'decent' a dwelling must meet the statutory minimum standard for housing (the 'fitness standard') and as such must be in a reasonable state of repair; have reasonably modern facilities and services (in terms of fitness and modernisation); and provide a reasonable degree of thermal comfort (see Appendix, Part 10: Decent home standard). Between 1996 and 2005 the number of non-decent homes in England fell from 9.1 million to 6.0 million. It should be noted that the total dwelling stock increased over the period as new homes were added. This may partly explain the decrease in the proportion of all dwellings classified as non decent, from 45 per cent to 27 per cent (Table 10.9). Over this period the proportion of social sector homes considered non-decent fell at a faster rate than the proportion in the private sector. The Government's target, set out in the *2003 Sustainable Communities Plan*, is to bring all social housing in England up to a decent standard by 2010.

The most common reason why dwellings in any sector failed the decent home standard in 2005 was not providing a reasonable level of thermal comfort. Compared with dwellings in other tenure groups, privately rented homes were the most likely to fail to meet the decent home standard for thermal comfort, disrepair and fitness. Between 1996 and 2005 there were improvements in the condition of housing stock in England across a range of facilities and services. Overall, the proportion of dwellings with central heating rose from 80 per cent to 88 per cent, those with full or partial double glazing rose from 59 per cent to 86 per cent, and the proportion with a second lavatory rose from 31 per cent to 38 per cent. Private rented dwellings were the least likely of all types of tenure to have central heating, or full or partial double glazing in 2005.

Households that are disadvantaged, either because they have limited resources to improve their living conditions or because they are more at risk from poor conditions because of their age or a long-term illness or disability, tend to be more likely than others to experience poor living conditions. In England in 2005, 26 per cent of lone-parent households with dependent children lived in non-decent homes and 23 per cent lived in a poor quality environment (Table 10.10). Homes are deemed as being in a poor quality environment if they have 'significant' or 'major' problems in any of the three environmental areas assessed. These are upkeep, management or misuse of private and public buildings and space (for example neglected buildings, graffiti and litter); road traffic or other transport (presence of intrusive motorways and main roads, railway or aircraft noise and heavy traffic) and abandonment or non-residential use (vacant or boarded up buildings and intrusive industry) (see Appendix, Part 10: Poor quality environments).

In contrast, 22 per cent of couple households with dependent children lived in non-decent homes and 16 per cent lived in a poor quality environment. This disparity is linked to relative levels of household vulnerability and area deprivation. According to the English House Condition Survey 2005, three-quarters of lone-parent households with dependent children are classed as vulnerable and these are concentrated in deprived neighbourhoods, (See Appendix, Part 9: Indices of Deprivation 2004), with more than 40 per cent of all vulnerable households with children living in the 20 per cent most deprived areas in England. The private sector housing in these areas is more likely to be non-decent and in serious disrepair than elsewhere, and such areas also comprise a high proportion of social sector housing where homes are much more likely to have a poor quality environment.

Among all households there were marked differences in experience of poor living conditions by age of the oldest householder. Households where the oldest resident was aged 85 and over were the most likely to live in non-decent homes (40 per cent) and energy inefficient homes (16 per cent).

Table 10.9

Non-decent homes:[1] by tenure

England					Percentages
	1996	2001	2003	2004	2005
Private sector					
Owner-occupied	40	29	28	27	25
Privately rented	62	51	48	43	41
All private sector	43	32	30	29	27
Social sector					
Local authority	54	42	40	35	34
Registered social landlords	48	33	29	26	24
All rented from social sector	53	39	35	31	29
All tenures	45	33	31	29	27

1 See Appendix, Part 10: Decent home standard.

Source: English House Condition Survey, Communities and Local Government

Table 10.10

Poor living conditions: by type of household, 2005

England   Percentages

	Non-decent homes[1]	Poor quality environments[1]	Energy inefficient homes[1]	Homes in serious disrepair[2]
One-person households				
Under 60	35	20	10	11
Aged 60 and over	34	14	11	13
One-family households				
Couple no dependent children				
Under 60	25	16	11	9
Aged 60 and over	23	11	13	9
Couple with dependent children	22	16	8	8
Lone parent with dependent children	26	23	7	14
Other multi-person households	28	21	9	12
All households	27	16	10	10

1 See Appendix, Part 10: Decent home standard, Poor quality environments, and (for energy inefficient homes) Standard Assessment Procedure (SAP).
2 Based on the 10 per cent of all households in dwellings that have the highest repair costs per square metre.

Source: English House Condition Survey, Communities and Local Government

Households where the oldest resident was aged between 16 and 24 were the most likely to live in poor quality environments (28 per cent). From age 35 to 49 the proportion of people living in energy inefficient homes and homes in serious disrepair increased with age of the oldest householder.

As well as the condition of a person's home, aspects of the neighbourhood where they live can also be a source of problems or worry. In 2006/07 the most common aspect of their area that householders in England viewed as a serious problem was traffic (19 per cent) (Table 10.11). Among those

Table 10.11

Aspects of their neighbourhood householders viewed as a serious problem: by age,[1] 2006/07

England   Percentages[2]

	16–24	25–34	35–44	45–64	65 or over	All aged 16 or over
Traffic	12	17	19	21	19	19
Litter and rubbish in the streets	14	13	13	15	11	13
Teenagers hanging around on the street	15	18	16	13	8	13
Vandalism and hooliganism	11	11	10	10	8	10
Crime	14	13	12	11	7	10
People using or dealing drugs	9	10	10	10	5	9
Noise (excluding noisy neighbours)	8	7	6	7	6	7
Dogs	8	8	8	6	5	7
Graffiti	5	5	5	5	4	5
People being drunk or disruptive	8	8	6	5	2	5
Neighbours (including noisy neighbours)	7	6	5	5	2	4

1 Age of household reference person. See Appendix, Part 7: Household reference person.
2 Percentages do not sum to 100 because respondents could give more than one answer.

Source: Survey of English Housing, Communities and Local Government

10

aged 16 to 24, teenagers hanging around the streets (15 per cent), crime, and litter and rubbish (both 14 per cent) were cited as the most serious problems. Those aged 65 and over were the least likely to identify serious problems with their area, with the exception of traffic and noise (excluding noisy neighbours) for which the proportions viewing these as a problem in their area were the same as those for 35 to 44 year olds. Overall satisfaction with the neighbourhood varies by tenure. In England 89 per cent of owner-occupiers reported that they were 'satisfied' with their area in 2006/07 compared with 80 per cent of those who were renting in the social sector. More than twice as many of those living in social rented accommodation (19 per cent) cited crime as a serious problem in their area compared with those who were owner-occupiers (8 per cent). The proportion of householders considering crime to be a problem in their area fell from 58 per cent in 2001/02 to 48 per cent in 2004/05, and fell again to 45 per cent in 2006/07.

Housing mobility

In 2006/07 around one in ten of all households in England moved to their current home within the previous 12 months. Of these the most common types of move were from one owned property to another or from one privately rented property to another (Table 10.12). Overall movement within each of the three most common types of tenure was more likely than movement between them; 69 per cent of households

that owned their home outright had previously done so. Almost two-fifths (37 per cent) of all those moving had previously been in privately rented accommodation, showing how important this sector is in facilitating mobility within the housing market. Of the newly formed households, almost half (48 per cent) moved into the private rented sector, 32 per cent became owner-occupiers and 20 per cent became social renters.

More than one-half (56 per cent) of households in England in 2006/07 that moved in the past 12 months moved less than 5 miles. There were variations in the distance moved by tenure. Those renting in the social sector were more likely than any other group to move less than 5 miles (71 per cent), reflecting the fairly limited opportunities to move to another local authority area. In contrast, 14 per cent of private renters who moved in the past 12 months moved 50 miles or more, and a further 9 per cent moved into Great Britain, from Northern Ireland or abroad.

People have different reasons for moving. In 2006/07 in England the most common reason given for moving in the year before interview was the desire for different accommodation (20 per cent), with three-quarters of these wanting to move to larger or better accommodation. Personal reasons, which include divorce or separation and marriage or cohabitation, were the second most common reason (20 per cent). The desire to move to a better area (11 per cent), to live independently (10 per cent) and job-related reasons (also 10 per cent) were

Table 10.12

Households resident under one year: current tenure by previous tenure,[1] 2006/07

England

Percentages

| | | Previous tenure | | | | | |
| | | Owner-occupied | | Rented from social sector | | | |
	New household	Owned outright	Owned with a mortgage	Local authority	Housing association	Rented privately	All tenures
Current tenure							
Owner-occupied							
Owned outright	3	69	18	1	0	10	100
Owned with a mortgage	17	3	51	0	1	29	100
Rented from social sector							
Local authority	23	3	2	42	12	17	100
Housing association	17	4	6	11	39	24	100
Rented privately	20	4	14	3	3	56	100
All tenures	18	9	24	6	6	37	100

1 See Appendix, Part 10: Tenure.

Source: Survey of English Housing, Communities and Local Government

Table 10.13

Main reasons[1] for moving: by post-move tenure,[2] 2006/07

England   Percentages

	Owned outright	Owned with mortgage	Rented from social sector	Rented privately	All tenures
Different accommodation					
Wanted larger or better house or flat	9	23	15	10	15
Wanted smaller or cheaper house or flat	23	2	5	4	5
Personal reasons					
Divorce or separation	2	5	6	8	6
Marriage or cohabitation	3	9	1	5	5
Other personal reasons	18	4	14	8	8
To move to a better area	17	12	11	10	11
To live independently	5	12	12	9	10
Job-related reasons	1	8	1	17	10
Wanted to buy	3	17	0	0	6
Accommodation no longer available	0	-	7	9	5
Couldn't afford mortgage or rent	0	-	2	1	1
Better school for children	0	2	0	-	1
Other reasons	18	5	26	18	15
All households (=100%) (thousands)	166	727	398	966	2,256

1 Respondents were asked to give their main reason only, although more than one reason could apply.
2 Current tenure of all household reference persons who moved in the year before interview. See Appendix, Part 10: Tenure.

Source: Survey of English Housing, Communities and Local Government

other important factors in the decision to move home (Table 10.13).

Reasons for moving also varied by tenure. Among owner-occupiers, 23 per cent who owned their property outright moved because they wanted a smaller or cheaper house or flat, reflecting the high proportion of retired people in this group. However, among those buying with a mortgage, 23 per cent moved because they wanted a larger or better home. A far higher proportion of private renters than any other tenure group gave job-related reasons for their move (17 per cent).

The mobility of owner-occupiers is linked to the state of the housing market. Over the past 40 years the economy and the housing market have mirrored one another, with booms and slumps in one tending to contribute to the other. In 2006, 1.8 million property transactions took place in England and Wales, 16 per cent more than in 2005 (Figure 10.14). The number of property transactions in England and Wales rose during the 1980s, mainly as a result of existing owner-occupiers moving home. Market activity by first-time buyers and public

Figure 10.14

Property transactions[1]

England & Wales
Millions

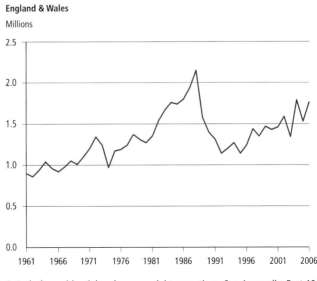

1 Includes residential and commercial transactions. See Appendix, Part 10: Property transactions.

Source: HM Revenue and Customs

10

sector tenants under the right to buy scheme were also factors, but contributed to a lesser extent. Changes to the mortgage lending market in the 1980s may also have been a contributing factor to the 1980s property boom, when new households opted for ownership rather than renting. Following sharp increases in the interest rate in the two years from 1988 (from around 7.4 per cent in mid-1988 to around 15 per cent two years later), the annual number of transactions halved from a peak of 2.2 million to 1.1 million by 1992, after which it fluctuated for several years in a generally upward direction. In Scotland there were 0.2 million transactions in 2006, a 6 per cent rise from 2005.

Housing market and finance

In 2006 the average price paid for a dwelling in the UK was £192,648, an increase of around 6 per cent from 2005 (Table 10.15). This was almost three times the average dwelling price compared with 1995, when it was £66,786.

In 2006, London, the South East and the East of England remained the most expensive regions in England in which to purchase property. However, with the exception of London, which had the second highest price increase from 2005, these areas recorded some of the lowest year on year price increases. Yorkshire and the Humber had the highest increase in England,

Figure 10.16

Distribution of dwelling prices

United Kingdom
Percentages

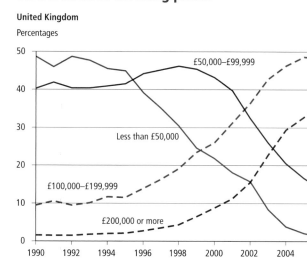

Source: Communities and Local Government

at 8 per cent. House price inflation in the UK was highest in Northern Ireland at 23 per cent, followed by Scotland at 11 per cent and Wales at 7 per cent. England had the lowest house price inflation in the UK at 6 per cent. Despite the larger increases in Northern Ireland and Scotland, average property prices there were among the lowest in the UK.

The increase in dwelling prices in the UK since the early 1990s can be seen in the changes in the distribution of prices paid. In 1990, 90 per cent of dwellings were bought for less than £100,000 and less than 2 per cent cost £200,000 or more (Figure 10.16). Until 2001 the majority of properties (58 per cent) continued to be bought for less than £100,000. In 2002 the number of properties costing £100,000 or more overtook those costing less than £100,000, and by 2006, more than one in three (37 per cent) dwellings bought in the UK cost more than £200,000, while 15 per cent cost less than £100,000. The distribution of house prices varies considerably by type of buyer. In 2006, 29 per cent of first-time buyers in the UK purchased their home for less than £100,000, compared with 7 per cent of former owner-occupiers. Conversely, almost one-half (49 per cent) of former owner-occupiers paid £200,000 or more for their home in 2006, compared with 17 per cent of first-time buyers.

In recent years steep increases in house prices have made affordability a particular concern for first-time buyers. Between 1996 and 2006 average prices paid by first-time buyers in the UK rose by around 200 per cent (not adjusting for inflation). The average price paid by first-time buyers in the UK in 2006 was £145,970, 3 per cent higher than in 2005 (Figure 10.17). The average price paid by former owner-occupiers rose by

Table 10.15

Average dwelling prices:[1] by region, 2006

United Kingdom

	All dwellings (£)	Percentage change 2005–06
United Kingdom	192,648	6.3
England	200,697	5.6
North East	139,481	6.7
North West	152,606	6.6
Yorkshire and the Humber	152,595	8.2
East Midlands	162,543	3.5
West Midlands	169,854	4.7
East	211,337	4.1
London	281,438	7.1
South East	240,655	4.7
South West	207,018	5.1
Wales	154,628	7.2
Scotland	139,080	11.3
Northern Ireland	159,637	23.1

1 See Appendix, Part 10: Mix adjusted prices.

Source: Regulated Mortgage Survey and BankSearch, Council of Mortgage Lenders

Figure 10.17

Average dwelling prices:[1] by type of buyer

United Kingdom

£ thousand

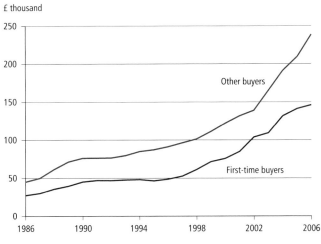

1 Uses simple average prices. See Appendix, Part 10: Mix adjusted prices.

Source: Communities and Local Government

Figure 10.18

Reasons[1] given by private renters[2] for not yet buying a home, 2006/07

England

Percentages

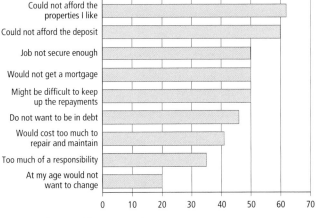

1 Respondents could give more than one reason.
2 Those who expect to buy their own property in the future.

Source: Survey of English Housing, Communities and Local Government

14 per cent to £239,042 over the same period, but this larger increase will have been compensated for by an increase in the price of the house they sold. In 2006 the average deposit paid by first-time buyers in the UK represented 16 per cent of the purchase price. This proportion has been falling steadily since 2003 when it peaked at 23 per cent. This may in part reflect recent trends for mortgage lenders to offer loans at higher multiples of incomes (on average three times annual income in 2006) and repayment terms over longer periods than the traditional 25 years. These mortgage terms have the effect of increasing the amount first-time buyers are able to borrow whilst lowering typical monthly repayments. This helps to compensate for the increase in the average income of first-time buyers falling behind the increase in average dwelling prices since the mid-1990s. Between 1996 and 2006 the average declared income of first-time buyers increased by 106 per cent to reach £41,000 (see also Chapter 5: Income and wealth). Declared income is the income against which the mortgage was obtained and could include one income or joint incomes but is not necessarily the same as household income (as the mortgage could be secured against only one income in households where more than one person is earning).

Many people who plan to buy a home live in private rented accommodation. In England in 2006/07, the most common reasons for not yet buying a home, given by those who expected to buy eventually, were that they could not afford the property they liked (62 per cent) or they could not afford the deposit (60 per cent) (Figure 10.18). In 2006/07 half of those who expected to buy a home eventually had concerns that it might be difficult to keep up mortgage repayments compared

with just over one-third (36 per cent) in 2005/06. A further half felt that they would not get a mortgage and that their job was not secure enough to buy a home yet. Other common reasons for not yet buying were related to concerns over finance and job security. Sixteen per cent expected to buy within the next year and a further 18 per cent in one to two years' time.

Private renters who did not expect to buy their own property gave more reasons for not being able to do so than those who did expect to buy in the future. The most common reason given was that they would not get a mortgage (78 per cent) with 75 per cent concerned that it might be difficult to keep up the repayments, a 19 per cent increase since 2005/06.

Housing costs constitute a substantial proportion of household budgets. In 2005/06 the average monthly mortgage payment of owner-occupier households in England was £530.00, representing 20 per cent of average household disposable income. This compared with a peak of 27 per cent in 1990, during a period of high mortgage interest rates, and a low of 16 per cent in 1996. For first time buyers mortgage payments comprised 22 per cent of monthly income in 2006 compared with 28 per cent in 1990 and 17 per cent in 1996. These data include both interest only and repayment mortgages.

The proportion of monthly household income used to pay mortgages varied according to levels of household income. Owner-occupier households with the lowest incomes spent a far higher proportion of their monthly disposable income on mortgage payments than any other. In 2005/06

10

Table 10.19

Mortgage payments as a proportion of household disposable[1] income, 2005/06

England

Percentages

	Mortgage payments (£ per month)									
	Less than £100	£100 but less than £200	£200 but less than £300	£300 but less than £400	£400 but less than £500	£500 but less than £750	£750 but less than £1,000	£1,000 or over	All	As percentage of income
Disposable[1] income (£ per month)										
Less than 1,000	12	26	17	14	10	13	6	3	100	39
1,000 but less than 1,500	7	18	24	21	12	13	3	2	100	24
1,500 but less than 2,000	5	13	20	20	17	18	5	2	100	21
2,000 but less than 2,500	3	12	16	18	16	26	8	3	100	18
2,500 but less than 3,000	2	8	12	14	18	30	11	6	100	18
3,000 but less than 4,000	1	5	7	11	13	32	18	11	100	17
4,000 or over	1	3	6	6	9	23	19	33	100	14
All incomes	4	11	14	15	14	23	10	9	100	19

1 After deduction of income tax and national insurance contributions.

Source: Labour Force Survey, Office for National Statistics

owner-occupier households in England with a monthly disposable income of less than £1,000 spent an average 39 per cent of it on mortgage payments (Table 10.19). In contrast, households with a monthly disposable income of £4,000 or more spent an average 14 per cent of it on mortgage payments. One-third of households in this income group made monthly mortgage payments of £1,000 or more. This was at least three times the proportion of those in any other income group.

For most owner-occupiers their home represents their most valuable financial asset (see also Chapter 5: Income and wealth). Releasing equity from the value of a home can be a relatively inexpensive and convenient way of borrowing money (see also Chapter 6: Expenditure). In 2005/06 it was reported that almost 5 per cent (656,000) of owner-occupiers in England had withdrawn equity from their home within the previous three years. The average amount released by each homeowner was £33,300. Home improvements or renovations was the most common reason for withdrawing equity (56 per cent), followed by paying off debts (29 per cent) and buying new goods for the property (15 per cent) (Table 10.20). Those who withdrew more than £20,000 were far more likely than those withdrawing less to use the proceeds towards financing the purchase of another property for themselves in the UK (10 per cent compared with 2 per cent), or to invest or save (17 per cent compared with 8 per cent). The most

common methods of equity release borrowing were to increase the size of the current mortgage through a further advance or top-up (used in 33 per cent of cases) or to remortgage the current home (used in 27 per cent of cases).

Table 10.20

Owner-occupier uses[1] of equity released from their properties, 2006/07

England

Percentages

Home improvements/renovations	56
Pay off debts	29
Buy new goods for the property	15
Invest or save	13
Buy a car or other vehicle	12
Pay for a holiday	7
Finance towards buying another property for self in UK	6
Finance for a business	3
Finance towards buying another property for self abroad	2
Finance towards buying a property for other family member	2
Pay for university costs	2
Pay for school fees	1
Other	10

1 Percentages sum to more than 100 as respondents could have used the equity withdrawn from their home in more than one way.

Source: Survey of English Housing, Communities and Local Government

Chapter 11

Environment

- In England in 2007, 33 per cent of adults strongly or tended to agree that they found it hard to change their habits to be more environmentally-friendly. (Figure 11.1)

- The year 2007 saw the wettest May to July period in the 241-year England and Wales rainfall series, with 387.6 mm of rain. (Page 152)

- In 2006, the UK generated over 18,000 GWh of electricity from renewable sources, almost three and a half times more than in 1991. (Table 11.8)

- Between 1971 and 2005 in the UK, domestic energy used for lighting and appliances increased 136 per cent and energy used for cooking fell by 35 per cent. (Figure 11.10)

- UK emissions of carbon monoxide in the air fell by 71 per cent between 1990 and 2005. (Figure 11.11)

- In 2006/07, 58 per cent of municipal waste in England was disposed to landfill, down from 84 per cent in 1996/97. Recycling rates increased from 7 to 31 per cent over the same period. (Figure 11.15)

DATA

Download data by clicking the online pdf

www.statistics.gov.uk/socialtrends38

Human activities affect the physical environment and natural resources at both the local and global level. The way we live now, mainly in industrial and commercial towns and conurbations, has led to huge pressures on land, wildlife, the atmosphere and waters. The Government has developed environment-related policies and regulations and the UK has a strategy for sustainable development to protect the environment and reduce the negative impacts that human activity can have.

Environmental concerns and behaviour

According to the Survey of Public Attitudes and Behaviours towards the Environment, carried out by the Department for Environment, Food and Rural Affairs (Defra) in 2007, environment and pollution was the fourth most important issue after crime, health and education that adults in England felt the Government should address. Nearly one-fifth (19 per cent) of adults felt that environment and pollution issues were important, although this had fallen from one-quarter (25 per cent) in 2001.

When asked to agree or disagree with statements on the environment and climate change, two-thirds (68 per cent) of respondents strongly agreed or tended to agree that humans were capable of finding ways to overcome the world's environmental problems (Table 11.1). However, nearly two in ten (18 per cent) strongly agreed or tended to agree that it takes too much effort to do things that are environmentally friendly. Around six in ten people tended to disagree or strongly disagreed with statements that 'the effects of climate

change are too far in the future to really worry me' (62 per cent) and 'scientists will find a solution to global warming without people having to make big changes in their lifestyles' (63 per cent).

One-third (33 per cent) of respondents strongly or tended to agree that they found it hard to change their habits to be more environmentally friendly, while nearly three in ten adults strongly or tended to agree with non-environmentally friendly statements such as 'I don't believe my behaviour and everyday lifestyle contribute to climate change' (29 per cent) or 'the environment is a low priority for me compared with a lot of other things in my life' (28 per cent).

Popular measures that around eight in ten people thought would have a major or medium impact on the UK contribution to climate change, if most people were willing to do them, were recycling, cutting down gas and electricity use at home, using a more fuel efficient car, using a car less and improving/installing insulation at home. People were shown some changes that they might have made to their lifestyles and asked if they performed these actions at the time of their interview. Defra found that 71 per cent of people in England said that they recycled their waste more than they had done before, rather than throwing things away, and intended to keep it up (Table 11.2), while 65 per cent wasted less food than they did, and 58 per cent cut down gas and electricity for use at home. Around three in ten (29 per cent) used a car less or took fewer flights than they did previously and intended to keep it up. A similar proportion of people did not really want to use a car less or fly less (24 per cent and 32 per cent respectively).

Table 11.1

Attitudes towards the environment and climate change,[1] 2007

England   Percentages

	Strongly agree	Tend to agree	Neither agree nor disagree	Tend to disagree	Strongly disagree
Humans are capable of finding ways to overcome the world's environmental problems	24	44	19	11	4
I don't believe my behaviour and everyday lifestyle contribute to climate change	8	21	25	35	12
The effects of climate change are too far in the future to really worry me	7	14	17	36	26
The environment is a low priority for me compared with a lot of other things in my life	7	21	26	33	15
Scientists will find a solution to global warming without people having to make big changes to their lifestyles	5	13	19	36	27
I find it hard to change my habits to be more environmentally-friendly	5	28	24	33	10
Climate change is beyond control – it's too late to do anything about it	5	12	19	39	25
It takes too much effort to do things that are environmentally friendly	3	15	21	42	18

1 Percentages use the total number of people who gave one of the five options as a base and do not include those that answered 'don't know'.

Source: Department for Environment, Food and Rural Affairs

Table 11.2

Proportion of people engaging in environmentally friendly behaviours,[1] 2007

England   Percentages

	Recycling more	Wasting less food	Cutting down gas and electricity use at home	Reducing water use at home	Buying food produced locally rather than abroad	Using a car less	Flying less
Already doing this and intend to keep it up	71	65	58	52	38	29	29
Already doing this, but probably won't manage to keep it up	6	8	8	7	7	6	4
Thinking about doing this	12	12	14	14	18	13	8
Thought about doing this, but probably won't do it	4	4	6	7	9	13	8
Tried doing this but I've given up	1	2	1	1	2	2	1
Haven't really thought about doing this	5	6	9	13	21	13	19
Don't really want to do this	1	3	5	6	5	24	32

1 The base for these proportions varies as those who answered 'not applicable' or 'don't know' are excluded. For example, those without a car were classed as not applicable for the 'using a car less' option.

Source: Department for Environment, Food and Rural Affairs

However, a further 13 per cent were thinking about using a car less and 8 per cent were considering flying less.

Global warming and climate change

The temperature of the Earth is determined by a balance between energy from the sun and radiation from the surface of the Earth to space. Some of this outgoing radiation is absorbed by naturally occurring gases such as water vapour and carbon dioxide. This creates a greenhouse effect that keeps the surface of the Earth around 33 degrees Celsius (°C) warmer than it would otherwise be and helps to sustain life.

Both global and local average temperatures have risen over the long term since the late 19th century, though there have been fluctuations around this trend (Figure 11.3). For this purpose, local is defined as the triangular area of the UK enclosed by Bristol, Lancashire and London and is otherwise referred to as 'central England'. Over the last century, global surface temperatures increased by 0.3°C to 0.6°C, beyond the range of estimated average temperatures experienced on Earth over the last 1,000 years. Ten of the warmest years globally have all occurred in the last 12 years (1995 to 2006), with 1998 the hottest year since records began in 1850. The year 2006 was the sixth warmest year and it would have been warmer but for unusually cold ocean temperatures in the equatorial Pacific also known as 'La Niña'. Current climate models predict that global temperatures will rise by between 1.4 and 5.8°C by the end of the 21st century, which will affect sea levels and weather patterns.

During the 20th century, the annual mean temperature for central England warmed by about 1°C. The 1990s were

exceptionally warm in central England by historical standards, and about 0.6°C warmer than the 1961–1990 average temperature. The warmest year ever measured in central England was 2006, with an annual average temperature of 10.84°C. It also included the warmest month ever (July) where the mean temperature was 19.7°C and a record temperature for September (a mean temperature of 16.8°C). Records for 2007 were not available at the time of printing. The highest single temperature ever recorded in the UK was in August

Figure 11.3

Difference in average surface temperature: deviation from 1961–90 average[1]

Global and Central England

Degrees Celsius

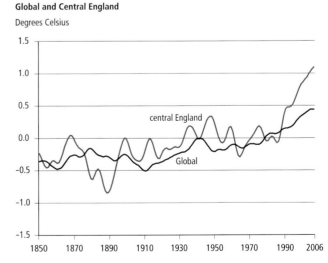

1 Data are smoothed to remove short-term variation from a time series to get a clearer view of the underlying changes.

Source: Hadley Centre for Climate Prediction and Research

11

2003 when temperatures peaked at 38.5°C at the observing station at Brodgate near Faversham in Kent. Climate change models suggest that the average temperature across the UK could increase by between 2.0°C and 3.5°C by the 2080s, with the level of warming dependent on future global greenhouse gas emissions.

Although the UK overall does not suffer from a lack of rain, water is a resource that needs to be managed carefully, particularly as climate change models predict that the UK will experience a change in rainfall patterns. On average, rainfall across the UK is usually well distributed through the year, but summer rainfall was greater than winter rainfall for extended periods during the 19th century. In contrast since the 1960s there has been a tendency towards wetter winters and drier summers in England and Wales (Figure 11.4). Between 1995 and 2004 winter rainfall had, on average, exceeded summer rainfall by almost 100 millimetres, the greatest margin in records stretching back to 1766. However, more recent years have not conformed to this pattern. Dry winters in 2004/05 and 2005/06 resulted in severe drought conditions and although the 2006/07 winter rainfall was in the normal range, the late spring and early summer rainfall in 2007 was remarkable. The year 2007 saw the wettest May to July period in the 241-year England and Wales rainfall series with 387.6 mm of rain, and triggered widespread and severe flooding.

Climate change predictions suggest that winters across the UK may become wetter and summers drier. In south east England

Figure 11.4

Winter and summer rainfall[1,2]

England & Wales

Millimetres

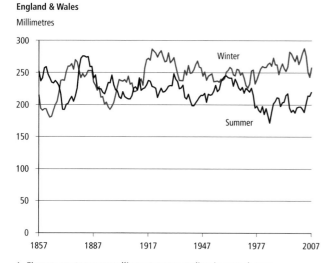

1 Figures are ten-year rolling averages ending in year shown.
2 Winter is December to February, summer is June to August.

Source: Climate Research Unit, University of East Anglia; Hadley Centre for Climate Prediction and Research; Centre for Ecology & Hydrology (CEH-Wallingford)

these changes could be as much as a 50 per cent reduction in summer precipitation by the 2080s. However, there is considerable uncertainty about future rainfall patterns and given the natural variability of the UK climate any short-term trends should be treated with caution.

Changes in seasonal patterns of rainfall and temperature have important implications for water resources and flood risk. An increase in rainfall over the winter – when evaporation losses are lowest – would generally be beneficial for water resources but could increase flood frequency. On the other hand lower summer rainfall can, as in 1995 and 2003, lead to pressure on water resources (for example, increased demands for irrigation and garden watering) particularly during hot summers. Hot, dry summers also result in exceptionally dry soils. Autumn and winter rainfall must then restore soil moisture before water becomes available for the recovery of river flows and the replenishment of reservoirs and aquifers (underground sources of water).

Flooding is a natural feature, which regularly brings disruption and damage to different parts of the UK. Floods vary in scale from water running off a saturated hillside to rivers bursting their banks. The impacts of floods range from waterlogged fields and impassable roads and railways to widespread inundation of houses and commercial property and, occasionally, loss of life. Normally the risk of a flood during the summer is diminished by dry soil conditions. However, in 2007 the record May to July rainfall ensured that soils remained close to saturation across much of England and Wales and storm totals exceeding 100 mm in parts of the North East and the South Midlands triggered a sequence of major flood events. Typically these included localised flash floods (mostly in urban areas), extremely high flows in river catchments, and subsequently, extensive floodplain floods as the runoff concentrated in the major rivers of southern Britain (including the Severn, the Warwickshire Avon, the Bedford Ouse, the Trent and the Thames). This caused transport disruption, the inundation of many houses, commercial property and vehicles; extensive crop damage and the need to move livestock to higher ground. According to the Association of British Insurers, the cost to the insurance industry was estimated to be around £3 billion.

In 2001 the Intergovernmental Panel on Climate Change (IPCC) reported strong new evidence that most of the warming over the last 50 years was attributable to human activities. The predominant factor among these activities was the emission of 'greenhouse gases', such as carbon dioxide, methane and nitrous oxide. The final part of the IPCC Fourth Assessment Report *Climate Change 2007* was published in November 2007.

11

Figure 11.5

Emissions of greenhouse gases[1]

United Kingdom

Million tonnes of carbon dioxide equivalent

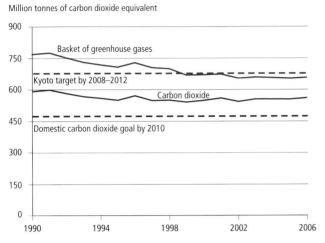

1 See Appendix, Part 11: Global warming and climate change.

Source: Department for Environment, Food and Rural Affairs; AEA Energy and Environment

Figure 11.6

Carbon dioxide emissions: by end user

United Kingdom

Million tonnes of carbon dioxide equivalent

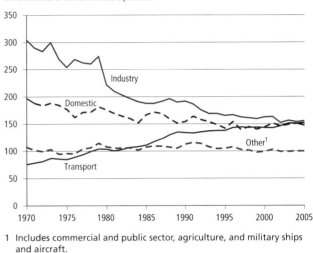

1 Includes commercial and public sector, agriculture, and military ships and aircraft.

Source: AEA Energy and Environment

The report stated that urgent action must be taken to reduce greenhouse gas emissions or climate change will intensify and have a dramatic effect on the natural world and human society.

Under the Kyoto Protocol, the UK has a legally binding target to reduce its emissions of a 'basket' of six greenhouse gases by 12.5 per cent over the period 2008 to 2012. This reduction is against 1990 emission levels for carbon dioxide, methane and nitrous oxide, and 1995 levels for hydrofluorocarbons, perfluorocarbons and sulphur hexafluoride. Additionally, the Government intends to move beyond that target towards a goal of reducing carbon dioxide emissions to 20 per cent below 1990 levels by 2010. In 2006 emissions of the 'basket' of six greenhouse gases, weighted by global warming potential (see Appendix, Part 11: Global warming and climate change), were about 15.3 per cent below the base year level (Figure 11.5). However, emissions had not fallen since 2002, mainly a result of increased carbon dioxide emissions from industry and transport.

Carbon dioxide (CO_2) accounted for around 85 per cent of greenhouse gas emissions within the UK in 2006. In 2005 the industry and the transport sectors each accounted for 28 per cent of emissions, and domestic users accounted for a further 27 per cent (Figure 11.6). For these data, emissions from power stations that generate electricity are allocated to the sectors using that electricity.

Between 1970 and 2005 estimated carbon dioxide emissions fell by 19 per cent. Much of this decline came from a reduction

in emissions attributable to industry, which fell steeply in the late 1970s and early 1980s, declined more steadily from that point, and then levelled off from 1997. The overall result was a 49 per cent reduction in emissions from industry between 1970 and 2005. Emissions by domestic users declined by 25 per cent over the same period, while those attributable to transport more than doubled – a 101 per cent increase. Furthermore, these transport data do not include figures for international aviation and shipping. Between 1990 and 2005, emissions from aviation fuel use more than doubled. CO_2 emissions from domestic aviation increased by 7 per cent between 2004 and 2005. International aviation emissions increased by 6 per cent over the same period reflecting an increase in the number of flights (see also Chapter 12: Transport).

Use of resources

One way that global warming can be tackled is by using renewable sources of energy. Renewable energy utilises natural resources such as sunlight, wind, tides and geothermal heat, which are naturally replenished. Renewable energy technologies range from solar power, wind power, and hydroelectricity to biomass and biofuels for transportation. None of these forms of generation, except biomass, involves the production of carbon dioxide, and biomass generation produces only the carbon that the material has absorbed from the atmosphere while growing.

Under its Renewables Obligation (the Government's key measure to encourage renewable energy generation), the UK Government is committed to increasing the contribution of

11

electricity from renewable sources. By providing market incentives for renewable energy, the UK has a challenging target that by 2010, 10 per cent of licensed electricity sales will be from renewable sources. The EU-wide target is that 22 per cent of electricity generated in the EU should be generated from renewable sources by 2010. In 2005 renewable sources accounted for around 6 per cent of electricity generated in the UK (Table 11.7). This was among the lowest proportions in the EU-27 where the average was 17 per cent. Latvia, Austria and

Sweden produced the greatest proportions (71 per cent, 64 per cent and 53 per cent respectively). Cyprus and Malta produced no electricity from renewable sources and were wholly dependent on petroleum products. The UK figure reflects its historical use of coal and gas, the absence of high mountains, which facilitate large scale hydro generation, and the lack of extensive forests needed for biomass generation. There is, however, scope to develop extensive wind and wave power in the UK.

Table 11.7

Electricity generation: by fuel used, EU comparison, 2005

Percentages

	Coal and lignite	Petroleum products	Natural and derived gases	Nuclear	Renewable sources and waste[1]	All fuels (=100%) (thousand GWh[2])
Germany	43	2	12	27	16	578
France	5	1	4	78	11	550
United Kingdom	34	1	39	20	6	381
Italy	14	15	51	-	19	291
Spain	27	8	27	20	18	282
Sweden	-	1	1	45	53	155
Poland	91	1	3	-	4	144
Netherlands	23	2	61	4	9	96
Belgium	9	2	29	54	5	83
Czech Republic	58	-	6	31	5	76
Finland	15	1	17	33	34	68
Austria	11	3	22	-	64	62
Greece	59	15	13	-	13	56
Romania	36	3	16	9	36	56
Portugal	33	19	29	-	20	45
Bulgaria	39	1	5	43	12	40
Denmark	42	4	24	-	30	34
Hungary	20	1	35	39	5	33
Slovakia	17	2	8	56	16	29
Ireland	35	13	43	-	9	24
Lithuania	-	3	20	70	7	14
Slovenia	33	-	2	40	25	14
Estonia	91	-	7	-	1	9
Latvia	-	-	28	-	71	5
Cyprus	-	100	-	-	-	4
Luxembourg	-	-	76	-	24	4
Malta	-	100	-	-	-	2
EU-27 total	28	4	21	30	17	3,134

1 Non-renewable wastes included.
2 Gigawatt hours.

Source: Eurostat

In 2005 the UK was in the top ten EU countries in terms of the proportion of electricity generated using coal and lignite. More than one-third (34 per cent) of UK electricity was generated from coal and lignite. Poland and Estonia were the main users of coal and lignite, with 91 per cent of their electricity generated by this type of fuel. One-fifth (20 per cent) of the electricity produced in the UK in 2005 was generated by nuclear power stations, the same proportion as that produced by Spain and a similar proportion to Germany (27 per cent). France produced more than three-quarters (78 per cent) of its electricity from nuclear power and Lithuania just less than three-quarters (70 per cent). Nearly half of EU member states had no nuclear production capacity.

In 2006 electricity was generated from renewable sources on more than 1,200 sites around the UK (714 sites in England, 304 in Scotland, 102 in Wales and 83 in Northern Ireland). Scotland had the capacity to generate 24 per cent more electricity than England because of its considerable hydro resources.

In 2006, 89 per cent of the renewable energy produced in the UK was transformed into electricity. This was equivalent to 18,133 gigawatt hours (GWh) almost three and a half times more than 1991 (Table 11.8). Currently biofuels dominate the amount of electricity generated (9,295 GWh in 2006) followed by hydro (4,605 GWh) and wind and wave power (4,225 GWh) but wind power is the fastest growing source, with energy generation having more than quadrupled in the last five years.

Table 11.8

Generation of electricity: by renewable sources

United Kingdom   GWh[1]

	1991	2001	2006
Wind and wave	9	965	4,225
Solar photo-voltaics	..	2	7
Hydro	4,624	4,055	4,605
Biofuels			
Landfill gas	208	2,507	4,424
Sewage sludge digestion	328	363	463
Municipal solid waste combustion[2]	150	880	1,083
Co-firing with fossil fuels	..	..	2,528
Other biofuels[3]	1	776	797
Total	5,320	9,549	18,133

1 Gigawatt hours.
2 Biodegradable part only.
3 Includes electricity from farm waste digestion, poultry litter combustion, meat and bone combustion, straw and short rotation coppice.

Source: Department for Business, Enterprise and Regulatory Reform

Figure 11.9

Consumption of primary fuels[1] for energy use

United Kingdom

Million tonnes of oil equivalent

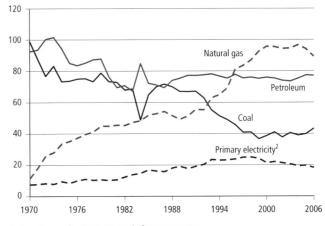

1 See Appendix, Part 11: Fuels for energy use.
2 Includes nuclear, hydroelectric and wind, wave and solar energy.

Source: Department for Business, Enterprise and Regulatory Reform

Fossil fuels accounted for more than 90 per cent of the total consumption of fuels used in the production of energy in the UK in 2006. The use of coal and petroleum for the production of energy fell between 1970 and 2006, by 56 per cent and 17 per cent respectively, although consumption of petroleum has remained relatively stable since 1988 (Figure 11.9). Natural gas consumption rose by 690 per cent between 1970 and 2006, while primary electricity production from nuclear energy, hydroelectricity and other non-thermal renewables have become increasingly important rising by 150 per cent, over the same period.

Domestic energy consumption increased by 32 per cent between 1971 and 2005, from 35.6 to 47.2 million tonnes of oil equivalent. However, in terms of energy use per household the increase was 1.5 per cent, from 1.87 to 1.90 tonnes of oil equivalent per household (22,100 kilowatt hours). Growth in the number of households, the proportion of households with central heating, and the ownership of household electrical appliances, have contributed to increased consumption over the period but growth in overall consumption has, to an extent been offset by improvements in energy efficiency (see also Chapter 2: Households and families and Chapter 10: Housing).

Most domestic energy consumption is used for space heating, which accounted for 60 per cent of final domestic energy use in the UK in 2005 (Figure 11.10 overleaf). The use of energy for space heating has increased at a slower rate than other energy demands due to improvements in levels of home insulation, double glazing and more efficient home heating. The other major areas of energy consumption in the domestic sector are

11

Figure 11.10

Domestic energy consumption: by final use

United Kingdom

Million tonnes of oil equivalent[1]

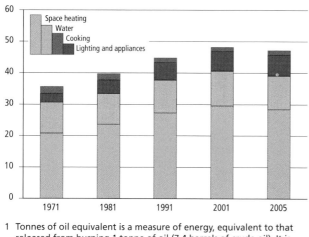

1 Tonnes of oil equivalent is a measure of energy, equivalent to that released from burning 1 tonne of oil (7.4 barrels of crude oil). It is approximately equal to 42 billion joules, or 11.6 megawatt hours.

Source: Department for Business, Enterprise and Regulatory Reform

for heating water, lighting and appliances, and cooking. Between 1971 and 2005, energy consumed by lighting and appliances in the UK increased by 136 per cent, reflecting the increasing number of electrical appliances in households. Energy use for cooking in the home fell by 35 per cent, perhaps partly explained by changes in technologies and lifestyle, with the greater availability of convenience food and people eating out more frequently in 2005 than in 1971.

Household energy use per person in the UK in 2004, at 0.75 tonnes of oil equivalent (toe), was broadly similar to other northern EU countries, such as Sweden (0.80 toe), Denmark (0.79 toe), France (0.78 toe) and the Netherlands (0.64 toe). Within the EU, northern countries generally have higher levels of energy use per household than southern countries, reflecting the higher proportion of household energy used for heating. Similarly, countries such as Iceland, Canada, Russia and the United States used considerably more energy, 2.42, 0.99, 0.94 and 0.90 tonnes of oil equivalent per person respectively in 2004.

Pollution

The term 'pollution' can be defined as a chemical or physical agent in an inappropriate location or concentration that causes damage or contamination. Air pollution comes from a variety of different sources. Fossil fuel combustion is the main source of air pollution in the UK, with road transport and power stations the largest contributors. Emissions of other pollutants are more evenly spread among different sources, although road

transport and electricity generation are again important contributors.

Emissions of the major air pollutants in the UK have generally been falling since the 1970s, and the rate of decline has accelerated since 1989 (Figure 11.11). Carbon monoxide (CO) is harmful because it reduces the capacity of the blood to carry and deliver oxygen around the body. Emissions of carbon monoxide fell by 32 per cent between 1970 and 1990, and by 71 per cent between 1990 and 2005. This was mainly the result of introducing catalytic converters in petrol cars.

Sulphur dioxide (SO_2) is an acid gas that can affect both human and animal health, and vegetation. It affects the lining of the nose, throat and lungs, particularly among those with asthma and chronic lung disease, and is one of the pollutants that form 'acid rain' leading to the destruction of crops and forests in the UK and elsewhere. Sulphur dioxide emissions fell by 81 per cent between 1990 and 2005, largely as a result of the reduction in coal use by power stations and the introduction of the desulphurisation of flue gas at some power stations. Following this change, the rate of decline slowed after 1999. Nitrogen oxides (NO_x) are also acid gases and have similar effects to sulphur dioxide. Emissions of nitrogen oxide pollutants fell by 45 per cent between 1990 and 2005, again mainly as a result of catalytic converters on petrol cars and reductions in emissions from large combustion plants. Emissions of particulate matter fell by 51 per cent between 1990 and 2005, due partly to a reduction in emissions from power stations, the installation of abatement equipment, and increased efficiency

Figure 11.11

Emissions of selected air pollutants[1]

United Kingdom

Million tonnes

Carbon monoxide

Sulphur dioxide

Nitrogen oxide

Volatile organic compounds

PM_{10}[2]

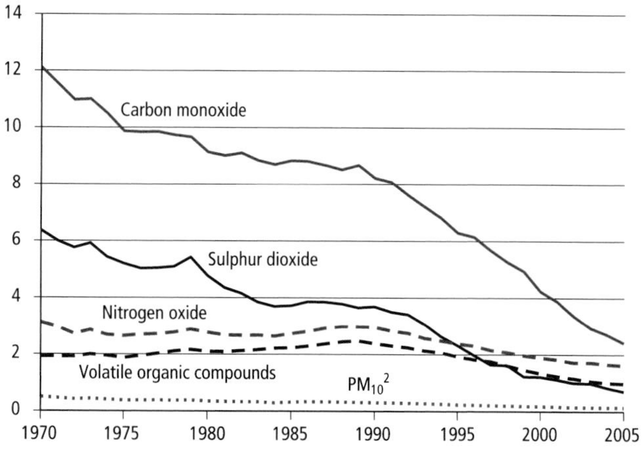

1 See Appendix, Part 11: Air pollutants.
2 Particulate matter that is less than 10 microns in diameter.

Source: Department for Environment, Food and Rural Affairs; AEA Energy and Environment

and use of natural gas for electricity generation.

The measurement of levels of ozone and particulate matter in the air is important as these two pollutants have significant impacts on public health through long-term exposure. They can cause biological mutations, poor lung development, breathing difficulties and premature death.

Particulate matter consists of very small liquid and solid particles floating in the air. Of greatest concern to public health are the particles small enough to be inhaled into the deepest parts of the lung. These particles are less than 10 microns in diameter – about one-seventh of the thickness of a human hair – and are known as PM_{10}. Annual average particulate levels monitored at urban background sites in the UK have generally decreased since 1993 when they were 36 microgrammes per cubic metre (Figure 11.12). In 2006 the level was 24 microgrammes per cubic metre, an increase from 22 in 2005. Annual average particulate levels monitored at roadside sites stood at 32 microgrammes per cubic metre, compared with 29 in 2005.

Ozone is not emitted directly into the atmosphere, but is a secondary pollutant produced by reactions between nitrogen dioxide, hydrocarbons and sunlight. Ozone levels are usually highest in rural areas, particularly in hot, still, sunny weather conditions, giving rise to 'summer smog'. Rural ozone levels averaged 74 microgrammes per cubic metre in 2006 compared

Figure 11.12

Air quality:[1] by levels of ozone and particulate matter[2]

United Kingdom

Microgrammes per cubic metre

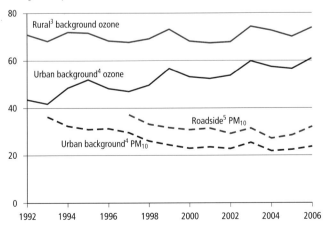

1 See Appendix, Part 11: Measuring air pollution.
2 Particulate matter that is less than 10 microns in diameter (PM_{10}).
3 Rural sites include monitoring sites in remote and rural areas.
4 Monitoring sites in suburban, central urban and industrial urban areas.
5 Includes kerbside monitoring sites and roadside sites next to major roads.

Source: Department for Environment, Food and Rural Affairs; AEA Energy and Environment

with 70 microgrammes per cubic metre in 2005 and 68 microgrammes per cubic metre in 1993. Urban background ozone levels were 61 microgrammes per cubic metre in 2006 compared with 57 in 2005.

The quality and quantity of water supplies are important to the health and well-being of both people and the natural environment. A number of factors affect the quality of rivers and other areas of water, including climate, fertiliser run-off, and industrial and sewage discharge. Lower than average rainfall, for example, can result in low river flows, and can have an adverse effect on river water quality by reducing the dilution of pollutants.

The Environment Agency monitors water pollution in England and Wales. There are four categories of pollution incidents. Category 1 incidents, classified as 'most severe', are defined as those that have a persistent and/or extensive effect on water quality. They may cause major damage to aquatic ecosystems; cause the closure of a drinking water abstraction plant; cause major damage to agriculture and/or commerce; or have a serious impact on the human population. Category 2 incidents, classified as 'severe', have similar but less serious effects. Category 3 incidents are relatively minor and if no impact on the environment has occurred, the incident is reported as Category 4 (see Appendix, Part 13: Water pollution incidents). In 2006 the Environment Agency recorded 22,034 incidents in England and Wales, of which 605 were category 1 or category 2 incidents to water. The most commonly identified sources of these incidents were the sewage and water industry (22 per cent), industry (12 per cent) and agriculture (11 per cent).

Since 1993 the number of category 1 incidents in England and Wales has fallen by nearly three-quarters (74 per cent) to 86 in 2006 (Figure 11.13 overleaf). The number of category 2 incidents have also fallen over the same period, by 92 per cent to 519.

Pollution from the land and rivers can also affect the seas around the UK. The microbiological quality of bathing waters can be polluted by sewage effluent, storm water overflows and river-borne pollutants that could affect human health, as well as pollutants from shipping and other seaborne activities. The European Commission (EC) Bathing Water Directive sets compulsory limits on acceptable levels for a number of physical, chemical and microbiological pollutants in bathing waters, with total and faecal coliforms being the most important. Coliforms are bacteria that inhabit the intestines of humans and other vertebrates.

Nearly 97 per cent of coastal bathing waters in the UK complied with the mandatory EC Bathing Water Directive coliform standards during the bathing season (see Appendix, Part 13:

11

Figure 11.13

Water pollution incidents: by category[1]

England & Wales

Number of incidents

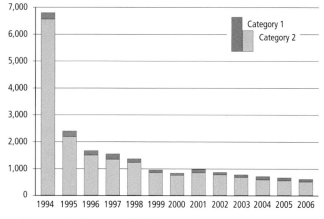

1 Category 1 incidents are classified as 'most severe' and have a persistent or extensive effect on water quality. Category 2 incidents are classified as 'severe' and have similar but less serious effects.

Source: Department for Environment, Food and Rural Affairs

Table 11.14

Coastal bathing water – compliance with EC bathing water directive coliform standards[1,2]

United Kingdom   Percentages

	Mandatory compliance		Guideline compliance	
	2006	2007	2006	2007
United Kingdom	99.6	96.5	76.1	71.3
England[3]	99.8	97.8	76.2	72.8
North East	98.2	94.5	80.0	72.7
North West	100.0	90.9	28.1	36.4
Anglian	100.0	100.0	71.8	71.8
Thames	100.0	100.0	75.0	50.0
Southern	100.0	100.0	78.2	82.1
South West	100.0	98.4	84.3	78.0
Wales	98.8	97.5	88.8	86.3
Scotland	100.0	88.1	55.7	49.2
Northern Ireland	100.0	91.3	87.5	47.8

1 During the bathing season. See Appendix, Part 11: Bathing waters.
2 EC Bathing Water Directive 76/160/EEC.
3 Environment Agency regions. The boundaries of the Environment Agency regions are based on river catchment areas and not county borders.

Source: Environment Agency; Scottish Environment Protection Agency; Environment and Heritage Service, Northern Ireland

Bathing waters) in 2007 (Table 11.14). There was 97.8 per cent compliance in England, 97.5 per cent in Wales, 91.3 per cent in Northern Ireland and 88.1 per cent in Scotland. Although bathing water quality has generally increased steadily since the late 1990s, levels of compliance dropped in some areas of the UK in 2007 compared with 2006, following the exceptional summer 2007 rainfall (see also Figure 11.4). The increased flow of water washed pollution into coastal waters through the sewage network and from diffuse sources, particularly agriculture, thereby impacting on overall water quality. However, coastal bathing waters in the Anglian, Thames and Southern regions in England achieved full compliance with the Directive in 2007.

Compliance with more stringent guideline standards which form part of the requirements for Blue Flag beach status awarded by the Foundation for Environmental Education, was 71.3 per cent for the UK in 2007. In Wales 86.3 per cent of coastal bathing waters met this guideline standard, compared with 72.8 per cent in England, 49.2 per cent in Scotland and 47.8 per cent in Northern Ireland. Again some of these results were lower than in 2006 for the reasons mentioned above, however the general trend towards improved bathing water quality is expected to continue as further improvements are made to sewerage infrastructure affecting coastal waters, and through tackling diffuse pollution.

Other than full compliance with the EC Directive for water quality, for a beach to be awarded a Blue Flag, environmental standards are set relating to the provision of litter bins, beach cleansing, and safety. In the UK there were 136 beaches with Blue Flag status in 2006, compared with 12 when the award scheme started in 1987.

In 2006 there were 219 pollution incidents in England and Wales that had a serious impact on land quality. This is a fall of 55 per cent since 2002 and the lowest number on record. The waste management industry caused 14 per cent of serious (category 1 and 2) land pollution incidents in 2006. Many of the other sources of incidents could not be identified, especially where waste had been disposed of illegally or fly-tipped.

Waste management

The collection and disposal of domestic waste, litter and rubbish from public areas, as well as some commercial waste, is the responsibility of local authorities throughout the UK. Most of this municipal waste has traditionally been disposed to landfill, a method that makes little use of the waste and produces greenhouse gases, mainly carbon dioxide and methane.

11

Figure 11.15

Management of municipal waste: by method

England
Million tonnes

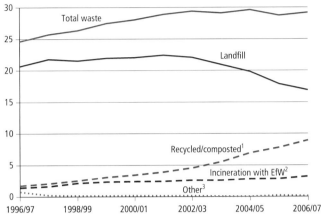

1 Includes household and non-household sources collected for recycling or for centralised composting; home composting estimates are not included in this total.
2 Energy from waste. Includes refuse derived fuel.
3 Includes incineration without energy from waste and other disposal that excludes any processing before waste is sent to landfill or materials reclamation.

Source: Department for Environment, Food and Rural Affairs

The total amount of municipal waste produced in England rose from around 24.6 million tonnes in 1996/97 to peak at nearly 29.6 million tonnes in 2004/05. In 2006/07 it stood at 29.2 million tonnes, an increase of 19 per cent since 1996/97 (Figure 11.15).

In 2006/07, 58 per cent of this municipal waste was disposed to landfill, down from 84 per cent in 1996/97. Recycling increased over the same period, from 7 per cent to 31 per cent of total municipal waste, while waste disposed of through burning and using the incineration process to produce energy increased from 6 per cent to 11 per cent of total municipal waste.

Around 89 per cent of municipal waste in England was generated by households in 2006/07. This represented 25.9 million tonnes of waste, equivalent to 509 kilogrammes of household waste per person over the year. The amount of household waste collected for recycling or composting (excluding home-composting) in 2006/07, at 8.0 million tonnes, was 17 per cent higher than in 2005/06. Recycling or composting includes materials taken to civic amenity sites (local authority dumps) and other drop-off points such as bottle banks provided by the local authority, as well as material collected directly from households.

In 2006/07 compost was the largest component of recycled household waste in England, at 36 per cent of the total. The next largest component was paper and card (19 per cent). Glass made up 10 per cent, while co-mingled collections – that is collection of a number of recyclable materials in the same box or bin (for example paper, cans and plastics) – together with other materials (such as wood, furniture and oils) made up 15 per cent.

The Government target for England, set in *Waste Strategy for England 2007*, is to recycle or compost at least 40 per cent of household waste by 2010. The recycling rate for household waste in England rose from 11 per cent in 2000/01 to 31 per cent in 2006/07.

There was a wide variation in household recycling rates achieved by waste disposal authorities or councils across England and Wales in 2006/07. The rates varied between 12 per cent in Tower Hamlets in London and 13 per cent in Blaenau Gwent and the Isles of Scilly to 49 per cent in Cambridgeshire, with over half of authorities achieving a rate of more than 28 per cent (Map 11.16). Eleven waste disposal authorities or councils had a household waste recycling rate of less than

Map 11.16

Household waste recycling:[1] by waste disposal authority,[2] 2006/07

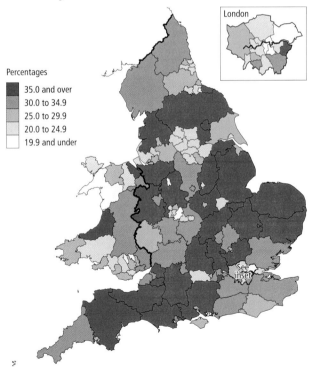

1 Includes composting.
2 Mainly counties or unitary authorities. Metropolitan districts in West Yorkshire, South Yorkshire, Tyne and Wear and West Midlands. Data are collected separately for Wigan Metropolitan District and Isles of Scilly Local Authority District. London contains statutory joint waste authorities and London boroughs.

Source: Department for Environment, Food and Rural Affairs; Welsh Assembly Government

20 per cent. In Northern Ireland the highest household recycling rates were in Antrim Borough Council and Banbridge District Council (47 per cent and 45 per cent respectively). Belfast City Council had the lowest recycling rate (19 per cent).

A regional comparison of the composition of materials collected for recycling in England in 2006/07 showed a wide variation, reflecting a combination of differences in local recycling amenities, policy and public attitudes. For example, 26 per cent of materials collected in London and 28 per cent in the North East were for composting, compared with 43 per cent in the West Midlands, while 4 per cent of materials collected in the West Midlands was co-mingled compared with 28 per cent in London.

Countryside, farming and wildlife

Nearly three-quarters (74 per cent) of the land area in the UK is used for agriculture (Table 11.17), and much of the 'natural' landscape is the product of many centuries of human intervention. Across the UK, Wales has the largest proportion of agricultural land (79 per cent), while England has the smallest (72 per cent). There is considerable variety in the use to which agricultural land is put. In England, 30 per cent of total land area is covered by crops and bare fallow, compared with 7 per cent in Scotland, 4 per cent in Northern Ireland and 3 per cent in Wales. In 2006, 466 thousand hectares in the UK was set-aside land. This is a scheme where the EU pays farmers a subsidy to leave land uncultivated to reduce overall production. Around three-quarters of land in Wales (75 per cent) and Northern Ireland (73 per cent) is given over to grasses and rough grazing, while Scotland and Wales contain

the most forest and woodland (17 per cent and 14 per cent respectively).

In 2006 the UK was the fourth largest producer of cereal and oilseed crops in the EU after France, Germany and Poland. The most common cereal crops grown in the UK were wheat and barley. Wheat, which is used in bread, cakes and many other food products, was the most widely grown arable crop covering nearly 2 million hectares in 2006 (Table 11.18). Around 15.5 million tonnes of wheat are grown each year. Barley was grown on nearly 1 million hectares, producing an output of 6 million tonnes. Around one-third of this is used in the production of malt, a key ingredient of beer and whisky. Oil seed rape was grown on about 0.5 million hectares producing around 1.5 million tonnes of seed. This is crushed to extract oil for the food and animal feed industries. Oats were grown on 4 per cent of the total land that cereals were grown in the UK (0.1 million hectares). Around one-half of the crop milled is used for human consumption, for example, in breakfast cereals. Potatoes and horticulture, including vegetables, fruits, and plants and flowers, were grown on the remaining 0.3 million hectares.

Organic farming is a form of agriculture that avoids or largely excludes the use of synthetic fertilisers and pesticides, plant growth regulators, and livestock feed additives. As far as possible, organic farmers rely on crop rotation, crop residues, animal manures and mechanical cultivation to maintain soil productivity, supply plant nutrients and control weeds, insects and other pests. In January 2007, 498,646 hectares in the UK were fully organic, and a further 121,137 hectares were in conversion. England had the largest area of organically

Table 11.17

Land by agricultural and other uses, 2006[1]

United Kingdom
Percentages

	Agricultural land			Forest and woodland	Urban land and land not otherwise specified	Total land[2] (=100%) (thousand hectares)	Inland water[2] (thousand hectares)
	Crops and bare fallow	Grasses and rough grazing	Other				
England	30	39	4	9	19	13,028	76
Wales	3	75	1	14	8	2,073	13
Scotland	7	68	2	17	6	7,792	169
Northern Ireland	4	73	1	6	16	1,358	64
United Kingdom	19	53	3	12	14	24,251	325

1 For definitions of categories, see Appendix, Part 11: Land use.
2 As at January 2001.

Source: Department for Environment, Food and Rural Affairs; Ordnance Survey; Forestry Commission; Forest Service

Table 11.18

Agricultural land area: by crops grown, 2006

United Kingdom	Thousand hectares
Cereals	2,861
Wheat	1,833
Barley	881
Oats	121
Rye and mixed corn	10
Triticale	13
Other arable crops (excluding potatoes)	1,192
Oilseed rape	500
Sugar beet not for stockfeeding	130
Hops	1
Peas for harvesting dry and field beans	231
Linseed	33
Other crops	297
Potatoes	140
Horticulture	166
Vegetables grown in the open	119
Orchard fruit[1]	23
Soft fruit[2]	10
Plants and flowers[3]	12
Glasshouse crops	2
Total	4,359

1 Includes non-commercial orchards.
2 Includes wine grapes.
3 Hardy nursery stock, bulbs and flowers.

Source: Department for Environment, Food and Rural Affairs

Figure 11.19

Population of wild birds:[1] by species group

United Kingdom

Index numbers (1970=100)

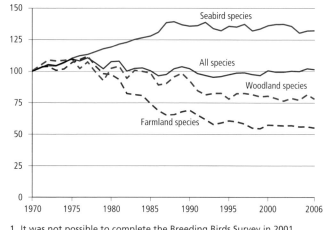

1 It was not possible to complete the Breeding Birds Survey in 2001 because of restrictions imposed during the outbreak of foot-and-mouth disease. Estimates for that year are based on the average for 2000 and 2002 for individual species.

Source: British Trust for Ornithology; Royal Society for the Protection of Birds; Department for Environment, Food and Rural Affairs

managed land in the UK with 296,386 hectares (48 per cent). Scotland had 38 per cent of the UK's organically managed land, Wales 13 per cent and Northern Ireland 1 per cent.

Wild bird populations are good indicators of the general state of the environment, as they have a wide range of habitats and tend to be at or near the top of the food chain. The size of the total population of the UK's breeding bird species has been relatively stable over the last 36 years. However, the trends for different species groups vary. The steepest decline has been in the population of farmland species, in 2006 this was around 55 per cent of its 1970 value, although the population has remained fairly stable since the 1990s (Figure 11.19). Some farmland species such as the goldfinch have recovered from large declines in the 1980s, and farmland generalists, such as the wood pigeon, have maintained their populations. The birds most at risk are those that feed mainly or solely on farmland, such as the skylark, where populations were at their lowest level in 2006, having declined by over 60 per cent since 1970.

The woodland bird population was around 20 per cent lower in 2006 than in the early 1970s, with the main decrease taking place in the late 1980s and early 1990s. This was probably due to changes in woodland structure, which included increases in woodland age, reduction in active management and the possibility of increased deer browsing. Birds that breed or feed mainly in woodland, such as the lesser redpoll, willow tit and tree pipit, showed the greatest declines in population of all woodland birds. Since 1976 seabird populations have generally increased, rising by 32 per cent over the period. However populations of some species such as the herring gull, arctic skua and kittiwake declined over the period.

Although populations of the more common farmland and woodland birds have declined, rare bird populations such as species of owls and eagles, which are not included in this index, have been either stable or rising. This reflects conservation efforts focused on these rare species, and also some species possibly benefiting from climate change in the southern areas of the country.

Fish are a traditional food resource and are a vital element of the ocean's ecosystem. Trends in spawning stock vary from species to species and stocks can fluctuate substantially over relatively short periods. Most stocks have been over-exploited, with some at near historically low levels. For example, the spawning stock of North Sea cod fell from 157,000 tonnes in 1963 to 36,000 tonnes in 2005, a decrease of 77 per cent

11

(Figure 11.20). The North Sea herring population was seriously affected by over-fishing in the 1970s. The closure of the North Sea fishery between 1978 and 1982 allowed spawning stocks to recover. From the late 1980s there was another decline in North Sea herring stocks. Stocks recovered again from the mid-1990s and in 2004 the spawning stock was at the highest level recorded for 40 years. In 2005 stocks declined slightly, to an estimated 1.7 million tonnes.

The main factor affecting the decline in fish stocks is over-fishing. Pollution to the sea is another factor, although this has little overall impact because concentrations of contaminants in sea water are generally low. To prevent over-exploitation of fish stocks there must be a balance between fishing activity and the natural ability of fish stocks to regenerate. Biomass estimates are used to evaluate whether the spawning population of each stock is sustainable. In 2005, 35 per cent of the 26 assessed fish stocks around the UK were categorised as being at full reproductive capacity and being harvested sustainably. This means that for 65 per cent of the assessed stocks, spawning levels were insufficient to guarantee stock replenishment.

Figure 11.20

North Sea fish stocks

Thousand tonnes

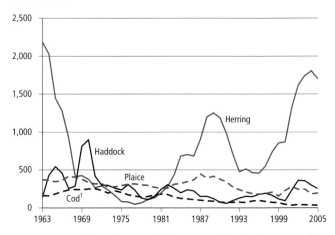

1 No assessment for cod was possible in 2005 and so the data were taken from the 2004 Advisory Committee on Fishery Management report.

Source: Centre for Environment, Fisheries and Agriculture Science; International Council for the Exploration of the Sea; Department for Environment, Food and Rural Affairs

11

Chapter 12

Transport

- The total distance travelled by people within Great Britain increased by 94 per cent between 1971 and 2006, to 812 billion passenger kilometres. (Table 12.1)

- Walking accounted for 52 per cent of trips to school by children aged five to ten in Great Britain in 2006, while 41 per cent were made by car or van. (Figure 12.4)

- The number of people licensed to drive a car in Great Britain increased by more than 14 million between 1975/76 and 2006 to just under 34 million. (Page 167)

- The proportion of households with regular use of two cars in Great Britain increased fourfold between 1971 and 2006, to 26 per cent. (Figure 12.8)

- Between 1987 and 2007, motoring costs in the UK measured by the retail prices index (RPI) rose by 85 per cent in real terms, while the cost of fares and other travel costs rose by 130 per cent. (Figure 12.14)

- In November 2007 the UK was the fourth most expensive country in the EU-25 in which to buy premium unleaded petrol, at 100.5 pence per litre. (Figure 12.15)

DATA

Download data by clicking the online pdf

www.statistics.gov.uk/ socialtrends38

Most people use some form of transport in their daily lives, to travel to and from work, to go shopping, to travel to other countries for holidays and for various social and leisure activities. During the last ten years, there has been little change in long-term trends in many areas of transport and travel. The distance travelled by each person in a year continued to increase, and the number of cars on the roads continued to rise.

Travel patterns

In 2006 people in Great Britain travelled a total of 812 billion passenger kilometres by road, rail and air (Table 12.1). This was almost double the 419 billion passenger kilometres travelled in 1971. Travel by car, van and taxi more than doubled between 1971 and 2006 from 313 to 686 billion passenger kilometres and accounted for around 84 per cent of all passenger kilometres travelled in 2006. However, the rapid increase in distance travelled that occurred in the 1980s was replaced by more gradual growth from the early 1990s. The total distance travelled by car rose by an average of nearly 5 per cent a year in the 1980s compared with an annual average of 1 per cent between 1991 and 2006.

Travel by bus and coach declined between 1971 and 2006. Around one in seven (14 per cent) of all journeys in 1971 was by bus and coach, accounting for 60 billion passenger kilometres. This declined to a low of 43 billion passenger kilometres in

Table 12.1

Passenger transport: by mode

Great Britain				Billion passenger kilometres	
	1971	1981	1991	2001	2006
Road[1]					
Car and van[2]	313	394	582	654	686
Bus and coach	60	48	44	47	50
Bicycle	4	5	5	4	5
Motorcycle	4	10	6	5	6
All road	381	458	637	710	747
Rail[3]	35	34	39	47	55
Air[4]	2	3	5	8	10
All modes	419	495	681	765	812

1 Road transport data from 1993 onwards are not directly comparable with earlier years. See Appendix, Part 12: Road traffic.
2 Includes taxis.
3 Data for rail relate to financial years.
4 Data for air are domestic flights only and include Northern Ireland, Channel Islands and the Isle of Man.

Source: Department for Transport

1992 but has since risen to around 50 billion passenger kilometres in 2006, accounting for around 6 per cent of all travel.

Rail travel grew from 35 billion to 55 billion passenger kilometres between 1971 and 2006, although there were fluctuations in between, but fell as a proportion of all distances travelled, from 8 per cent to 7 per cent. Rail travel declined during the 1970s, reaching a low point of 31 billion passenger kilometres in 1982 then rose to 41 billion in 1988, before declining again in the early 1990s. Between 1998 and 2006, distances travelled by rail rose again, by an average of 3 per cent a year and reached 55 billion passenger kilometres in 2006.

The distance travelled by domestic air flights is five times that travelled in 1971, accounting for 10 billion passenger kilometres in 2006. Although air travel showed the fastest growth of any means of transport over the period, it represents 1 per cent of the total distance travelled within Great Britain.

The largest proportion of trips made in Great Britain in 2006 were by car. More than 660,000 trips (63 per cent) were made by car, 41 per cent by car drivers and 22 per cent by car passengers (Table 12.2). Commuting or business was the main reason for driving a car, accounting for more than one-quarter (28 per cent) of all trips, while the main reason for trips by car passengers (40 per cent) was leisure activities. Walking accounted for nearly one-quarter (24 per cent) of all trips, by any mode.

Shopping trips were also the main reason for people using local bus services in 2006 with three in ten (30 per cent) bus trips being made for this purpose, followed by leisure, and commuting or business (both 20 per cent). Local bus journeys accounted for 6 per cent of all trips, while journeys by rail accounted for 2 per cent. The main purpose for more than half (54 per cent) of rail trips was commuting or business. Most trips made by bicycle were for commuting or business (35 per cent) or leisure (34 per cent).

How people travel to work varies across England. This is affected by a variety of factors, such as availability and reliability of public transport, access to a motor vehicle, availability of parking and the location of a person's workplace compared with where they live. In the last quarter of 2006, 70 per cent of trips to work in England were made by car or van. Such trips have a major impact on the volume of traffic on the roads (see Figure 12.9 later in this chapter for more information on traffic flows). In 2006, Warrington ranked the highest in terms of the proportion travelling to work by car or van, with 89 per cent of people doing so (Table 12.3), followed by Milton Keynes (87 per cent), Stockton-on-Tees (85 per cent)

Table 12.2

Trips per person per year: by main mode[1] and trip purpose,[2] 2006

Great Britain　　　　　　　　　　　　　　　　　　　　　　　　　　　　　　　　　　　　Percentages

	Car driver	Walk	Car passenger	Local bus	Rail[3]	Bicycle	Other[4]	All modes
Leisure	23	19	40	20	24	34	39	26
Shopping	21	22	20	30	10	13	14	21
Commuting/business	28	8	8	20	54	35	22	19
Education/escort education	5	18	10	17	6	10	14	10
Personal business	10	10	11	10	4	7	9	10
Other escort	13	5	11	3	1	1	3	9
Other, including walking trips	-	18	-	-	-	-	-	4
All purposes (=100%) (thousands)	430	249	228	65	24	16	25	1,037

1　Mode used for the longest part of the trip.
2　See Appendix, Part 12: National Travel Survey.
3　Rail includes London Underground.
4　Other includes motorcycles, taxis and other private and public transport.

Source: National Travel Survey, Department for Transport

and Worcestershire (84 per cent). In comparison just over half (53 per cent) of people travelling to work used a car or van in Portsmouth and less than one half (47 per cent) in Outer London. The lowest ranking area in England was Inner London, where one-fifth (20 per cent) of people travelled to work by car or van. The most commonly used transport to travel to work in Inner London was the London Underground or light rail, used by 26 per cent of commuters.

The way that people travel to work also varies by socio-economic group. In Great Britain, small employers and own account workers, (see Appendix, Part 1: National Statistics Socio-economic Classification (NS-SEC)), were the most likely of all groups to drive to work in a car or van (87 per cent) while the most likely to travel by train, underground or metro were people in higher managerial and professional occupations (15 per cent). In contrast, people in semi-routine occupations were the least

Table 12.3

Travel to work by car or van:[1] by selected local authority, 2006[2]

England　　　　　　　　　　　　　　　　　　　　　　　　　　　　　　　　　　　　　Percentages

Most likely			Least likely		
1	Warrington	89	1	Inner London	20
2	Milton Keynes	87	2	Outer London	47
3	Stockton-on-Tees	85	3	Portsmouth	53
4	Worcestershire	84	4	York	55
5	Warwickshire	84	5	Reading	57
6	North Somerset	84	6	Nottingham	59
7	Northumberland	83	7	City of Kingston upon Hull	59
8	Halton	83	8	Brighton and Hove	60
9	Dorset	82	9	Southampton	62
10	Staffordshire	82	10	Leicester	64

1　Number of people who travel to work by car or van as a percentage of all persons who travel to work. Excludes those on government training schemes and those working from home or using their home as a work base.
2　Data are for unitary authorities and counties at October to December (Q4) 2006.

Source: Labour Force Survey, Office for National Statistics

12

likely to drive to work (60 per cent) and among the least likely to travel by train, underground or metro (2 per cent). People in semi-routine and routine occupations were most likely to walk to work, 19 per cent and 17 per cent respectively.

Since the late 1980s the way that children travel to school has changed for both primary and secondary school pupils. In the period 1989–91, walking accounted for 62 per cent of trips to school by children aged five to ten in Great Britain, while 27 per cent were by car or van (Figure 12.4). In 2006 walking accounted for 52 per cent of trips to school for this age group, while 41 per cent were made by car or van. Among children aged 11 to 16 the proportion of trips to school made on foot decreased from 48 per cent in 1989–91 to 41 per cent in 2006, with a corresponding increase in the proportion made by car, from 14 to 20 per cent.

The proportion of trips to school by other modes of transport, which are mainly trips by private or local bus, remained relatively stable for children in both age groups. In 2006 these other modes accounted for a much higher proportion of trips to school among children aged 11 to 16 (38 per cent) than among children aged 5 to 10 (8 per cent).

The average length of trips to school has increased. In the period 1995/97 the average trip to school for children aged five to ten in Great Britain was 2.0 kilometres. This rose to

Figure 12.4

Trips[1] to and from school: by age of child and selected mode[2]

Great Britain

Percentages

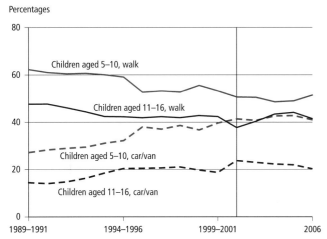

1 Trips of under 80 kilometres (50 miles) only. See Appendix, Part 12: National Travel Survey.
2 From 1995–97 data are weighted to account for non-response bias. Data prior to 2002 are averages for three years combined. Due to methodological changes short walks were under-recorded in 2002 and to a lesser extent in 2003. Under-recording of short walks affects the average time and length of trips, especially for walking and school trips.

Source: National Travel Survey, Department for Transport

Figure 12.5

Average distance travelled by bicycle:[1] by age and sex, 2005–06

Great Britain

Kilometres

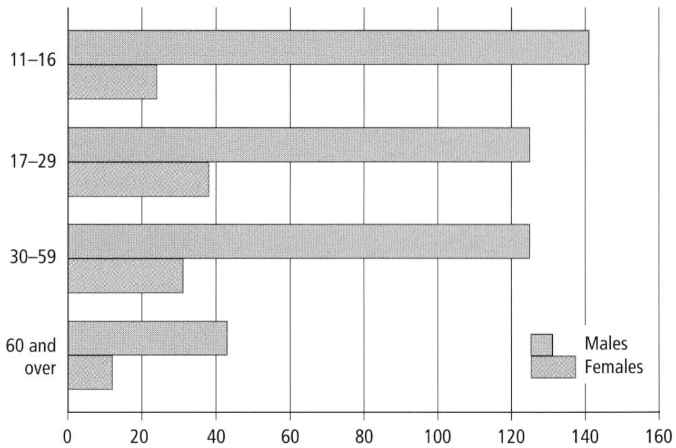

1 See Appendix, Part 12: National Travel Survey.

Source: National Travel Survey, Department for Transport

2.4 kilometres in 2006. For children aged 11 to 16 the average distance to school increased from 4.7 to 5.4 kilometres between 1995/97 and 2006. Trips to and from school normally take place at the same time each day, and can have a major impact on the level of traffic in residential areas during these times. In 2006 the proportion of cars taking children to school, known as the 'school-run' reached a peak at 08:45 on weekdays in school term time, accounting for 18 per cent of all car trips in urban areas at this time.

The average distance travelled by bicycle in Great Britain has declined over the past ten years for both males and females across nearly all age groups. On average, males aged 11 to 16 travelled greater distances by bicycle than females of the same age. Boys aged 11 to 16 travelled further than any other age group in 2005–06, averaging 141 kilometres per person per year (Figure 12.5). However, between 1995–97 and 2005–06 the largest decline in distances cycled was among boys and girls aged 11 to 16 (34 per cent and 39 per cent respectively). Men aged 17 and over travelled an average of 105 kilometres in 2005–06 compared with 27 kilometres for women, a decrease of 13 per cent and 9 per cent respectively since 1995–97. Women aged between 17 and 29 were the only group of either sex to travel a greater average distance by bicycle in 2005–06 than in 1995–97 and this age group also averaged the longest distance of any other female age group (38 kilometres).

Motor vehicles

Adults aged 18 and over in Great Britain were asked in 2006 whether they agreed with the statements 'many of the

Table 12.6

Attitudes to using transport for short journeys:[1] by sex and mode, 2006

Great Britain   Percentages

	Men			Women		
	Walk	Bus	Bicycle	Walk	Bus	Bicycle
Agree[2]	35	28	39	33	29	32
Neither agree nor disagree	9	7	9	8	9	9
Disagree[3]	46	56	43	49	54	50
Never travel less than 2 miles by car	7	6	6	7	6	5
Can't choose	3	2	3	4	2	3

1 Adults aged 18 and over were asked if they agreed or disagreed with the statement 'many of the journeys of less than two miles that I now make by car I could just as easily walk', 'go by bus' or 'cycle'. Excludes those who did not answer.
2 Those who said they either agreed or agreed strongly.
3 Those who said they either disagreed or disagreed strongly.

Source: British Social Attitudes Survey, National Centre for Social Research

journeys of less than two miles (3 kilometres) that I now make by car I could just as easily walk' or 'go by bus' or 'cycle'. Between 43 per cent and 56 per cent of men and 49 to 54 per cent of women disagreed or disagreed strongly with the statements and showed preference for using a car for a short journey rather than walking, taking a bus or cycling (Table 12.6). However, around one-third of both men and women (35 per cent and 33 per cent respectively) agreed or strongly agreed that they could walk the distance and 39 per cent of men and 32 per cent of women agreed or strongly agreed that they could cycle. Less than three in ten of both men and women agreed that they could make the journey by bus.

Around two-thirds of men and women agreed or agreed strongly that everyone should reduce how much they use their cars for the sake of the environment (64 per cent and 69 per cent respectively) (see also Chapter 11: Environment, Table 11.2). More than one-half of men (54 per cent) and women (57 per cent) disagreed or strongly disagreed that car users should pay higher taxes. However, 71 per cent of men and 64 per cent of women agreed that people who drive cars that are better for the environment should pay less to use the roads than people whose cars are more harmful to the environment. Less than one-fifth of both men and women (16 per cent and 17 per cent respectively) agreed or strongly agreed with the statement that 'anyone reducing their own car use will help the environment is wrong as one person doesn't make any difference'.

The number of people licensed to drive a car in Great Britain increased by more than 14 million between 1975/76 and 2006 to just under 34 million. Men are more likely than women to hold a full car driving licence although the gap is narrowing. In 1975/76 nearly seven in ten (69 per cent) of men held a licence

compared with nearly three in ten (29 per cent) women. In 2006, 81 per cent of men held a full driving licence compared to 63 per cent of women. The difference was particularly marked in older age groups. Among people aged 70 and over, the proportion with a driving licence was more than twice as high among men than women in 2006 (76 per cent compared with 31 per cent) (Figure 12.7). Overall, the proportion of men and women aged 17 to 20 holding a licence has increased over the period 1975/76 to 2006 from 28 per cent to 34 per cent. However, the number of licence holders aged 17 to 20 has

Figure 12.7

Full car driving licence holders:[1] by sex and age

Great Britain

Percentages

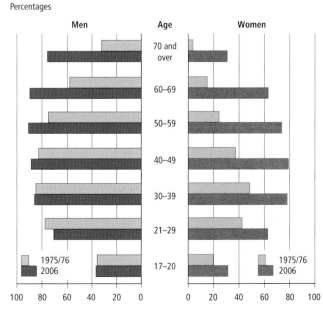

1 See Appendix, Part 12: National Travel Survey.

Source: National Travel Survey, Department for Transport

Figure 12.8

Households with regular use of a car[1]

Great Britain
Percentages

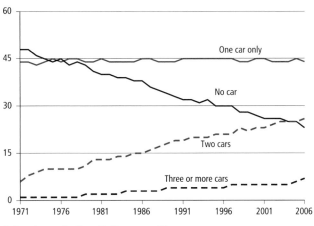

1 See Appendix, Part 12: Car ownership.

Source: General Household Survey (Longitudinal), Office for National Statistics

decreased since the early 1990s from 54 per cent to 37 per cent for men and from 42 per cent to 31 per cent for women. Possible reasons for this decline could include the cost of lessons, the cost of buying and insuring a car, the increase in the proportion who are students (see Chapter 3: Education and training) and the increasing difficulty of passing the driving test. However, this downward trend may now be reversing as in 2005 the percentage of both men and women holding licences saw the first increase since the early 1990s with 37 per cent and 27 per cent holding a licence respectively.

The increase in people licensed to drive is reflected in the growth of households with regular use of two or more cars. Since the early 1970s the percentage of households in Great Britain with access to one car has remained stable, at around 45 per cent over the period to 2006 (Figure 12.8). However, the proportion of households without regular use of a car more than halved, from 48 per cent in 1971 to 23 per cent in 2006, while the proportion of households with access to two cars increased more than fourfold, from 6 per cent to 26 per cent over the period. The proportion of households with regular use of three or more cars steadily increased to 7 per cent in 2006, an increase of 6 percentage points from 1971.

Rural households were more likely than urban households to have two or more cars (see Appendix, Part 12: Area type classification). Around one-half (51 per cent) of all rural households in Great Britain had two or more cars in 2006, compared with around one in three households in most urban

areas, around one in four in metropolitan built up areas and around one in six households in London boroughs.

In Great Britain, the higher a household's income, the more likely it is to have access to a car. Less than one-half (49 per cent) of households in the lowest quintile group of the income distribution had access to at least one car in 2006 (see Chapter 5: Income and wealth, analysing income distribution box for more on quintiles). This proportion rose to 65 per cent for those in the next quintile group and reached 91 per cent for households in the highest quintile group.

The number of cars on the roads of Great Britain varies at different times of the day and week. On weekdays in 2006 between 08:00 and 09:00 and 17:00 and 18:00 the number of cars on roads were at their highest mainly because of the daily commute to and from work and to a lesser extent the morning school run (Figure 12.9). At these peak hours car traffic was around 25 per cent higher than between the hours of 10:00 and 16:00. After 18:00 the flow of cars reduced with the lowest levels of traffic occurring between the hours of 23:00 and 06:00. Patterns in car flow follow a different pattern at the weekend. On Saturdays there were more cars on the road between the hours of 10:00 and 15:00 than at any other time of the day. The flow peaked at nearly twice the flow per average hour (192 per cent) at 12:00. On Sundays there were more cars on the road between 11:00 and 19:00 than at any other time of day, peaking at 17:00. Possible reasons for these weekend peaks might include shopping trips,

Figure 12.9

Distribution of cars on all roads: by time of day,[1] 2006

Great Britain
Index numbers (Flow per average hour = 100)

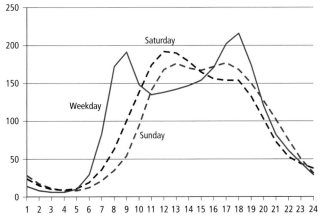

1 Mean hourly total of aggregated counts of vehicles on different types of roads throughout Great Britain in a week. See Appendix, Part 12: Road traffic.

Source: Department for Transport

Table 12.10

Average daily flow[1] of motor vehicles: by class of road[2]

Great Britain   Thousands

	1983	1988	1993	1998	2001	2006
Motorways	31.2	49.6	58.2	68.7	71.6	76.4
All 'A' roads	11.3	13.7	11.3	12.4	12.6	13.3
Urban major roads	17.2	19.4	19.2	20.2	20.1	20.3
Rural major roads	8.7	11.3	8.9	10.0	10.3	11.1
All major roads[3]	..	..	14.4	16.3	16.7	17.7
All minor roads	1.1	1.3	1.3	1.3	1.4	1.4
All roads	2.1	2.9	2.9	3.2	3.3	3.5

1 Flow at an average point on each class of road.
2 Motorways include trunk motorways and principal motorways. Urban major roads include roads in built up areas prior to 1993. Rural major roads include roads in non-built up areas prior to 1993. See Appendix, Part 12: Road traffic.
3 Includes all trunk and principal motorways and 'A' roads.

Source: National Road Traffic Survey, Department for Transport

travelling to sports events and entertainment or returning from trips away.

In comparison, the number of goods vehicles on the roads were at their highest between 12:00 and 15:00 on weekdays, the flow peaking at just over double the flow per average hour (201 per cent). There were relatively low levels of goods vehicle traffic at weekends, with less distinction between the night and day.

Growth in the number of motor vehicles owned and the greater distances travelled by individuals, road haulage and public transport vehicles have led to an increase in the average daily flow of vehicles on Great Britain's roads. Between 1983 and 2006 the average daily traffic flow on all roads rose by nearly 66 per cent to 3,500 vehicles per day (Table 12.10). Motorways had the highest flow of vehicles, at 76,400 vehicles a day in 2006; this was more than double the 31,200 vehicles on motorways in 1983. There were also large increases in traffic flow on major roads in rural areas during the same period (27 per cent) while the increase on urban major roads was 18 per cent.

One of the ways to ease congestion on roads is to charge for road use, depending on the route taken. According to the British Social Attitudes Survey more than half of adults (55 per cent) in Great Britain in 2006 disagreed or disagreed strongly that people who drive on busy roads should pay more than people who drive on quiet roads. More than two-thirds (67 per cent) agreed or strongly agreed that it would be too complicated to charge drivers different amounts depending on when and where they drive.

Public transport

Passenger numbers on local buses have decreased over the past ten years in most parts of Great Britain, although overall, numbers have increased. The highest decrease was in the North East where passenger numbers fell by 24 per cent from 271 million to 206 million between 1996/97 and 2006/07 (Table 12.11). However, in London the number of passengers increased by 62 per cent from 1,230 million to 1,993 million over the same period. The East and South East regions together with Scotland also saw increases in passenger numbers of 13 per cent, 6 per cent and 1 per cent respectively.

Although passenger numbers on local buses in Wales decreased by 10 per cent overall between 1996/97 and 2006/07, the largest fall occurred between 1996/97 and 2001/02 after which numbers increased by 11 per cent by 2006/07 to 119 million passengers. The South West and Scotland also saw increases, of 6 per cent and 3 per cent respectively between 2001/02 and 2006/07. The highest increase, of 40 per cent, over this period was in London. Possible reasons for an increase in passenger numbers on London's buses were reductions in fares to people using the pre-pay Oyster card, the regularity of the bus service (around 8,000 buses running along 700 different routes) and the creation of more bus lanes giving greater reliability and faster journey times. The introduction

Table 12.11

Passengers on local buses: by area

Great Britain   Millions

	1996/97	2001/02	2006/07
Great Britain	4,455	4,455	4,972
England	3,844	3,881	4,371
North East	271	242	206
North West	587	516	498
Yorkshire and the Humber	431	387	376
East Midlands	215	212	210
West Midlands	462	455	402
East	162	178	183
London	1,230	1,422	1,993
South East	290	285	308
South West	196	185	195
Wales	133	108	119
Scotland	478	466	482

Source: Department for Transport

12

Figure 12.12

Passenger railway[1] journeys

Great Britain
Millions

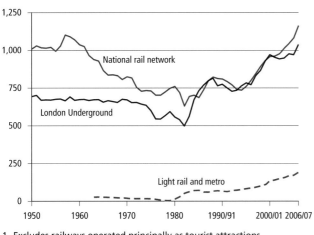

1 Excludes railways operated principally as tourist attractions.

Source: Department for Transport

of the congestion charge in February 2003 may also have led to increased passenger numbers on London's buses.

The number of journeys made on Great Britain's railway network (including underground and metro systems) rose by 173 million between 2005/06 and 2006/07 to 2.4 billion, an increase of 8 per cent (Figure 12.12). This is the highest year on

year increase since 1983 when passenger journeys rose by 140 million to slightly more than 1.3 billion. In every year since 2003/04 more than 1 billion passenger journeys were made on the national rail network. Prior to this, the last time passenger journeys were around this level was in 1961 just before the Beeching closures where more than 4,000 miles of railway and 3,000 stations were closed in the decade after 1963. Overall, use of national rail and the London Underground accounted for almost all rail journeys in 2006/07 (92 per cent).

Several new light railways and tram lines have been built or extended during the last ten years, such as the Croydon Tramlink in south London and the Metrolink in Manchester. Over the next decade, further extensions to the Docklands Light Railway are proposed as part of the transport system for the Olympic Games and Paralympic Games in 2012, alongside new lines and extensions elsewhere in the UK. Passenger journeys on light railways and trams more than doubled from around 80 million to 192 million between the mid-1990s and 2006/07.

The National Passenger Survey, conducted by Passenger Focus (the independent national rail consumer watchdog) in spring 2007 asked adult rail customers aged over 16 in Great Britain about their satisfaction with various aspects of travelling on the railways. Less than eight in ten (79 per cent) were satisfied with their rail journey and associated facilities overall (Table 12.13).

Table 12.13

Satisfaction with the railways, 2007[1]

Great Britain

Percentages

	Satisfactory or good	Neither satisfactory or unsatisfactory	Unsatisfactory or poor
Station facilities			
How request to station staff was handled	82	7	10
Provision of information about train times/platforms	76	13	12
Facilities and services	50	19	31
Facilities for car parking	46	16	38
Train facilities			
Length of time the journey was scheduled to take[2]	81	11	8
Frequency of the trains on that route	75	10	15
Punctuality/reliability[3]	77	8	15
Value for money for the price of ticket	40	21	39
Availability of staff	38	29	33
Toilet facilities	36	23	41
Overall satisfaction	79	13	9

1 Data are at spring 2007.
2 Relates to the speed of the journey.
3 The train arriving/departing on time.

Source: National Passenger Survey Spring 2007, Passenger Focus

This was a lower proportion than in spring 2006. When asked about station facilities, more than eight in ten (82 per cent) of customers were satisfied about how requests to station staff were handled, while 76 per cent were satisfied with the provision of information on train times and platform information. The two indicators that had the highest proportion of dissatisfied customers were facilities for car parking (38 per cent) and the general facilities and services at stations (31 per cent).

When asked about train facilities, more than eight in ten (81 per cent) customers were satisfied with the speed of the journey and more than three-quarters (77 per cent) were satisfied with punctuality and reliability. The indicators that had the highest proportion of dissatisfied customers were toilet facilities on the train (41 per cent), value for money for the price of the ticket (39 per cent) and the availability of staff on the train (33 per cent).

Prices and expenditure

Motoring costs in the UK as measured by the 'All motoring' component of the retail prices index (RPI) rose by 85 per cent between January 1987 and January 2007, compared with a rise in the 'All items' RPI measure of general inflation of 102 per cent (see also Chapter 6: Expenditure). Therefore motoring was relatively less expensive in 2007 than it was in 1987. This is mainly because the rise in the price of vehicles (6 per cent) was much less than the RPI rate of inflation (Figure 12.14). Vehicle tax and insurance rose by 189 per cent

during this period in real terms, although costs fell slightly in the mid-1990s, and maintenance costs rose by 204 per cent. The cost of petrol and oil more than doubled between 1987 and 2000. Four years later the cost was at a similar level, before rising to a peak in 2006 of 162 per cent above its 1987 level and then falling in 2007 to 156 per cent above the 1987 level.

Bus, coach and rail fares in the UK rose by considerably more than the rate of general inflation between 1987 and 2007. Bus and coach fares rose by 170 per cent and rail fares rose by 157 per cent. Overall, the 'All fares and other travel' index rose by 130 per cent.

In November 2007 the UK was the fourth most expensive country in the EU-25 in which to buy premium unleaded petrol, at 100.5 pence per litre (Figure 12.15 overleaf). This was the first time the average price had risen above £1.00 per litre in the UK. Premium unleaded petrol was most expensive in the Netherlands, at 107.4 pence per litre, while the cheapest price in the EU-25 was in Estonia, at 64.7 pence per litre. A litre of unleaded petrol in Estonia cost around one-third less on average than it did in the UK. The average price of unleaded petrol in the UK was more than 15 pence a litre more in November 2007 than in November 2006.

Across the EU-25, taxes and duties form a major component of petrol prices – 55 per cent on average in mid-November 2007. The tax component in the UK was the highest in the EU, at 65 per cent. Finland and Sweden had the next highest tax components, both at 62 per cent, while Malta and Cyprus had

Figure 12.14

Passenger transport prices[1]

United Kingdom

Index numbers (1987=100)

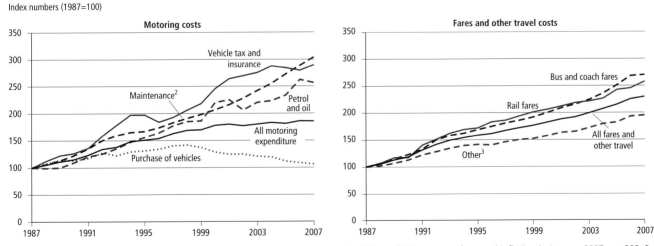

1 At January each year based on the retail prices index (RPI). For comparison, the 'All items' RPI measure of general inflation in January 2007 was 202. See Appendix, Part 6: Retail prices index.
2 Includes spare parts and accessories, roadside recovery services, MOT test fee, car service, labour charges and car wash.
3 Includes taxi and minicab fares, self-drive and van hire charges, ferry and sea fares, air fares, road tolls, purchase of bicycles/boats and car park charges.

Source: Office for National Statistics

Figure 12.15

Premium unleaded petrol[1] prices: EU comparison, mid-November 2007

Pence per litre[2]

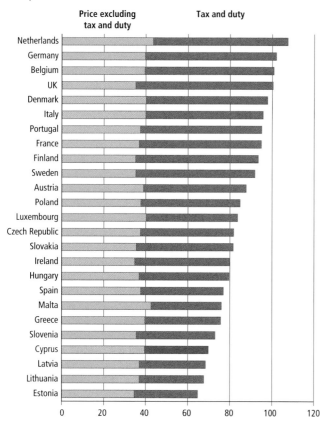

1 Unleaded petrol which is rated at 95 Research Octane Number. Does not include super unleaded petrol.
2 Prices converted to pounds sterling using mid-month exchange rates.

Source: Department for Business Enterprise and Regulatory Reform

the lowest, at 44 per cent and 43 per cent respectively. As with unleaded petrol, the major component of the price of diesel in the UK was tax and duty (63 per cent), above the EU-25 average of 47 per cent. Slovakia had the second largest component of tax on diesel, at 53 per cent and Cyprus had the lowest tax component, at 38 per cent. A litre of diesel in the UK cost an average 104.2 pence in November 2007 and as with unleaded petrol, this was the first time that UK average prices for diesel have risen above £1.00 per litre.

Transport safety

The Government has set targets to help bring about substantial improvements in road safety. By 2010, in Great Britain, the aim is to reduce the number of people killed or seriously injured in road accidents compared to the average for figures for a number of indicators in 1994–98. Similar targets exist for Northern Ireland (see Appendix, Part 12: Road safety).

The casualty rate per 100 billion vehicle kilometres for people killed or seriously injured has fallen throughout all the regions of Great Britain between the period 1994–1998 and 2006 (Table 12.16). In 2006 the region with the largest percentage change from the 1994–98 average, showing a reduction of 53 per cent in casualties was the West Midlands, with the second largest decrease at 46 per cent in the East Midlands. Within England, the smallest reduction was found in the North East, at 32 per cent. Scotland and Wales also had reductions in casualty rates, 46 per cent and 9 per cent respectively. There was only a small percentage change over the period in Wales, however, compared with other areas the rate in 1994–1998 was already low (8.5 per billion vehicle kilometres) in comparison to Scotland (10.6 per billion kilometres) and England (10.8 per billion kilometres).

One way to reduce the likelihood of road casualties is through use of speed cameras and red-light cameras. According to the British Social Attitudes Survey in 2006 more than one-half (55 per cent) of adults who were current car drivers in Great Britain agreed or agreed strongly that speed cameras save lives. Over 9 in 10 (93 per cent) agreed or strongly agreed that people should drive within the speed limit.

Alcohol is a major contributor to road accidents. The *Road Safety Act 1967* established a legal alcohol limit for drivers, set at 80 mg of alcohol in 100 ml of blood and made it an offence to drive when over this limit. The 1967 Act also gave the police

Table 12.16

Killed or seriously injured casualty rate: by region

Great Britain			Rate per 100 billion vehicle kilometres
	1994–98 average	2006	Percentage change
England	10.8	6.3	–41.7
North East	8.4	5.7	–32.0
North West	10.8	6.5	–39.9
Yorkshire and the Humber	11.5	7.6	–34.4
East Midlands	11.4	6.2	–46.1
West Midlands	11.0	5.2	–53.0
East	10.2	5.9	–42.4
London	21.2	11.7	–44.7
South East	7.9	5.1	–36.0
South West	7.9	5.1	–35.5
Wales	8.5	7.8	–8.6
Scotland	10.6	5.8	–45.5

Source: Department for Transport; Welsh Assembly Government; Scottish Government

the power to carry out breath testing in order to determine whether an individual's alcohol level is above the limit of 35 mcg of alcohol in 100 ml of breath. For many years there have been national publicity campaigns discouraging drink driving, involving television, radio, newspaper and other forms of advertising. The total number of casualties from road accidents involving illegal alcohol levels in the UK fell sharply between the mid-1980s and early 1990s, from 27,200 in 1986 to 15,600 in 1993 (Figure 12.17). Between 1999 and 2002 the number of casualties rose to 20,900 before falling to less than 15,000 in 2006. The total number of deaths from accidents involving illegal alcohol levels declined steadily from around 1,000 in 1986 to approximately 600 a year in the early to mid-1990s. Following a further decline to around 500 deaths in 1998 and 1999, the total number of deaths from accidents involving illegal alcohol levels has remained relatively stable at approximately 600 a year between 2000 and 2006. Over the same period in the 1980s and 1990s serious injuries decreased by more than one-half, and in 2006 the number fell to just over 2,000.

According to the British Social Attitudes Survey, more than four-fifths (84 per cent) of adults in Great Britain in 2006 agreed or agreed strongly with the statement that if someone has drunk any alcohol they should not drive. Three-quarters (75 per cent) agreed or strongly agreed that anyone caught drink-driving should be banned for at least five years. More than two-thirds (68 per cent) of adults agreed or agreed strongly that most people don't know how much alcohol they can drink before being over the legal drink-drive limit.

Figure 12.17

Casualties from road accidents involving illegal alcohol levels: by severity

United Kingdom
Thousands

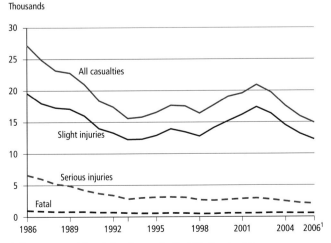

1 Data are provisional. See Appendix, Part 12: Road safety.
Source: Department for Transport; Police Service of Northern Ireland

Table 12.18

Passenger death rates:[1] by mode of transport[2]

Great Britain			Rate per billion passenger kilometres		
	1981	1991	1996	2001	2005
Motorcycle	115.8	94.6	108.4	112.1	96.9
Walk	76.9	69.8	55.9	47.5	36.2
Bicycle	56.9	46.5	49.8	32.5	33.6
Car	6.1	3.7	3.0	2.8	2.6
Van	3.7	2.1	1.0	0.9	0.6
Bus or coach	0.3	0.6	0.2	0.2	0.2
Rail[3]	1.0	0.8	0.4	0.3	0.1
Water	0.4	0.0	0.8	0.4	0.3
Air	0.2	0.0	0.0	0.0	0.0

1 See Appendix, Part 12: Passenger death rates.
2 Motorcycle, bicycle, car and van includes driver and passenger fatalities. Water includes fatalities on UK registered merchant vessels. Air includes fatalities involving UK registered airline aircraft in UK and foreign airspace.
3 Financial years. Includes train accidents and accidents occurring through movement of railway vehicles.

Source: Department for Transport

The safety levels of most forms of transport in Great Britain are much improved compared with the levels of the early 1980s, and improvements in most areas have continued since the early 1990s. Motorcycling, walking and cycling have the highest fatality rates per kilometre travelled than any other form of transport in Great Britain (Table 12.18). In 2005 the highest death rate was for motorcycle users, at 96.9 deaths per billion passenger kilometres travelled. This was around 37 times greater than the death rate for car users.

Almost all deaths in transport accidents in Great Britain occur on the roads. In 2005 there were 271,000 casualties on the roads, resulting in 3,200 deaths. In 2005, 52 per cent of those killed were occupants of cars, 21 per cent were pedestrians, 18 per cent were motorcycle users and 5 per cent were cyclists.

The UK has a good record for road safety compared with most other EU countries. According to the Organisation for Economic Co-operation and Development, across the EU-25 the UK had one of the lowest road death rates for all persons, at 5.5 per 100,000 population in 2005 (Table 12.19 overleaf). Lithuania had the highest recorded road death rate for all persons, at 22.2 per 100,000 population. The EU-25 average was 10.6 per 100,000 population. The UK rate was also substantially lower than those for other industrialised nations such as the United States (14.7 per 100,000 population), Republic of Korea (13.2 per 100,000) and New Zealand (9.9 per 100,000).

12

Table 12.19

Road deaths: EU comparison, 2005

Rate per 100,000 population

	All persons	Children[1]		All persons	Children[1]
Lithuania	22.2	..	Austria	9.4	1.9
Latvia	19.2	..	Italy	9.3	..
Greece	15.0	2.8	France	8.8	1.2
Poland	14.3	2.6	Finland	7.2	2.3
Cyprus	13.6	..	Germany	6.5	1.3
Slovenia	12.9	3.5	Denmark	6.1	1.3
Hungary	12.7	2.2	United Kingdom	5.5	1.2
Czech Republic	12.6	2.7	Sweden	4.9	0.6
Estonia	12.6	5.8	Netherlands	4.6	1.0
Portugal	11.8	1.9	Malta	4.2	4.2
Belgium	10.4	2.1	EU-25 average	10.6	..
Slovakia	10.4	..			
Spain	10.3	1.9			
Luxembourg	9.9	..			
Ireland	9.7	1.1			

1 Aged 0–14.

Source: International Road Traffic and Accident Database (Organisation for Economic Co-operation and Development); International Transport Forum; Eurostat and CARE (EU road accidents database)

The UK also has a relatively good record in terms of the number of road accidents involving children. In 2005 the UK road accident death rate for children aged under 15 was 1.2 deaths per 100,000 population. Estonia had the highest rate in the EU-25, of 5.8 per 100,000 population. The UK rate was again lower than other industrialised nations, with New Zealand reporting a rate of 3.5 per 100,000 population and the United States and Republic of Korea reporting rates of 3.2 and 3.1 per 100,000 population respectively.

The UK had the sixth lowest recorded rate in the EU-25 for all pedestrian deaths in 2005, at 1.2 pedestrian deaths per 100,000 population. The lowest in the EU-25 was the Netherlands, at 0.5 per 100,000 population, while Poland had the highest, at 4.6 per 100,000 population. The number of child-pedestrian deaths showed similar rankings. The UK had the fifth lowest rate of 0.6 per 100,000 of population, while Sweden had the lowest rate of all EU-25 member states, at 0.2 per 100,000 of population. Poland had the highest rate, at 1.1 per 100,000 population.

International travel

UK residents made a record number of trips abroad in 2006, with 69.5 million visits. This was more than three times as many as 25 years ago. The use of air travel has grown consistently over this period. In 1982 air travel accounted for 58 per cent of all modes of travel abroad by UK residents, while in 2006 this had increased to more than 80 per cent. Trips made by sea have declined over the same period from 42 per cent to 12 per cent. Holidays accounted for nearly two-thirds (65 per cent) of trips made abroad by UK residents (Table 12.20) (see also Chapter 13: Lifestyles and social participation). A further 17 per cent of all trips were to visit friends and family overseas, and 13 per cent were business trips. The total number of trips made abroad by UK residents was more than double the number of overseas residents visiting the UK in 2006.

Table 12.20

International travel: by mode of travel and purpose of visit, 2006

United Kingdom

Percentages

	UK residents[1]				Overseas residents[2]			
	Air	Sea	Channel Tunnel	All modes	Air	Sea	Channel Tunnel	All modes
Holiday	66	68	55	65	30	41	40	32
Visiting friends and relatives	18	13	13	17	32	18	20	29
Business	13	8	19	13	27	30	30	28
Other	3	10	13	5	12	10	10	12
All purposes (=100%) (millions)	56.5	8.4	4.7	69.5	24.6	4.9	3.3	32.7

1 Visits abroad by UK residents.
2 Visits to the UK by overseas residents.

Source: International Passenger Survey, Office for National Statistics

There were a record number of visits to the UK by overseas residents in 2006. At 32.7 million visits, the number was nearly three times more than in 1982. Of these, around three-quarters were made by air and the remainder were made by sea or through the Channel Tunnel. Holidays accounted for around one-third (32 per cent) of all trips to the UK by overseas residents, followed by visiting friends and relatives in the UK (29 per cent) and business trips (28 per cent).

According to Sea Passenger Statistics 2006 produced by the Department for Transport, around 23 million passengers travelled on international routes to and from the UK by sea in 2006. This was a fall of 32 per cent since 1996. The largest falls in passenger numbers were at ports in the Thames area and Kent (37 per cent). Competition from the Channel Tunnel, which opened in 1994, and cheaper air travel have caused the downward trend in sea passenger journeys since the mid-1990s (see Appendix, Part 12: Sea passengers on short sea routes).

In 2006 around 90 per cent of all air terminal passengers (excluding those in transit) entering or leaving UK airports were travelling to or from overseas countries. The number of people travelling by plane over the last two decades was both a continuation, and an acceleration of a long-term trend. Between 1980 and 2006 the number of international terminal passengers at UK airports increased more than fourfold from 43 million to 186 million, while the number of domestic passengers rose from 8 million to 25 million over the same period (Figure 12.21).

Figure 12.21

Passengers at UK civil airports

United Kingdom

Millions

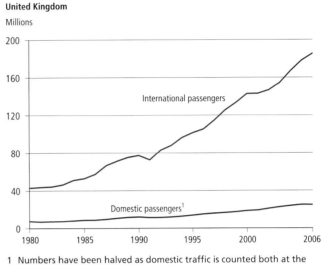

1 Numbers have been halved as domestic traffic is counted both at the airport of arrival and at the airport of departure.

Source: Civil Aviation Authority

According to the Civil Aviation Authority, in 2006 passenger traffic at the five main London airports (Heathrow, Gatwick, Stansted, Luton and London City Airport) grew by 2 per cent since 2005 to 137 million passengers and by more than 50 per cent since 1996. Outside London, regional airport traffic increased by 4 per cent from 2005. Among the ten largest regional airports, the fastest growing were Liverpool and Nottingham East Midlands (both showing 13 per cent growth over the period). Manchester Airport handled the most passengers of the regional airports (22 million).

12

Chapter 13

Lifestyles and social participation

- In the UK, 81 per cent of homes had a digital television service at the end of the first quarter in 2007, a rise of 65 percentage points since 2000. (Figure 13.2)

- Excluding the National Lottery draw, around 23 million people in Great Britain participated in gambling in the 12 months prior to interview in 2006 and 2007, around 1 million more than in 1999. (Page 183)

- In 2005/06, 31 per cent of adults in England had not participated in sport in the previous 12 months. Nearly half stated their health not being good enough as the main reason. (Figure 13.13)

- In 2006, 48 per cent of adults in Great Britain felt it was more important to have close ties with family than to have close friends. (Page 186)

- More than one-half (53 per cent) of formal volunteers in England in 2006/07 got involved because they wanted to improve things or help people. (Figure 13.16)

- The average charitable donation made by each adult in the UK in 2006/07 in a four-week period was £16. The total amount donated was £9.5 billion. (Page 188)

People engage in many different activities in their spare time. Some visit places of entertainment and cultural activity such as the theatre or a library. Many go on day trips, or away on holidays. Other activities involve interaction with technology, such as watching television and listening to the radio, and more recently the Internet. Although modern technology seems ever present in everyday life traditional forms of leisure, such as reading books or going to the cinema, remain popular. Many individuals participate in sports and physical activities in their leisure time, spend time with friends and family, help other people or participate in religious worship.

Leisure and entertainment

According to the Taking Part Survey, the most common leisure activity for more than eight in ten (82 per cent) adults aged 16 and over in England in 2005/06 was watching television, followed by spending time with family and friends (75 per cent) (Figure 13.1).

Figure 13.1

Activities performed in free time,[1] 2005/06

England
Percentages

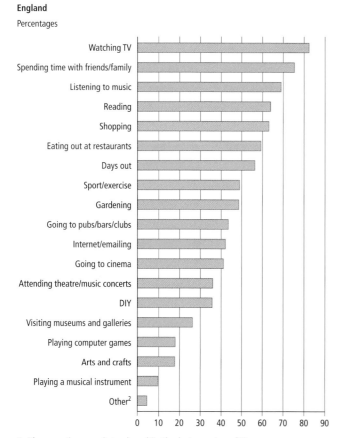

1 The question was introduced in the last quarter of the survey. Engagement in some of the activities here is also asked about later in the questionnaire. Prevalence rates differ slightly due to the format and definition of questions/activities. Percentages do not add up to 100 per cent as respondents could give more than one answer.
2 Includes puzzles, games and academic study.

Source: Taking Part: The National Survey of Culture, Leisure and Sport, Department for Culture, Media and Sport

Traditional solo activities such as listening to music and reading were enjoyed by more than six in ten adults (69 per cent and 64 per cent respectively). Around six in ten adults shopped and ate out at restaurants, while activities around the home, such as gardening and DIY, were performed by 49 per cent and 36 per cent of adults respectively. Cultural activities, including attending theatre or music concerts and visiting museums and galleries, were popular with 36 per cent and 26 per cent of adults respectively.

With digital television services providing more channels and programmes than the analogue equivalent, as well as advanced interactive shows and games and high definition channels, the television is likely to remain a popular medium of entertainment for years to come. More than eight in ten homes (81 per cent) in the UK had a digital television service at the end of the first quarter of 2007 (Figure 13.2), a rise of 65 percentage points since 2000. Other than a greater choice of channels, this rise was possibly in anticipation of the digital switchover which takes place between 2008 and 2012. During this period, television services in the UK will move over to a digital signal and the analogue television broadcast signal will be switched off. Much of the recent growth in digital television services was driven by the take up of Freeview, the free to air digital terrestrial service. In 2003, 6 per cent of households had this service connected to their main television set. This increased more than fivefold to 33 per cent of households in 2007. More than one-half of people with a digital television device connected to their main set paid a subscription to a satellite or cable service provider at the end of the first quarter of 2007.

Figure 13.2

Household take up of digital television: by type of service[1]

United Kingdom
Percentages

1 Data are at the end of the first quarter in each year.
Source: Ofcom

According to Ofcom (the independent regulator for the UK communications industries), Freeview was the most common way of receiving a digital television service on the main television set at home at the end of the second quarter of 2007.

According to the Taking Part Survey, more than one-quarter (27 per cent) of adults in England in 2005/06 watched television for an average of two hours per day, with 23 per cent watching for around three hours. The most popular type of television programmes viewed were the news (national or local), watched by 65 per cent of viewers, followed by films (61 per cent), comedy (54 per cent) and live sport coverage (51 per cent).

A digital television set can also transmit digital radio stations. One-third of adults in the UK in 2007 had listened to radio through a digital television at least once. However, most are likely to listen to a radio set. Radio is a secondary medium; it may be listened to while people do other things such as working or commuting. The way radio broadcasts are received has changed over the years from long and medium wave transmissions through to frequency modulation (FM) transmissions to digital services. According to Radio Joint Audience Research Limited, the average time spent listening to the radio by people in the UK aged four and over in the first quarter of 2007 was 19 hours and 24 minutes per week (Figure 13.3). Average listening time increases with age. Those aged 4 to 14 listened to the least amount of radio (9 hours and 30 minutes per week), compared with 23 hours and 18 minutes for those aged 55 and over. Men aged 15 and over listened to slightly more radio per week than women of the same age, 22 hours and 12 minutes compared with 19 hours and 48 minutes. Between 2001/02 and 2006/07 radio listening fell among most age groups, with the largest fall (17 per cent) among 25 to 34 year olds. This could be a result of consuming other new media and audio such as iPods. The only group to increase listening over the period were those aged 55 and over (up 6 per cent), and this age group accounted for more than one-third of all radio listening (35 per cent). This could partly be a result of the increased ratio of the population in this age group and their listening habits compared with those in the group in 2001/02.

In the first quarter of 2007 almost all (99 per cent) homes in the UK had at least one radio set, with over two-thirds (68 per cent) having two or more sets. Analogue sets were the most widely used radio device, used daily or weekly by more than nine in ten (92 per cent) adults. However, regular use of other modes of radio is rising. Nearly two in ten people (18 per cent) used a Digital Audio Broadcasting (DAB) set on a daily or weekly basis in the first quarter of 2007 (an increase of

Figure 13.3

Radio listening: by age, 2007[1]

United Kingdom

Average weekly listening hours

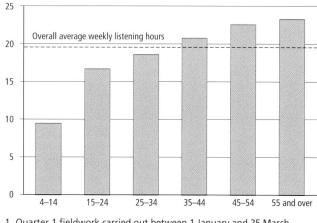

1 Quarter 1 fieldwork carried out between 1 January and 25 March.

Source: Radio Joint Audience Research Limited

7 percentage points from 2006), 15 per cent listened to radio through a digital television on a daily or weekly basis and 12 per cent listened through the Internet on a daily or weekly basis. In the first quarter of 2003, 1 per cent of homes had a DAB radio; by the first quarter of 2007 this had increased to 17 per cent. Almost one in five (19 per cent) adults aged 15 and over without DAB radio reported that they were likely to buy a set within six months.

The Internet allows people to listen to radio content in different ways, such as live listening, listen again services and podcasting (see Appendix, Part 13: Definitions). Broadband Internet services make these services quicker and easier to use.

In 2007 more than eight in ten (84 per cent) households in the UK with Internet access had a broadband connection, this was equivalent to 51 per cent of all households in the UK. Overall 15.2 million households (61 per cent) had some kind of Internet access (see Appendix, Part 13: Internet connection). More than two-thirds (67 per cent) of adults aged 16 and over in the UK accessed the Internet in the three months prior to interview in 2007, while a further 6 per cent stated they had used it at some time. More than one-quarter (27 per cent) of adults who had used the Internet in the last 3 months stated that they would like to use the Internet more often. The most common reasons for not doing so were lack of time (52 per cent) and lack of skills or knowledge (21 per cent).

The most common activity of adults in the UK that had used the Internet in the three months prior to interview in 2007 was finding information about goods and services (86 per cent), closely followed by sending or receiving emails (85 per cent)

Table 13.4

Selected uses of the Internet: by age, 2007[1]

United Kingdom

Percentages

	16–24	25–44	45–54	55–64	65 and over	All aged 16 and over
Finding information about goods and services	83	88	89	86	75	86
Sending/receiving email	84	87	86	86	80	85
Using services related to travel and accommodation	52	67	69	63	56	63
Obtaining information from public authority websites	30	51	49	50	36	46
Internet banking	34	52	46	43	31	45
Looking for information about education	54	38	36	19	-	36
Playing/downloading games/images/films/music	58	40	25	14	-	35
Downloading official forms	21	34	34	35	22	31
Seeking health-related information	20	31	34	23	18	27
Sending completed official forms	18	27	29	26	-	25
Downloading software	33	26	22	17	-	24
Selling goods or services	21	23	13	-	-	17
Telephoning over the Internet	15	13	10	-	-	12
Doing an online course	-	8	8	-	-	6

1 Adults who used the Internet in the three months prior to interview. Data were collected in January, February and March 2007 for England, Wales and Scotland, and May 2007 for Northern Ireland.

Source: Omnibus Survey, Office for National Statistics

(Table 13.4). These two activities were also the most common use of the Internet across all age groups. Young people aged 16 to 24 were more likely than any other age group to play or download games, images, films or music and look for information about education. Using services related to travel and accommodation and obtaining information from public authority websites were more popular activities among those aged over 24, particularly among the 25 to 64 year olds. Internet banking was also a common activity for this age group. Of all the activities surveyed three were performed more by women than men: seeking health-related information; looking for information related to education, training or courses and doing an online course in any subject.

In 2007, 53 per cent of adults in the UK had ever purchased goods or services over the Internet. Of these, 93 per cent had bought goods or services online in the 12 months prior to interview. Nearly one-half (45 per cent) were aged 25 to 44, with nearly one-third (32 per cent) aged 45 to 64. At least 40 per cent of all age groups up to the age of 64 had purchased films, music or DVDs. Other common purchases online among those aged 16 to 24 were clothes or sports goods (41 per cent) and tickets for events (40 per cent). For those aged 25 and over, other common purchases were travel, accommodation or holidays (49 per cent) and household goods (43 per cent). There was generally little difference between the types of purchases

made by men and women online, apart from computer software/ hardware and electronic equipment, which men were more likely to purchase than women (45 per cent compared with 28 per cent) and food or groceries, which women were more likely to purchase (24 per cent compared with 17 per cent).

Competition from Internet entertainment and social networking and multi-channel television services may have contributed to falling cinema admissions. In 2006, there were 157 million visits to UK cinemas, 4.9 per cent less than in 2005 and a fall for a second successive year. Almost six in ten (57 per cent) people aged 15 and over went to the cinema at least once during the year, while nearly two in ten (17 per cent) went once a month or more. There was no difference between men and women attending the cinema at least once a year, although men were more likely than women to go once a month or more –19 per cent of men compared with 14 per cent of women.

The likelihood of attending the cinema at least once a year fell with age. In the UK in 2006 nearly nine in ten (87 per cent) children aged 7 to 14 saw a film at the cinema compared with around three in ten (32 per cent) people aged 55 and over (Figure 13.5). Nearly three in ten (28 per cent) children aged 7 to 14 also went to the cinema at least once a month or more. Of all children who attended the cinema in 2006, most

Figure 13.5

Cinema attendance: by age, 2006

United Kingdom

Percentages

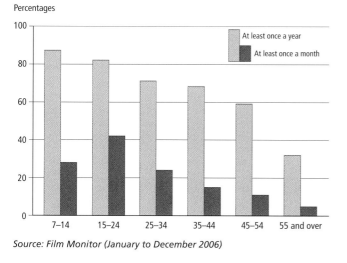

Source: Film Monitor (January to December 2006)

(93 per cent) aged four to nine were accompanied to the cinema by an adult. Children started to go to the cinema with friends between the ages of 12 to 14 years. One in two children in this age group had been to the cinema with friends, and nearly seven in ten had been with friends and siblings. Young people aged 15 to 24 were the most likely of all age groups to go to the cinema often, 42 per cent of this age group attended the cinema at least once a month or more compared with 9 per cent of those aged 35 and over.

Males preferred action-led films such as *United 93* and *V for Vendetta*, while drama with females in the leading roles were popular with women, such as *The Devil wears Prada* and *The Queen*. The top five grossing films in the UK in 2006 were *Casino Royale*, *Pirates of the Caribbean: Dead Man's Chest*, *The Da Vinci Code*, *Ice Age 2* and *Borat: Cultural Learnings of America for Make Benefit Glorious Nation of Kazakhstan*.

Cultural activities

The *Da Vinci Code* by Dan Brown was the most borrowed adult fiction book in public libraries in the UK between July 2005 and June 2006, followed by *Nights of Rain and Stars* by Maeve Binchy. The most borrowed children's books were *Harry Potter and the Half Blood Prince* by JK Rowling and *Clean Break* by Jacqueline Wilson, who had 13 titles in the top 20 most borrowed children's fiction titles. *You Are What You Eat* by Gillian McKeith was the most borrowed adult non-fiction title, perhaps reflecting increasing awareness and interest in self-image, diet and food. The most borrowed adult classic title was JD Salinger's *Catcher in the Rye* and for children, *The Witches* by Roald Dahl. Overall, the majority of books lent to adults were fiction (46 per cent) followed by

lifestyle, sport and leisure (8 per cent) and health and personal development (3 per cent). Books on the arts were the fourth most popular at 2 per cent.

According to the Taking Part Survey, nearly one-half of all adults (48 per cent) in England attended a library in the 12 months prior to interview in 2005/06. More than one-third (34 per cent) of these attended at least once a month, while a further 28 per cent went three or four times during the year. Adults aged 16 to 44 were more likely to visit a public library than those aged over 45 and women were more likely to go than men. Adults from lower managerial and professional occupations had a higher rate of attendance at a public library than those in any other socio-economic classified group (see Appendix, Part 1: National Statistics Socio-economic Classification (NS-SEC). More than one-half (56 per cent) of this group visited a library in the 12 months prior to interview in 2005/06 (Figure 13.6), followed by 53 per cent of those in higher managerial and professional occupations and 52 per cent of those in intermediate occupations. Less than four in ten adults working in routine occupations (36 per cent) visited a library over the same period.

The main reasons for visiting a library in England were to borrow, return or renew books (56 per cent) and to accompany children (10 per cent). Other reasons include browsing or reading (8 per cent) and using computers or the Internet (6 per cent). More than one-half of adults (52 per cent) had

Figure 13.6

Attendance at a public library: by socio-economic classification,[1] 2005/06[2]

England

Percentages

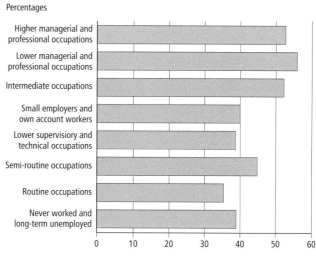

1 See Appendix, Part 1: National Statistics Socio-economic Classification (NS-SEC).
2 In the 12 months prior to interview.

Source: Taking Part: The National Survey of Culture, Leisure and Sport, Department for Culture, Media and Sport

Table 13.7

Top ten arts events attended:[1] by age, 2005/06

England

Percentages

	16–24	25–44	45–64	65 and over	All aged 16 and over
Theatre performance[2]	29	37	42	31	36
Carnival and street arts[3]	28	31	27	16	26
Live music event[4]	34	29	25	8	24
Exhibition of art, photography or sculpture	16	23	26	16	22
Craft exhibition	5	14	21	17	15
Classical music performance	3	5	12	12	8
Culturally specific festival	6	7	6	2	6
Jazz performance	4	5	7	5	6
Event connected with books or writing	3	5	6	3	5
Opera or operetta	2	3	6	6	4

1 Attendance during the 12 months prior to interview. Percentages do not add up to 100 per cent as respondents could give more than one answer.
2 Theatre includes play/drama and other theatre.
3 Carnival and street arts have been merged.
4 Excluding jazz and classical music performances.

Source: Taking Part: The National Survey of Culture, Leisure and Sport, Department for Culture, Media and Sport

not visited a library in the 12 months prior to interview in 2005/06. Three in ten (30 per cent) of these stated that they did not need to go, while nearly two in ten (19 per cent) said they were not really interested. Preferring to purchase their own books was a reason given by 7 per cent of non-attendees.

Around two-thirds (67 per cent) of adults aged 16 and over in England attended an arts event in the 12 months prior to interview in 2005/06. Nearly one-half (49 per cent) attended once or twice, while around one-third (34 per cent) attended three or four times. The most common types of art events attended were any type of theatre performances, attended by 36 per cent, carnival and street arts (26 per cent) and live musical events (24 per cent) (Table 13.7). Overall, arts attendance among people aged 25 to 64 was higher than among those in younger and older age groups, but this varied among the different kinds of events. For example, people aged 45 to 64 were more likely than other age groups to attend a theatre performance (42 per cent), while live music events were more likely to be attended by those aged 16 to 24 (34 per cent). One-third of adults had not attended an arts event in the 12 months prior to interview. The main reasons given were that they were not really interested (31 per cent), they had difficulty finding time (29 per cent) and their health was not good enough to attend (16 per cent). In Northern Ireland a theatrical production of a drama was the most popular arts event attended according to the Continuous Household Survey in 2005/06. Nearly one-quarter (24 per cent) of adults attended in the 12 months prior to interview.

More than one-half of adults (53 per cent) in England had participated in an arts activity in the 12 months prior to interview in 2005/06. Of these, nearly one-half (46 per cent) participated at least once a week. The most common type of arts activity participation was buying original/handmade crafts (16 per cent), painting, drawing, printmaking and sculpture (13 per cent) and textile crafts (13 per cent). Women were more likely to participate than men, 58 per cent compared with 48 per cent. Not surprisingly, the main reason for participating in an arts activity was enjoyment (62 per cent), while finding the activity relaxing and learning or developing skills were reasons for 8 per cent and 7 per cent of participants respectively. Adults who were encouraged as a child to participate in an art activity, such as reading books that were not required for school or religious studies, drawing and painting, writing stories, poems, plays or music, and playing a musical instrument, acting, singing or dancing, were more likely to participate in the arts as adults than those who were not encouraged as a child, 57 per cent compared with 39 per cent.

Gambling

According to the 2007 British Gambling Prevalence Survey the National Lottery draw is the most popular gambling activity. Nearly six in ten adults (57 per cent) purchased tickets for the National Lottery draw in Great Britain in the 12 months prior to interview (Table 13.8). Overall, 68 per cent of adults participated in some form of gambling activity in the 12 months prior to interview, a fall from 72 per cent in 1999. This fall is mainly because fewer people played the National Lottery draw. The proportion of people buying a lottery ticket fell from 65 per cent in 1999 to 57 per cent in 2007. However, excluding the National Lottery draw, 48 per cent (around 23 million people) participated in another form of gambling in the 12 months prior to interview, about 1 million more than in 1999.

Men were more likely than women to participate in gambling activities, 71 per cent compared with 65 per cent in the 12 months prior to interview. Of all those who participated, men participated in more than or nearly equal proportions to women in all but one activity, bingo, which was played by 10 per cent of women compared with 4 per cent of men. Men were more likely than women to bet on horse races, play slot machines and have a private bet with friends or colleagues. Men also participated in more gambling activities than women; 18 per cent of men compared with 10 per cent of women participated in four or more activities in the year prior to interview.

People also use modern technology to participate in gambling activities remotely. According to the Gambling Commission survey on remote gambling, over the four quarters to September 2007, 9 per cent of adults in Great Britain

Table 13.8

Participation in selected gambling activities: by sex, 2007[1]

Great Britain   Percentages

	Men	Women	Total[2]
National Lottery draw	59	56	57
Scratchcards	19	20	20
Horse races[3]	22	13	17
Slot machines	19	10	14
Another lottery	12	12	12
Private betting (e.g. with friends, colleagues)	15	6	10
Bingo	4	10	7
Betting with a bookmaker (other than on horse or dog races)[3]	10	3	6
Dog races[3]	7	3	5
Online betting with a bookmaker on any event or sport	6	1	4
Table games in a casino	6	2	4
Football pools	5	2	3

1 In the 12 months prior to interview.
2 Includes those for whom sex was not known.
3 Does not include bets made online.

Source: British Gambling Prevalence Survey 2007, Gambling Commission

Figure 13.9

Participation in remote gambling:[1] by age

Great Britain

Percentages

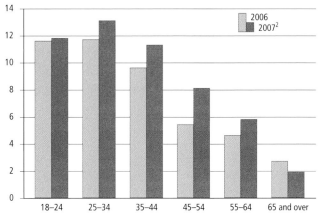

1 In at least one form of remote gambling, in the month prior to interview. Includes Internet through a personal computer, laptop or handheld device, Wireless Application Protocol/Internet or text (SMS) on a mobile phone and interactive/digital television.
2 Data are an average of figures for December 2006, March 2007, June 2007 and September 2007.

Source: Gambling Commission

participated in gambling through a computer, mobile phone or interactive/digital television. Since 2006, there has been an increase in participation across all age groups up to the age of 64 (Figure 13.9). Those participating in remote gambling were more likely to be aged 18 to 44 than to be in any age group over 45, with 12 per cent of adults aged 18 to 24 participating, 13 per cent of those aged 25 to 34 and 11 per cent of those aged 35 to 44. Remote gamblers were more likely to be men than women. Nearly double the proportion of men than women gambled remotely, 11 per cent compared with 6 per cent. The most common way to gamble remotely was on the Internet, through a personal computer, laptop or handheld device (7 per cent of all adults), followed by Internet or text (SMS) on a mobile phone (3 per cent) and through an interactive/digital television service (2 per cent), though participants may have used one or all of these modes. The three main types of activity were the National Lottery draw, where 6 per cent of all adults gambled remotely, betting on sports such as horses, greyhounds and football and poker rooms/tournaments (2 per cent).

Holidays and sporting activities

UK residents made a record 45.3 million holiday trips abroad in 2006. The number of trips abroad has increased over two and a half times (153 per cent) since 1986 and is a continuation of the rise in overseas holidays over the last three decades from 6.7 million in 1971. Most holiday trips were taken during the

July to September quarter, when almost twice as many were taken than during the January to March quarter. Spain was the most popular destination, accounting for nearly three in ten holidays (28 per cent). France was the second most popular destination (16 per cent of all holidays). As in recent years eight of the ten most popular holiday destinations were in the EU. The exceptions were North America where 6 per cent of all holidays (2.7 million visits) were taken, of which the vast majority were in the United States (2.4 million visits), and Turkey where 3 per cent of holidays (1.2 million visits) were taken (Figure 13.10). UK residents made 1.9 million holiday visits to the continent of Africa (4 per cent of all holidays), where the majority of holidays were taken in Egypt. Nearly 3 per cent (1.3 million visits) of holiday trips were to Asia, where the most common destinations were India and Thailand (0.4 million visits and 0.3 million visits respectively).

Tourism visits or trips to the countryside, the coast or towns and cities are another leisure pursuit. Tourism visits are defined as round trips made from home for leisure purposes that last three hours or more and are not taken regularly. According to Natural England, nearly two in ten adults (17 per cent) in England made a tourism visit in the week prior to interview in 2005. The majority of trips were to inland towns and cities (77 per cent), while 16 per cent were to the countryside and 7 per cent were to a seaside coast or seaside town or city.

The main activity undertaken on tourism trips in England in 2005 was eating and drinking (Table 13.11), and was the main focus for one-quarter (25 per cent) of all trips. Shopping was another common activity occupying nearly two in ten trips

Figure 13.10

Holidays abroad by UK residents:[1] by selected non-EU destination, 2006

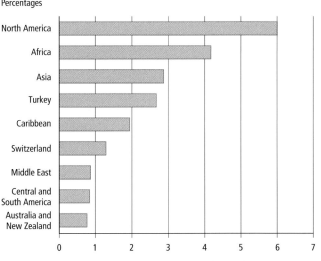

United Kingdom

Percentages

1 Proportion of all holidays taken abroad by residents of the UK.

Source: International Passenger Survey, Office for National Statistics

(18 per cent), followed by visiting friends and relatives at their home (14 per cent) and entertainment, for example trips to theatre or cinema (12 per cent). The main activity undertaken varied by destination type. Shopping and entertainment were more likely activities on trips to inland towns or cities than on trips to the seaside or countryside, where trips were more likely to involve walking or a visit to a leisure attraction or place of interest.

Table 13.11

Top ten activities undertaken on a tourism trip:[1] by selected main destination type, 2005

England

Percentages

	Inland town/city	Seaside town/city	Countryside	Seaside coast	All tourism visits
Eating/drinking out	25	28	25	10	25
Shopping	22	4	3	2	18
Visiting friends/relatives at their home	14	10	12	12	14
Entertainment (e.g. cinema, theatre)	14	8	6	1	12
Visiting leisure attraction/place of interest	5	11	11	7	7
Hobby or special interest	5	4	9	7	6
Walking/hill walking/rambling	3	12	15	14	6
Watching live sport/live event	3	1	2	0	3
Taking part in sports or active pursuits	3	1	4	1	3
Driving/sightseeing/picnicing	2	5	5	9	3

1 Tourism trips are round trips that start from and return to home for leisure purposes that last three hours or more and are not taken regularly.

Source: Leisure Visits Survey, Natural England

The average distance travelled on a tourism trip was 32.8 miles, although distances varied by destination. The furthest distances travelled were trips to the seaside/coast, an average 61.3 miles compared with 28.4 miles to inland towns/cities. Trips lasted an average of 5 hours and 18 minutes in total with an average of 3 hours and 24 minutes spent at the main destination.

According to the Active People Survey, 21 per cent of adults (8.5 million people) regularly took part in sport and active recreation in England in 2005/06. Regular participation is defined as participating in at least 30 minutes of sport and active recreation (including walking and cycling) of at least moderate intensity on at least three occasions a week in the four weeks prior to interview.

Rates of regular participation in sport and active recreation vary among local and unitary authorities in England. Map 13.12 shows the levels of sports participation and club membership in England in 2005/06 split into four groupings, with each group containing similar numbers of local authorities. The highest rate of regular participation in a sport or active recreation in 2005/06 was in the Isles of Scilly where over three in ten (32 per cent) participated (this was based on a sample

size of less than 1,000 people). Richmond-upon-Thames in London had the next highest rate, where nearly three in ten adults (30 per cent) participated, followed by Macclesfield in the North West (29 per cent), and Kensington and Chelsea in London and Hart in the South East (both 28 per cent). The lowest participation rate of 14 per cent was in Boston in the East Midlands, closely followed by Newham, and Barking and Dagenham (both in London) and Sandwell in the West Midlands, where participation was between 14 and 15 per cent.

One-quarter (25 per cent) of adults in England were members of a club where they took part in sport in the four weeks prior to interview in 2005/06. Membership of a club also varied among local authorities in England. The highest rate was in Elmbridge in the South East where nearly four in ten (37 per cent) adults belonged to a club, followed by Wokingham in the South East (37 per cent) and Kensington and Chelsea in London (36 per cent). The lowest club membership rate of 17 per cent was in Newham in London and Easington in the North East.

According to the Taking Part Survey, nearly seven in ten (69 per cent) adults aged 16 and over in England participated in at least one type of active sport in the 12 months prior to

Map 13.12

Sport participation[1] and club membership:[2] by local authority,[3] 2005/06

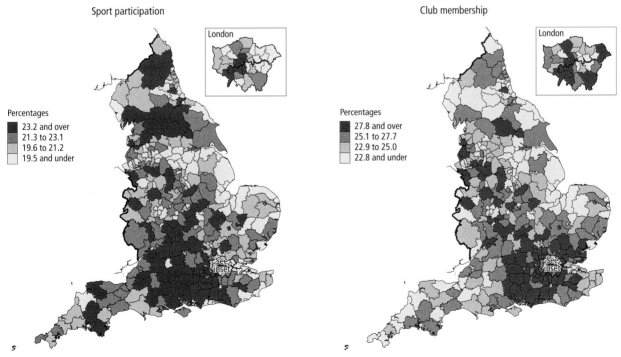

1 The proportion of the adult population participating in at least 30 minutes of sport and active recreation (including recreational walking and cycling) of at least moderate intensity on at least three occasions a week.
2 The proportion of the adult population who are a member of a club where they took part in a sport in the four weeks prior to interview.
3 Local and unitary authorities.

Source: The Active People Survey, Sport England

interview in 2005/06. Excluding walking, the most popular sporting activity was indoor swimming and diving, with 31 per cent of adults participating. This was most popular among both men and women (27 per cent and 35 per cent respectively) and especially among women aged between 16 and 44, where nearly one-half (48 per cent) participated. The second most popular category of sporting activity for men was snooker, pool or billiards, 22 per cent of men participated compared with 7 per cent of women, while for women it was health, fitness, gym or conditioning activities such as abdominal and thigh exercises (21 per cent). As well as snooker, pool or billiards, outdoor football was considerably more popular with men than women, 19 per cent of men had played during the previous 12 months compared with 3 per cent of women. Conversely 16 per cent of women participated in keep-fit, aerobics and dance exercise, compared with 5 per cent of men.

Of the 31 per cent of adults in England who had not participated in an active sport during the 12 months prior to interview in 2005/06 nearly one-half stated that their main reason for not participating was that their health was not good enough (Figure 13.13). More than one-third (36 per cent) were either not really interested in participating (18 per cent) or found it difficult to find the time (also 18 per cent). Adults who participated in at least one sport in the 12 months prior to interview gave many factors that would make them participate more often. Just under four in ten (39 per cent) stated they would participate if they were less busy, while just over one in ten (11 per cent) felt cheaper admission prices for venues such as gyms or clubs would encourage them to participate more often. Other factors included having someone to go with and more free time (9 per cent and 6 per cent respectively).

In Scotland nearly one-half (48 per cent) of all adults participated at least once in a sport (excluding walking) in the four weeks prior to interview in 2004–06, according to sportscotland. Nearly six in ten (57 per cent) men and four in ten (40 per cent) women participated. Swimming was the most popular sport; 16 per cent of all adults went swimming in the four weeks prior to interview. This was also the most popular sport for women where 19 per cent participated, while for men, indoor or outdoor football was the most popular sport, also with 19 per cent participating. Swimming or diving was also the most popular sport for men in Northern Ireland according to the Continuous Household Survey in 2005/06 where one-fifth (20 per cent) of men participated in the 12 months prior to interview. The most popular sport for women in Northern Ireland was keep fit, aerobics, yoga or dance, where nearly one-quarter (24 per cent) participated.

Figure 13.13

Main reason for non-participation in an active sport,[1] 2005/06

England

Percentages

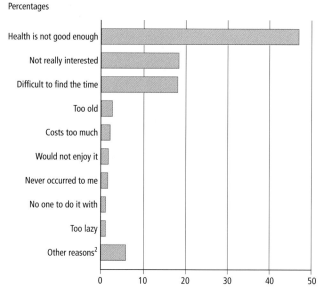

1 In the 12 months prior to interview.
2 Other reasons include 'don't know', 'fear of injury' and 'changing facilities are not good enough'.

Source: Taking Part: The National Survey of Culture, Leisure and Sport, Department for Culture, Media and Sport

Social participation

Cultivating and developing relationships and friendships is an important part of life. According to the 2006 British Social Attitudes Survey, nearly one-half (48 per cent) of people aged 18 and over in Great Britain felt that it was more important to have close ties with their family than to have close friends, while 13 per cent felt that it was more important to have close friends than close family ties. Nearly four in ten (39 per cent) felt that it was neither more important to have closer ties with family than friends nor more important to have close friends.

In 2005 the British Social Attitudes Survey asked how much time was spent with friends and family. Women tended to spend more time with both family and friends than men, 65 per cent stated that they saw members of their family or other relatives weekly or nearly every week and 63 per cent saw friends, compared with 57 per cent and 58 per cent respectively for men (Table 13.14). More than one in ten men (11 per cent) spent social time with their work colleagues weekly or nearly every week compared with 8 per cent of women. Part of this difference was probably because more men than women work and so this part of the question applied to more men than women. One-quarter (25 per cent) of men very rarely or never socialised with work colleagues, compared

Table 13.14

Amount of time spent with friends and family:[1] by sex, 2005

Great Britain   Percentages

	Weekly or nearly every week	Once or twice a month	A few times a year	Very rarely or never	Does not apply
Men					
Members of family or other relatives	57	19	18	5	1
Friends	58	27	11	2	1
Work colleagues	11	18	26	25	21
People known through groups or organisations	17	14	17	22	30
Women					
Members of family or other relatives	65	17	15	2	1
Friends	63	26	7	3	1
Work colleagues	8	17	25	17	33
People known through groups or organisations	16	14	13	18	38

1 Adults aged 18 and over. Those who said 'don't know' are excluded.

Source: British Social Attitudes Survey, National Centre for Social Research

Figure 13.15

Methods used to find either a casual or long-term date or partner,[1,2] 2007

Great Britain

Percentages

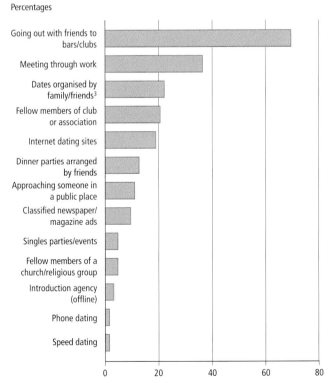

1 Methods used at any time in the past. Does not include those who responded 'none of these', 'prefer not to say' and 'don't know'. Data were collected in March 2007.
2 Percentages do not add up to 100 per cent as respondents could give more than one answer.
3 Includes blind dates.

Source: YouGov

with 17 per cent of women. A similar proportion of both men and women spent time regularly with people that they knew through groups or organisations (17 per cent of men compared with 16 per cent of women).

Looking for a date or partner is something that most people do during their life-time (see Chapter 2: Households and families for evidence of the proportion of people who are married/ living with partner). Adults aged 18 and over in Great Britain were asked in a survey by YouGov to select a method that they had used at any time to find a casual or long-term date or partner. Of those adults who used a 'method', going out with friends to bars and clubs was the most common way to meet a casual or long-term partner, with seven in ten (70 per cent) doing so, followed by meeting someone at work, with nearly four in ten (37 per cent) doing so (Figure 13.15). More than two in ten (22 per cent) of these adults went on dates organised by family and friends, and a similar proportion (21 per cent) had dates organised by fellow members of a club or organisation. Nearly one-fifth (19 per cent) of these adults used Internet dating sites, which were more popular than the traditional introduction agencies that work offline, used by just 3 per cent.

Volunteering

One way that individuals contribute to their community is through volunteering, from formal volunteering activities which is giving unpaid help through groups, clubs or organisations to benefit other people or the environment, to informal activities which is giving unpaid help as an individual to people who are not relatives. According to the Citizenship Survey, over seven in ten (73 per cent) adults in England had volunteered (either formally or informally) at least once in the 12 months prior to interview in April to June 2007. Just under half (48 per cent) had volunteered at least once a month. Between 2001 and April to June 2007, the overall levels of volunteering have not changed. However, levels of formal volunteering at least once a year have risen over this period from 39 per cent to 45 per cent, while informal volunteering fell from 67 per cent to 63 per cent. Women were more likely to volunteer at least once a month than men (53 per cent of women compared to 42 per cent of men).

There are many reasons why individuals volunteer. According to the Helping Out Survey, more than one-half (53 per cent) of formal volunteers in England in 2006/07 got involved because they wanted to improve things or help people (Figure 13.16). Around four in ten felt that either the cause was important or they had time to spare that could be used in this way. Three in ten did voluntary work to meet people and make friends. Family or friends' connections with volunteering influenced some individuals, nearly three in ten people volunteered help for an activity that was connected with family or friends'

interests and more than two in ten volunteered because their family or friends were volunteers. More than one-quarter (27 per cent) volunteered to use their existing skills, while 19 per cent volunteered to learn new skills.

The main types of organisations helped by formal volunteers in 2006/07 were educational establishments such as schools or universities, helped by around three in ten (31 per cent). Nearly one-quarter (24 per cent) of volunteers helped out with religious organisations and more than one-fifth (22 per cent) helped sports and exercise organisations and health and disability organisations.

The most common reason given by just over eight in ten (82 per cent) adults who did not volunteer was that they did not have enough spare time. People were also put off by bureaucracy (49 per cent) and worried about risk and liability (47 per cent).

Charity

Many organisations that people volunteer to help are charities, and the time and expertise of volunteers are crucial to charitable organisations. Giving gifts of money to charity is also a prominent way of caring for others and supporting various causes. According to the Charities Aid Foundation and the National Council of Voluntary Organisations, the average donation made by each adult in the UK in 2006/07 in a four-week period was £16 and the total amount donated was estimated to be £9.5 billion. Over half (54 per cent) of adults gave at least once a month, with women more likely to give than men, 59 per cent compared with 48 per cent. Those with the highest socio-economic status were more likely to give, 66 per cent of those in professional or managerial occupations donated to charity in a typical month compared with 47 per cent of those in routine or manual occupations (see Appendix, Part 1: National Statistics Socio-economic Classification (NS-SEC) and also Chapter 8: Social protection).

The cause that received the greatest proportion of donations was medical research at 17 per cent of total donations. This was closely followed by religious causes with 16 per cent of the total money. Overseas projects attracted 9 per cent of the total amount given.

People use different methods to give monetary aid to charity. In 2006/07 nearly one-half of all donors (48 per cent) in the UK gave cash, although this method generated around one-sixth (18 per cent) of the total amount donated (Figure 13.17). Similarly, nearly one quarter (23 per cent) of people bought a raffle ticket or lottery ticket (other than the National Lottery),

Figure 13.16

Selected reasons for starting formal volunteering,[1] 2006/07

England
Percentages

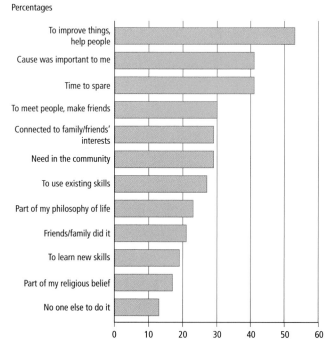

1 Percentages do not add up to 100 per cent as respondents could give more than one answer. Those who said 'don't know' or refused to respond are excluded.

Source: Helping Out: A national survey of volunteering and charitable giving, Cabinet Office

Figure 13.17

Methods of giving to charity: by proportion of donors and total amount given, 2006/07

United Kingdom
Percentages

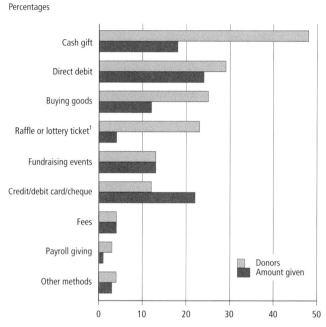

1 Not including the National Lottery.

Source: UK Giving 2007: Charities Aid Foundation; National Council for Voluntary Organisations

and this generated 4 per cent of the total amount donated. The method yielding the largest amount was donated by direct debit, standing order or covenant. More than one-quarter (29 per cent) of all donors used this method, which generated 24 per cent of the total. This method is particularly useful for easy conversion to tax efficiency through Gift Aid (allowing charities to reclaim the basic rate tax on the amount donated) and supporting charitable causes online through designated charity websites. Between 2002/03 and 2006/07 the amount of Gift Aid paid out to charities increased by 64 per cent, from £506 million to £828 million. Donations by credit/debit card or cheque also yielded a large amount. This method was used by 12 per cent of donors and accounted for 22 per cent of the total amount donated.

Religion

Belonging to a religion can provide a spiritual element and a moral framework to a person's life, as well as involving contact with other individuals and participation in the local community. According to the British Social Attitudes Survey, more than one-half (54 per cent) of the population in Great Britain claimed to belong to a religion in 2006, a fall of 3 percentage points since 1996. Of these, 48 per cent claimed to be Christian and the majority, 22 per cent, belonged to the Church of

Table 13.18

Belonging to a religion[1,2]

Great Britain		Percentages
	1996	2006
Christian		
Church of England/Anglican	29.3	22.2
Christian – no denomination	4.7	9.6
Roman Catholic	8.9	9.0
Presbyterian/Free-Presbyterian/ Church of Scotland	3.8	2.5
Baptist/Methodist	3.0	2.4
United Reform Church (URC)/ Congregational	0.8	0.1
Brethren	0.1	-
Other Protestant/other Christian	2.2	1.7
Non-Christian		
Islam/Muslim	1.8	3.3
Hindu	0.6	1.4
Jewish	0.3	0.5
Sikh	0.2	0.2
Buddhist	0.5	0.2
Other non-Christian	0.4	0.4
No religion	42.6	45.8
Refusal/not answered/didn't know	0.8	0.6

1 Respondents were asked 'Do you regard yourself as belonging to any particular religion?' and those who said yes were asked which religion.
2 See Appendix, Part 13: Measurement of religion.

Source: British Social Attitudes Survey, National Centre for Social Research

England (Table 13.18). After Christians, the largest religious group in Great Britain was Muslim (3 per cent). Overall, the largest percentage rise was for people who stated that they were Christian with no denomination (up 4.9 percentage points since 1996). In Northern Ireland 98 per cent of adults claimed to belong to a religion according to the Continuous Household Survey in 2005/06. Nearly two-fifths (39 per cent) were Roman Catholic, 24 per cent were Presbyterian and 17 per cent belonged to the Church of Ireland.

When people were asked how often they attended services or meetings connected with their religion in Great Britain (apart from special occasions such as weddings, funerals and baptisms) 55 per cent stated that they never or practically never attended. Men were more likely than women to not attend, 59 per cent compared with 52 per cent in 2006. Religious meetings or services were attended once a week or more by 13 per cent of men and 15 per cent of women.

European society has great religious and philosophical diversity. According to a Eurobarometer survey in 2005, nearly four in five (79 per cent) citizens of the EU-25 held religious or spiritual beliefs. More than one-half (52 per cent) believed in God and more than one-quarter (27 per cent) believed in some sort of spirit or life force. Less than one in five (18 per cent) did not believe that there was any sort of spirit, God or life force. More than nine in ten (95 per cent) of Maltese respondents stated that they believed in a God, the greatest proportion of the population than in any EU member state (Figure 13.19). Romania and Cyprus had the next greatest proportion of people believing in God (90 per cent). Belief in God was also widespread in Greece, Portugal and Poland, where around 80 per cent of people stated that they believed in a God, followed by Italy and Ireland, at 74 per cent and 73 per cent of their populations respectively. In contrast, in Estonia and the Czech Republic, less than one in five stated that they believed in a God. In these countries, at least one in two believed that there was some sort of spirit or life force (54 per cent and 50 per cent respectively). In the UK nearly four in ten (38 per cent) people believed in a God, a further four in ten (40 per cent) believed in some sort of spirit or life force and two in ten (20 per cent) did not believe there is any sort of spirit, God or life force.

Figure 13.19

Belief in God:[1] EU comparison, 2005

Percentages

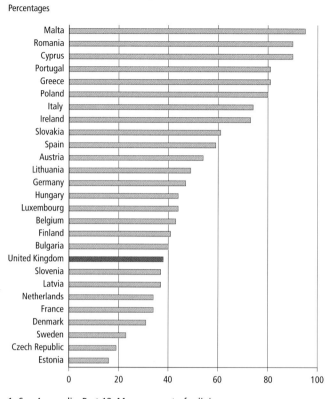

1 See Appendix, Part 13: Measurement of religion.

Source: Eurobarometer, European Commission

References, further reading and websites

Chapter 1: Population

References and further reading

Annual Report of the Registrar General for Northern Ireland, Northern Ireland Statistics and Research Agency, available at:
www.nisra.gov.uk/demography/default.asp?cmsid=20_45_100&cms=demography_Publications_Registrar+General+Annual+Reports&release

Annual Report of the Registrar General for Scotland, General Register Office for Scotland, available at:
www.gro-scotland.gov.uk/statistics/index.html

Asylum Statistics United Kingdom, 2006, Home Office, available at:
www.homeoffice.gov.uk/rds/pdfs07/hosb1407.pdf

Birth Statistics, England and Wales (Series FM1), ONS, Internet only publication, available at:
www.statistics.gov.uk/statbase/Product.asp?vlnk=5768

Census 2001: First results on population for England and Wales, ONS, TSO, available at:
www.statistics.gov.uk/census2001/downloads/pop2001ew.pdf

Control of Immigration: Statistics, United Kingdom, 2006, TSO, available at:
www.official-documents.gov.uk/document/cm71/7197/7197.pdf

Europe in Figures – Population, Eurostat, available at:
www.epp.eurostat.ec.europa.eu/cache/ITY_OFFPUB/KS-CD-06-001-01/EN/KS-CD-06-001-01-EN.PDF

Focus on Ethnicity and Religion, ONS, Palgrave Macmillan, available at:
www.statistics.gov.uk/StatBase/Product.asp?vlnk=14629

Health Statistics Quarterly, ONS, Palgrave Macmillan, available at:
www.statistics.gov.uk/statbase/Product.asp?vlnk=6725

International Migration Statistics (Series MN), ONS, Internet only publication, available at:
www.statistics.gov.uk/statbase/Product.asp?vlnk=507

Key Population and Vital Statistics (Series VS/PP1), ONS/TSO, available at:
www.statistics.gov.uk/statbase/Product.asp?vlnk=539

Mid-year Population Estimates, Northern Ireland, Northern Ireland Statistics and Research Agency, available at:
www.nisra.gov.uk/demography/default.asp?cmsid=20_21_24&cms=demography_Popula_Mid-Year+Population+Estimates

Mortality Statistics for England and Wales (Series DH2), ONS, Internet only publication, available at:
www.statistics.gov.uk/statbase/Product.asp?vlnk=618

National Population Projections, UK (Series PP2), ONS, available at:
www.statistics.gov.uk/StatBase/Product.asp?vlnk=8519

Persons Granted British Citizenship, United Kingdom, 2006, Home Office, available at:
www.homeoffice.gov.uk/rds/pdfs07/hosb0807.pdf

Population Projections, Northern Ireland, Northern Ireland Statistics and Research Agency, available at:
www.nisra.gov.uk/demography/default.asp?cmsid=20_21_25&cms=demography_Population%20statistics_Population+Projections&release

Population Projections, Scotland, General Register Office for Scotland, available at:
www.gro-scotland.gov.uk/statistics/publications-and-data/popproj/projected-population-of-scotland-(2006-based)/index.html

Population Projections for Wales (sub-national), Welsh Assembly Government / Welsh Office Statistical Directorate, available at:
http://new.wales.gov.uk/topics/statistics/theme/population/pop-project/?lang=en

Population Trends, ONS, Palgrave Macmillan, available at:
www.statistics.gov.uk/STATBASE/Product.asp?vlnk=6303

Scotland's population 2006, The Registrar General's Annual Review of Demographic Trends, General Register Office for Scotland, available at:
www.gro-scotland.gov.uk/statistics/publications-and-data/population-estimates/index.html

Who are the 'Mixed' ethnic group? Ben Bradford, ONS, Internet only, available at:
www.statistics.gov.uk/CCI/article.asp?ID=1580&Pos=1&ColRank=1&Rank=224

World Population Prospects: The 2006 Revision, United Nations, available at:
www.un.org/esa/population/publications/wpp2006/wpp2006.htm

Other useful websites

National Statistics
www.statistics.gov.uk

Eurostat
www.europa.eu.int/comm/eurostat

General Register Office for Scotland
www.gro-scotland.gov.uk

Government Actuary's Department
www.gad.gov.uk

Home Office Immigration and Asylum Statistics
www.homeoffice.gov.uk/rds/immigration1.html

National Institute for Demographic Studies, France (INED)
www.ined.fr/en/homepage_of_ined_website/

National Institute for Statistics and Economic Studies, France (INSEE)
www.insee.fr/en/home/home_page.asp

National Institute for Statistics, Italy (ISTAT)
www.istat.it/english/

Northern Ireland Statistics Research Agency
www.nisra.gov.uk

Scottish Government
www.scotland.gov.uk

Statistics Belgium
www.statbel.fgov.be/

United Nations Population Division
www.un.org/esa/population/unpop.htm

Welsh Assembly Government
www.wales.gov.uk

Chapter 2: Households and families

References and further reading

Abortion Statistics, England and Wales: 2006, Department of Health available at:
www.dh.gov.uk/en/Publicationsandstatistics/Publications/Publicationsstatistics/DH_075697

Abortion Statistics, 2006, ISD Scotland, available at:
www.isdscotland.org/isd/4871.html

Adoption Statistics (Series FM2), Office for National Statistics, available at:
www.statistics.gov.uk/statbase/Product.asp?vlnk=581

Adoption: The new approach, Department of Health, available at:
www.dh.gov.uk/en/publicationsandstatistics/publications/publicationspolicyandguidance/dh_4006581

Annual Report of the Registrar General for Northern Ireland, Northern Ireland Statistics and Research Agency, available at:
www.nisra.gov.uk/demography/default.asp?cmsid=20_45_48&cms=demography_Publications_Registrar+General+Report+2003&release=

Annual Report of the Registrar General for Scotland, General Register Office for Scotland, available at:
www.gro-scotland.gov.uk/statistics/index.html

Birth Statistics, England and Wales (Series FM1), ONS, available at:
www.statistics.gov.uk/statbase/Product.asp?vlnk=5768

Continuous Household Survey, Northern Ireland Statistics and Research Agency available at:
www.csu.nisra.gov.uk/surveys/survey.asp?id=1

Europe in Figures – Population, Eurostat, available at:
www.epp.eurostat.ec.europa.eu/cache/ITY_OFFPUB/KS-CD-06-001-01/EN/KS-CD-06-001-01-EN.PDF

Focus on Families, ONS, available at:
www.statistics.gov.uk/focuson/families

Focus on People & Migration, ONS, available at:
www.statistics.gov.uk/focuson/#Migration

Focus on Religion, ONS, available at:
www.statistics.gov.uk/focuson/Religion

General Household Survey, ONS, available at:
www.statistics.gov.uk/ghs

Health Statistics Quarterly, ONS, available at:
www.statistics.gov.uk/statbase/Product.asp?vlnk=6725

HFEA Guide to infertility, Human Fertilisation and Embryology Authority, available at:
www.hfea.gov.uk/en/406.html

Influences on young women's decisions about abortion or motherhood, Joseph Rowntree Foundation, available at:
www.jrf.org.uk/knowledge/findings/socialpolicy/684.asp

Marriages Abroad, Government Actuary's Department, available at:
www.gad.gov.uk/Demography_Data/Marital_status_projections/2003/marriages_abroad.asp

Population and Societies, Issue No. 422, April 2006, National Institute of Demographic Studies (France), available at:
www.ined.fr/fichier/t_telechargement/4439/telechargement_fichier_en_pop_and_soc_english_422.pdf

Population Trends, ONS, available at:
www.statistics.gov.uk/statbase/Product.asp?vlnk=6303

Rise in ageing population and people living alone drives household growth, Communities and Local Government, available at:
www.communities.gov.uk/news/corporate/riseageing

Study reveals variations in local proportions of pregnant young women choosing abortion, Joseph Rowntree Foundation, available at:
www.jrf.org.uk/pressroom/releases/300604.asp

Summary statistics on children in care and children adopted from care, British Association for Adoption & Fostering, available at:
www.baaf.org.uk/info/stats/index.shtml

Teenage conceptions:statistics and trends, Brook, available at:
www.brook.org.uk/content/Fact2_TeenageConceptions.pdf

Other useful websites

National Statistics
www.statistics.gov.uk

British Association for Adoption & Fostering
www.baaf.org.uk

Communities and Local Government
www.communities.gov.uk

Department of Health
www.dh.gov.uk

Eurostat
www.europa.eu.int/comm/eurostat

General Register Office for Scotland
www.gro-scotland.gov.uk

Government Actuary's Department
www.gad.gov.uk

Human Fertilisation and Embryology Authority
www.hfea.gov.uk

Northern Ireland Statistics and Research Agency
www.nisra.gov.uk

Scottish Government
www.scotland.gov.uk

United Nations Population Division
www.un.org/esa/population

Welsh Assembly Government
www.wales.gov.uk

Chapter 3: Education and training

References and further reading

British Social Attitudes, Hard copy, National Centre for Social Research, available at:
www.natcen.ac.uk/natcen/pages/op_socialattitudes.htm#bsa

Education at a Glance, OECD Indicators 2007, Organisation for Economic Co-operation and Development, available at:
www.oecd.org/document/30/0,3343,en_2649_39263238_39251550_1_1_1_1,00.html

Evaluation of Curriculum Online Report of the third survey of schools, BECTA ICT Research for the Department for Education and Skills, available at:
http://partners.becta.org.uk/upload-dir/downloads/page_documents/curriculum_online_third_survey0406.pdf

Harnessing Technology Review 2007: Progress and impact of technology in education, BECTA, available at:
http://partners.becta.org.uk/index.php?section=rh&catcode=_re_rp_02&rid=14409

Research Report: 2006 Childcare and Early Years Providers Survey Overview Report, BMRB Social Research for the Department of Children, Schools and Families, available at:
www.dfes.gov.uk/research/data/uploadfiles/DCSF-RR009%20v2.pdf

Research Report: 2006 Childcare and Early Years Providers Surveys, Primary schools with nursery and reception classes, BMRB Social Research for the Department for Children, Schools and Families, available at:
www.dfes.gov.uk/research/data/uploadfiles/DCSF-RW014.pdf

Research Report: 2006 Childcare and Early Years Providers Surveys, Nursery schools, BMRB Social Research for the Department for Children, Schools and Families, available at:
www.dfes.gov.uk/research/data/uploadfiles/DCSF-RW012.pdf

Scottish Survey of Achievement: 2006 Social Subjects (Enquiry Skills) and Core Skills – Supporting Evidence, The Scottish Government, available at:
www.scotland.gov.uk/Resource/Doc/195029/0052389.pdf

Statistical Volume: Education and Training Statistics for the United Kingdom 2007, Internet only publication, Department for Children, Schools and Families, available at:
www.dfes.gov.uk/rsgateway/DB/VOL/v000761/index.shtml

Workforce Training in England 2006, IFF Research Ltd for the Department for Education and Skills, available at:
www.dfes.gov.uk/research/data/uploadfiles/RR848.pdf

Other useful websites

National Statistics
www.statistics.gov.uk

Becta
www.becta.org.uk

Department for Children, Schools and Families Homepage/Trends/Research and Statistics gateway
www.dcsf.gov.uk
www.dcsf.gov.uk/trends
www.dcsf.gov.uk/rsgateway

Department of Education, Northern Ireland
www.deni.gov.uk

Department for Employment and Learning, Northern Ireland
www.delni.gov.uk

Department for Innovation, Universities and Skills
www.dius.gov.uk

Higher Education Statistics Agency
www.hesa.ac.uk

Learning and Skills Council
www.lsc.gov.uk

National Centre for Social Research
www.natcen.ac.uk

National Foundation for Educational Research
www.nfer.ac.uk

Office for Standards in Education
www.ofsted.gov.uk

Organisation for Economic Co-operation and Development
www.oecd.org

Scottish Government
www.scotland.gov.uk

Welsh Assembly Government
www.wales.gov.uk

Chapter 4: Labour market

References and further reading

Changing job quality in Great Britain 1998–2004, Department of Business, Enterprise and Regulatory Reform available at:
www.berr.gov.uk/files/file35846.pdf

Characteristics of public sector workers, ONS, available at:
www.statistics.gov.uk/elmr/05_07/downloads/ELMR_0507Millard_Machin.pdf

The first fair treatment at work survey, Department of Business, Enterprise and Regulatory Reform available at:
www.berr.gov.uk/files/file38386.pdf

Labour disputes in 2006, ONS, available at:
www.statistics.gov.uk/elmr/06_07/downloads/ELMR06_07Hale.pdf

Labour Market Guide, ONS, available at:
www.statistics.gov.uk/about/data/guides/LabourMarket/

Labour market summary for the UK household population by country of birth, ONS, available at:
www.statistics.gov.uk/articles/nojournal/Birthcountry.pdf

Local area labour markets: Statistical indicators July 2007, ONS, available at:
www.statistics.gov.uk/downloads/theme_labour/LALM_statistical_indicators_Jul07.pdf

Lone parents in employment, ONS, available at:
www.statistics.gov.uk/cci/nugget.asp?id=409

Public sector employment, ONS, available at:
www.statistics.gov.uk/pdfdir/pse0907.pdf

The third work-life balance employee survey: Main findings, Department of Business, Enterprise and Regulatory Reform available at:
www.berr.gov.uk/files/file38388.pdf

Work and worklessness among households, ONS, available at:
www.statistics.gov.uk/pdfdir/work0807.pdf

Other useful websites

National Statistics
www.statistics.gov.uk

Department for Business, Enterprise and Regulatory Reform
www.berr.gov.uk

Department for Enterprise, Trade and Investment Northern Ireland
www.detini.gov.uk

Department for Work and Pensions
www.dwp.gov.uk

Eurostat
www.europa.eu.int/comm/eurostat

Jobcentre Plus
www.jobcentreplus.gov.uk

Learning and Skills Council
www.lsc.gov.uk

Scottish Government
www.scotland.gov.uk

Welsh Assembly Government
www.wales.gov.uk

Chapter 5: Income and wealth

References and further reading

Annual Survey of Hours and Earnings, Internet only publication, ONS, available at:
www.statistics.gov.uk/StatBase/Product.asp?vlnk=13101

Blanden, J. P. Gregg and S. Machin (April 2005), *Intergenerational Mobility in Europe and North America*, Sutton Trust

Brewer M, Goodman A, Myck M, Shaw J and Shephard A (2004) *Poverty and Inequality in Britain: 2004*, Commentary no. 96, Institute for Fiscal Studies

Changing Households: The British Household Panel Survey, Institute for Social and Economic Research

Clark T and Leicester A (2004) *Inequality and two decades of British tax and benefit reforms*, Fiscal Studies, vol. 25, pp 129–58

Economic and Labour Market Trends, ONS, Palgrave Macmillan, available at:
www.statistics.gov.uk/StatBase/Product.asp?vlnk=308

Eurostat National Accounts ESA, Eurostat

Family Resources Survey, Department for Work and Pensions

Fiscal Studies, Institute for Fiscal Studies

For Richer, For Poorer, Institute for Fiscal Studies

Households Below Average Income, 1994/95–2005/06 (revised), Department for Work and Pensions

Income and Wealth. The Latest Evidence, Joseph Rowntree Foundation

Monitoring Poverty and Social Exclusion, Joseph Rowntree Foundation

Opportunity for All Annual Report, Department for Work and Pensions

The Pensioners' Incomes Series, Department for Work and Pensions available at:
www.dwp.gov.uk/asd/pensioners_income.asp

Pension Trends, ONS, Palgrave Macmillan, available at:
www.statistics.gov.uk/StatBase/Product.asp?vlnk=14173

Quarterly Savings Survey, National Savings and Investments

United Kingdom National Accounts (The Blue Book), ONS, Palgrave Macmillan, available at:
www.statistics.gov.uk/StatBase/Product.asp?vlnk=1143

Other useful websites

Centre for Economic Performance
www.cep.lse.ac.uk/

Department for Children, Schools and Families
www.dcsf.gov.uk

Department for Work and Pensions
www.dwp.gov.uk

Eurostat
www.europa.eu.int/comm/eurostat

HM Revenue and Customs
www.hmrc.gov.uk

HM Treasury
www.hm-treasury.gov.uk

Institute for Fiscal Studies
www.ifs.org.uk

Institute for Social and Economic Research
www.iser.essex.ac.uk

National Centre for Social Research
www.natcen.ac.uk

National Savings and Investments
www.nsandi.com

Women and Equality Unit
www.womenandequalityunit.gov.uk

Chapter 6: Expenditure

References and further reading

Consumer Trends, Internet only publication, ONS, available at:
www.statistics.gov.uk/consumertrends

Family Spending, ONS, Palgrave Macmillan, available at:
www.statistics.gov.uk/StatBase/Product.asp?vlnk=361

Financial Risk Outlook Report, 2007, Financial Services Authority

Focus on Consumer Price Indices, ONS, Palgrave Macmillan, available at:
www.statistics.gov.uk/StatBase/Product.asp?vlnk=867

Households Below Average Income, 1994/95–2005/06, Department for Work and Pensions

Other useful websites

APACS – The UK Payments Association
www.apacs.org.uk

Bank of England
www.bankofengland.co.uk

Department for Environment, Food and Rural Affairs
www.defra.gov.uk/

Department for Work and Pensions
www.dwp.gov.uk/

Financial Services Authority
www.fsa.gov.uk/

Insolvency Service
www.insolvency.gov.uk

Chapter 7: Health

References and further reading

Alcohol-related deaths 1991–2006, ONS, available at:
www.statistics.gov.uk/CCI/nugget.asp?ID=1091&Pos=1&ColRank=28&Rank=1000

Alcohol-related death rates by deprivation in England and Wales 1999–2003, Health Statistics Quarterly, 2007, no 33, pp 19-22, available at:
www.statistics.gov.uk/downloads/theme_health/hsq33web.pdf

Alcohol-related death rates in the countries of the UK and regions of England 1991–2004, Health Statistics Quarterly, 2007, no 33, pp 9-10, available at:
www.statistics.gov.uk/downloads/theme_health/hsq33web.pdf

Annual Report of the Registrar General for Northern Ireland, Northern Ireland Statistics and Research Agency, available at:
www.nisra.gov.uk/demography/default.asp?cmsid=20_45_100&cms=demography_Publications_Registrar+General+Annual+Reports&release

Annual Report of the Registrar General for Scotland, General Register Office for Scotland, available at:
www.gro-scotland.gov.uk/statistics/annrep/index.html

At Least Five a Week – Evidence on the Impact of Physical Activity and its Relationship to Health, A Report from the Chief Medical Officer, Department of Health, available at:

www.dh.gov.uk/PublicationsAndStatistics/Publications/PublicationsPolicyAndGuidance/PublicationsPolicyAndGuidanceArticle/fs/en?CONTENT_ID=4080994&chk=1Ft1Of

Babb P and Quinn M (2000) *Cancer Trends in England and Wales, 1950–1999,* Health Statistics Quarterly, no 8, pp 5-19, available at:
www.statistics.gov.uk/CCI/article.asp?ID=1493

Choosing Health – Making Healthy Choices Easier, Cm6374, TSO, available at:
www.dh.gov.uk/PublicationsAndStatistics/Publications/PublicationsPolicyAndGuidance/PublicationsPolicyAndGuidanceArticle/fs/en?CONTENT_ID=4094550&chk=aN5Cor

Coleman MP, Babb P et al, *Cancer Survival Trends in England and Wales 1971–1995: Deprivation and NHS Region,* available at:
www.lshtm.ac.uk/ncdeu/cancersurvival/trends/index.htm

A Complex Picture – HIV and other Sexually Transmitted Infections in the United Kingdom: 2006, Health Protection Agency Centre for Infections, available at:
www.hpa.org.uk/publications/PublicationDisplay.asp?PublicationID=55

Contraception and Sexual Health, 2006/07, ONS, Palgrave Macmillan, available at:
www.statistics.gov.uk/downloads/theme_health/contraception2006-07.pdf

Family Food - Report on the Expenditure and Food Survey, Department for Environment, Food and Rural Affairs, available at:
www.statistics.defra.gov.uk/esg/publications/efs/default.asp

Focus on Health 2006, ONS, available at:
www.statistics.gov.uk/downloads/theme_compendia/foh2005/08_Cancer.pdf

General Household Survey (Longitudinal) 2006, Internet only publication, ONS, available at: www.statistics.gov.uk/ghs

Geographic Variations in Health, ONS, Palgrave Macmillan, available at:
www.statistics.gov.uk/downloads/theme_health/DS16/ds16.asp

Goddard E, *Estimating alcohol consumption from survey data: updated method of converting volumes to units, National Statistics Methodology Series NSM 37 (ONS 2007),* ONS, available at:
www.statistics.gov.uk/statbase/product.asp?vlnk=15067

Health Expectancies in the United Kingdom 2003, Health Statistics Quarterly, no 33, pp 69-70, ONS, available at:
www.statistics.gov.uk/downloads/theme_health/hsq33web.pdf

Health in Scotland 2006: The Annual Report of the Chief Medical Officer on the State of Scotland's Health, Scottish Executive, available at:
www.scotland.gov.uk/Publications/2007/11/15135302/0

Health Statistics Wales, Welsh Assembly Government, available at:
http://new.wales.gov.uk/topics/statistics/publications/publication-archive/hsw2007/?lang=en

Health Survey for England, Information Centre for health and social care, available at:
www.ic.nhs.uk/statistics-and-data-collections/health-and-lifestyles-related-surveys/health-survey-for-England

Key Health Statistics from General Practice 1998, ONS, Palgrave Macmillan, available at:
www.statistics.gov.uk/downloads/theme_health/Key_Health_Stats_1998.pdf

Mapping the Issues HIV and other Sexually Transmitted Infections in the United Kingdom: 2005, Health Protection Agency Centre for Infections, available at:
www.hpa.org.uk/publications/2005/hiv_sti_2005/default.htm

Measuring deprivation in England and Wales using 2001 Carstairs scores, Health Statistics Quarterly, no 31, ONS, available at:
www.statistics.gov.uk/downloads/theme_health/HSQ31.pdf

Mental health of Children and Young People in Great Britain 2004, ONS, Palgrave Macmillan, available at:
www.statistics.gov.uk/downloads/theme_health/GB2004.pdf

Mortality Statistics for England and Wales (Series DH1 2,3,4), Internet only publications ONS, available at:
www.statistics.gov.uk/statbase/Product.asp?vlnk=620
www.statistics.gov.uk/statbase/Product.asp?vlnk=618
www.statistics.gov.uk/statbase/Product.asp?vlnk=6305
www.statistics.gov.uk/statbase/Product.asp?vlnk=621

The NHS Cancer Plan 2000, NHS, available at:
www.dh.gov.uk/prod_consum_dh/groups/dh_digitalassets/@dh/@en/documents/digitalasset/dh_4014513.pdf

On the State of the Public Health: The Annual Report of the Chief Medical Officer of the Department of Health, Department of Health, available at:
www.dh.gov.uk/en/Publicationsandstatistics/Publications/AnnualReports/DH_076817

Population Trends, ONS, Palgrave Macmillan, available at:
www.statistics.gov.uk/statbase/Product.asp?vlnk=6303

Psychiatric Morbidity Survey among Adults Living in Private Households 2000, ONS, TSO, available at:
www.statistics.gov.uk/downloads/theme_health/psychmorb.pdf

Quinn M, Wood H, Cooper N and Rowan S (2005) *Cancer Atlas of the United Kingdom and Ireland 1991–2000*, ONS, Palgrave Macmillan, available at:
www.statistics.gov.uk/statbase/Product.asp?vlnk=14059

Report of the Chief Medical Officer, Department of Health, Social Services and Public Safety, Northern Ireland, available at:
www.dhsspsni.gov.uk/index/phealth/cmoannualreport.htm

Results of the ICD-10 bridge coding study, England and Wales, 1999, Health Statistics Quarterly, no 14, pp 75-83, available at:
www.statistics.gov.uk/downloads/theme_health/HSQ14_v4.pdf

Smoking-related Behaviour and Attitudes 2006, Internet only publication ONS, available at:
www.statistics.gov.uk/downloads/theme_health/smoking2006.pdf

Statistical Publications on aspects of Health and Personal social services activity in England (various), Department of Health, available at:
www.dh.gov.uk/en/Publicationsandstatistics/index.htm

Tackling Health Inequalities: Status Report on the Programme for Action, Department of Health, available at:
www.dh.gov.uk/en/Publicationsandstatistics/Publications/PublicationsPolicyAndGuidance/DH_062903

Testing Times: HIV and other Sexually Transmitted Infections in the United Kingdom 2007, Health Protection Agency Centre for Infections, available at:
www.hpa.org.uk/infections/topics_az/hiv_and_sti/publications/AnnualReport/2007/default.htm

Tuberculosis in the UK. Annual report on tuberculosis surveillance and control in the UK 2007, Health Protection Agency, available at:
www.hpa.org.uk/publications/PublicationDisplay.asp?PublicationID=110

United Kingdom Health Statistics 2006, ONS, Palgrave Macmillan, available at:
www.statistics.gov.uk/downloads/theme_health/ukhs2/ukhs2_rel1_superseded.pdf

Welsh Health: Annual Report of the Chief Medical Officer, Welsh Assembly Government, available at:
http://new.wales.gov.uk/topics/health/ocmo/communications/cmo-reports/annualreport2006/?lang=en

World Health Statistics, World Health Organisation, available at:
www.who.int/whosis/en/

Other useful websites

National Statistics
www.statistics.gov.uk

Department for Environment, Food and Rural Affairs
www.defra.gov.uk

Department of Health
www.dh.gov.uk

Department of Health, Social Services and Public Safety, Northern Ireland
www.dhsspsni.gov.uk/stats&research/index.asp

General Register Office for Scotland
www.gro-scotland.gov.uk

Government Actuary Department
www.gad.gov.uk

Health Protection Agency
www.hpa.org.uk

Information Centre for health and social care
www.ic.nhs.uk

Information Services Division Scotland
www.isdscotland.org

Northern Ireland Cancer Registry
www.qub.ac.uk/nicr

Northern Ireland Statistics and Research Agency
www.nisra.gov.uk

Scottish Government
www.scotland.gov.uk

Welsh Assembly Government
www.wales.gov.uk

Welsh Cancer Intelligence and Surveillance Unit
www.velindre-tr.wales.nhs.uk/wcisu

Chapter 8: Social protection

References and further reading

Annual Statistical Publication Notices (various including 'Children's Social Work Statistics 2004-05), Scottish Executive, available at:
www.scotland.gov.uk/statistics/

Benefit expenditure and caseload information, Department for Work and Pensions, available at: www.dwp.gov.uk/asd/asd4/expenditure.asp

British Social Attitudes – The 24th Report, National Centre for Social Research, Sage publications, available at:
www.natcen.ac.uk/natcen/pages/nm_pressreleases.htm

Charity Trends 2007, Charities Aid Foundation, published by CaritasData, available at: www.cafonline.org/charitytrends

Clarke A, *Referrals, assessments and children and young people on child protection registers, England (First Release)*, Department for Education and Skills, available at:
www.dfes.gov.uk/rsgateway/DB/SFR/s000692/index.shtml

Community Care Statistics 2006: Home Help/Care Services for Adults, England - NHS, available at:
www.ic.nhs.uk/statistics-and-data-collections/social-care/adult-social-care-information/community-care-statistics-2006:-help-care-services-for-adults-england

Community Care Statistics 2006: Referrals, Assessments and Packages of Care for Adults, England – National Report and CSSR Tables, available at:
www.ic.nhs.uk/statistics-and-data-collections/social-care/adult-social-care-information/community-care-statistics-2006:-referrals-assessments-and-packages-of-care-for-adults-england--national-report-and-cssr-tables

ESSPROS Manual 1996, Eurostat

Family Resources Survey, Department for Work and Pensions, available at:
www.dwp.gov.uk/asd/frs

General Household Survey 2005, Internet only publication, ONS, available at: www.statistics.gov.uk/ghs

Health Statistics Wales, Welsh assembly Government, available at:
www.wales.gov.uk/topics/statistics/publications/hsw2007/?lang=en

Hospital Statistics for Northern Ireland, Department of Health, Social Services and Public Safety, Northern Ireland, available at
www.dhsspsni.gov.uk/stats-cib-children_order_bulletin

Hoxhallari, Conolly and Lyon (2007) *Families with children in Britain: Findings from the 2005 Families and Children Study (FACS)*, Department for Work and Pensions, Corporate Document Services, available at:
www.dwp.gov.uk/asd/asd5/rports2007-2008/rrep424.pdf

Mooney E, Fitzpatrick M, Orr J and Hewitt R (2006) *Children Order Statistical Bulletin*, Department of Health, Social Services and Public Safety, Northern Ireland, available at:
www.dhsspsni.gov.uk/stats-cib-children_order_bulletin

Personal Social Services Survey of Home Care Users in England Aged 65 or Over: 2005-06 Available at:
www.ic.nhs.uk/statistics-and-data-collections/social-care/adult-social-care-information/personal-social-services-survey-of-care-users-in-england-aged-65-or-over:-2005-06

Social Services Statistics Wales, Local Government Data Unit, available at:
www.dataunitwales.gov.uk

Other useful websites

National Statistics
www.statistics.gov.uk

Charities Aid Foundation
www.cafonline.org

Department for children, schools and families
www.dcsf.gov.uk

Department of Health, Social Services and Public Safety, Northern Ireland
www.dhsspsni.gov.uk

Department for Social Development, Northern Ireland
www.dsdni.gov.uk

Department for Work and Pensions
www.dwp.gov.uk

Eurostat
www.eurostat.eu.int

The Information Centre for health and social care
www.ic.nhs.uk

Local Government Data Unit
www.dataunitwales.gov.uk
www.unedddatacymru.gov.uk

Scottish Government
www.scotland.gov.uk

Welsh Assembly Government
www.wales.gov.uk

Chapter 9: Crime and justice

References and further reading

Attitudes, perceptions and risks of crime: Supplementary Volume 1 to Crime in England and Wales 2006/07, Home Office available at:
www.homeoffice.gov.uk/rds/pdfs07/hosb1907.pdf

Crime in England and Wales 2006/07, Home Office, available at:
www.homeoffice.gov.uk/rds/crimeew0607.html

Crime in England and Wales 2005/06, Home Office, available at:
www.homeoffice.gov.uk/rds/crimeew0506.html

Criminal Justice System Strategic plan 2008-2011, Office for Criminal Justice Reform (OCJR), available at:
www.cjsonline.gov.uk/downloads/application/pdf/1_Strategic_Plan_ALL.pdf

Digest 4: Information on the Criminal Justice System in England and Wales (1999), Home Office, available at:
www.homeoffice.gov.uk/rds/digest41.html

Digest of Information on the Northern Ireland Criminal Justice System 4, TSO, available at:
www.nio.gov.uk/digest_information_on_the_ni_criminal_justice_system_4.pdf

A Guide to anti-social behaviour orders and acceptable behaviour contracts (2007), Home Office, available at:
www.crimereduction.homeoffice.gov.uk/asbos/asbos9.pdf

HM Prison Service Annual Report and Accounts, TSO, available at:
www.official-documents.gov.uk/document/hc0607/hc07/0717/0717.asp

Home Office Departmental Report 2007, TSO, available at:
www.homeoffice.gov.uk/documents/ho-annual-report-07

Home Office Research Findings, Home Office, available at:
www.homeoffice.gov.uk/rds/pubsintro1.html

Home Office Statistical Bulletins, Home Office, available at:
www.homeoffice.gov.uk/rds/hosbpubs1.html

Homicides, Firearm offences and Intimate Violence 2005/2006: Supplementary Volume 1 to Crime in England and Wales 2005/2006, Home Office, available at:
www.homeoffice.gov.uk/rds/pdfs07/hosb0207.pdf

Mobile phone theft, plastic card and identity fraud: Findings from the British Crime survey 2005/2006, Home Office, available at:
www.homeoffice.gov.uk/rds/pdfs07/hosb1007.pdf

New Publication of Offender Management Caseload Statistics, Ministry of Justice, available at:
www.justice.gov.uk/publications/statistics.htm
www.justice.gov.uk/publications/prisonandprobation.htm

Northern Ireland Crime Survey, Northern Ireland Office, available at:
www.csu.nisra.gov.uk/surveys/survey.asp?id=52

Northern Ireland Judicial Statistics, Northern Ireland Court Service, available at:
www.courtsni.gov.uk/en-GB/Publications/Targets_and_Performance/

Police Service of Northern Ireland Annual Statistics, 2006/07, Police Service of Northern Ireland, available at:
www.psni.police.uk/index/statistics_branch.htm

Population in Custody: Monthly tables, Ministry of Justice, available at:
www.justice.gov.uk/publications/populationincustody.htm

Recorded Crime in Scotland 2006/07, Scottish Government, available at:
www.scotland.gov.uk/Publications/2007/08/30141914/0

Report of the Northern Ireland Prison Service, TSO, available at:
www.official-documents.gov.uk/document/hc0506/hc12/1251/1251.asp

Review of Police Forces' Crime Recording Practices, Home Office, available at:
www.homeoffice.gov.uk/rds/pdfs/hors204.pdf

Scotland crime and justice statistics, Scottish Government, available at:
www.scotland.gov.uk/Topics/Statistics/Browse/Crime-Justice

Scottish Crime and Victimisation Survey 2006, Scottish Government, available at:
www.scotland.gov.uk/Publications/2007/10/12094216/13

Sentencing Statistics, 2006 England and Wales (annual), available at:
www.justice.gov.uk/publications/prisonandprobation.htm

Other useful websites

Courts Service
www.hmcourts-service.gov.uk

Criminal Justice System
www.cjsonline.org

Crown Prosecution Service
www.cps.gov.uk

Department of Constitutional Affairs
www.dca.gov.uk

Home Office
www.homeoffice.gov.uk

Ministry of Justice
www.justice.gov.uk

Northern Ireland Court Service
www.courtsni.gov.uk

Northern Ireland Office
www.nio.gov.uk

Northern Ireland Prison Service
www.niprisonservice.gov.uk

Police Service of Northern Ireland
www.psni.police.uk

Prison Service for England and Wales
www.hmprisonservice.gov.uk

Scottish Government
www.scotland.gov.uk

Scottish Prison Service
www.sps.gov.uk

Welsh Assembly Government
www.wales.gov.uk

Chapter 10: Housing

References and further reading

Bate R, Best R and Holmans A (Editors) (2000) *On the Move: The Housing Consequences of Migration*, Joseph Rowntree Foundation, YPS, available at: www.jrf.org.uk/knowledge/findings/housing/820.asp

e-digest Statistics about: land Use and Land Cover – Urbanisation in England, Department for Environment, Food and Rural Affairs (DEFRA), available at: www.defra.gov.uk/environment/statistics/land/lduse.htm

English House Condition Survey 2005, Communities and Local Government, TSO, available at: www.communities.gov.uk/publications/housing/englishhousesurveyannual

General Household Survey (Longitudinal) 2006, Internet only publication, ONS, available at: www.statistics.gov.uk/ghs

Housing in England: Survey of English Housing, Communities and Local Government, TSO, available at: www.communities.gov.uk/publications/housing/Surveyenglishhousing

Housing Statistics 2006, Communities and Local Government, TSO, available at: www.communities.gov.uk/news/corporate/housingstatistics

Local Housing Statistics, Internet only publication, Communities and Local Government, available at: www.communities.gov.uk/housing/housingresearch/housingstatistics/housingstatisticsby/locallevelstatistics/

New Projections of households for England and the Regions to 2029 (2007), Communities and Local Government, TSO, available at: www.communities.gov.uk/news/corporate/new-projection-households

Northern Ireland House Condition Survey, Northern Ireland Housing Executive, available at: www.nihe.gov.uk/HCS

Northern Ireland Housing Statistics, 2005/06, Department for Social Development, Northern Ireland, available at: www.dsdni.gov.uk/index/stats_and_research.htm

Scottish House Condition Survey, Scottish Government, available at: www.scotland.gov.uk/Topics/Statistics/SHCS

Statistical Bulletins on Housing, Scottish Executive, available at: www.scotland.gov.uk/Topics/Housing

Welsh House Condition Survey 1998, Welsh Assembly Government, available at: http://new.wales.gov.uk/topics/statistics/publications/whcs98/?lang=en

Welsh Housing Statistics, Welsh Assembly Government, available at: http://new.wales.gov.uk/topics/statistics/theme/housing/?lang=en

Other useful websites

National Statistics
www.statistics.gov.uk

Communities and Local Government
www.communities.gov.uk

Council of Mortgage Lenders
www.cml.org.uk

Department for Social Development in Northern Ireland
www.dsdni.gov.uk

Department for Work and Pensions
www.dwp.gov.uk

Land Registry
www.landreg.gov.uk

Northern Ireland Statistics and Research Agency
www.nisra.gov.uk

Scottish Government
www.scotland.gov.uk

Social Exclusion Unit
www.socialexclusionunit.gov.uk

Welsh Assembly Government
www.wales.gov.uk

Chapter 11: Environment

References and further reading

Agriculture in the United Kingdom 2006, Department for Environment, Food and Rural Affairs, TSO, available at: www.statistics.defra.gov.uk/esg/publications/auk/default.asp

Air Quality Strategy for England, Scotland, Wales and Northern Ireland, Department for Environment, Food and Rural Affairs, TSO, available at: www.defra.gov.uk/environment/airquality/index.htm

Digest of United Kingdom Energy Statistics 2007, Department for Business, Enterprise and Regulatory Reform, TSO, available at: www.berr.gov.uk/energy/statistics/publications/dukes/page39771.html

e-Digest of Environmental Statistics, Department for Environment, Food and Rural Affairs, available at: www.defra.gov.uk/environment/statistics/index.htm

Energy Trends, Department for Business, Enterprise and Regulatory Reform, available at: www.berr.gov.uk/energy/statistics/publications/trends/index.html

Environmental Facts and Figures, Environment Agency, Internet only publication, available at: www.environment-agency.gov.uk/yourenv/eff/

The Environment in your Pocket, Department for Environment, Food and Rural Affairs, available at: www.defra.gov.uk/environment/statistics/eiyp/index.htm

General Quality Assessment, Environment Agency, available at: www.environment-agency.gov.uk/yourenv/eff/1190084/water/213902/river_qual/gqa2000/

Hydrological Summaries for the United Kingdom, Centre for Ecology and Hydrology Wallingford and British Geological Survey, available at: www.ceh.ac.uk/data/nrfa/water_watch.html

Municipal Waste Statistics, Department for Environment, Food and Rural Affairs, available at: www.defra.gov.uk/environment/statistics/wastats/

Organic Statistics UK, Department for Environment, Food and Rural Affairs, available at: www.statistics.defra.gov.uk/esg/statnot/orguk.pdf

Quarterly Energy Prices, Department for Business, Enterprise and Regulatory Reform, available at: www.berr.gov.uk/energy/statistics/publications/prices/index.html

State of the Environment Report 2006, Scottish Environment Protection Agency, available at:
www.sepa.org.uk/publications/state_of/index.htm

Survey of Public Attitudes to Quality of Life and to the Environment: 2007, Department for Environment, Food and Rural Affairs, available at:
www.defra.gov.uk/environment/statistics/pubatt/index.htm

Sustainable Development Indicators in your Pocket 2007, Department for Environment, Food and Rural Affairs, available at:
www.sustainable-development.gov.uk/progress/index.htm

Other useful websites

Centre for Ecology and Hydrology
www.ceh-nerc.ac.uk

Department for Business, Enterprise and Regulatory Reform
www.berr.gov.uk

Department for Environment, Food and Rural Affairs
www.defra.gov.uk

Department of the Environment Northern Ireland
www.doeni.gov.uk

Environment Agency
www.environment-agency.gov.uk

Eurostat
www.europa.eu.int/comm/eurostat

Northern Ireland Statistics and Research Agency
www.nisra.gov.uk

Scottish Environment Protection Agency
www.sepa.org.uk

Scottish Government
www.scotland.gov.uk

Welsh Assembly Government
www.wales.gov.uk

Chapter 12: Transport

References and further reading

British Social Attitudes – The 24th Report, National Centre for Social Research, Sage publications, available at:
www.natcen.ac.uk/natcen/pages/nm_pressreleases.htm

Driving Standards Agency Annual Report and Accounts 2005/06, Driving Standards Agency, TSO, available at:
www.official-documents.gov.uk/document/hc0506/hc11/1172/1172.asp

European Union Energy and Transport in Figures, 2005, European Commission, available at:
www.ec.europa.eu/dgs/energy_transport/figures/pocketbook/

Focus on Personal Travel: 2005 edition, Department for Transport, TSO, available at:
www.dft.gov.uk/pgr/statistics/datatablespublications/personal/focuspt/2005/focusonpersonaltravel2005edi5238

General Household Survey (Longitudinal) 2006, Internet only publication, ONS, available at: www.statistics.gov.uk/ghs

Injury Road Traffic Collision Statistics Annual Report 2005, Police Service of Northern Ireland, available at:
www.psni.police.uk/rtc_report-4.pdf

National Passenger Survey Spring 2007, Passenger Focus, available at:
www.passengerfocus.org.uk/your-experiences/content.asp?dsid=496

National Rail Trends 2005-2006 Yearbook, Office of Rail Regulator, available at: www.rail-reg.gov.uk/server/show/nav.1528

National Travel Survey Bulletins, Department for Transport, available at:
www.dft.gov.uk/pgr/statistics/recentforthcomingpublications/recentpublications

A New Deal for Transport: Better for Everyone (2005), Department for Transport, TSO, available at:
www.dft.gov.uk/about/strategy/whitepapers/previous/anewdealfortransportbetterfo5695

Northern Ireland Transport Statistics Annual 2006-2007, Department for Regional Development Northern Ireland, available at:
www.drdni.gov.uk/annual_transport_statistics_2006-07_publication.pdf

Office of Rail Regulation Annual report 2005-06, Office of Rail Regulation, available at: www.rail-reg.gov.uk/upload/pdf/290.pdf

Road Accidents Scotland 2006, Scottish Executive, available at:
www.scotland.gov.uk/Publications/2007/11/20143740/0

Road Casualties Great Britain 2006 – Annual Report, Department for Transport, TSO, available at:
www.dft.gov.uk/pgr/statistics/datatablespublications/accidents/casualtiesgbar/roadcasualtiesgreatbritain2006

Road Casualties: Wales 2006, Welsh Assembly Government, available at:
http://new.wales.gov.uk/topics/statistics/publications/rcw2006/?lang=en

Scottish Transport Statistics: No 25 2006 Edition, Scottish Executive, available at: www.scotland.gov.uk/Publications/2006/12/15135954/0

Securing the Future - UK Government sustainable development strategy (2005), Department for Environment, Food and Rural Affairs, TSO, available at:
www.sustainable-development.gov.uk/publications/uk-strategy/index.htm

Traffic Speeds and Congestion 2006, Department for Transport, available at: www.dft.gov.uk/pgr/statistics/datatablespublications/roadstraffic/speedscongestion/roadstatstsc/roadstats06tsc

Transport Statistics Bulletins and Reports, Department for Transport, available at:
www.dft.gov.uk/pgr/statistics/recentforthcomingpublications/recentpublications

Transport Statistics for Great Britain 2007, Department for Transport, TSO, available at:
www.dft.gov.uk/pgr/statistics/datatablespublications/tsgb/2007edition/transportstatisticsforgreatb2007

Transport Trends 2007, Department for Transport, TSO, available at:
www.dft.gov.uk/pgr/statistics/datatablespublications/trends/current/transporttrends2007

Travel Trends, ONS, Palgrave Macmillan, available at:
www.statistics.gov.uk/statbase/Product.asp?vlnk=1391

Vehicle Licensing Statistics 2006, Department for Transport, available at:
www.dft.gov.uk/pgr/statistics/datatablespublications/vehicles/licensing/vehiclelicensingstatistics2006

Vehicle Speeds in Great Britain 2005, Department for Transport, available at:
www.dft.gov.uk/pgr/statistics/datatablespublications/roadstraffic/speedscongestion/vehiclespeedsgb/vehiclespeedsingreatbritain2005a

Welsh Transport Statistics, Welsh Assembly Government, available at:
http://new.wales.gov.uk/topics/statistics/theme/transport/?lang=en

Other useful websites

National Statistics
www.statistics.gov.uk

Civil Aviation Authority, Economic Regulation Group
www.caa.co.uk/homepage.aspx

Department for Business Enterprise and Regulatory Reform
www.berr.gov.uk

Department of the Environment Northern Ireland
www.doeni.gov.uk

Department for Regional Development Northern Ireland
www.drdni.gov.uk

Department for Transport
www.dft.gov.uk

European Commission Directorate-General Energy and Transport
www.ec.europa.eu/dgs/energy_transport/index_en.html

National Centre for Social Research
www.natcen.ac.uk

Office of Rail Regulation
www.rail-reg.gov.uk

Passenger Focus
www.passengerfocus.org.uk

Scottish Government
www.scotland.gov.uk

Welsh Assembly Government
www.wales.gov.uk

Chapter 13: Lifestyles and social participation

References and further reading

Active People Survey 2005/06, Sport England, available at:
www.sportengland.org/active_people

British Gambling Prevalence Survey 2007, Heather Wardle, Kerry Sproston, Jim Orford, Bob Erens, Mark Griffiths, Rebecca Constantine, Sarah Pigott, available at:
www.gamblingcommission.gov.uk/Client/detail.asp?ContentId=288

The Communications Market 2007, Ofcom, available at:
www.ofcom.org.uk/research/cm/cmr07/

England Leisure Visits 2005, Natural England, available at:
www.countryside.gov.uk/LAR/Recreation/visits/index.asp

Eurobarometer – Social values, Science and Technology, June 2005, European Commission, available at:
www.ec.europa.eu/public_opinion/archives/eb_special_en.htm

Helping Out, a national survey of volunteering and charitable giving, 2006/07, Cabinet Office, available at:
www.cabinetoffice.gov.uk/third_sector/Research_and_statistics/third_sector_research/helping_out.aspx

2005 Home Office Citizenship Survey, Communities and Local Government, available at:
www.communities.gov.uk/communities/racecohesionfaith/communitycohesion/strategy/citizenshipsurvey/

RSU Statistical Yearbook, UK Film Council, available at:
http://rsu.ukfilmcouncil.org/?y=2006

Survey Data on Remote Gambling Participation, The British Gambling Commission, available at:
www.gamblingcommission.gov.uk/Client/detail.asp?Contentid=184

Taking Part: The National Survey of Culture, Leisure and Sport, Department of Culture, Media and Sport, available at:
www.culture.gov.uk/Reference_library/rands/taking_part_survey/

Travel Trends: Data tables on the 2006 International Passenger Survey, available at:
www.statistics.gov.uk/downloads/theme_transport/TravelTrends2006.pdf

UK Giving 2007, Charities Aid Foundation and National Council of Voluntary Organisations, available at:
www.cafonline.org/ukgiving

Other useful websites

Cabinet Office
www.cabinetoffice.gov.uk

Charities Aid Foundation
www.cafonline.org

Communities and Local Government
www.communities.gov.uk

Department for Culture, Media and Sport
www.culture.gov.uk

Eurobarometer
www.ec.europa.eu/public_opinion

Gambling Commission
www.gamblingcommission.gov.uk

National Centre for Social Research
www.natcen.ac.uk

Natural England
www.countryside.gov.uk/

Ofcom
www.ofcom.org.uk

Pearl and Dean
www.pearlanddean.com

Public Lending Right
www.plr.uk.com

Radio Joint Audience Research Ltd
www.rajar.co.uk

Sport England
www.sportengland.org

Sport Scotland
www.sportscotland.org.uk

The UK Film Council
www.ukfilmcouncil.org.uk

YouGov
www.yougov.com

Geographical areas

The European Union, 1 January 2007

- Countries which joined the EU on 1 January 2007
- EU-25 members
- Non-EU members

Azores (Portugal)

Madeira Islands (Portugal)

Canary Islands (Spain)

Sweden
Finland
Estonia
Latvia
Lithuania
Denmark
Ireland
Netherlands
United Kingdom
Belgium
Germany
Poland
Luxembourg
Czech Republic
Slovakia
Austria
Hungary
Romania
France
Slovenia
Bulgaria
Italy
Portugal
Spain
Greece
Malta (not to scale)
Cyprus

Government Office Regions

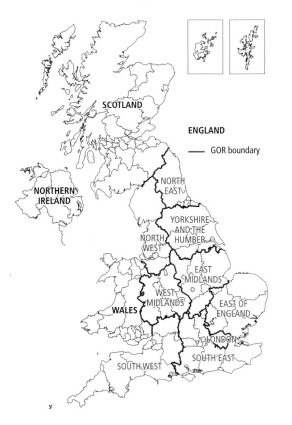

SCOTLAND

ENGLAND
— GOR boundary

NORTHERN IRELAND

NORTH EAST
YORKSHIRE AND THE HUMBER
NORTH WEST
EAST MIDLANDS
WEST MIDLANDS
WALES
EAST OF ENGLAND
LONDON
SOUTH WEST
SOUTH EAST

Strategic Health Authorities

SCOTLAND

ENGLAND
— Strategic Health Authority boundary

NORTHERN IRELAND

North East England
North West
Yorkshire and the Humber
West Midlands
East Midlands
WALES
East of England
South Central
London
South West
South East Coast

Waste Disposal Authorities

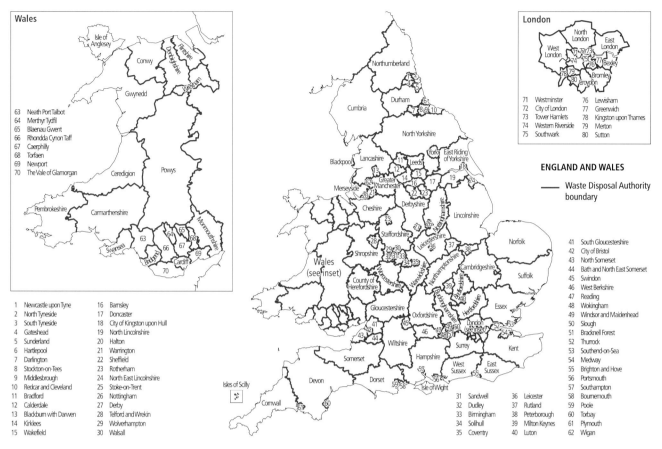

Wales

63	Neath Port Talbot
64	Merthyr Tydfil
65	Blaenau Gwent
66	Rhondda Cynon Taff
67	Caerphilly
68	Torfaen
69	Newport
70	The Vale of Glamorgan

London

71	Westminster	76	Lewisham
72	City of London	77	Greenwich
73	Tower Hamlets	78	Kingston upon Thames
74	Western Riverside	79	Merton
75	Southwark	80	Sutton

ENGLAND AND WALES

—— Waste Disposal Authority boundary

41	South Gloucestershire
42	City of Bristol
43	North Somerset
44	Bath and North East Somerset
45	Swindon
46	West Berkshire
47	Reading
48	Wokingham
49	Windsor and Maidenhead
50	Slough
51	Bracknell Forest
52	Thurrock
53	Southend-on-Sea
54	Medway
55	Brighton and Hove
56	Portsmouth
57	Southampton
58	Bournemouth
59	Poole
60	Torbay
61	Plymouth
62	Wigan

1	Newcastle upon Tyne	16	Barnsley
2	North Tyneside	17	Doncaster
3	South Tyneside	18	City of Kingston upon Hull
4	Gateshead	19	North Lincolnshire
5	Sunderland	20	Halton
6	Hartlepool	21	Warrington
7	Darlington	22	Sheffield
8	Stockton-on-Tees	23	Rotherham
9	Middlesbrough	24	North East Lincolnshire
10	Redcar and Cleveland	25	Stoke-on-Trent
11	Bradford	26	Nottingham
12	Calderdale	27	Derby
13	Blackburn with Darwen	28	Telford and Wrekin
14	Kirklees	29	Wolverhampton
15	Wakefield	30	Walsall

31	Sandwell	36	Leicester
32	Dudley	37	Rutland
33	Birmingham	38	Peterborough
34	Solihull	39	Milton Keynes
35	Coventry	40	Luton

Environment Agency regions

ENGLAND and WALES

—— Environment Agency region boundary

To obtain basic facts on the type of areas used in *Social Trends*, as well as more specialist information on topics such as boundary change visit the ONS Beginners' Guide to UK Geography at: **www.statistics.gov.uk/geography/beginners_guide.asp.**

Local or Unitary Authorities[1]

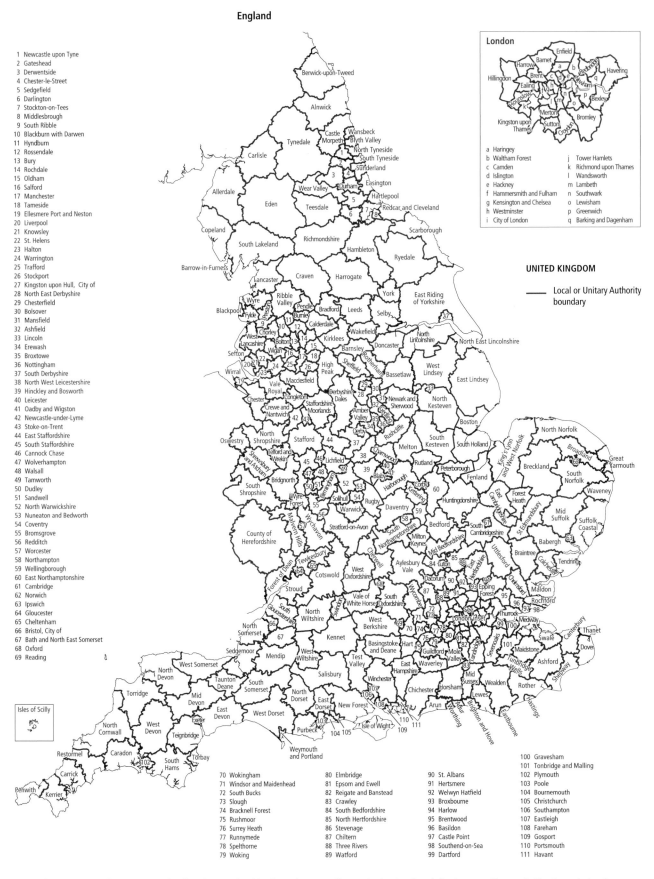

England

1 Newcastle upon Tyne
2 Gateshead
3 Derwentside
4 Chester-le-Street
5 Sedgefield
6 Darlington
7 Stockton-on-Tees
8 Middlesbrough
9 South Ribble
10 Blackburn with Darwen
11 Hyndburn
12 Rossendale
13 Bury
14 Rochdale
15 Oldham
16 Salford
17 Manchester
18 Tameside
19 Ellesmere Port and Neston
20 Liverpool
21 Knowsley
22 St. Helens
23 Halton
24 Warrington
25 Trafford
26 Stockport
27 Kingston upon Hull, City of
28 North East Derbyshire
29 Chesterfield
30 Bolsover
31 Mansfield
32 Ashfield
33 Lincoln
34 Erewash
35 Broxtowe
36 Nottingham
37 South Derbyshire
38 North West Leicestershire
39 Hinckley and Bosworth
40 Leicester
41 Oadby and Wigston
42 Newcastle-under-Lyme
43 Stoke-on-Trent
44 East Staffordshire
45 South Staffordshire
46 Cannock Chase
47 Wolverhampton
48 Walsall
49 Tamworth
50 Dudley
51 Sandwell
52 North Warwickshire
53 Nuneaton and Bedworth
54 Coventry
55 Bromsgrove
56 Redditch
57 Worcester
58 Northampton
59 Wellingborough
60 East Northamptonshire
61 Cambridge
62 Norwich
63 Ipswich
64 Gloucester
65 Cheltenham
66 Bristol, City of
67 Bath and North East Somerset
68 Oxford
69 Reading

70 Wokingham
71 Windsor and Maidenhead
72 South Bucks
73 Slough
74 Bracknell Forest
75 Rushmoor
76 Surrey Heath
77 Runnymede
78 Spelthorne
79 Woking

80 Elmbridge
81 Epsom and Ewell
82 Reigate and Banstead
83 Crawley
84 South Bedfordshire
85 North Hertfordshire
86 Stevenage
87 Chiltern
88 Three Rivers
89 Watford

90 St. Albans
91 Hertsmere
92 Welwyn Hatfield
93 Broxbourne
94 Harlow
95 Brentwood
96 Basildon
97 Castle Point
98 Southend-on-Sea
99 Dartford

100 Gravesham
101 Tonbridge and Malling
102 Plymouth
103 Poole
104 Bournemouth
105 Christchurch
106 Southampton
107 Eastleigh
108 Fareham
109 Gosport
110 Portsmouth
111 Havant

London

a Haringey
b Waltham Forest
c Camden
d Islington
e Hackney
f Hammersmith and Fulham
g Kensington and Chelsea
h Westminster
i City of London
j Tower Hamlets
k Richmond upon Thames
l Wandsworth
m Lambeth
n Southwark
o Lewisham
p Greenwich
q Barking and Dagenham

UNITED KINGDOM

—— Local or Unitary Authority boundary

1 Local or unitary authorities in England, unitary authorities in Wales, council areas in Scotland and district council areas in Northern Ireland.

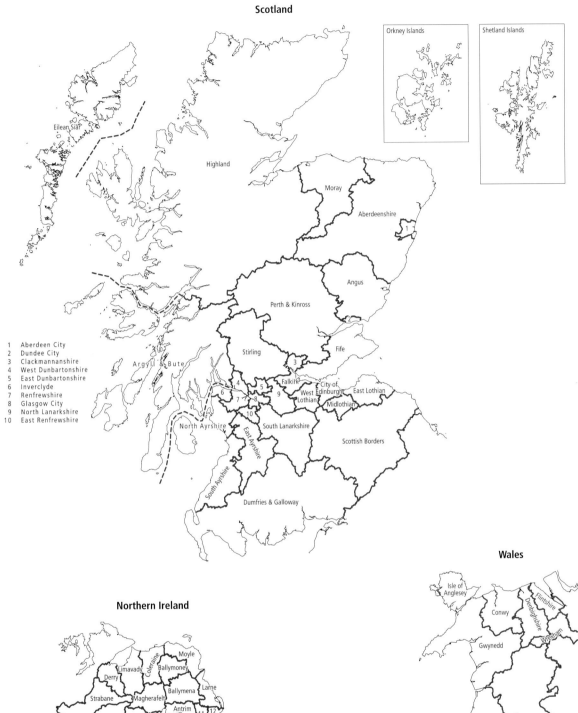

Scotland

Orkney Islands

Shetland Islands

Eilean Siar

Highland

Moray

Aberdeenshire

Angus

Perth & Kinross

Argyll & Bute

Stirling

Fife

Falkirk

City of Edinburgh

West Lothian

East Lothian

Midlothian

North Ayrshire

East Ayrshire

South Lanarkshire

Scottish Borders

South Ayrshire

Dumfries & Galloway

1 Aberdeen City
2 Dundee City
3 Clackmannanshire
4 West Dunbartonshire
5 East Dunbartonshire
6 Inverclyde
7 Renfrewshire
8 Glasgow City
9 North Lanarkshire
10 East Renfrewshire

Northern Ireland

Moyle

Limavady

Coleraine

Ballymoney

Derry

Ballymena

Larne

Strabane

Magherafelt

Antrim

11 12

Omagh

Cookstown

Belfast

Ards

Dungannon

Craigavon

Lisburn

14

Fermanagh

Armagh

Banbridge

Down

Newry and Mourne

11 Newtownabbey
12 Carrickfergus
13 North Down
14 Castlereagh

Wales

Isle of Anglesey

Conwy

Flintshire

Denbighshire

Wrexham

Gwynedd

Powys

Ceredigion

Pembrokeshire

Carmarthenshire

Monmouthshire

Neath Port Talbot

Rhondda Cynon Taf

Caerphilly

Torfaen

Newport

Swansea

Bridgend

Cardiff

The Vale of Glâmorgan

15 Merthyr Tydfil
16 Blaenau Gwent

Major surveys

	Frequency	Sampling frame	Type of respondent	Coverage	Effective sample size[1] (most recent survey included in *Social Trends*)	Response rate (percentages)
Annual Population Survey	Continuous	Postcode Address File	All adults in household	UK	370,000 individuals	[2]
Annual Survey of Hours and Earnings	Annual	HM Revenue & Customs PAYE records	Employee	UK	142,000 employees	82
British Crime Survey	Annual	Postcode Address File	Adult in household	E&W	47,138 addresses	75
British Social Attitudes Survey	Annual	Postcode Address File	One adult per household	GB	7,915 addresses	54[3]
Census of Population	Decennial	Detailed local	Adult in household	UK	Full count	98
Citizenship Survey	Continuous	Postcode Address File	One adult per household	E&W	2,156 core and 1,255 boost (quarter 1)[4]	58[4]
Continuous Household Survey	Continuous	Valuation and Lands Agency Property	All adults in household	NI	3,980 addresses	65
English House Condition Survey	Continuous[5]	Postcode Address File	Any one householder	E	37,716 addresses	56[5]
Expenditure and Food Survey	Continuous	Postcode Address File in GB, Valuation and Lands Agency list in NI	All adults in households aged 16 and over[6]	UK	10,929 addresses[6]	57[6]
Families and Children Study	Annual	Child benefit records[7]	Recipients of child benefit (usually mothers)	GB	6,976 families[7]	84[7]
Family Resources Survey	Continuous	Postcode Address File	All members in household	UK	44,973 households	63
General Household Survey	Continuous	Postcode Address File	All adults in household	GB	9,731 households	73[8]
Health Survey for England	Continuous	Postcode Address File	All household members	E	6,367 households	71[8]
International Passenger Survey	Continuous	International passengers	Individual traveller	UK[9]	276,000 individuals	89
Labour Force Survey	Continuous	Postcode Address File	All adults in household	UK	52,000 households	69[10]
Longitudinal Study of Young People in England	Annual	School records	Young person and his/her parents/guardians	E	13,115 households	87[11]
Mental Health of Children and Young People, 2004	Ad hoc[12]	Child benefit records	Parents, children if aged 11–16, teachers	GB	7,977 families	76[12]
National Passenger Survey	Twice yearly	Passengers at 650 stations	Railway passengers	GB	50,000 individuals	37
National Travel Survey	Continuous	Postcode Address File	All household members	GB	13,687 households per year	61[13]
Northern Ireland Crime Survey	Continuous	Land and Property Services Agency (LPSA) list of domestic addresses	One adult aged 16 and over in private households	NI	5,932 addresses	64
Omnibus Survey	Continuous	Postcode Address File	Adults aged 16 and over living in private households	GB	Approximately 12,000[14]	66

	Frequency	Sampling frame	Type of respondent	Coverage	Effective sample size[1] (most recent survey included in *Social Trends*)	Response rate (percentages)
Psychiatric Morbidity Survey	Ad hoc	Postcode Address File	Adults aged 16 to 74 years living in private households	GB	15,804 addresses	69
Retail Sales Inquiry	Continuous	Inter Departmental Business Register[15]	Retailers	GB	Approximately 5,000	63[15]
Survey of English Housing	Continuous	Postcode Address File	Household	E	29,800 households	64
Scottish Crime and Victimisation Survey	Annual	Postcode Address File	One adult aged 16 and over in private households	S	4,988	71
Survey of Personal Incomes	Annual	HM Revenue & Customs PAYE, Claims and Self-assessment records	Individuals/taxpayers	UK	520,000 individuals	[16]
Taking Part Survey	Continuous	Postcode Address File	One adult aged 16 and over in private households and, where appropriate, one child aged between 11 and 15	E	28,117 adults aged 16 and over	55
Work and Pensions Longitudinal Study	Quarterly	Benefit claimants	Benefit claimants/ beneficiaries	GB	All benefit claimants	[16]

1 Effective sample size includes nonrespondents but excludes ineligible households.
2 The Annual Population Survey includes the English Local Labour Force Survey, Welsh Local Labour Force Survey, Scottish Labour Force Survey, Annual Population Survey 'Boost' and waves 1 and 5 of the Quarterly Labour Force Survey.
3 Response rate refers to 2006 survey.
4 First quarter of 2007 only.
5 Although the EHCS runs on a continuous basis, its reporting is based on a rolling two year sample. The EHCS response combines successful outcomes from two linked surveys where information is separately gathered about the household and the dwelling for each address.
6 There is an optional diary for children aged 7 to 15 in Great Britain. Basic sample for Great Britain only. Response rate refers to Great Britain.
7 The overall response rate is given, which is the number of interviews as a proportion of the total initial sample.
8 Response rate for fully and partially responding households.
9 Includes UK and overseas residents.
10 Response rate to first wave interviews of the quarterly LFS over the period April to June 2007.
11 Response rate quoted refers to wave 2, which was conducted in 2005.
12 A similar survey was carried out in 1999. Response rate based on number of families approached for interview.
13 Sixty-one per cent of eligible households were recorded as being 'fully productive'. However, a further 7 per cent co-operated partially with the survey, and the data from these households can be used on a limited basis.
14 Achieved sample size per Omnibus cycle. The Omnibus interviews at one household per sampled address and one adult per household. Data are weighted to account for the fact that respondents living in smaller households would have a greater chance of selection.
15 Average response rate for 2006.
16 Response rate not applicable as data are drawn from administrative records.

Symbols and conventions

Reference years	Where, because of space constraints, a choice of years has to be made, the most recent year or a run of recent years is shown together with the past population census years (2001, 1991, 1981, etc) and sometimes the mid-points between census years (1996, 1986, etc). Other years may be added if they represent a peak or trough in the series.
Financial year	For example, 1 April 2005 to 31 March 2006 would be shown as 2005/06.
Academic year	For example, September 2005 to July 2006 would be shown as 2005/06.
Combined years	For example, 2003–06 shows data for more than one year that have been combined.
Geography	Where possible *Social Trends* uses data for the UK as a whole. When UK data are not available, or data from the constituent countries of the UK are not comparable, data for Great Britain or the constituent countries are used. Constituent countries can advise where data are available that are equivalent but not directly comparable with those of other constituent countries.
Units on tables	Where one unit predominates it is shown at the top of the table. All other units are shown against the relevant row or column. Figures are shown in italics when they represent percentages.
Rounding of figures	In tables where figures have been rounded to the nearest final digit, there may be an apparent discrepancy between the sum of the constituent items and the total as shown.
Provisional and estimated data	Some data for the latest year (and occasionally for earlier years) are provisional or estimated. To keep footnotes to a minimum, these have not been indicated; source departments will be able to advise if revised data are available.
Billion	This term is used to represent one thousand million.
Household reference person	Sometimes it is necessary to select one person in a household to indicate the general characteristics of the household. For this purpose the household reference person has replaced the head of household in all government-sponsored household surveys after 2000–01. The household reference person is identified during the interview and is:
	a. the householder (in whose name the accommodation is owned or rented); or
	b. in households with joint householders, the person with the highest income or, if both householders have the same income, the oldest householder.
Seasonal adjustment	Unless otherwise stated, unadjusted data have been used.
Dependent children	Those aged under 16, or single people aged 16 to 18 who have not married and are in full-time education unless otherwise indicated.
State pension age (SPA)	The age at which pensions are normally payable by the state pension scheme, currently 65 for men and 60 for women.
EU	Unless otherwise stated, data relate to the enlarged European Union of 27 countries (EU-27) as constituted since 1 January 2007. EU-25 refers to the 25 members of the EU before enlargement.
Ireland	Refers to the Republic of Ireland and does not include Northern Ireland.
Sources	Sources are usually listed as the name by which the source is currently known. In some instances, requests have been made to show the source name at the time the data were compiled. Specific instances have been recorded in relevant appendix entries.

Symbols   The following symbols have been used throughout *Social Trends*:

    .. not available

    . not applicable

    * data have been suppressed to protect confidentiality

    - negligible (less than half the final digit shown)

    0 nil

Dotted lines (…) on charts, when joined with solid lines represent periods in the series for which data are not available.

Appendix

Part 1: Population

Population estimates and projections

The estimated and projected populations are of the resident population of an area, that is all those usually resident there, whatever their nationality. Members of HM Forces stationed outside the UK are excluded; members of foreign forces stationed in the UK are included. Students are taken to be resident at their term-time addresses. Figures for the UK do not include the population of the Channel Islands or the Isle of Man.

The population estimates for mid-2001 to mid-2006 are based on results from the 2001 Census and have been updated to reflect subsequent births, deaths, net migration and other changes. The estimates used in this publication were released on 24 August 2006.

The most recent set of national population projections published for the UK are based on the populations of England, Wales, Scotland and Northern Ireland at mid-2006. These were released on 23 October 2007 and further details can be found on the Office for National Statistics website **www.statistics.gov.uk**

Classification of ethnic groups

The recommended classification of ethnic groups for National Statistics data sources was changed in 2001 to bring it broadly in line with the 2001 Census.

There are two levels to this classification. Level 1 is a classification into five main ethnic groups. Level 2 provides a finer, more detailed classification of Level 1. The preference is for the Level 2 categories to be adopted wherever possible. The two levels and the categories are in the box below.

Direct comparisons should not be made between the figures produced using this new classification and those based on the previous classification.

Further details can be found on the National Statistics website: **www.statistics.gov.uk/ about/classifications/downloads/ns_ ethnicity_statement.doc**

Experimental statistics

These are statistics that are in the testing phase and are not fully developed. Defining what is experimental and non-experimental is largely a matter of statistical judgement, but typically experimental series arise when:

- they are being produced part way through a well defined development programme – whether these statistics are new or changed versions of existing statistics

- statistics are new but still subject to testing in terms of their volatility and ability to meet customer needs

- statistics do not yet meet the rigorous quality standards of National Statistics or

- a rich variety of new measures is available from a new set of statistics, with components that have considerable immediate value to users. These users are aware of the statistics' theoretical quality and can make use of them before the Office for National Statistics has completed all operational testing. The testing is designed to fully validate the measures to the standard expected of National Statistics

Further details can be found on the National Statistics website: **www.statistics.gov.uk/cci/ nugget.asp?id=173**

National Statistics Socio-economic Classification (NS-SEC)

From 2001 the National Statistics Socio-economic Classification (NS-SEC) was adopted for all official surveys, in place of social class based on occupation and socio-economic group. NS-SEC is itself based on the Standard Occupational Classification 2000 (SOC2000) and details of employment status (whether as employer, self employed or employee).

The NS-SEC is an occupationally based classification designed to provide coverage of the whole adult population. The version of the classification, which will be used for most analyses, has eight classes, the first of which can be subdivided. These are:

National Statistics Socio-economic Classification (NS-SEC)

1. Higher managerial and professional occupations, subdivided into:
    1.1 Large employers and higher managerial occupations
    1.2 Higher professional occupations
2. Lower managerial and professional occupations
3. Intermediate occupations
4. Small employers and own account workers
5. Lower supervisory and technical operations
6. Semi-routine occupations
7. Routine occupations
8. Never worked and long-term unemployed

The classes can be further grouped into:

i. Managerial and professional occupations	1, 2
ii. Intermediate occupations	3, 4
iii. Routine and manual occupations	5, 6, 7
iv. Never worked and long term unemployed	8

Classification of ethnic groups

Level 1	Level 2
White	White
	British
	Irish
	Other White background
	All White groups
Mixed	White and Black Caribbean
	White and Black African
	White and Asian
	Other Mixed background
	All Mixed groups
Asian or Asian British	Indian
	Pakistani
	Bangladeshi
	Other Asian background
	All Asian groups
Black or Black British	Caribbean
	African
	Other Black background
	All Black groups
Chinese or other ethnic Group	Chinese
	Other ethnic group
	All Chinese or Other groups
All ethnic groups	All ethnic groups
Not stated	Not stated

Users have the option to include these classes in the overall analysis or keep them separate. The long-term unemployed are defined as those unemployed and seeking work for 12 months or more. Members of HM Forces, who were shown separately in tables of social class, are included within the NS-SEC. Residual groups that remain unclassified include students and those with inadequately described occupations.

Further details can be found on the National Statistics website: www.statistics.gov.uk/methods_quality/ns_sec/default.asp

International migration estimates

An international migrant is defined as someone who changes his or her country of usual residence for a period of at least a year, so that the country of destination becomes the country of usual residence. The richest source of information on international migrants comes from the International Passenger Survey (IPS), which is a sample survey of passengers arriving at, and departing from, the main UK air and sea ports and the Channel Tunnel. This survey provides migration estimates based on respondents' intended length of stay in the UK or abroad.

Adjustments are made to account for people who do not realise their intended length of stay. An estimate is made for the number of people who initially come to or leave the UK for a short period but subsequently stay for a year or longer ('visitor switchers'). The number of people who intend to be migrants, but who in reality stay in the UK or abroad for less than a year ('migrant switchers') are also estimated.

Data from other sources are used to supplement the IPS migration estimates. Home Office asylum seeker data are used to estimate the number of asylum seekers and their dependants who enter or leave the country without being counted in the IPS. Estimates of migration between the UK and Ireland are made using information from the Irish Central Statistics Office.

Data in Figure 1.12 are from Total International Migration (TIM), which is based mainly on IPS data. This includes adjustments for those whose intended length of stay changes so their migrant status changes (migrant/visitor switchers), asylum seekers and their dependants not identified by the IPS, and flows between the UK and Ireland. Estimates are based on a revised methodology that has changed the geographical distribution of immigrants. This has only been applied from 1999.

Internal migration estimates

The estimates of internal migration presented in this volume are based on data provided by the National Health Service Central Register (NHSCR), which records movements of patients between former Health Authority (HA) areas in England and Wales. Using this data source, the definition of an internal migrant is someone who moves from one former HA to another and registers with a different doctor. Historically, internal migration estimates were only available at the former HA level; these were equivalent to shire counties, metropolitan districts and groupings of London boroughs. HA-level migration estimates are available from 1975 on a quarterly rolling year basis.

Internal migration estimates by age and sex became available for all local authority areas in 1999. By obtaining a download from each patient register and by combining all the patient register extracts together, the Office for National Statistics creates a total register for the whole of England and Wales. Comparing records in one year with those of the previous year enables identification of people who have changed their postcode. Estimates at local authority level are made by constraining the migration estimates from the patient registers with the NHSCR estimates at the former HA level.

It has been established that internal migration data under-report the migration of men aged between 16 and 36. Currently, however, there are no suitable sources of data available to enable adjustments or revisions to be made to the estimates. Further research is planned on this topic and new data sources may become available in the future.

Refugees

The criteria for recognition as a refugee, and hence the granting of asylum, are set out in the 1951 United Nations Convention relating to the Status of Refugees, extended in its application by the 1967 Protocol relating to the Status of Refugees. The Convention defines a refugee as a person who 'owing to a well-founded fear of being persecuted for reasons of race, religion, nationality, membership of a particular social group or political opinion, is outside the country of his [or her] nationality and unable or, owing to such fear, is unwilling to avail himself [or herself] of the protection of that country; or who, not having a nationality and being outside the country of his [or her] former habitual residence … is unable or, owing to such fear, is unwilling to return to it'.

Part 2: Households and families

Multi-sourced tables

Tables 2.1, 2.2, 2.3 and 2.6 have multiple sources. To create long time series it is necessary to combine these sources even though they are not always directly comparable. Most of the multi-sourced tables include a combination of the General Household Survey (GHS) (Longitudinal), the Labour Force Survey (LFS) and the Census. For further information about the GHS see below and for the LFS see Appendix, Part 4: Labour Force Survey.

Households

Although definitions differ slightly across surveys and the census, they are broadly similar.

A household is a person living alone or a group of people who have the address as their only or main residence and who either share one meal a day or share the living accommodation.

Students: those living in halls of residence are recorded under their parents' household and included in the parents' family type in the Labour Force Survey (LFS), although some surveys/projections include such students in the institutional population.

In the General Household Survey (GHS) (Longitudinal) (see below), young people aged 16 and over who live away from home for purposes of either work or study and come home only for holidays are not included at the parental address.

Families

Children: Never-married people of any age who live with one or both parent(s). They include stepchildren and adopted children (but not foster children) and also grandchildren, where the parent(s) are absent.

Dependent children: In the 1971 and 1981 Censuses, dependent children were defined as never-married children in families who were either under 15 years of age, or aged 15 to 24 and in full-time education. In the 1991 Census, the Labour Force Survey (LFS) and the General Household Survey (GHS) (Longitudinal), dependent children are childless never-married children in families who are aged under 16, or aged 16 to 18 and in full-time education and living in the household and, in the 1991 Census, economically inactive (see Glossary in Chapter 4: Labour Market on page 47). In the 2001 Census a dependent child is a person aged under 16 in a household (whether or not in a family) or aged 16 to 18, in full-time education and living in a family with their parent(s).

A family: A married or cohabiting couple, either with or without their never-married child or children (of any age), including couples with no children or a lone parent together with his or her never-married child or children, provided they have no children of their own. A family could also consist of a grandparent(s) with their grandchild or grandchildren if the parents of the grandchild or grandchildren are not usually resident in the household. In the LFS, a family unit can also comprise a single person. LFS family units include non-dependent children (who can in fact be adult) those aged 16 and over and not in full-time education, provided they are never married and have no children of their own in the household.

One family and no others: A household comprises one family and no others if there is only one family in the household and there are no non-family people.

Multi-family household: A household containing two or more people who cannot be allocated to a single family as defined in 'a family' above. This includes households with two or more unrelated adults and can also include a grandparent(s) with their child or children and grandchild or grandchildren in one household.

A lone-parent family: In the census is a father or mother together with his or her never-married child or children. A lone-parent family in the LFS consists of a lone parent, living with his or her never-married child or children, provided these children have no children of their own living with them. A lone-parent family in the GHS consists of a lone parent, living with his or her never-married dependent child or children, provided these children have no children of their own. Married lone mothers whose husbands are not defined as resident in the household are not classified as lone parents. Evidence suggests the majority are separated from their husband either because he usually works away from home or for some other reason that does not imply the breakdown of the marriage.

General Household Survey

The General Household Survey (GHS) (Longitudinal) is an interdepartmental multi-purpose continuous survey carried out by the Office for National Statistics (ONS) collecting information from people living in private households in Great Britain. The survey has run continuously since 1971, except for breaks in 1997/78 (when the survey was reviewed) and 1999/2000 when the survey was redeveloped.

In 2005 the GHS adopted a new sample design in line with European requirements, changing from a cross-sectional to a longitudinal design. The purpose of this change was to help monitor European social policy by comparing poverty indicators and changes over time across the European Community. The GHS design changed to a four-yearly rotation where respondents are followed up and re-interviewed up to four times. Around 75 per cent of the people surveyed in 2006 had also completed an interview in 2005.

Between April 1994 and April 2005, the GHS was conducted on a financial year basis, with fieldwork spread evenly across the year April–March. However, in 2005 the survey period reverted to the calendar year. The 2006 survey ran from January to December.

Further details of the methodological changes made during 2005 can be found in the appendices to the GHS at www.statistics.gov.uk/ghs

The GHS collects information on a range of topics. These are:

- smoking
- drinking
- households, families and people
- housing and consumer durables
- marriage and cohabitation
- occupational and personal pension schemes

The GHS provides authoritative estimates in the topics of smoking and drinking. A detailed summary and a longer report on these topics can be found at: www.statistics.gov.uk/ghs

Civil partnership

The Civil Partnership Act 2004 came into force on 5 December 2005 and enables same-sex couples to obtain legal recognition of their relationship. Couples who form a civil partnership have a new legal status, that of 'civil partner'.

Civil partners have equal treatment to married couples in a range of legal matters, including:

- tax, including inheritance tax
- employment benefits
- most state and occupational pension benefits
- income-related benefits, tax credits and child support
- duty to provide reasonable maintenance for your civil partner and any children of the family
- ability to apply for parental responsibility for your civil partner's child
- inheritance of a tenancy agreement
- recognition under intestacy rules
- access to fatal accidents compensation

- protection from domestic violence
- recognition for immigration and nationality purposes

True birth order

At registration, the question on previous live births is not asked where the birth occurred outside marriage. At the registration of births occurring within marriage, previous live births occurring outside marriage and where the woman had never been married to the father are not counted. The information collected on birth order, therefore, has been supplemented to give estimates of overall true birth order, which includes births both within and outside marriage. These estimates are obtained from the General Household Survey (Longitudinal), see above.

Conceptions

Conception statistics used in Table 2.18 include pregnancies that result in either a maternity at which one or more live births or stillbirths occur, or a legal abortion under the Abortion Act 1967. Conception statistics do not include miscarriages or illegal abortions. Dates of conception are estimated using recorded gestation for abortions and stillbirths, and assuming 38 weeks gestation for live births.

Part 3: Education and training

Stages of education

Education takes place in several stages: early years, primary, secondary, further and higher education, and is compulsory for all children in the UK between the ages of 5 (4 in Northern Ireland) and 16. The non-compulsory fourth stage, further education, covers non-advanced education, which can be taken at both further (including tertiary) education colleges, higher education institutions and increasingly in secondary schools. The fifth stage, higher education, is study beyond GCE A levels and their equivalent, which, for most full-time students, takes place in universities and other higher education institutions.

Early years education
In recent years there has been a major expansion of early years education. Many children under five attend state nursery schools or nursery classes within primary schools. Others may attend playgroups in the voluntary sector or in privately run nurseries. In England and Wales many primary schools also operate an early admissions policy where they admit children under five into what are called 'reception classes'. The Education Act 2002 extended the National Curriculum (see below) for England to include the foundation stage. The foundation stage was introduced in September 2000 and covers children's education from the age of three to the end of the reception year, when most are just five and some almost six years old. The Early Years Foundation Stage (EYFS), which is due to come into force in September 2008, will be a single framework for care, learning and development for children in all registered early years settings from birth to five. The EYFS will build on and replace the *Birth to three matters* framework, as well as the *Curriculum Guidance for the Foundation Stage*, and the

Organisation of compulsory school years

	Pupil ages	Year group
England and Wales		
Key Stage 1	5–7	1–2
Key Stage 2	7–11	3–6
Key Stage 3	11–14	7–9
Key Stage 4	14–16	10–11
Northern Ireland		
Key Stage 1	4/5–8	1–4
Key Stage 2	8–11	5–7
Key Stage 3	11–14	8–10
Key Stage 4	14–16	11–12
Scotland		
(Curriculum	4/5–6/7	P1–P3
following	6/7–6/8	P3–P4
national	6/8–9/10	P4–P6
guidelines from	9/10–/1011	P6–P7
ages 5 to 14)	10/11–12/13	P7–S2
NQ[1]	13/14–14/15	S3–S4

1 Standard Grades are part of the National Qualifications (NQ) framework in Scotland. They are broadly equivalent to GCSEs.

National Standards for Under 8s Day Care and Childminding.

Figure 3.1 covers children in early years education in maintained nursery and primary schools. Other provision also takes place in independent and special schools and in non-school education settings in the private and voluntary sector, such as nurseries (which usually provide care, education and play for children up to the age of five), playgroups and pre-schools (which provide childcare, play and early years education, usually for children aged between two and five), children's centres (for children under five), and through accredited childminders. In Scotland data are based on children who are registered for early years education at the time of the annual Pre-school Education and Daycare Census, as a proportion of all those who are eligible for early years education. For more information on data for Scotland see: www.scotland.gov.uk/Topics/Statistics/Browse/Children/PubPreSchoolEdChildcare

Primary education
The primary stage covers three age ranges: nursery (under 5), infant (5 to 7 or 8) and junior (8 or 9 to 11 or 12). In Scotland and Northern Ireland there is generally no distinction between infant and junior schools. Most public sector primary schools take both boys and girls in mixed classes. It is usual to transfer straight to secondary school at age 11 (in England, Wales and Northern Ireland) but in England some children make the transition through middle schools catering for various age ranges between 8 and 14. Depending on their individual age ranges middle schools are classified as either

primary or secondary. In Scotland, pupils start school based on their age as at the end of February rather than at the start of the academic year, and so generally start secondary school at age 11 or 12.

Secondary education
Public provision of secondary education in an area may consist of a combination of different types of school, the pattern reflecting historical circumstances and the policy adopted by the local authority. Comprehensive schools largely admit pupils without reference to ability or aptitude and cater for all the children in a neighbourhood, but in some areas they co-exist with grammar, secondary modern or technical schools. In Northern Ireland post-primary education is provided by grammar schools and non-selective secondary schools. In England the Specialist Schools Programme helps schools, in partnership with private sector sponsors and supported by additional government funding, to establish distinctive identities through their chosen specialisms. Specialist schools have a focus on their chosen subject area but must meet the National Curriculum requirements and deliver a broad and balanced education to all pupils. Any maintained secondary school in England can apply to be designated as a specialist school in one of ten specialist areas: arts, business and enterprise, engineering, humanities, languages, mathematics and computing, music, science, sports, and technology. Schools can also combine any two specialisms. Academies, operating in England, are publicly funded independent local schools that provide free education. They are all ability schools established by sponsors from business, faith or voluntary groups working with partners from the local community. The Department for Children, Schools and Families (DCSF) Secretary of State announced in July 2007, that future academies (that is not including those with a signed agreement, although they could if they wished), would be required to follow the National Curriculum programmes of study in English, mathematics, and information and communication technology (ICT). This is different to the previous model whereby academies had to teach English, mathematics, ICT and science to all pupils.

Special schools
Special schools (day or boarding) provide education for children who require specialist support to complete their education, for example, because they have physical or other difficulties. Many pupils with special educational needs are educated in mainstream schools. All children attending special schools are offered a curriculum designed to overcome their learning difficulties and to enable them to become self-reliant. Since December 2005 special schools in England have also been able to apply for the special educational needs (SEN) specialism, under the Specialist Schools Programme (see Secondary education above). They can apply for a curriculum specialism, but not for both the SEN and a curriculum specialism.

Pupil referral units
Pupil referral units (PRUs) are legally a type of school established and maintained by a local authority to provide education for children of

compulsory school age who may otherwise not receive suitable education. The aim of such units is to provide suitable alternative education on a temporary basis for pupils who may not be able to attend a mainstream school. The focus of the units should be to get pupils back into a mainstream school. Pupils in the units may include: teenage mothers, pupils excluded from school, school-phobics and pupils in the assessment phase of a statement of special educational needs (SEN).

Further education
The term further education may be used in a general sense to cover all non-advanced courses taken after the period of compulsory education, but more commonly it excludes those staying on at secondary school and those in higher education, that is doing courses in universities and colleges leading to qualifications above GCE A level, Higher Grade (in Scotland), General National Vocational Qualifications/National Vocational Qualifications (GNVQ/NVQ) level 3, and their equivalents. Since 1 April 1993, sixth form colleges in England and Wales have been included in the further education sector.

Further education figures for 2005/06 shown in Table 3.9 are whole year counts. However, over the period covered in the table, there is a mixture of whole year and annual snapshot counts, as well as a combination of enrolment and headcounts. There are also other factors, such as mode of study, the inclusion/exclusion of students funded by specific bodies or at certain types of institutions, which have not been constant over time.

Higher education
Higher education (HE) is defined as courses that are of a standard that is higher than GCE A level, the Higher Grade of the Scottish Certificate of Education/National Qualification, GNVQ/NVQ level 3 or the Edexcel (formerly BTEC) or SQA National Certificate/Diploma. There are three main levels of HE courses:

- postgraduate courses leading to higher degrees, diplomas and certificates, including postgraduate certificates of education (PGCE) and professional qualifications that usually require a first degree as entry qualification

- undergraduate courses, which include first degrees, first degrees with qualified teacher status, enhanced first degrees, first degrees obtained concurrently with a diploma, and intercalated first degrees (where first degree students, usually in medicine, dentistry or veterinary medicine, interrupt their studies to complete a one-year course of advanced studies in a related topic)

- other undergraduate courses, which include all other HE courses, for example Higher National Diplomas and Diplomas in HE

As a result of the *1992 Further and Higher Education Act,* former polytechnics and some other HE institutions were designated as universities in 1992/93. Students normally attend HE courses at HE institutions, but some attend at further education colleges. In Scotland, around one-fifth of HE students study at a college. Some also attend institutions that do not receive public grants (such as the University of Buckingham) and these numbers are excluded from the tables.

Up to 2000/01, figures for HE students in Table 3.9 are annual snapshots taken around November or December each year, depending on the type of institution, except for Scotland further education colleges from 1998/99, for which counts are based on the whole year. From 2001/02, figures for HE institutions are based on the Higher Education Statistics Agency (HESA) 'standard registration' count, and are not directly comparable with previous years. The Open University is included in these estimates.

Main categories of educational establishments

Educational establishments in the UK are administered and financed in several ways. Most schools are controlled by local authorities (LAs), which are part of the structure of local government, but some are 'assisted', receiving grants direct from central government sources and being controlled by governing bodies that have a substantial degree of autonomy. Completely outside the public sector are non-maintained schools run by individuals, companies or charitable institutions.

Up to March 2001, further education (FE) courses in FE sector colleges in England and Wales were largely funded through grants from the respective Further Education Funding Councils (FEFCs). In April 2001, however, the Learning and Skills Council (LSC) took over the responsibility for funding the FE sector in England, and the National Council for Education and Training for Wales (part of Education and Learning Wales – ELWa) did so for Wales. The LSC in England is also responsible for funding provision for FE and some non-prescribed higher education in FE sector colleges; in addition, it funds some FE provided by LA maintained and other institutions referred to as 'external institutions'. From April 2006 FE funding in Wales, became the responsibility of the Welsh Assembly Government. The Scottish Further and Higher Education Funding Council (SFC) funds FE colleges in Scotland, while the Department for Employment and Learning funds FE colleges in Northern Ireland.

Higher education (HE) courses in HE establishments are largely publicly funded through block grants from the HE funding councils in England and Scotland, the Higher Education Funding Council in Wales, and the Department for Employment and Learning in Northern Ireland. In addition, some designated HE, mainly Higher National Diplomas (HND)/ Higher National Certificates (HNC) is funded by these sources. The FE sources mentioned above fund the remainder.

Numbers of school pupils are shown in Table 3.3. Nursery school figures for Scotland before 1998/99 only include data for local authority pre-schools. Data from 1998/99 include partnership pre-schools. However, from 2005/06 figures refer to centres providing pre-school education as an LA centre or in partnership with the LA only. Secondary 'Other' schools largely consist of middle schools in England, and secondary intermediate schools in Northern Ireland. 'Special schools' include maintained and non-maintained sectors, while 'public sector schools' and 'non-maintained schools' totals exclude special schools.

The 'All schools' total includes pupil referral units (see under 'Stages of education'), which accounted for around 16,000 pupils in 2006/07.

Special educational needs data

Information for England presented in Figure 3.6 is mainly drawn from two sources: the Schools' Census (SC) and the SEN2 Survey. Figures sourced from SC and the SEN2 Survey are not directly comparable.

The SC has collected information on pupils with special educational needs (SEN) on the census date in January from schools since 1985. It is completed by schools and records those pupils with and without statements who are educated at the school, regardless of which local authority (LA) is responsible. Figures for pupils with SEN without statements were collected from maintained primary and secondary schools for the first time in 1995.

The SEN2 Survey has collected information on children with statements on the census date in January and new statements made in the previous calendar year from LAs since 1984. SEN2 is completed by LAs and records those children for whom the LA is responsible (regardless of whether they are educated in the LA's own maintained schools, in schools in other LAs, in the non-maintained or independent sectors or educated other than at school).

In January 2002 the SC introduced a major change in that primary, secondary and special schools reported data at an individual pupil level for the first time. While the overall collection of pupil level data for these schools was successful, it is possible that some discontinuity in the time series data has resulted from this underlying change in data collection. For instance, the national trend in SEN pupils with statements between 2001 and 2002 in SC is different from that shown in the SEN2 survey. While there are valid reasons as to why the figures will be different between these surveys, it is unusual for the trends to differ to this degree.

Qualifications

England, Wales and Northern Ireland
In England, Wales and Northern Ireland the main examination for school pupils at the minimum school leaving age is the General Certificate of Secondary Education (GCSE), which can be taken in a wide range of subjects. This replaced the GCE O Level and Certificate of Secondary Education (CSE) examinations in 1987 (1988 in Northern Ireland). In England, Wales and Northern Ireland the GCSE is awarded in eight grades, A* to G, the highest four (A* to C) being regarded as equivalent to O level grades A to C or CSE grade 1.

GCE A level is usually taken after a further two years of study in a sixth form or equivalent, passes being graded from A (the highest) to E (the lowest).

In September 2000, following the Qualifying for Success consultation in 1997, a number of reforms were introduced to the qualifications structure for young people aged 16 to 19. Under these reforms, students were encouraged to follow a wide range of subjects in their first year of post-16 study, with students expected to study four Advanced Subsidiaries (AS) before

progressing three of them on to full A levels in their second year. New specifications introduced in 2001 are in place and A levels now comprise units, normally six for a full A level and three for the AS level, which is one-half a full A level. The full A level is normally taken either over two years (modular) or as a set of exams at the end of the two years (linear). In addition, students are encouraged to study a combination of both general and vocational advanced level examinations.

The AS qualification equates to the first year of study of a traditional A level, while the programmes of study in the second year of the full A level are called 'A2' and represent the harder elements of the traditional A level. The AS is a qualification in its own right, whereas A2 modules do not make up a qualification in their own right, but when taken together with the AS units they comprise a full A level.

Scotland
In Scotland, National Qualifications (NQs) are offered to students. These include Standard Grades, National Courses and National Units. The Standard Grade is awarded in seven grades, through three levels of study: Credit (1 or 2), General (3 or 4) and Foundation (5 or 6). Students who do not achieve grade 1 to 6, but do complete the course, are awarded a grade 7. Standard Grade courses are made up of different parts called 'elements', with an exam at the end. National Courses are available at Intermediate, Higher and Advanced Higher, and consist of National Units that are assessed by the school/college, plus an external assessment. Grades are awarded on the basis of how well a student does in the external assessment, having passed all of the National Units. Pass grades are awarded at A, B and C. Grade D is awarded to a student who just fails to get a grade C. In Figure 3.13, Standard Grades 1 to 3 and Intermediate 2 grades A to C are equivalent to GCSE grades A* to C. Standard Grades 4 to 6, Intermediate 1 grades B to C or Access 3 (pass) are equivalent to grades D to G only at GCSE level. Intermediate courses can be taken as an alternative to Standard grade or as a stepping stone to Higher. Access units are assessed by the school/college, with no exam involved. Groups of units in a particular subject area can be built up at Access 2 and 3 to lead to 'cluster awards'. In Scotland pupils generally sit Highers one year earlier than pupils in the rest of the UK sit A levels.

Vocational qualifications
After leaving school, people can study towards higher academic qualifications such as degrees. However, a large number of people choose to study towards qualifications aimed at a particular occupation or group of occupations – these qualifications are called vocational qualifications.

Vocational qualifications can be split into three groups: National Vocational Qualifications (NVQs), General National Vocational Qualifications (GNVQs) and vocationally related qualifications.

- NVQs are based on an explicit statement of competence derived from an analysis of employment requirements. They are awarded at five levels. Scottish Vocational Qualifications (SVQs) are the Scottish equivalent

- GNVQs are a vocational alternative to GCSEs and GCE A levels. General Scottish Vocational Qualifications (GSVQs) are the Scottish equivalent. They are awarded at three levels: Foundation, Intermediate and Advanced. Advanced GNVQs were redesigned and relaunched as Vocational A levels or, more formally, Advanced Vocational Certificates of Education (VCEs) and, as well as being available at AS level and full A level, there are also double awards (counting as 12 units)

- There are a large number of other vocational qualifications, which are not NVQs, SVQs, GNVQs or GSVQs. For example, a Business and Technology Education Council (BTEC) Higher National Diploma (HND) or a City & Guilds craft award

Other qualifications (including academic qualifications) are often expressed as being equivalent to a particular NVQ level so that comparisons can be easily made:

- An NVQ level 1 is equivalent to one or more GCSEs at grade G (but is lower than five GCSE grades A* to C), BTEC general certificate, a Youth Training certificate, other Royal Society of Arts (RSA), City & Guilds craft qualifications

- An NVQ level 2 is equivalent to five GCSEs at grades A* to C, an Intermediate GNVQ, an RSA diploma, a City & Guilds craft or a BTEC first or general diploma

- An NVQ level 3 is equivalent to two A levels, an advanced GNVQ, International Baccalaureate, an RSA advanced diploma, a City & Guilds advanced craft, an Ordinary National Diploma (OND) or Ordinary National Certificate (ONC) or a BTEC National Diploma

- An NVQ level 4 is equivalent to a first degree, a HND or HNC, a BTEC Higher Diploma, an RSA Higher Diploma, a nursing qualification or other higher education qualification below a higher degree

- An NVQ level 5 is equivalent to a higher degree

The National Curriculum

Under the *Education Reform Act 1988* a National Curriculum has been progressively introduced into primary and secondary schools in England and Wales. This consists of English (or the option of Welsh as a first language in Wales), mathematics and science. The second level of curriculum additionally comprises the so-called 'foundation' subjects, such as history, geography, art, music, information technology, design and technology, and physical education (and Welsh as a second language in Wales). The *Education Act 2002* extended the National Curriculum for England to include the foundation stage. It has six areas of learning:

- personal

- social and emotional development

- communication, language and literacy

- mathematical development

- knowledge and understanding of the world

- physical development and

- creative development

Measurable targets have been defined for four key stages, corresponding to ages 7, 11, 14 and 16. Pupils are assessed formally at the ages of 7, 11 and 14 by a mixture of teacher assessments and by national tests (statutory testing at Key Stages 1 to 3 has been abolished in Wales with the last tests taking place in 2005 at Key Stage 3) in the core subjects of English, mathematics and science (and in Welsh speaking schools in Wales, Welsh as a first language), though the method varies between subjects and countries. Sixteen-year-olds are assessed by the GCSE examination. Statutory authorities have been set up for England and for Wales to advise the Government on the National Curriculum and promote curriculum development generally.

Northern Ireland has its own common curriculum that is similar but not identical to the National Curriculum in England and Wales. Assessment arrangements in Northern Ireland became statutory from September 1996 and Key Stage 1 pupils are assessed at age eight.

Expected attainment levels in England

England	Attainment expected
Key Stage 1	Level 2 or above
Key Stage 2	Level 4 or above
Key Stage 3	Level 5 or above
Key Stage 4	GCSE

In Scotland, there is no statutory national curriculum and responsibility for the management and delivery of the curriculum belongs to education authorities and head teachers. Pupils aged 5 to 14 study a broad curriculum based on national guidelines, which set out the aims of study, the ground to be covered and the way the pupils' learning should be assessed and reported. Progress is measured by attainment of six levels based on the expectation of the performance of the majority of pupils on completion of certain stages between the ages of 5 and 14: Primary 3 (age 7/8), Primary 4 (age 8/9), Primary 7 (age 11/12) and Secondary 2 (age 13/14). It is recognised that pupils learn at different rates and some will reach the various levels before others.

The 5 to 14 curriculum areas in Scotland are:

- language
- mathematics
- environmental studies
- expressive arts
- religious and moral education with personal and social development and
- health education

In Secondary 3 and 4, it is recommended that the core curriculum of all pupils should include study within the following eight modes:

- language and communication
- mathematical studies and applications
- scientific studies and applications
- social and environmental studies
- technological activities and applications

- creative and aesthetic activities
- physical education and
- religious and moral education

For Secondary 5 and 6 these eight modes are important in structuring the curriculum, although it is not expected that each pupil will study under each mode but that the curriculum will be negotiated. The Scottish curriculum 3 to 18 is being reviewed under *A Curriculum for Excellence*.

Adult education

The establishment of the LSC (Learning and Skills Council) in March 2001 led to changes in the arrangements for planning and funding of learning opportunities for adults in England, as well as in data collection. Since 2003/04, adult and community learning data have been collected by the LSC and incorporated into the Individualised Learner Record (ILR). The ILR covers learners in further education and on work based learning for young people. Data in Table 3.17 are taken from the ILR.

Classification of the Functions of Government (COFOG)

In 2007 Her Majesty's Treasury (HMT) changed the presentation of public expenditure statistical analysis (PESA) categories to bring analysis in closer alignment to the UN Classification of the Functions of Government (COFOG). COFOG describes the functions of government in ten categories (general public services; defence; public order and safety; economic affairs; environment protection; housing and community amenities; health; recreation, culture and religion; education; and social protection) and within these categories there is a further breakdown of the functions into sub-sets. Departmental expenditure is allocated to these sub-sets, which create the overall function categories.

Expenditure data from 1987/88 in Figure 3.20 are based on COFOG.

For further details on the classification see: www.hm-treasury.gov.uk/media/2/7/natstat_techpesa04.pdf

Departmental changes

Since June 2007 the remit of the former Department for Education and Skills (DfES) has been split between the Department for Children, Schools and Families (DCSF) and the Department for Innovation, Universities and Skills (DIUS). DCSF became responsible for education, children and youth issues – in short, everything affecting people up to the age of 19. DIUS became responsible for adult learning, further and higher education, skills, science and innovation.

Part 4: Labour market

Labour Force Survey

The Labour Force Survey (LFS) is the largest regular household survey in the UK and much of the labour market data published are measured by the LFS. The concepts and definitions used in the LFS are agreed by the International Labour

Organisation (ILO), an agency of the United Nations. The definitions are used by EU member states and members of the Organisation for Economic Co-operation and Development.

On 24 August 2006 the Office for National Statistics (ONS) published the 2005-based mid-year population estimates for the UK and on 7 September 2006 ONS published the 2006 Q2 experimental population estimates for England and Wales. These revised population estimates have been incorporated into LFS estimates used in the following tables and figures 4.1, 4.2, 4.3, 4.4, 4.8, 4.10, 4.11, 4.14, 4.17, 4.18 and 4.19. The following LFS sourced tables and figures are based on population estimates published in spring 2003: 4.5, 4.12, 4.15 and 4.20.

An EU requirement exists whereby all member states must have a labour force survey based on calendar quarters. The UK LFS complied with this from May 2006. The survey previously used seasonal quarters where, for example, the March–May months covered the spring quarter, June–August was summer and so forth. This has now changed to calendar quarters where micro data are available for January–March (Q1), April–June (Q2), July–September (Q3) and October–December (Q4). However, because of data availability issues, all the data in Figure 4.20 are at autumn with the exception of 2006, which are at Q4.

ONS has produced a set of historical estimates covering the monthly periods between 1971 and 1991, which are fully consistent with post-1992 LFS data. The data cover headline measures of employment, unemployment, economic activity, economic inactivity and hours worked. These estimates were published on an experimental basis in 2003 and following further user consultation and quality assurance, these estimates were made National Statistics. As such, they represent ONS's best estimate of the headline labour market series over this period. The labour market chapter uses data from these estimates only where headline data are reported (Figures 4.1, 4.4, 4.14 and 4.17) since the historical estimates are not yet available for subgroups of the population, other than by sex and for key age groups.

Annual Population Survey

The Annual Population Survey (APS) was introduced in 2004. The APS included all the data of the annual local area Labour Force Survey (LFS), as well as a further sample boost aimed at achieving a minimum number of economically active respondents in the sample in each local authority district in England. This sample boost was withdrawn after 2005. The first APS covered the calendar year 2004, rather than the annual local area LFS period of March to February. Also, the annual local area LFS data are published only once a year, whereas the APS data are published quarterly, with each publication including a year's data. Like the local area LFS data set, the APS data are published by local authority area. However, the APS data contain an enhanced range of variables providing a greater level of detail than the LFS about the resident household population of an area, in particular on ethnic group, health and sex.

For more information on local area labour market statistics, see: 'Local area labour markets: statistical indicators July 2007', www.statistics.gov.uk/StatBase/Product.asp?vlnk=14160

Eurostat rates

There are differences between Eurostat and the Office for National Statistics in the age bases used in calculating published employment and unemployment rates.

In Table 4.7, which uses Eurostat data, the numerators for the employment rates of the UK and Spain are those aged 16 to 64 and the denominators are also those aged 16 to 64. However, although the numerators for the remaining rates are also those aged 16 to 64, the denominators are those aged 15 to 64.

In Table 4.16, which also uses Eurostat data, the numerator for the unemployment rates of the UK and Spain are those aged 16 to 74 and the denominators are also 16 to 74. However, although the numerators for the remaining rates are also those aged 16 to 74, the denominators are those aged 15 to 74.

For more information see: http://europa.eu.int/estatref/info/sdds/en/strind/emploi_index.htm

Standard Occupational Classification 2000 (SOC2000)

The Standard Occupational Classification (SOC2000) was first published in 1990 (SOC90) to replace both the Classification of Occupations 1980, and the Classification of Occupations and Dictionary of Occupational Titles. SOC90 was revised and updated in 2000 to produce SOC2000. There is no exact correspondence between SOC90 and SOC2000 at any level.

The two main concepts that SOC2000 is used to investigate are:

• kind of work performed and
• the competent performance of the tasks and duties

The structure of SOC2000 is four-tier covering:

• major groups/numbers
• sub-major groups/numbers
• minor groups/numbers and
• unit groups/numbers (occupations)

For example, the group/number breakdown for the occupation of a chemist is as follows:

• major group	2	Professional occupations
• sub-major group	21	Science and technology professionals
• minor group	211	Science professionals
• unit group	2111	Chemists

SOC2000 comprises 9 major groups, 25 sub-major groups, 81 minor groups and 353 unit groups (occupations). The major groups are:

• managers and senior officials
• professional occupations
• associate professional and technical occupations
• administrative and secretarial occupations
• skilled trades occupations
• personal service occupations
• sales and customer service occupations
• process, plant and machine operatives
• elementary occupations

For more information on SOC2000 see: www.statistics.gov.uk/methods_quality/ns_sec/soc2000.asp

Standard Industrial Classification 2003

A Standard Industrial Classification (SIC) was first introduced into the UK in 1948 for use in classifying business establishments and other statistical units by the type of economic activity in which they are engaged. The classification provides a framework for the collection, tabulation, presentation and analysis of data and its use promotes uniformity. In addition, it can be used for administrative purposes and by non-government bodies as a convenient way of classifying industrial activities into a common structure.

Since 1948 the classification has been revised in 1958, 1968, 1980, 1992 and 2003. Figure 4.9 uses the SIC 2003. Revision is necessary because over time new products and the new industries to produce them emerge, and shifts of emphasis occur in existing industries. It is not always possible for the system to accommodate such developments and so the classification is updated.

For further information about SIC see: www.statistics.gov.uk/methods_quality/sic/downloads/UK_SIC_Vol1(2003).pdf

Public sector employment

Public sector employment comprises employment in central government, local government and public corporations as defined for the UK National Accounts. Data are collected from public sector organisations through the Office for National Statistics Quarterly Public Sector Employees Survey and other sources. Employment estimates for the private sector are derived as the difference between Labour Force Survey employment estimates for the whole economy (not seasonally adjusted) and the public sector employment estimates.

The public sector employment estimates given in Figure 4.10 include a number of workers with a second job in the public sector whose main job is in the private sector or in a separate public sector organisation. The private sector estimate will thus tend to be correspondingly understated by a small percentage.

Model-based estimates of unemployment

On 28 July 2006 the Office for National Statistics launched model-based estimates of unemployment for unitary and local authorities as National Statistics. These estimates are the best available for total unemployment in these areas. For local areas, even the annual local area

Labour Force Survey or Annual Population Survey have small samples. This means that estimates for these areas are likely to be less reliable than those for larger areas, since the sampling variability is high. In particular, this affects estimates of events that are uncommon, like unemployment. A statistical model was developed to provide reliable unemployment estimates for all local authorities.

For more information, see: 'Local area labour markets: statistical indicators July 2007', www.statistics.gov.uk/StatBase/Product.asp?vlnk=14160

Labour disputes

Statistics of stoppages of work caused by labour disputes in the UK relate to disputes connected with terms and conditions of employment. Small stoppages involving fewer than ten workers or lasting less than one day are excluded from the statistics unless the aggregate number of working days lost in the dispute is 100 or more. Disputes not resulting in a stoppage of work are not included in the statistics.

Workers involved and working days lost relate to persons both directly and indirectly involved (unable to work although not parties to the dispute) at the establishments where the disputes occurred. People laid off and working days lost at establishments not in dispute, for example because of resulting shortages of supplies, are excluded.

There are difficulties in ensuring complete recording of stoppages, in particular for short disputes lasting only a day or so, or involving only a few workers. Any under-recording would affect the total number of stoppages much more than the number of working days lost.

For more information, see 'Labour disputes in 2006', pp 25–36, Economic & Labour Market Review, June 2007. www.statistics.gov.uk/elmr/06_07/downloads/ELMR06_07Hale.pdf

Labour market statistics

For more information on labour market statistics, sources and analysis, including information about all aspects of the Office for National Statistics' labour market outputs, see the Labour Market Review 2006 www.statistics.gov.uk/labourmarketreview/ and the online Guide to Labour Market Statistics www.statistics.gov.uk/about/data/guides/LabourMarket/

Department of Trade and Industry (DTI) / Department for Business, Enterprise and Regulatory Reform (BERR)

BERR was created on the 28 June 2007 with the disbanding of the DTI. This involved the removal of the Office of Science and Innovation (moved to the Department of Innovation, Universities and Skills), and the arrival of the Better Regulation Office from the Cabinet Office.

The footnotes to 4.13, 4.20 and 4.21 state the source as DTI as the original reports were published before the creation of BERR. Web links to the reports (see References and further reading) connect with either DTI or BERR in the web address.

Part 5: Income and wealth

Household income data sources

The data for the household sector as derived from the National Accounts have been compiled according to the definitions and conventions set out in the European System of Accounts 1995 (ESA95). Estimates for the household sector cannot be separated from the sector for non-profit institutions serving households and so the data in *Social Trends* cover both sectors. The most obvious example of a non-profit institution is a charity. This sector also includes many other organisations of which universities, trade unions, and clubs and societies are the most important. Non-profit making bodies receive income mainly in the form of property income (that is, investment income) and of other current receipts. The household sector differs from the personal sector, as defined in the National Accounts prior to the introduction of ESA95, in that it excludes unincorporated private businesses apart from sole traders. The household sector also includes people living in institutions such as nursing homes, as well as people living in private households. More information is given in *United Kingdom National Accounts Concepts, Sources and Methods* published by The Stationery Office and is available on the Office for National Statistics (ONS) website: **www.statistics.gov.uk/ downloads/theme_economy/Concepts_ Sources_&_Methods.pdf.**

In ESA95, household income includes the value of national insurance contributions and pension contributions made by employers on behalf of their employees. It also shows property income (that is, income from investments) net of payments of interest on loans. In both these respects, national accounts' conventions diverge from those normally used when collecting data on household income from household surveys. Employees are usually unaware of the value of the national insurance contributions and pension contributions made on their behalf by their employer, and so such data are rarely collected. Payments of interest are usually regarded as items of expenditure rather than reductions of income. In Figure 5.1, household income excludes employers' national insurance and pension contributions and includes property income gross of payment of interest on loans, to correspond more closely with the definition generally used in household surveys.

Survey sources differ from the National Accounts in a number of other important respects. They cover the population living in households and some cover certain parts of the population living in institutions such as nursing homes, but all exclude non-profit making institutions. Survey sources are also subject to under-reporting and non-response bias. In the case of household income surveys, investment income is commonly underestimated, as is income from self-employment. All these factors mean that the survey data on income used in most of this chapter are not entirely consistent with the National Accounts household sector data.

Households Below Average Income (HBAI)

Information on the distribution of income based on the Family Resources Survey is provided in the Department for Work and Pensions (DWP) publication *Households Below Average Income: 1994/95–2004/05,* available both in hard copy and on the DWP website: **www.dwp.gov.uk/ asd/hbai.asp.** This publication provides estimates of patterns of personal disposable income in Great Britain, and of changes in income over time. It attempts to measure people's potential living standards as determined by disposable income. Although as the title would suggest, HBAI concentrates on the lower part of the income distribution, it also provides estimates covering the whole of the income distribution.

In 2002/03 the Family Resources Survey was extended to cover Northern Ireland. Now that three years of data are available, data presented from 2002/03 cover the UK rather than Great Britain. Estimates for the UK are very similar to those for Great Britain.

Disposable household income includes all flows of income into the household, principally earnings, benefits, occupational and private pensions, and investments. It is net of tax, employees' national insurance contributions, council tax, contributions to occupational pension schemes (including additional voluntary contributions), maintenance and child support payments, and parental contributions to students living away from home.

Two different measures of disposable income are used in HBAI: before and after housing costs are deducted. This is principally to take into account variations in housing costs that do not correspond to comparable variations in the quality of housing. Housing costs consist of rent, water rates, community charges, mortgage interest payments, structural insurance, ground rent and service charges.

Equivalisation scales

The Department for Work and Pensions (DWP), the Office for National Statistics (ONS), the Institute for Fiscal Studies (IFS) and the Institute for Social and Economic Research (ISER) all use McClements equivalence scales in their analysis of the income distribution, to take into account variations in the size and composition of households. This reflects the common sense notion that a household of five adults will need a higher income than will a single person living alone to enjoy a comparable standard of living. An overall equivalence value is calculated for each household by summing the appropriate scale values for each household member. Equivalised household income is then calculated by dividing household income by the household's equivalence value. The scales conventionally take a couple as the reference point with an equivalence value of one; equivalisation therefore tends to increase relatively the incomes of single person households (since their incomes are divided by a value of less than one) and to reduce incomes of households with three or more persons. For further information see *Households Below Average Income 1994/95–2004/05* available on the DWP website: **www.dwp.gov.uk/asd/ hbai.asp.** There are two McClements equivalence scales, one for adjusting incomes before housing costs and one for adjusting income after housing costs, see table below.

The DWP and IFS both use different scales for adjustment of income before and after the deduction of housing costs.

Gini coefficient

The Gini coefficient is the most widely used summary measure of the degree of inequality in an income distribution. The first step is to rank the distribution in ascending order. The coefficient can then best be understood by considering a graph of the cumulative income share against the cumulative share of households – the Lorenz curve. This would take the form of a diagonal line for complete equality where all households had the same income, while complete inequality where one household received all the income and the remainder received none would be represented by a curve comprising the horizontal axis and the right-hand vertical axis. The area between the Lorenz curve and the diagonal line of complete equality and inequality gives the value of the Gini coefficient. As inequality increases (and the Lorenz curve bellies out) so does the Gini coefficient until it reaches its maximum value of 1 with complete inequality.

Pensioners' income

Information on the income of pensioners based on the Family Resources Survey is provided in

McClements equivalence scales:

Household member	Before housing costs	After housing costs
First adult (head)	0.61	0.55
Spouse of head	0.39	0.45
Other second adult	0.46	0.45
Third adult	0.42	0.45
Subsequent adults	0.36	0.40
Each dependant aged:		
0–1	0.09	0.07
2–4	0.18	0.18
5–7	0.21	0.21
8–10	0.23	0.23
11–12	0.25	0.26
13–15	0.27	0.28
16 or over	0.36	0.38

the Department for Work and Pensions (DWP) publication *Pensioners' Income Series*, the latest year of which is 2004/05 available both in hard copy and on the DWP website: **www.dwp.gov. uk/asd/asd6/pensioners_income.asp**. It contains estimates and interpretation of trends in the levels and sources of pensioners' incomes in Great Britain over time.

A pensioner benefit unit, or family, is one where the head is over state pension age. The head of the benefit unit is either the household reference person, where he or she belongs to the benefit unit, or the first person listed at interview in the benefit unit – for couples it is usually the man.

In 2002/03 the Family Resources Survey was extended to cover Northern Ireland. Now that three years of data are available, data presented for pensioners income from 2002/03 cover the UK rather than Great Britain. Estimates for the UK are very similar to those for Great Britain.

Earnings surveys

The Annual Survey of Hours and Earnings (ASHE) replaced the New Earnings Survey (NES) from October 2004. ASHE improves on NES by extending the coverage of the survey sample, introducing weighting and publishing estimates of quality for all survey outputs. The new survey methodology produces weighted estimates, using weights calculated by calibrating the survey responses to totals from the Labour Force Survey (see also Appendix, Part 4: Labour Force Survey) by occupation, sex, region and age. The survey sample has been increased to include employees changing jobs between the survey sample identification and the survey reference date. The new survey design also produces outputs that focus on median rather than mean levels of pay. Full details of the methodology of ASHE can be found on the Office for National Statistics website at: **www.statistics.gov.uk/articles/nojournal/ ASHEMethod_article.pdf**

Back series using ASHE methodology applied to NES data sets are available for 1997 to 2004 at: **www.statistics.gov.uk/statbase/Product. asp?vlnk=13101**. However, it is not possible to adjust NES data sets to allow for the supplementary information collected by ASHE. Thus 2004 data are available on two bases, with and without this information, whereas estimates from 2005 onwards only include the supplementary information.

Model-based estimates of income

The Office for National Statistics (ONS) has produced a set of model-based income estimates for wards in England and Wales on boundaries consistent with the 2001 Census. Model-based estimates have been produced for four different income types:

- total weekly household income (unequivalised)

- net weekly household income (unequivalised)

- net weekly household income before housing costs (equivalised) and

- net weekly household income after housing costs (equivalised)

The methodology used to produce the model-based estimates is relatively new and as a result may be subject to consultation, modification and further development. In view of this ongoing work the current model-based estimates are published as experimental statistics (see also Appendix, Part 1: Experimental statistics). The modelling methodology enables survey data to be combined with census and administrative data to produce estimates at a lower geographical level than is possible with survey data alone. Since the estimates are model-based they are different to standard direct estimates obtained from surveys and from statistics provided by administrative sources. These estimates are dependent upon correctly specifying the relationship between weekly household income and the census/administrative information. The main limitation of estimates for small areas is that they are subject to variability. ONS has produced confidence intervals associated with the model-based estimates to make the accuracy of the estimates clear. These ward estimates are constrained to the published Family Resources Survey estimates for each Government Office Region within England and for Wales. Further information on the methodology may be found in **www.neighbourhood.statistics.gov.uk/ dissemination/**.

Net wealth of the household sector

Revised balance sheet estimates of the net wealth of the household (and non-profit institutions) sector were published in an article in *Economic Trends* November 1999 **www.statistics.gov.uk/cci/article.asp?ID=41 &Pos=1&ColRank=1&Rank=1**.

These figures are based on the new international system of national accounting and incorporate data from new sources. Office for National Statistics quarterly estimates of net financial wealth (excluding tangible and intangible assets) are published in *Financial Statistics*.

Part 6: Expenditure

Household expenditure

The estimates of household final consumption expenditure that appear in the National Accounts measure expenditure on goods and services by UK residents. This includes the value of income in kind; imputed rent for owner-occupied dwellings; and the purchase of second-hand goods less the proceeds of sales of used goods. Excluded are interest and other transfer payments; all business expenditure; and the purchase of land and buildings (and associated costs).

Expenditure is classified according to the internationally recognised Classification of Individual Consumption by Purpose (COICOP), which has 12 categories of household expenditure:

- food and non-alcoholic beverages

- alcoholic beverages and tobacco

- clothing and footwear

- housing, water and fuel

- household goods and services

- health

- transport

- communication

- recreation and culture

- education

- restaurants and hotels

- miscellaneous goods and services

In addition, household final consumption expenditure includes expenditure by UK resident households that takes place abroad, and excludes expenditure by non-residents in the UK.

Estimates of household final consumption expenditure are produced using a range of data sources. Both value and volume estimates are available, which provide reliable information about how expenditure has changed over time.

Until September 2003 UK economic growth was calculated using 'fixed base aggregation'. Under this method the detailed estimates for growth for different parts of the economy were summed to a total by weighting each component according to its share of total expenditure in 1995. The year from which this information was drawn was updated at five-yearly intervals. Since September 2003 UK economic growth has been calculated by 'annual chain-linking'. This uses information updated every year to give each component the most relevant weight that can be estimated. This method has been used for estimating change in household expenditure since 1971.

For further details see *Consumer Trends* at: **www.statistics.gov.uk/consumertrends**

Expenditure and Food Survey

Estimates of household expenditure are also available directly from the Expenditure and Food Survey (EFS) and are published in *Family Spending*. The EFS covers all private households (that is, not people living in institutions such as prisons, retirement homes or in student accommodation) and provides information about how expenditure patterns differ across different types of households. However, unlike the National Accounts estimates (see 'Household expenditure' above), only estimates of the value of expenditure are available (that is, current price estimates) and the survey results are not intended to be used to measure change over time.

The EFS was created in April 2001, by merging the Family Expenditure Survey (FES) with the National Food Survey (NFS). The EFS continues to produce the information previously provided by the FES. From January 2006 survey results are published for calendar years (rather than financial years), in anticipation of the EFS' integration within the Continuous Population Survey (CPS).

The EFS also uses the Classification of Individual Consumption by Purpose (COICOP, see above), although the definition of household expenditure is not exactly the same as that used in the National Accounts. For example, there are some differences in the treatment of housing-related expenditure. Within the National Accounts, an estimate of imputed rent for owner-occupied dwellings is included in the category 'Housing, water and fuel'. Results from the EFS do not include imputed rent for owner occupiers but mortgage interest payments are included in an additional category 'Other expenditure items'.

For further details see *Family Spending* at: www.statistics.gov.uk/familyspending

Retail sales index

The retail sales index (RSI) is a measurement of monthly movements in the average weekly retail turnover of retailers in Great Britain. All retailers selected for the Retail Sales Inquiry are asked to provide estimates of total retail turnover, including sales from stores, e-commerce (including over the Internet), mail order, stalls and markets, and door-to-door sales. Retail turnover is defined as the value of sales of goods to the general public for personal and household use.

The sample is addressed to approximately 5,000 retailers of all sizes every month. All of the largest 900 retailers are included in the sample together with a random sample of smaller retailers. Estimates are produced for each type of store by size-band. These detailed estimates are aggregated to produce estimates of weekly sales for 17 retail sectors, the main industry aggregates and retailing as a whole.

Headline data are presented in constant prices (volume) seasonally adjusted and at current prices (value) non-seasonally adjusted. For further details see retail sales at: www.statistics.gov.uk/rsi

Retail prices index

The retail prices index (RPI) is the most long-standing measure of inflation in the UK. It measures the average change from month to month in the prices of goods and services purchased by most households in the UK. The spending pattern on which the index is based is revised each year, mainly using information from the Expenditure and Food Survey (EFS, see above). It covers the goods and services purchased by private households, excluding:

- high income households, defined as those households with a total income within the top 4 per cent of all households, as measured by each quarter's EFS and

- 'pensioner' households, which derive at least three quarters of their total income from state pensions and benefits

It is considered that such households are likely to spend their money on atypical things and including them in the scope of the RPI would distort the overall average. Expenditure patterns of one-person and two-person 'pensioner' households differ from those of the households that the RPI is based on. Separate indices have been compiled for such pensioner households since 1969, and quarterly averages are published in *Focus on Consumer Price Indices*, available on the National Statistics website. They are chained indices constructed in the same way as the RPI. It should, however, be noted that the pensioner indices exclude housing costs.

A guide to the RPI can be found on the National Statistics website: **www.statistics.gov.uk/rpi**

Consumer prices index

The consumer prices index (CPI) is the main measure of inflation used within the Government's monetary policy framework. Prior to 10 December 2003, this index was published as the harmonised index of consumer prices.

The methodology of the CPI is similar to that of the RPI but differs in the following ways:

- in the CPI, the geometric mean is used to aggregate the prices at the most basic level, whereas the RPI uses arithmetic means

- a number of RPI series are excluded from the CPI, most particularly, those mainly relating to owner occupiers' housing costs (for example, mortgage interest payments, house depreciation, council tax and buildings insurance)

- the coverage of the CPI indices is based on the Classification of Individual Consumption by Purpose (COICOP, see above), whereas the RPI uses its own bespoke classification

- the CPI includes series for university accommodation fees, foreign students' university tuition fees, unit trust and stockbrokers charges, none of which are included in the RPI

- the index for new car prices in the RPI is imputed from movements in second-hand car prices, whereas the CPI uses a quality adjusted index based on published prices of new cars

- the CPI weights are based on expenditure by all private households, foreign visitors to the UK and residents of institutional households. In the RPI, weights are based on expenditure by private households only, excluding the highest income households, and pensioner households mainly dependent on state benefits

- in the construction of the RPI weights, expenditure on insurance is assigned to the relevant insurance heading. For the CPI weights, the amount paid out in insurance claims is distributed among the COICOP headings according to the nature of the claims expenditure with the residual (that is, the service charge) being allocated to the relevant insurance heading

A guide to the CPI can be found on the National Statistics website: **www.statistics.gov.uk/cpi**

Internationally, the CPI is known as the harmonised index of consumer prices (HICP). HICPs are calculated in each member state of the European Union (EU), according to rules specified in a series of European regulations developed by Eurostat in conjunction with the EU member states. HICPs are used to compare inflation rates across the EU. Since January 1999 the European Central Bank (ECB) has used HICPs as the measure of price stability across the euro area.

Further details can be found on the ECB website: **www.ecb.int/mopo/html/index.en.html**

CPI estimates for years prior to 1996 had to be estimated using available data sources. For 1988 to 1995 the CPI was estimated from archived RPI price quotes and historical weights data, and aggregated up to the published COICOP

weights. Therefore, the estimated CPI is based on the RPI household population and not all private households, and it does not account for all items included in the official CPI.

For more information about how these historical estimates were produced see the 'Harmonised Index of Consumer Prices: Historical Estimates' paper in *Economic Trends,* no. 541.

Purchasing power parities

The international spending power of sterling depends both on exchange rates and on the ratios of prices between the UK and other countries (measured by purchasing power parities). Spending power can be measured by comparative price levels, which are defined as the ratios of purchasing power parities to exchange rates. They provide a measure of the differences in price levels between countries, by indicating the number of units of a common currency needed to buy the same volume of goods and services in each country.

Part 7: Health

Expectation of life

The expectation of life is the average total number of years that a person of that age could be expected to live, if the rates of mortality at each age were those experienced in that year. The mortality rates that underlie the expectation of life figures are based, up to 2006, on total deaths occurring in each year for England and Wales, and the total deaths registered in each year in Scotland and Northern Ireland.

Healthy life expectancy and disability-free life expectancy

Healthy life expectancy and disability-free life expectancy are summary measures of population health that combine mortality and ill-health. In contrast to life expectancy, these two indicators measure both the quality and quantity of life. Essentially they partition life expectancy into the following two components:

- years lived free from ill-health or disability

- years lived in ill-health or with disability

Life expectancy indicators are independent of the age structure of the population and represent the average health expectation of a synthetic birth cohort experiencing current rates of mortality and ill-health over their lifetime.

Healthy life expectancy (HLE) at birth is defined as the number of years that a newly born baby can expect to live in good or fairly good health if he or she experienced the current mortality rates and 'good' or 'fairly good' health rates, based on self-assessed general health for different age groups during their lifespan. The calculation of HLE uses Government Actuary's Department data on life expectancy, and the General Household Survey (GHS) (Longitudinal) and census data on self-assessed health, specifically responses to the question 'Over the last 12 months would you say your health has on the whole been good, fairly good, or not good?' 'Good' and 'Fairly good' responses are taken as a positive measure of health. The GHS was not conducted in either 1997 or 1999. The resulting modifications to the annual series of healthy life expectancy data are:

- no data points were calculated for the years 1996,1998 and 2000

- the data points for 1997 and 1999 were each calculated using two years of GHS health data: 1997 on 1996 and 1998 data, and 1999 on 1998 and 2000 data

Furthermore, HLE estimates for 2001 and 2002 were calculated using the revised methodology to incorporate improved population estimates from the 2001 Census and changes in weighting methodology in the GHS. They are therefore not directly comparable with previous years. However, the level of change was small and the new series can be used to monitor trends over the longer term.

Disability-free life expectancy, defined as expected years lived without limiting long-standing illness, is calculated in exactly the same way as healthy life expectancy, with the difference that it uses the GHS age-sex rates of 'without limiting long-standing illness' instead of the rates of 'good/fairly good health'.

Self-reported illness

The General Household Survey (Longitudinal) includes two measures of self-reported illness:

Chronic illness: Respondents aged 16 and over are asked whether they have any long-standing illness or disability that has troubled them for some time. Information about children is collected from a responsible adult, usually the mother. Those who report a long-standing condition, either on their own behalf or that of their children, are asked whether it limits their activities in any way.

Acute sickness: Respondents are asked whether they had to cut down on their normal activities in the two weeks before interview as a result of illness or injury (this is known as 'restricted activity').

Standardised rates

Directly age-standardised incidence rates enable comparisons to be made between geographical areas over time, and between the sexes, which are independent of changes in the age structure of the population. In each year the crude rates in each five-year age group are multiplied by the European standard population (see below) for that age group. These are then summed and divided by the total standard population for these age groups to give an overall standardised rate.

International Classification of Diseases

The International Classification of Diseases (ICD) is a coding scheme for diseases and causes of death. The Tenth Revision of the ICD (ICD10) was introduced for coding the underlying cause of death in Scotland from 2000 and in the rest of the UK from 2001. The causes of death included in Figure 7.4 correspond to the following ICD10 codes: circulatory diseases I00–I99: cancer C00–D48: and respiratory diseases J00–J99. Rates for 2000 are for England and Wales only.

The data presented in Figure 7.4 cover three different revisions of the ICD. Although they have been selected according to codes that are

ICD 9		ICD 10	
Code 151	Stomach	C16	Stomach
Code 153	Colon	C18	Colon
Code 154	Rectum	C19–C20	Rectum
Code 153,154	Colorectal	C18–C21	Colorectal
Code 162	Lung	C33-C34	Lung
Code 174	Breast	C50	Breast
Code 179	Uterus	C54	Uterus
Code 183	Ovary	C56–C57	Ovary
Code 185	Prostate	C61	Prostate
Code 188	Bladder	C67	Bladder
C00–C97	excluding C44	All malignant cancers excluding non-melanoma skin cancer	

comparable, there may still be differences between years that are the result of changes in the rules used to select the underlying cause of death. This can be seen in deaths from respiratory diseases where different interpretation of these rules were used to code the underlying cause of death from 1983 to 1992, and from 2001 onwards in England and Wales, and 2000 onwards in Scotland.

The cancer trends data presented in Figure 7.15 and Table 7.16 correspond to the following two sets of cancer specific ICD9 and ICD10 codes. ICD9 codes correspond to the period up to 1994, ICD10 codes correspond to the period from 1995 when the coding for cancer incidence was changed.

Body mass index

The body mass index (BMI) shown in Figure 7.10, is the most widely used index of obesity among adults aged 16 and over. The BMI standardises weight for height and is calculated as weight (kg)/height (m)^2. Underweight is defined as a BMI of less than 18.5, desirable over 18.5 to less than 25, overweight 25 to less than 30 and obese 30 and over.

There is ongoing debate on the definition of overweight and obesity in children. For children, BMI changes substantially with age, rising steeply in infancy, falling during the pre-school years and then rising again into adulthood. For this reason, child BMI needs to be assessed against standards that make allowance for age. Because of differences in growth rates, it is not possible to apply a universal formula in calculating obesity and overweight in children. The 1990 UK national BMI percentile classification is therefore used, which gives a BMI threshold for each age above which a child is considered overweight or obese. Those children within the 85th to 95th percentile are classified as overweight and those above the 95th percentile are classified as obese, compared with 1990 BMI UK reference data. The percentiles are given for each sex and age. According to this method, 15 per cent of children had a BMI within the 85th to 95th percentile in 1990, and 5 per cent of children were above the 95th percentile, and were thus classified as overweight or obese respectively. Increases over 15 per cent and 5 per cent in the proportion of children who exceed the reference 85th and 95th percentiles, over time, indicate an upward trend in the prevalence of those overweight and obese.

Alcohol consumption

Estimates of alcohol consumption in surveys are given in standard units derived from assumptions about the alcohol content of different types of drink, combined with information from the respondent about the volume drunk. Following recent changes to the type of alcoholic drinks available, the alcohol content of drinks, and variable quantities, it became necessary to reconsider the assumptions made in obtaining estimates of alcohol consumption.

The changes in conversion factor are discussed in detail in a paper in the National Statistics Methodology series, which also includes a table giving the original and updated factors for converting alcohol volume to units. See Goddard E, Estimating alcohol consumption from survey data: updated method of converting volumes to units, National Statistics Methodology Series NSM 37 (Office for National Statistics 2007), also available at: **www.statistics.gov.uk/statbase/product. asp?vlnk=15067**

It was clear from the research undertaken that all surveys, including the General Household Survey (GHS) (Longitudinal), have been undercounting the number of units in some types of drink – predominantly wine, but also to a lesser degree beer, lager and cider. For example, using the latest method one-half pint of strong beer, larger or cider has 2 units, the number of units in a glass of wine depends on the size of glass and is counted as 2 units if the glass size is unspecified and bottle of alcopops has 1.5 units.

Household reference person

From April 2000 the General Household Survey (see Appendix, Part 2) adopted the term 'household reference person' in place of 'head of household'. As of April 2001 the Survey of English Housing (SEH) also adopted the term.

The household reference person (HRP) for both surveys is identified during the interview and is defined as the member of the household who:

- owns the household accommodation or

- is legally responsible for the rent of the accommodation or

- has the household accommodation as an emolument or perquisite or

- has the household accommodation by virtue of some relationship to the owner who is not a member of the household

The household reference person must always be a householder, whereas the head of household was always the husband for a couple household, who might not be a householder. If there are joint householders, the HRP will be the householder with the highest income. If two or more householders have exactly the same income the HRP is the eldest.

The definition of HRP used in survey data differs from that defined in the Reference persons box in Chapter 2: Households and families, which is based on economic activity and is used for vital statistics.

Alcohol-related causes of death

The Office for National Statistics (ONS) definition of alcohol-related deaths includes only those causes regarded as being most directly a result of alcohol consumption. Apart from deaths from accidental poisoning with alcohol, the definition excludes other external causes of deaths, such as road traffic deaths and other accidents.

For the years 1980–2000 the cause of death was defined using the International Classification of Diseases, Ninth Revision (ICD9) (see above). The codes used by ONS to define alcohol-related deaths are listed below:

291	Alcoholic psychoses
303	Alcohol dependence syndrome
305.0	Non-dependent abuse of alcohol
425.5	Alcoholic cardiomyopathy
571	Chronic liver disease and cirrhosis
E860	Accidental poisoning by alcohol

For the years 2001–03 the International Classification of Diseases, Tenth Revision (ICD10) was used. To maintain comparability with earlier years the following codes were used:

F10	Mental and behavioural disorders due to use of alcohol
I42.6	Alcoholic cardiomyopathy
K70	Alcoholic liver disease
K73	Chronic hepatitis, not elsewhere classified
K74	Fibrosis and cirrhosis of liver
X45	Accidental poisoning by and exposure to alcohol

Area deprivation

Alcohol–related deaths in England and Wales from 1999–2003 were allocated to the 2001 Census Standard Table ward of the deceased's usual residence. Each ward was then assigned a deprivation score using the Carstairs and Morris index. The Carstairs scores are an unweighted combination of four census variables:

- unemployment
- overcrowding where there is one or more persons per room as a proportion of all residents in the household

- car ownership and
- low social class where the economically active head of the household is in a partly skilled or unskilled occupation

Using the Carstairs scores, wards were ranked from least deprived to most deprived then divided into deprivation twentieths (5 per cent of the population) and fifths or quintiles (20 per cent of the population).

Further details can be found on the National Statistics website: www.statistics.gov.uk/ articles/ hsq/HSQ31deprivation_using_ carstairs.pdf

European standard population

The age distribution of the European standard population is presented in the table below.

Age	Population
Under 1	1,600
1–4	6,400
5–9	7,000
10–14	7,000
15–19	7,000
20–24	7,000
25–29	7,000
30–34	7,000
35–39	7,000
40–44	7,000
45–49	7,000
50–54	7,000
55–59	6,000
60–64	5,000
65–69	4,000
70–74	3,000
75–79	2,000
80–84	1,000
85 and over	1,000
Total	100,000

Relative survival rates

Relative cancer survival varies with age at diagnosis, and the age profile of cancer patients changes with time. In some circumstances it is not possible to estimate age standardised survival because there are too few patients in one or more age groups.

Overall (all ages) survival estimates are age standardised to improve their comparability over time using standard weights given in Chapter 3 of *Cancer Survival Trends in England and Wales 1971–1995 deprivation and NHS region*. It is published by The Stationary Office and is available at: www.lshtm.ac.uk/ncdeu/ cancersurvival/trends/ bookcdrominvestigators.htm.

ACORN

ACORN (A Classification of Residential Neighbourhoods) is a classification combining geographical and demographic characteristics to distinguish different types of people in different areas of Great Britain. ACORN classifies areas according to various census characteristics.

The ACORN classification has 5 categories, 17 groups and 56 types. The analysis in Figure 7.17 uses the five highest level categories. Further information on ACORN can be found at www.caci.co.uk/acorn/

Mental disorders

The data presented in Figure 7.17 were coded using the term 'mental disorder' as defined by the International Classification of Diseases Tenth Revision (ICD-10, see above) to imply a clinically recognisable set of symptoms or behaviours, associated in most cases with considerable distress and substantial interference with personal functions.

New HIV diagnoses database

The HIV and AIDS new diagnoses database at the Health Protection Agency Centre for Infections collects information on new HIV diagnoses, first AIDS diagnoses and deaths in HIV-infected individuals.

Numbers of new HIV diagnoses are presented by year of diagnoses. Numbers will include individuals who have an existing infection as well as those who have a newly acquired infection. Therefore, the number of new HIV diagnoses cannot be used to estimate incidence.

As reporting of new HIV diagnoses is voluntary a reporting delay needs to be considered. Data for a given year will increase substantially for a period of at least one year after the end of that calendar year. For example, 2007 data will substantially increase from the end of 2007 until the end of 2008 as more diagnoses are input onto the database. Taking this into consideration it is worth noting the archive date of the data presented. For example, data presented for 2006 from an end-June 2007 archive will be more complete than data taken from an end-December 2006 archive.

Part 8: Social protection

Expenditure on social protection benefits

Cash benefits
Income support: Periodic payments to people with insufficient resources. Conditions for entitlement may be related to personal resources and to nationality, residence, age, availability for work and family status. The benefit may be paid for a limited or an unlimited period. It may be paid to the individual or to the family, and be provided by central or local government.

Other cash benefits: Support for destitute or vulnerable people to help alleviate poverty or assist in difficult situations. These benefits may be paid by private non-profit organisations.

Benefits in kind
Accommodation: Shelter and board provided to destitute or vulnerable people, where these services cannot be classified under another function. This may be short term in reception centres, shelters and others, or on a more regular basis in special institutions, boarding houses, reception families, and others.

Rehabilitation of alcohol and drug abusers: Treatment of alcohol and drug dependency aimed at reconstructing the social life of the abusers, making them able to live an independent life. The treatment is usually provided in reception centres or special institutions.

Other benefits in kind: Basic services and goods to help vulnerable people, such as counselling, day shelter, help with carrying out daily tasks, food, clothing and fuel. Means-tested legal aid is also included.

General practitioners

General practitioner (GP) retainers are practitioners who provide service sessions in general practice. They are employed by GP partnerships to undertake sessions and are allowed to work a maximum of four sessions of approximately one-half a day each week. GP registrars are fully registered practitioners who are being trained for general practice under an arrangement approved by the Secretary of State for Health.

The Personal Medical Services (PMS) contract with GPs was introduced in 1998 as a local alternative to the national General Medical Services (GMS) contract. PMS contracts are locally negotiated contracts between the primary care trust (PCT) and the PMS provider enabling, for example, flexible provision of services in accordance with specific local circumstances.

In-patient activity

In Table 8.13 in-patient data for England are based on finished consultant episodes (FCEs). Data for Wales, Scotland and Northern Ireland are based on deaths and discharges and transfers between specialities (between hospitals in Northern Ireland).

An FCE is a completed period of care of a patient using a bed, under one consultant, in a particular National Health Service (NHS) Trust or directly managed unit. If a patient is transferred from one consultant to another within the same hospital, this counts as an FCE but not a hospital discharge. If a patient is transferred from one hospital to another provider, this counts as an FCE and a hospital discharge. Data for England, Wales and Northern Ireland exclude NHS beds and activity in joint-user and contractual hospitals. For Scotland, data for joint-user and contractual hospitals are included.

Pension schemes

A pension scheme is a plan offering benefits to members upon retirement. Schemes are provided by the state, employers and insurance firms, and are differentiated by a wide range of rules governing membership eligibility, contributions, benefits and taxation.

Occupational pension scheme: An arrangement (other than accident or permanent health insurance) organised by an employer (or on behalf of a group of employers) to provide benefits for employees on their retirement and for their dependants on their death.

Personal pension scheme: A scheme where the contract to provide contributions in return for retirement benefits is between an individual and an insurance firm, rather than between an individual and an employer or the state. Individuals may choose to join such schemes for example, to provide a primary source of retirement income for the self-employed, or to provide a secondary income to employees who are members of occupational schemes. These schemes may be facilitated (but not provided) by an employer.

Stakeholder pension scheme: Available since 2001, a flexible, portable, defined-contribution personal pension arrangement (provided by insurance companies with capped management charges) that must meet the conditions set out in the *Welfare Reform and Pensions Act 1999* and be registered with the Pensions Regulator. They can be taken out by an individual or facilitated by an employer. Where an employer of five or more staff offers no occupational pension and an employee earns more than the lower earnings limit (the entrance level for paying tax), the provision of access to a stakeholder scheme with contributions deducted from payroll is compulsory.

Benefit units

A benefit unit is a single adult or couple living as married and any dependent children, where the head is below state pension age (60 for women and 65 for men). A pensioner benefit unit is a single person over state pension age or a couple where one or both adults are over state pension age.

Registered childcare places

Registered places are the number of children who may attend the provision at any one time. Registered places are not the number of places occupied, nor the number of children who may benefit from receiving places through providers offering sessions at different times of the day. The number of registered places on the Office for Standards in Education, Children's Services and Skills (Ofsted) and Welsh Assembly Government (WAG) databases, is likely to be higher than the actual number of registered places, as not all providers will immediately inform Ofsted/Welsh Assembly Government that they have ceased their provision. For around 3 per cent of providers, the database does not hold the number of registered places. In these cases, the number of places has been estimated and included in the figures shown.

Registered providers are the number of settings offered by providers registered on the Ofsted/ WAG databases at the time data are published. As not all providers inform Ofsted/WAG when they have ceased provision, this number is likely to be higher than the actual number of providers.

Childminders: Childminders are registered to look after one or more children under the age of eight, to whom they are not related, on domestic premises, for reward, and for a total of more than two hours in any day.

Full day care: Facilities that provide day care for children under eight for a continuous period of four hours or more in any day in premises that are not domestic premises. Includes day nurseries and children's centres, and some family centres.

Out of school day care: Facilities that provide day care for children under eight, which operate during one or more of the following periods: before school, after school, during the school holidays. The total care provided is for more than two hours in any day and for more than five days a year. Open access schemes are included.

Sessional day care: Facilities that provide day care for children under eight for a session that is less than a continuous period of four hours in any day in premises that are not domestic premises. Where two sessions are offered in any one day, individual children must not attend more than five sessions in a week.

Crèche day care: Facilities that provide occasional care for children under eight and are provided on particular premises on more than five days a year. They need to be registered where they run for more than two hours a day, even when individual children attend for shorter periods.

All: Around 3,300 providers offer more than one type of day care, for example operating both full day care and sessional day care. This provision is included separately under each of the headings in Table 8.19 to reflect the total number of settings available for childcare.

Part 9: Crime and justice

Prevalence rates and incidence rates

Prevalence rates show the percentage of the British Crime Survey (BCS) sample who were victims of an offence once or more during the year. Unlike the BCS incidence rates, they only take account of whether a household or person was a victim of a specific crime once or more in the recall period, but not of the number of times victimised. Prevalence rates are taken as equivalent to 'risk'.

Incidence rates describe the number of crimes experienced per household or adult in the BCS or police recorded crime statistics.

Types of offences in England and Wales

The figures are compiled from police returns to the Home Office or directly from court computer systems.

In England and Wales, indictable offences cover those offences that can only be tried at the Crown Court and include the more serious offences.

Summary offences are those for which a defendant would normally be tried at a magistrates' court and are generally less serious – the majority of motoring offences fall into this category. Triable-either-way offences are triable either on indictment or summarily.

Recorded crime statistics broadly cover the more serious offences. Up to March 1998 most indictable and triable-either-way offences were included, as well as some summary ones; from April 1998, all indictable and triable-either-way offences were included, plus a few closely related summary ones.

Recorded offences are the most readily available measures of the incidence of crime, but do not necessarily indicate the true level of crime. Many less serious offences are not reported to the police and cannot, therefore, be recorded. Moreover, the propensity of the public to report offences to the police is influenced by a number of factors and may change over time.

From 2000, some police forces have changed their systems to record the allegations of victims unless there is credible evidence that a crime has not taken place. In April 2002, the National Crime Recording Standard (NCRS, see below) formalised these changes across England and Wales.

There have been changes to the methodology of the British Crime Survey (BCS). Between 1982 and 2001 the survey was carried out every two years, and reported on victimisation in the previous calendar year. From 2001/02 onwards the surveys cover the financial year of interviews and report on victimisation in the 12 months before interview, on an annual basis.

This change makes the BCS estimates more comparable with figures collected by the police. Because of the significant changes taking place in both these measures of crime, direct comparisons with figures for previous years cannot be made.

Types of offences in Northern Ireland

In recording crime, the Police Service of Northern Ireland broadly follows the Home Office rules for counting crime. As from 1 April 1998 notifiable offences are recorded on the same basis as those in England and Wales. Before the revision of the rules, criminal damage offences in Northern Ireland excluded those where the value of the property damaged was less than £200.

See 'Availability and comparability of data from constituent countries' entry below for information on the differences in the legal system in Scotland compared with England and Wales and Northern Ireland.

National Crime Recording Standard

Changes in the counting rules for recorded crime on 1 April 1998 affected both the methods of counting and the coverage for recorded crime and had the effect of inflating the number of crimes recorded. For some offence groups – more serious violence against the person and burglary – there was little effect on the number recorded. However, the changes have had more effect on figures for minor violence and criminal damage.

In April 2002 the National Crime Recording Standard (NCRS) was introduced in England and Wales with the aim of taking a more victim-centred approach and providing more consistency between forces. Before 2002, police forces in England and Wales did not necessarily record a crime that was reported if there was no evidence to support the claim of the victim. Therefore crimes recorded from 1 April 2002 are not comparable with earlier years.

It is not possible to assess the effect of NCRS on recorded firearm crimes. NCRS inflated the overall number of violence against the person and criminal damage offences, but has less effect on the number of robberies, Many firearm offences are among the less serious categories,

and these types of offences are among those most affected by NCRS.

The introduction of the NCRS may have had an effect on the recorded crime detection rate, but this is difficult to quantify.

Scottish Crime Recording Standard
In April 2004, the Association of Chief Police Officers in Scotland (ACPOS) implemented the Scottish Crime Recording Standard (SCRS) following recommendations from Her Majesty's Inspectorate of Constabulary (HMIC), which means that no corroborative evidence is required initially to record a crime-related incident as a crime if so perceived by the victim. In consequence of this more victim-oriented approach, the HMIC expected the SCRS to increase the numbers of minor crimes recorded by the police, such as minor crimes of vandalism and minor thefts. However, the HMIC also expected that the SCRS would not have much impact on the figures for the more serious crimes, such as serious assault, sexual assault, robbery or housebreaking.

Unfortunately it was not possible to estimate the exact impact of SCRS on the recorded crime figures. Around the time that the standard was implemented police also introduced centralised call centres, which encouraged the reporting of incidents to the police. The Scottish Government had hoped that the underlying trends in crime would be monitored through a new, much larger, Scottish Crime and Victimisation Survey (SCVS), but this has not proved possible.

Availability and comparability of data from constituent countries

There are a number of reasons why recorded crime statistics in England and Wales, Northern Ireland and Scotland cannot be directly compared:

Different legal systems: The legal system operating in Scotland differs from that in England and Wales, and Northern Ireland. For example, in Scotland children aged under 16 accused of offending are normally dealt with by the Children's Hearings system rather than the courts.

Differences in classification: There are significant differences in the offences included within the recorded crime categories used in Scotland and the categories of notifiable offences used in England, Wales and Northern Ireland. Scottish figures are divided into 'offences' (less serious criminal acts) and 'crimes' (the more serious criminal acts). The seriousness of an act is *generally* based on the maximum sentence that can be imposed. Scottish figures of 'crime' have therefore been grouped in an attempt to approximate to the classification of notifiable offences in England, Wales and Northern Ireland.

Counting rules: In all parts of the UK, only the main offence occurring within an incident is counted.

Burglary: This term is not applicable to Scotland where the term used is 'housebreaking' and includes domestic as well as commercial premises.

Theft from vehicles: In Scotland data have only been separately identified from January 1992.

The figures include theft by opening lock-fast places from a motor vehicle and other theft from a motor vehicle.

Comparable crimes

Comparable crimes are a set of offences that are covered by both the British Crime Survey (BCS) and police recorded crime. Various adjustments are made to the recorded crime categories to maximise comparability with the BCS. Comparable crime is used to compare trends in police and BCS figures, and to identify the amount of crime that is not reported to the police and not recorded by them. The comparable subset includes common assaults (and assaults on a constable), and vehicle interference and tampering. More than three-quarters (79 per cent) of BCS offences reported through interviews in the 2006/07 interview sample fall into categories that can be compared with crimes recorded under the new police coverage of offences adopted from 1 April 1998. With the introduction of new police counting rules in 1998/99, the 'old' comparable subset that was used, up to and including the 1998 BCS, was updated as it excluded common assaults, other household theft and other theft of personal property.

Violent crime

Violent crime as measured by the British Crime Survey (BCS) is classified according to the relationship between the victim and the offender, and includes domestic violence, mugging, violence committed by strangers and acquaintance violence. Domestic violence includes all violent incidents (except muggings) that involve partners, ex-partners or other relatives. Mugging includes robbery, attempted robbery and snatch theft. Violence committed by strangers includes common assaults and woundings in which the victim did not know any of the offenders in any way. Acquaintance violence includes common assaults and woundings in which the victim knew one or more of the offenders, at least by sight.

Intimate violence

Intimate violence includes domestic violence, sexual assault and stalking and is categorised by the relationship of the victim to the offender and by the type of offence. See below for categories:

Partner abuse (non-sexual): non-sexual emotional or financial abuse, threats or physical force by a current or former partner.

Family abuse (non-sexual): non-sexual emotional or financial abuse, threats or physical force by a family member other than a partner (father/mother, step-father/ mother or other relative).

Sexual assault: indecent exposure, sexual threats and unwanted touching ('less serious'), rape or assault by penetration including attempts ('serious'), by any person including a partner or family member.

Stalking: two or more incidents – causing distress, fear or alarm – of obscene/threatening unwanted letters or phone calls, waiting or loitering around home or workplace, following or watching, or interfering with or damaging personal property by any person including a partner or family member.

Indices of Deprivation 2004

Local area deprivation is measured in this report using the Indices of Deprivation 2004 (England). There are seven domains of deprivation:

- income
- employment
- health and disability
- education, skills and training
- barriers to housing and services
- living environment and
- crime

There are a number of indicators of deprivation in each of these domains, such as level of unemployment and incapacity benefit claimants, which are combined into a single deprivation score for each local area on that domain. In order to examine how deprivation varies across the country the local areas are ranked according to their scores on a domain and divided into ten equally sized groups, called deciles: those areas in the first decile are the most deprived areas on the domain of interest, those in the tenth decile are the least deprived. Table 9.7 presents data divided into five equally sized groups (quintiles) ranging from the least deprived 20 per cent of areas to the most deprived 20 per cent of areas.

An Index of Multiple Deprivation is also available which combines all seven separate domains (see above) into one index; this has not been used here to examine the risk of being a victim of crime by the level of deprivation as it includes the crime domain; deprived areas using this index are, by definition, those areas that have higher levels of crime.

Different indices exist for Wales, Scotland and Northern Ireland. Further information can be found here: www.neighbourhood.statistics. gov.uk/dissemination/Info.do?page=about neighbourhood/indicesofdeprivation/ indices-of-deprivation.htm

Anti-social behaviour indicators

The British Crime Survey (BCS) measures 'high' levels of perceived anti-social behaviour from responses to seven individual anti-social behaviour strands:

- noisy neighbours or loud parties
- teenagers hanging around on the streets
- rubbish or litter lying around
- vandalism, graffiti and other deliberate damage to property
- people using or dealing drugs
- people being drunk or rowdy in public places
- abandoned or burnt-out cars

Perceptions of anti-social behaviour are measured using a scale based on answers to the seven questions as follows:

- 'very big problem' = 3

- 'fairly big problem' = 2
- 'not a very big problem' = 1 and
- 'not a problem at all' = 0

The maximum score for the seven questions is 21. Respondents with 'high' levels of perceived anti-social behaviour are those who score 11 or more on this scale.

Sentences and orders

The following are the main sentences and orders that can be imposed upon people found guilty. Some types of sentence or order can only be given to offenders in England and Wales in certain age groups. Under the framework for sentencing contained in the *Criminal Justice Acts 1991, 1993* and the *Powers of Criminal Courts (Sentencing) Act 2000* the sentence must reflect the seriousness of the offence. The following sentences are available for adults aged 18 and over (a similar range of sentences is available to juveniles aged 10 to 17):

Absolute and conditional discharge: A court may make an order discharging a person absolutely or (except in Scotland) conditionally where it is inexpedient to inflict punishment and, before 1 October 1992, where a probation order was not appropriate. An order for conditional discharge runs for a period of not more than three years as the court specifies, the condition being that the offender does not commit another offence within the period so specified. In Scotland a court may also discharge a person with an admonition.

Community sentences
The term '*community sentence*' refers to attendance centre orders, reparation orders, action plan orders, drug treatment and testing orders, community orders, community rehabilitation orders, community punishment orders, community punishment and rehabilitation orders, supervision orders, curfew orders and referral orders. Under the *Criminal Justice and Courts Services Act 2000*, certain community orders current at 1 April 2001 were renamed. Probation orders were renamed community rehabilitation orders, community service orders were renamed community punishment orders and combination orders were renamed community punishment and rehabilitation orders.

Attendance centre order: Available in England, Wales and Northern Ireland for young offenders and involves deprivation of free time.

Reparation order: Introduced under the *Powers of Criminal Courts (Sentencing) Act 2000*. This requires the offender to make an apology to the victim or to apologise in person. Maximum duration of the order is 24 hours and is only available to juveniles aged 10 to 18 in England and Wales.

Action plan order: An order imposed for a maximum of three months in England, Wales and Northern Ireland to address certain behavioural problems. This is again available for the younger age groups and is considered as early intervention to stop serious offending.

Drug treatment and testing order: This is imposed as a treatment order to reduce the person's dependence on drugs and to test if the

offender is complying with treatment. The length of order can run from six months to three years in England, Wales and Northern Ireland. This was introduced under the *Powers of Criminal Courts (Sentencing) Act 2000* for persons aged 16 and over. In Scotland, drug treatment and testing orders were introduced in phases on a court by court basis from 1999 onwards. They are now available in almost every Sheriff and High Court in Scotland.

Court orders: The term court orders used in the text includes all the above 'orders'. It does not include any pre or post release supervision.

Community sentences: This term refers to all court orders except for suspended sentence orders and deferred sentences, which may have a custodial component to the sentence.

Community order: For offences committed on or after 4th April 2005 the new community order, introduced under the *Criminal Justice Act 2003* (CJA03), replaced all existing community sentences for adults. Under this order, one or more of 12 possible requirements must be added, such as supervision, unpaid work and drug treatment. The Act also introduced a new suspended sentence order for offences that pass the custody threshold. One or more of the same set of 12 possible requirements must be added to this order. Unless considered dangerous, those sentenced to 12 months or more in custody, who will be released on licence at the halfway point of the sentence, will remain on licence, and subject to recall if they breach the conditions of their licence, for the entire remaining period of their sentence, instead of to the three-quarter point.

Community rehabilitation order: An offender sentenced to a community rehabilitation order is under the supervision of a probation officer (social worker in Scotland) whose duty it is to (in England and Wales and Northern Ireland) to advise, assist and befriend him or her, but the court has the power to include any other requirement it considers appropriate. A cardinal feature of the order is that it relies on the co-operation of the offender. Community rehabilitation orders may be given for any period between six months and three years inclusive.

Punishment order: An offender who is convicted of an offence punishable with imprisonment may be sentenced to perform unpaid work for not more than 240 hours (300 hours in Scotland), and not less than 40 hours. Twenty hours minimum community service are given for persistent petty offending or fine default. In Scotland the *Law Reform (Miscellaneous Provisions) (Scotland) Act 1990* requires that community service can only be ordered where the court would otherwise have imposed imprisonment or detention. Probation and community service may be combined in a single order in Scotland. Community punishment orders came into effect under the *Powers of Criminal Courts (Sentencing) Act 2000* when they replaced supervision orders.

Community punishment and rehabilitation order: The *Criminal Justice Act 1991* introduced the combination order in England and Wales only, which combines elements of both probation supervision and community service. Meanwhile, Article 15 of the Criminal Justice

(NI) Order 1996 introduced the combination order to Northern Ireland. The *Powers of Criminal Courts (Sentencing) Act 2000* brought into effect the community punishment and rehabilitation order, known as the combination order, which requires an offender to be under a probation officer and to take on unpaid work.

Detention and imprisonment
Detention and training order: This was introduced for juveniles aged 10 to 18 under the *Powers of Criminal Courts (Sentencing) Act 2000*. It is for juveniles who have committed a serious crime. They can serve the sentence at a young offender institution or at a local authority establishment, or local authority secure training centre. The sentence given is from 4 to 24 months, but sentences can run consecutively.

Imprisonment: Is the custodial sentence for adult offenders. Home Office or Scottish Executive consent is needed for release or transfer. In the case of mentally disordered offenders, hospital orders, which may include a restriction order, may be considered appropriate.

A new disposal, the 'hospital direction', was introduced in 1997. The court, when imposing a period of imprisonment, can direct that the offender be sent directly to hospital. On recovering from the mental disorder, the offender is returned to prison to serve the balance of their sentence.

The *Criminal Justice Act 1991* abolished remission and substantially changed the parole scheme in England and Wales. Those serving sentences of under four years, imposed on or after 1 October 1992, are subject to automatic conditional release and are released, subject to certain criteria, halfway through their sentence. Home detention curfews result in selected prisoners being released up to two months early with a tag that monitors their presence during curfew hours. Those serving sentences of four years or longer are considered for discretionary conditional release after having served half their sentence, but are automatically released at the two-thirds point of sentence.

The *Crime (Sentences) Act 1997*, implemented on 1 October 1997, included, for persons aged 18 or over, an automatic life sentence for a second serious violent or sexual offence unless there are exceptional circumstances. All offenders serving a sentence of 12 months or more are supervised in the community until the three-quarters point of sentence. A life sentence prisoner may be released on licence subject to supervision and is always liable to recall.

In Scotland the *Prisoners and Criminal Proceedings (Scotland) Act 1993* changed the system of remission and parole for prisoners sentenced on or after 1 October 1993. Those serving sentences of less than four years are released unconditionally after having served half of their sentence, unless the court specifically imposes a supervised release order that subjects them to social work supervision after release. Those serving sentences of four years or more are eligible for parole at half sentence. If parole is not granted then they will automatically be released on licence at the two-thirds point of sentence subject to days added for breaches of prison rules. All such prisoners are liable to be

'recalled on conviction' or for breach of conditions of licence, if between the date of release and the date on which the full sentence ends he/she commits another offence that is punishable by imprisonment, or breaches his/her licence conditions, then the offender may be returned to prison for the remainder of that sentence whether or not a sentence of imprisonment is also imposed for the new offence.

Management of Offenders, etc (Scotland) Act 2005 introduced home detention curfew in Scotland. From the 3 July 2006, certain prisoners serving less than four years and assessed as presenting a low risk of re-offending, can be released on licence between two weeks and four months early. They are subject to electronically monitored restrictions on their movements for up to 12 hours per day for the remainder of their sentence.

Custody probation order: An order unique to Northern Ireland reflecting the different regime there that applies in respect of remission and the general absence of release on licence. The custodial sentence is followed by a period of supervision for a period of between one and three years.

Fully suspended sentences: These may only be passed in exceptional circumstances. In England, Wales and Northern Ireland, sentences of imprisonment of two years or less may be fully suspended. A court should not pass a suspended sentence unless a sentence of imprisonment would be appropriate in the absence of a power to suspend. The result of suspending a sentence is that it will not take effect unless during the period specified the offender is convicted of another offence punishable with imprisonment. Suspended sentences are not available in Scotland.

Fines
The *Criminal Justice Act 1993* introduced new arrangements on 20 September 1993 whereby courts are required to fit an amount for the fine that reflects the seriousness of the offence and that takes account of an offender's means. This system replaced the more formal unit fines scheme included in the *Criminal Justice Act 1991*. The Act also introduced the power for courts to arrange deduction of fines from income benefit for those offenders receiving such benefits. The *Law Reform (Miscellaneous Provision) (Scotland) Act 1990* as amended by the *Criminal Procedure (Scotland) Act 1995* provides for the use of supervised attendance orders by selected courts in Scotland. The *Criminal Procedure (Scotland) Act 1995* also makes it easier for courts to impose a supervised attendance order in the event of a default and enables the court to impose a supervised attendance order in the first instance for 16 and 17-year-olds.

Prison population

Population in custody includes those held in prison or police cells. They include prisoners on remand (both untried and those who have been convicted but remain unsentenced), prisoners under sentence and non-criminal prisoners (for example those held under the *1971 Immigration Act*). They also include those held in police cells.

Imprisonment (or Detention) for Public Protection (IPP)

The new indeterminate sentence of imprisonment (or detention) for public protection came into effect on 4 April 2005 and applies to offenders who are convicted of a serious offence (that is a specified sexual or violent offence carrying a maximum penalty of ten years' imprisonment or more) and who are considered by the court to pose a 'significant risk to members of the public, of serious harm'.

Re-offenders

The measurement of re-offending has undergone a change from the previous publication, owing to the availability of a more comprehensive data source. In previous years, the measurement of re-offending was restricted to the measurement of reconviction, that is where an offender both committed an offence and was convicted in court within two years. This has been a useful measure, but changes in the speed of securing convictions can result in artificial changes to the reconviction rates. The availability of a more comprehensive database allows the measurement of re-offending within two years that then leads to conviction regardless of the two-year period. That is, offenders who re-offended within two years can now be counted, even if their conviction is secured beyond the two-year period. In so doing, the distorting effect of the speeding up or slowing down of securing convictions through the criminal justice system is removed. Figures in the chapter include offenders aged 18 and over on the day of release from prison or from starting community sentence who re-offended within a two-year period and were subsequently convicted in court.

Police

Police Community Support Officers (PCSOs) are paid officers who have different roles in different forces. The main responsibilities of a PCSO are to patrol a beat and interact with the public and offer assistance to police officers at crime scenes and major events. They provide a visible and reassuring presence on the streets and have a role in tackling the menace of anti-social behaviour.

The Special Constabulary is a force of trained volunteers who work with and support their local police. Once trained they have the same powers as regular officers and provide a link between the regular police and the local community.

Each partnership has a designated officer (DO) who oversees the information-sharing process. Designated officers are responsible for data protection (subject access) issues, ensuring the confidentiality and security of information at all stages, ensuring compliance with legislation, auditing and monitoring exchanges and dealing with complaints

Courts system in England and Wales

The courts system consists of civil courts (including the High Court and county courts, see below), the magistrates' courts and Crown courts, each of which preside over different types of crimes and complaints.

Civil courts

The main civil courts are the High Court and the county courts. The High Court is divided into three divisions:

- the Queen's Bench Division deals with disputes relating to contracts, general commercial matters and breaches of duty – known as 'liability in tort' – covering claims of negligence, nuisance or defamation

- the Chancery Division deals with disputes relating to land, wills, companies and insolvency

- the Family Division deals with matrimonial matters, including divorce, and the welfare of children

Magistrates' courts also have some civil jurisdiction, mainly in family proceedings. Most appeals in civil cases go to the Court of Appeal (Civil Division) and may go from there to the House of Lords. Since July 1991, county courts have been able to deal with all contract and tort cases and actions for recovery of land, regardless of value. Cases are presided over by a judge who almost always sits without a jury. Jury trials are limited to specified cases, for example, actions for libel.

Magistrates' courts
Virtually all criminal cases start in a magistrates' court and more than 95 per cent of cases are also completed here. In addition, magistrates' courts deal with many civil cases, mostly family matters plus liquor licensing and betting and gaming work. Cases in the magistrates' courts are usually heard by panels of three magistrates (Justices of the Peace). The youth court is a specialised form of magistrates' court where almost all 10 to 17-year-olds will have their case dealt with. As in the magistrates' court, the case will be heard by magistrates or by a district judge (magistrates' courts).

Crown Court

The Crown Court deals with more serious criminal cases transferred from the magistrates' court such as murder, rape and robbery. It also hears appeals against decisions made in the magistrates' courts and deals with cases sent from magistrates' courts for sentence.

Part 10: Housing

Housebuilding completions

Housebuilding statistics cover building of all permanent dwellings, including houses, bungalows and flats. In principle a dwelling is regarded as completed when it becomes ready for occupation, whether it is occupied or not. In practice there are instances where the timing could be delayed and some completions are missed, for example, because no completion certificates were requested by the owner.

Tenure definition for housebuilding is only slightly different from that used for dwelling stock figures (see below). For further information on the methodology used to calculate stock by tenure and tenure definitions, see Appendix B Notes and Definitions in the Communities and Local Government annual volume *Housing Statistics* or the housing statistics page of the

Communities and Local Government website, at **www.communities.gov.uk**.

Public and private sectors

All local authority dwellings are public sector dwellings.

'Social sector' housing includes all local authority (or public) housing as well as registered social landlord (RSL) and housing association (HA) housing. For housing data, RSLs/HAs are generally separated out to identify the extent of social housing.

Where the term 'private sector' is used in housing policy and housing statistics, it generally means the 'private housing' sector or non-social housing sector, that is owner-occupied dwellings and those rented privately, including those that go with a job or business and not those owned by RSLs/HAs.

For housebuilding starts and completions data, especially the former, there is a small possibility that some dwellings built for RSLs/HAs could have been counted as 'private enterprise' and vice versa. This is because sometimes the builders themselves are not sure of the precise ownership or the ownership may keep evolving and it is not final until it is sold.

Dwelling stock

The definition of a dwelling follows the census definition applicable at that time. Currently the 2001 Census is used, which defines a dwelling as 'structurally separate accommodation'. This was determined primarily by considering the type of accommodation, as well as separate and shared access to multi-occupied properties.

In all stock figures vacant dwellings are included but non-permanent dwellings are generally excluded. For housebuilding statistics, only data on permanent dwellings are collected.

Estimates of the total dwelling stock, stock changes and the tenure distribution in the UK are made by Communities and Local Government for England, the Scottish Government, the Welsh Assembly Government, and the Northern Ireland Department for Social Development. These are primarily based on census output data for the number of dwellings (or households converted to dwellings) from the censuses of population for the UK. Adjustments are carried out if there are specific reasons to do so. Census year figures are based on outputs from the censuses. For years between censuses, the total figures are obtained by projecting the base census year's figure forward annually. The increment is based on the annual total number of completions plus the annual total net gain from other housing statistics, that is, conversions, demolitions and changes of use.

Estimates of dwelling stock by tenure category are based on other sources where it is considered that for some specific tenure information, these are more accurate than census output data. In this situation it is assumed that the other data sources also contain vacant dwellings, but it is not certain and it is not expected that these data are very precise. Thus the allocation of vacant dwellings to tenure categories may not be completely accurate and the margin of error for tenure categories is wider than for estimates of total stock.

For local authority stock, figures supplied by local authorities are more reliable than those in the 2001 Census. Similarly, it was found that the Housing Corporation's own data are more accurate than census output data for the registered social landlord (RSL) stock. Hence only the privately rented or with a job or business tenure data were taken directly from the census. The owner-occupied data were taken as the residual of the total from the census. For non-census years, the same approach was adopted except for the privately rented or with a job or business, for which Labour Force Survey (see Appendix, Part 4: Labour Force Survey) results were used.

In the Survey of English Housing, data for privately rented unfurnished accommodation include accommodation that is partly furnished.

For further information on the methodology used to calculate stock by tenure and tenure definitions for the UK, see Appendix B Notes and Definitions in the Communities and Local Government annual volume *Housing Statistics* or the housing statistics page of the Communities and Local Government website at: **www.communities.gov.uk**

Housing green paper

The housing green paper, *Homes for the future: more affordable, more sustainable*, published in July 2007, set out a 13-year programme of action to supply 2 million homes by 2016 and 3 million by 2020. These homes are net additional to the stock and include new build, converted properties and change of use. The paper also announced plans to build eco-towns, small new towns intended to exploit the potential to create complete new settlements to achieve zero carbon development and more sustainable living, and further growth points in addition to the existing growth points and growth areas.

The green paper builds upon previous housing programmes, notably the Sustainable Communities Plan, *Sustainable Communities: Building for the Future*, which identified four major growth areas – Thames Gateway; Milton Keynes and the South Midlands; London Stansted, Cambridge and Peterborough; and Ashford.

Tenure

There are up to four tenure categories for dwelling stock and household figures. These are:

- owner-occupied (or private enterprise in the case of housebuilding statistics, that is dwellings built for owner occupiers or for private landlords, whether persons or companies). This includes accommodation that is owned outright or bought with a mortgage

- rented privately (defined as all non-owner-occupied property other than that rented from local authorities and registered social landlords (RSLs), plus that rented from private or public bodies by virtue of employment. This includes property occupied rent-free by someone other than the owner),

- rented from RSLs, but for stock figures non-registered Housing Associations are excluded and subsumed within owner-occupied

rented from local authorities. In Scotland dwellings rented from local authorities include those rented from Scottish Homes, formerly the Scottish Special Housing Association

See Public and private sectors (above) for further definition of the sectors.

Sales and transfers of local authority dwellings

Right to buy was established by the *Housing Act 1980* and was introduced across Great Britain in October 1980. In England large scale voluntary transfers (LSVTs) of stock have been principally to housing associations/registered social landlords (RSLs). Figures include transfers supported by estate renewal challenge funding (ERCF). The figures for 1993 include 949 dwellings transferred under Tenants' Choice. In Scotland LSVTs to RSLs and the small number of transfers to housing associations are included.

Homeless at home

Homeless at home refers to any arrangement where a household for whom a duty has been accepted by the local authority (eligible for assistance, unintentionally homeless and in priority need) is able to remain in, or return to the accommodation from which they are being made homeless, or temporarily stay in other accommodation found by the household. Such schemes may locally be referred to as: Direct Rehousing; Prevention of Homelessness; Concealed Household Schemes; Prevention of Imminent Homelessness Schemes; Impending Homeless Schemes; and Pre-eviction Schemes.

Decent home standard

Government targets set for 2010 are to bring all social housing in England into a decent condition and to increase the proportion of vulnerable households in private sector housing living in homes that are in decent condition. Vulnerable households are those in receipt of means tested or disability related benefits.

A decent home is one that:

- meets the current statutory minimum for housing (the 'fitness standard' for the reporting period of the data presented in Table 10.10)

- is in a reasonable state of repair

- has reasonably modern facilities and services and

- provides a reasonable degree of thermal comfort, that is it has efficient heating and effective insulation

Poor quality environments

The identification of poor quality environments is based on surveyors' observed assessments of the severity of problems in the immediate environment of the home. The problems assessed fall into three groups:

- the upkeep, management or misuse of private and public buildings and space (scruffy or neglected buildings; poor condition housing; graffiti; scruffy gardens or landscaping; litter; rubbish or dumping; vandalism; dog or other excrement; nuisance from street parking)

- road traffic or other transport (presence of intrusive motorways and main roads; railway or aircraft noise; heavy traffic; ambient air quality)

- abandonment or non-residential use (vacant sites; vacant or boarded up buildings; intrusive industry; nonconforming use of domestic premises such as running car repair, scrap yard or haulage business)

A home is regarded as having a poor quality environment of a given type if it is assessed to have 'significant' or 'major' problems in respect of any of the specific environmental problems assessed and grouped under that type. The overall assessment of households with poor quality environments is based on whether the home has any of the three types of problems.

Standard Assessment Procedure

The Standard Assessment Procedure (SAP) is an index based on calculated annual space and water heating costs for a standard heating regime for a home and is expressed on a scale of 1 (highly energy inefficient) to 100 (highly energy efficient with 100 representing zero energy cost).

The detailed methodology for calculating the SAP to monitor the energy efficiency was comprehensively updated in 2005 to reflect developments in the energy efficiency technologies and knowledge of dwelling performance. The rating scale was revised to run between 1 and 100 under the 2005 methodology. Under the 2001 methodology the scale ran between 1 and 120. Therefore, a SAP rating under the 2001 methodology is not comparable with the one calculated under the 2005 methodology.

Energy inefficient homes are those assessed with a SAP rating of 30 or below.

Property transactions

The figures are based on the number of particular delivered (PD) forms processed and stamp duty land tax certificates issued. They relate to the transfer or sale of any freehold interest in land or property, or the grant or transfer of a lease of at least 21 years and 1 day. In practice there is an average lag of about one month between the transaction and the date when the PD form is processed.

Mix adjusted prices

Information on dwelling prices at national and regional levels are collected and published by Communities and Local Government on a monthly basis. Until August 2005 data came from a sample survey of mortgage completions, the Survey of Mortgage Lenders (SML). The SML covered around 50 banks and building societies that are members of the Council of Mortgage Lenders (CML). From September 2005 data come from the Regulated Mortgage Survey (RMS), which is conducted by BankSearch and the CML.

Data before the first quarter of 2002 were derived from a 5 per cent sample of completions data and were calculated on an old mix adjusted methodology. As a consequence of a significantly increased sample (to an average 25,000 cases per month), Communities and Local Government introduced a monthly series

in 2003 and also provided this data back to February 2002. The mix adjusted methodology was enhanced. The RMS collects 100 per cent of completions data from those mortgage lenders who take part (and as a result the sample size increased to around 50,000 from September 2005). Annual figures have been derived as an average of the monthly prices. The annual change in price is shown as the average percentage change over the year and is calculated from the house price index.

A simple average price will be influenced by changes in the mix of properties bought in each period. This effect is removed by applying fixed weights to the process at the start of each year, based on the average mix of properties purchased during the previous three years, and these weights are applied to prices during the year.

The mix adjusted average price excludes sitting tenant (right to buy) purchases, cash purchases, remortgages and further loans.

Part 11: Environment

Global warming and climate change

Emissions estimates for the UK are updated annually to reflect revisions in methodology and the availability of new information. These adjustments are applied retrospectively to earlier years and hence there are differences from the data published in previous editions of *Social Trends*.

In Figure 11.5, the Kyoto reduction targets cover a basket of six gases: carbon dioxide (CO_2), methane (CH_4), nitrous oxide (N_2O), hydrofluorocarbons (HFCs), perfluorocarbons (PFCs) and sulphur hexafluoride (SF_6). For the latter three gases signatories to the Protocol may choose to use 1995, rather than 1990, as the base year from which to calculate targets, since data for 1995 for these gases tend to be more widely available and more reliable than for 1990. The UK announced in its Climate Change Programme that it would use 1995 as the base year for the fluorinated gases – therefore the 'base year' emissions for the UK target differ slightly from UK emissions in 1990.

Emissions of the six greenhouse gases are presented based on their relative contribution to global warming. Limited allowance is given in the Protocol for the absorption of CO_2 by forests, which act as so-called carbon sinks.

Fuels for energy use

Energy use of fuel mainly comprises use for lighting, heating or cooling, motive power and power for appliances. Non-energy uses of fuel include chemical feedstock, solvents, lubricants, and road-making material.

Coal includes other solid fuels. Petroleum excludes marine bunkers. Natural gas includes colliery methane and non-energy use of natural gas up to 1998. Primary electricity includes nuclear, hydroelectric wind, wave and solar and imports of electricity via interconnectors net of exports.

Air pollutants

Volatile organic compounds (VOCs) comprise a wide range of chemical compounds including hydrocarbons, oxygenates and halogen-containing species. Methane (CH$_4$) is an important component of VOCs but its environmental impact derives principally from its contribution to global warming, see above.

Measuring air pollution

Volatile organic compounds (VOCs) are ozone precursors and comprise a wide range of chemical compounds including hydrocarbons, oxygenates and halogen containing species. Methane (CH$_4$) is an important component of VOCs but its environmental impact derives principally from its contribution to global warming. The major environmental impact of non-methane VOCs lies in their involvement in the formation of ground level ozone. Most VOCs are non-toxic or are present at levels well below guideline values. Others, such as benzene and 1, 3-butadiene, are of concern because of their potential impact on human health.

PM$_{10}$ is airborne particulate matter. Specifically, it is that fraction of 'black smoke' that is thought most likely to be deposited in the lungs. It can be defined as the fraction resulting from a collection from black smoke by a size selective sampler that collects smaller particles preferentially, capturing 50 per cent of 10 micron aerodynamic diameter particles, more than 95 per cent of 5 micron particles, and less than 5 per cent of 20 micron particles.

Water pollution incidents

Data shown in Figure 11.13 relate to substantiated reports of pollution and correspond to categories 1 and 2 in the Environment Agency's pollution incidents classification scheme for England and Wales. For Scotland the term 'significant incidents' is used and compares broadly with all of category 1 and most of category 2 used by the Environment Agency. In Northern Ireland the terms 'high severity' and 'medium severity' are used; these compare broadly with all of categories 1 and 2 used by the Environment Agency.

The Environment Agency defines four categories of pollution incidents.

Category 1: The most severe incidents, which involve one or more of the following:

- potential or actual persistent effect on water quality or aquatic life

- closure of potable water, industrial or agricultural abstraction necessary

- major damage to aquatic ecosystems

- major damage to agriculture and/or commerce

- serious impact on man, or

- major effect on amenity value

Category 2: Severe incidents, which involve one or more of the following:

- notification to abstractors necessary

- significant damage to aquatic ecosystems

- significant effect on water quality

- damage to agriculture and/or commerce

- impact on man, or

- impact on amenity value to public, owners or users

Category 3: Minor incidents, involving one or more of the following:

- a minimal effect on water quality

- minor damage to aquatic ecosystems

- amenity value only marginally affected, or

- minimal impact on agriculture and/or commerce

Category 4: Incidents where no impact on the environment occurred.

Bathing waters

Directive 76/160/EEC concerning the quality of bathing waters sets the following mandatory standards for the coliform parameters:

1. for total coliforms, 10,000 per 100 millilitres; and

2. for faecal coliforms 2,000 per 100 millilitres.

The directive requires that at least 95 per cent of samples taken for each of these parameters over the bathing season must meet the mandatory values. In practice this has been interpreted in the following manner: where 20 samples are taken only one sample for each parameter may exceed the mandatory values for the water to pass the coliform standards; where less than 20 samples are taken none may exceed the mandatory values for the water to pass the coliform standards.

The Bathing Water Directive also sets more stringent guideline microbiological standards. To comply with the guideline standards, bathing waters must not exceed values of 500 total coliforms per 100 ml and 100 faecal coliforms per 100 ml in 80 per cent of water quality samples, and 100 faecal streptococci per 100 ml in 90 per cent of samples taken.

Coliforms are microorganisms found in the intestinal tract of animals and human beings. When found in water it indicates fecal pollution and potentially hazardous bacterial contamination. Faecal streptococci are also natural inhabitants of the gut of humans and other warm-blooded animals. However, as they have a greater ability to survive outside of the gut, they could be used as an indicator of less recent contamination by sewage.

The bathing season is from mid-May to end-September in England and Wales, but is shorter in Scotland and Northern Ireland. Bathing waters that are closed for a season are excluded for that year.

The boundaries of the Environment Agency regions are based on river catchment areas and not county borders. In particular, the figures shown for Wales are for the Environment Agency Welsh Region, the boundary of which does not correspond to the boundary of Wales. See Geographic maps on page 203.

Land use

Land use refers to the main activity taking place on an area of land, for example, farming, forestry or housing. Land cover refers specifically to the make up of the land surface, for example, whether it comprises arable crops, trees or buildings.

In Table 11.17 the figures for agricultural land use are derived from the Agricultural and

Horticultural surveys carried out by the Department for Environment, Food and Rural Affairs (DEFRA) and the other UK Agricultural Departments in June each year. Data for 'Grasses and rough grazing' include sole right and common rough grazing and *Other'* agricultural land contains set aside and other land on agricultural holdings, for example farm roads, yards, buildings, gardens, ponds. Data exclude woodland on agricultural holdings, which is included in 'Forest and woodland'. Information on the area of forest and woodland in Great Britain is compiled by the Forestry Commission and covers both private and state-owned land. Estimates are based on the provisional results of the National Inventory of Woodland and Trees for 1995–99 and extrapolated forward using information about new planting and other changes. Data for Northern Ireland are compiled separately by the Forest Service, an agency of the Northern Ireland Department of Agriculture and Rural Development (DARD) and also cover both private and state-owned land. There is no comparable source of information on the amount of urban land in the UK, and the figures for the 'Urban land and land not otherwise specified' category are derived by subtracting land used for agricultural and forestry purposes from the land area. Figures include land used for urban and other purposes, for example transport and recreation, and non-agricultural, semi-natural environments, for example sand dunes, grouse moors and non-agricultural grasslands, and inland waters.

Part 12: Transport

Road traffic

Road traffic is estimated from a network of manual traffic counts, which count traffic for a single 12-hour period, and Automatic Traffic Counters, which count traffic 24 hours a day throughout the whole year. There are around 22,000 manual count points that are counted between every one to eight years, with around 9,000 counts carried out each year. There are around 190 Automatic Traffic Counters.

Improvements were made to the methodology used to estimate minor road traffic in 2004. From 2000 to 2003, trends in traffic flow, derived from a relatively small number of Automatic Traffic Counters, were used to update 1999 base-year estimates. For the annual estimates made from and including 2004, the trends were derived from a set of some 4,200 manual traffic counts instead.

For more details, see *How the National Road Traffic Estimates are made* from the Department for Transport, www.dft.gov.uk/matrix/forms/estimates.aspx

National Travel Survey

The National Travel Survey (NTS) is designed to provide a databank of personal travel information for Great Britain. It has been conducted as a continuous survey since July 1988, following ad hoc surveys since the mid-1960s. The NTS is designed to identify long-term trends and is not suitable for monitoring short-term trends.

In 2006 a weighting strategy was introduced to the NTS and applied retrospectively to data for

1995 onwards. The weighting methodology adjusts for non-response bias and also adjusts for the drop-off in the number of trips recorded by respondents during the course of the travel week. All results now published for 1995 onwards are based on weighted data, and direct comparisons cannot be made to previously published unweighted data.

During 2006 nearly 8,300 households provided details of their personal travel by filling in travel diaries over the course of a week. The drawn sample size from 2002 has nearly trebled compared with previous years following recommendations in a National Statistics Review of the NTS. This enables most results to be presented on a single year basis from 2002. Previously data was shown for a three-year period because of the smaller sample size.

Travel included in the NTS covers all trips by British residents within Great Britain for personal reasons, including travel in the course of work.

A trip is defined as a one-way course of travel having a single main purpose. It is the basic unit of personal travel defined in the survey. A round trip is split into two trips, with the first ending at a convenient point about halfway round as a notional stopping point for the outward destination and return origin. A stage is that portion of a trip defined by the use of a specific method of transport or of a specific ticket (a new stage being defined if either the mode or the ticket changes).

Cars are regarded as household cars if they are either owned by a member of the household, or available for the private use of household members. Company cars provided by an employer for the use of a particular employee (or director) are included, but cars borrowed temporarily from a company pool are not.

The main driver of a household car is the household member who drives the furthest in that car in the course of a year.

The purpose of a trip is normally taken to be the activity at the destination, unless that destination is 'home', in which case the purpose is defined by the origin of the trip. The classification of trips to 'work' is also dependent on the origin of the trip. The following purposes of trips are distinguished:

Commuting: Trips to a usual place of work from home, or from work to home.

Business: Personal trips in the course of work, including a trip in the course of work back to work. This includes all work trips by people with no usual place of work (for example, site workers) and those who work at or from home.

Education: Trips to school or college, etc, by full-time students, students on day-release and part-time students following vocational courses.

Escort: Used when the traveller has no purpose of his or her own, other than to escort or accompany another person; for example, taking a child to school. *Escort commuting* is escorting or accompanying someone from home to work or from work to home.

Shopping: All trips to shops or from shops to home, even if there was no intention to buy.

Personal business: Visits to services, for example, hairdressers, launderettes, dry-cleaners, betting shops, solicitors, banks, estate agents, libraries, churches; or for medical consultations or treatment, or for eating and drinking, unless the main purpose was social or entertainment.

Social or entertainment: Visits to meet friends, relatives, or acquaintances, both at someone's home or at a pub, restaurant, etc; all types of entertainment or sport, clubs, and voluntary work, non-vocational evening classes, political meetings, etc.

Holidays or day trips: Trips (within Great Britain) to or from any holiday (including stays of four nights or more with friends or relatives) or trips for pleasure (not otherwise classified as social or entertainment) within a single day.

Just walk: Walking for pleasure trips along public highways, including taking the dog for a walk and jogging.

Car ownership

The figures for household ownership include four-wheeled and three-wheeled cars, off-road vehicles, minibuses, motorcaravans, dormobiles, and light vans. Company cars normally available for household use are also included.

Area type classification

In the National Travel Survey (see above), households in Great Britain are classified according to whether they are within an urban area of at least 3,000 population or in a rural area. Urban areas are subdivided for the purpose of this publication as follows:

- London boroughs – the whole of the Greater London Authority

- Metropolitan built-up areas – the built-up areas of the former metropolitan counties of Greater Manchester, Merseyside, West Midlands, West Yorkshire, Tyne and Wear and Strathclyde (excludes South Yorkshire)

- Large urban – self-contained urban areas over 250,000 population

- Medium urban – self-contained urban areas over 25,000 but not over 250,000 population

- Small/medium urban – self-contained urban areas over 10,000 but not over 25,000 population

- Small urban – self-contained urban areas over 3,000 but not over 10,000 population

- Rural – all other areas, including urban areas, under 3,000 population

Prior to 1996, 'small urban' and 'small/medium urban' were combined into one category covering self-contained urban areas over 3,000 but not over 25,000 population.

England and Wales
The classification specifies urban areas based on the extent of urban development indicated on Ordnance Survey maps. An urban area is a tract of continuously built-up urban land extending 20 hectares or more. Urban areas thus defined but less than 200 metres apart are combined into a single urban area.

Scotland
In Scotland postcodes were classified as urban or rural using population density. Urban postcodes were then aggregated together to form localities using a minimum population of 500 together with other rules.

Road safety

The Government targets for Great Britain are that by 2010, compared with the average for a number of indicators in 1994–98, the proportion of people killed or seriously injured in road accidents per 100 million vehicle kilometres will be reduced by 40 per cent; the proportion of children killed or seriously injured, by 50 per cent, and the proportion of people slightly injured, by 10 per cent.

The Northern Ireland Road Safety Strategy 2002–2012 aims to reduce the proportion of people killed or seriously injured on Northern Ireland's roads each year by one-third, compared with the average for the period 1996–2000, and to reduce the proportion of children killed or seriously injured on Northern Ireland's roads each year by one-half.

Data for Great Britain in Figure 12.17 are provisional for 2006 and are derived from three sources. Two sources of data are used to assess the extent and characteristics of drink-drive accidents in Great Britain; the third source provides information on compliance with drink-drive restrictions. These sources are:

- coroners' data. Coroners in England and Wales and procurators fiscal in Scotland provide information about the level of alcohol in the blood of road accident fatalities aged 16 and over who die within 12 hours of a road accident.

- STATS19 breath test data. The personal injury road accident reporting system (STATS19) provides data on injury accidents in which the driver or rider survived and was also breath-tested at the roadside. If the driver or rider refused to provide a breath test specimen, then they are considered to have failed the test unless they are deemed unable to take the test for medical reasons.

- police force screening breath-test data. In England and Wales the Ministry of Justice provides information from breath tests carried out at the roadside following a moving traffic offence, road accident or suspicion of alcohol use.

Once the drink-drive accidents have been identified using coroners' and STATS19 data, then the resulting casualties in these accidents are identified from STATS19 data.

Completeness of data and reliability of estimates

Both sources of data from the police and coroners on drink-drive accidents are incomplete. In recognition of the uncertainty associated with the estimates produced from this data the numbers of accidents and casualties are rounded to the nearest ten.

Provisional and final estimates
As coroners' data are available for analysis a year later than the main road accident data, final estimates can only be made 18 months in arrears. Around 58 per cent of data expected to be available were available for inclusion in the provisional estimates. The provisional estimates

for serious and slight accidents depend on breath-test data and do not change in the final estimates. The coroners' data affect only the numbers of casualties from fatal accidents and these form a small proportion of serious and slight casualties. The estimates for fatalities depend mainly on coroners' data and are particularly susceptible to revision between the provisional and final figures.

Passenger death rates

Passenger fatality rates given in Table 12.18 can be interpreted as the risk a traveller runs of being killed, per billion kilometres travelled. The coverage varies for each mode of travel and care should be exercised in drawing comparisons between the rates for different modes.

The table provides information on passenger fatalities. Where possible travel by drivers and other crew in the course of their work has been excluded. Exceptions are for private journeys and those in company owned cars and vans where drivers are included.

Figures for all modes of transport exclude confirmed suicides and deaths through natural causes. Figures for air, rail and water exclude trespassers and rail excludes attempted suicides. Accidents occurring in airports, seaports and railway stations that do not directly involve the mode of transport concerned are also excluded, for example, deaths sustained on escalators or falling over packages on platforms.

The figures are compiled by the Department for Transport. Further information is available in the annual publications *Road Casualties Great Britain: Annual Report* and *Transport Statistics Great Britain*. Both are published by The Stationery Office and are available at: **www.dft.gov.uk/transtat**

The following definitions are used:

Air: Accidents involving UK registered airline aircraft in UK and foreign airspace. Fixed wing and rotary wing aircraft are included but air taxis are excluded. Accidents cover UK airline aircraft around the world not just in the UK.

Rail: Train accidents and accidents occurring through movement of railway vehicles in Great Britain. As well as national rail the figures include accidents on underground and tram systems, Eurotunnel and minor railways.

Water: Figures for travel by water include both domestic and international passenger carrying services of UK registered merchant vessels.

Road: Figures refer to Great Britain and include accidents occurring on the public highway (including footways) in which at least one road

vehicle or a vehicle in collision with a pedestrian is involved and which becomes known to the police within 30 days of its occurrence. Figures include both public and private transport.

Bus or coach: Figures for work buses are included. From 1 January 1994, the casualty definition was revised to include only those vehicles equipped to carry 17 or more passengers regardless of use. Prior to 1994 these vehicles were coded according to construction, whether or not they were being used for carrying passengers. Vehicles constructed as buses that were privately licensed were included under 'Bus and coach' but Public Service Vehicles (PSV) licensed minibuses were included under cars.

Car: Includes taxis, invalid tricycles, three-wheeled and four-wheeled cars and minibuses. Prior to 1999 motor caravans were also included.

Van: Vans mainly include vehicles of the van type constructed on a car chassis. From 1 January 1994 these are defined as those vehicles not 3.5 tonnes maximum permissible gross vehicle weight. Prior to 1994 the weight definition was not more than 1.524 tonnes unladen.

Two-wheeled motor vehicle: Mopeds, motor scooters and motorcycles (including motorcycle combinations).

Pedal cycle: Includes tandems, tricycles and toy cycles ridden on the carriageway.

Pedestrian: Includes persons riding toy cycles on the footway, persons pushing bicycles, pushing or pulling other vehicles or operating pedestrian controlled vehicles, those leading or herding animals, occupants of prams or wheelchairs, and people who alight safely from vehicles and are subsequently injured.

Sea passengers on short sea routes

The figures exclude cruise passengers, inter-island passengers and river crossings. Short sea international routes are generally those to Belgium, Denmark, Faroe Isles, Finland, France, Germany, Ireland, Netherlands, Norway, Spain and Sweden. Domestic routes are those between Great Britain and Northern Ireland, Isle of Man, Channel Islands, and Orkney and Shetland.

Part 13: Lifestyles and social participation

Definitions

Live listening: Any listening that takes place at the time of broadcast. It can be on the Internet

using the 'listen live' option on some websites, but also through AM/FM, DAB and digital television.

Listen again services: Listening to radio programmes that have already been broadcast through the Internet.

Podcasting: Involves making an audio file (usually in MP3 format) of content that is updated frequently (for example a weekly radio programme) available for automatic download so users can listen to the file at their convenience.

Internet connection

There are two types of Internet connection:

- Narrowband: The computer uses the telephone line to dial up an Internet connection. Because narrowband access uses normal telephone lines, the quality of the connection can vary and data rates are limited. A narrowband user cannot be online and use the telephone to make calls at the same time.

- Broadband: Broadband access to the Internet is many times faster than dial-up (narrowband) access, and is typically always on (so there is no need to dial up or 'connect' each time for access). There are several ways that a broadband connection can be delivered. The two most common methods are through cable or a digital subscriber line (DSL). Cable modems deliver an Internet connection through the same cables that deliver cable television, whereas a DSL line uses normal telephone lines. Broadband users can be online and use the telephone to make calls at the same time

Measurement of religion

The British Social Attitudes Survey (BSA) question *'Do you regard yourself as belonging to any particular religion?'* produces a much smaller proportion of Christians and a much larger proportion of people with no religion compared with the census question, *'What is your religion?'*. Part of the difference is because the two surveys cover different populations and a further difference is bought about by the different wording of the questions. The census question may suggest an expectation that people would have a religion while the BSA question introduced the possibility that people might not have a religion. For more information see *Focus on Ethnicity and Religion 2006*, available on the ONS website: **www.statistics. gov.uk/downloads/theme_compendia/ foer2006/FoER_main.pdf**

Index